Applied English Syntax

Foundations for Word, Phrase, and Sentence Analysis

ETTIEN KOFFI

St. Cloud State University

Kendall Hunt publishing company

Kendall Hunt
publishing company

www.kendallhunt.com
Send all inquiries to:
4050 Westmark Drive
Dubuque, IA 52004-1840

Copyright © 2010 by Kendall Hunt Publishing Company

ISBN 978-0-7575-7507-5

Printed in the United States of America
10 9 8 7 6 5 4 3 2 1

To my wife, *Kim*

To my son, *Jeremy*

To my daughter, *Tallie*

Contents

Preface

Applied English Syntax is unlike any other grammar textbook. It is unique both because of the scope of the material it covers and the methodology it uses. Behind each chapter of the book is the following equation:

PEDAGOGICAL GRAMMAR = TRADITIONAL GRAMMAR + PRESCRIPTIVE GRAMMAR + SOCIOLINGUISTICS + DESCRIPTIVE GRAMMAR

The inner workings of the equation will be fully explained and exemplified in Chapter 3. Suffice it to say for now that this multidimensional approach to grammar is the ideal tool that teachers need to bolster their confidence in teaching Language Arts or English as Second/Foreign Language. It is written intentionally to address the lack of confidence that plagues language professionals when it comes to answering students' grammar questions. Furthermore, the textbook uses a "clinical" approach in teaching grammar. It achieves this goal by training students to use four diagnostic tests. The first test is the semantic test. It is not foolproof but it gives a quick and rough idea about the lexical category of a word under consideration. The second test is the morphological test. It relies on affixation to identify word classes. The third test is the syntactic test. It derives clues from the environment in which a word occurs in order to determine its part of speech. Last but not least is the functional test. It uses evidence from within the sentence to help identify the function(s) of a word. Taken together, these four tests give teachers the linguistic background they need to teach grammar with confidence.

A brief statement about the organization of this book and the syntactic theory that undergirds it is in order before you dive into it. The book is divided into three major parts which you will find to be sensible. The first part, chapters 1 through 4, provides an overview of the historical and theoretical developments that have shaped the study of grammar over nearly three thousand years, and, specifically, for the last fifty years. Since knowledge is cumulative, this background is indispensable before proceeding further to the second and third parts of the book.

Chapters 5 to 10 constitute the bulk of the second part. Chapter 5 is a transition chapter that deals mainly with morphology and word formation processes. Morphology is so central to syntax that it would be unwise to omit it. From Chapter 6 onward, each chapter focuses on a major part of speech. By concentrating all the information relative to a specific part of speech in a single chapter, the reader has all he or she needs to know in one place. While this is certainly better than scattering information all over the book, such an approach has its challenges. Grammatical concepts are so interrelated that it is impossible to make clean breaks between parts of speech. However, the ease with which information related to a given part of speech can be retrieved from a single chapter far outweighs the inconvenience of not spelling out all the interrelatedness of grammatical concepts; a goal at which no grammar book has ever succeeded in any case. All the chapters have the same overall structure. Each begins with a definition, then moves quickly to semantic, morphological, syntactic, and functional tests that can help identify a word as a noun, an auxiliary verb, a main verb, an adjective, or an adverb.

The third part is comprised of four chapters. Each chapter focuses on a minor part of speech or an aspect of it. Thus, we deal with prepositions, coordinating conjunctions, subordinating conjunctions, and pronouns. The minor parts of speech, also called "function words" are trickier to package neatly because they come alive only when they are used in sentences. Though an attempt has been made to follow the same overall organization throughout the book, a great deal of attention has been devoted to syntactic constructions in this section. As a result, these four chapters are structured in a slightly different way. To be sure, the semantic aspects of function words are dealt with where warranted, but not as extensively as in the chapters on the major parts of speech. In addition, function words are morphologically impoverished. For this reason, only passing remarks are made about their form and word formation processes. This section of the book concludes with a chapter on transformational grammar and composition. The goal is to show that awareness of the various transformational operations discussed throughout the book can help improve students' writing skills.

The overall goal of this book is to enhance the teacher's grammatical awareness. No effort is spared in drawing his/her attention to grammatical aspects of pedagogical interest to students. It is a truism that when these tips and comments are integrated with a composition curriculum, the teacher will see a net improvement in students' writing. However, it should be borne in mind that this book is not about the writing process, but rather about the syntactic knowledge that students need to write grammatically well-formed sentences.

Let's conclude by saying something about the theoretical underpinnings of the book. I have taught college level syntax courses for over a decade. In so doing I have experimented with various approaches to syntax in undergraduate and first year graduate courses with little success. The tepid success is not to be blamed entirely on students' lack of prior grammatical knowledge rather on the fact that most textbooks do not use syntactic theories that correlate well with students' level of grammatical awareness. Such experiences have led me to conclude that for students who are taking their first semester-long course in syntax, the syntactic theory that is most suitable and relevant is the Extended Standard Theory. This theory states explicitly all the basic notions that students must have. Its formulas allow them to see for themselves how sentences are formed. Moreover, the Extended Standard Theory, more than any other syntactic theory, spells out clearly how the various components of grammar (semantics, syntax, morphology, and phonology) interact. Explaining to students the distinction between deep structure and surface structure and how transformations mediate between the two allows them to peak into the complexity of sentence generation. This explains why the bulk of this book is grounded in the Extended Standard Theory. However, I do not limit myself to this approach alone. More recent theories of syntax are used if they deal better with the issue under consideration. For instance, in Chapter 14, Government-Binding is used to account for the various issues involved in pronominal references. Chapter 15 draws on the Minimalist Program to highlight the importance of movement rules in composition.

Acknowledgments

Various versions of this book have been used in my undergraduate introduction to *English Syntax* course and in my graduate *Pedagogical Grammar* course. I owe a special debt of gratitude to the more than **200 students** who, over the course of eight semesters, have offered comments and suggestions in their anonymous course evaluations on how to improve the content of this book for their fellow students. Unfortunately, there is not enough space here to acknowledge their individual contributions. If you have taken a course with me and used this book as your textbook, you should know that your constant requests for clarification and your insatiable appetite for more and more examples have been instrumental in giving this book both depth and breadth of coverage. Without you, the student-centered approach taken in this book would not have been possible! Four former students of mine need to be singled out for special mention because of their invaluable help and insights. **Mrs. Rhoda Fagerland** of the Intensive English Center at Saint Cloud State University has read every single chapter of this book and made copious suggestions and editorial comments. I'm truly indebted to her expertise and friendship. It is with great gratitude that I acknowledge the resourcefulness of my former graduate assistants, **Mrs. Melissa Lindsey** and **Mrs. Amy Johnson** for their diligence in diagramming sentences, pinpointing errors, and providing various sorts of help along the way. More than **50 students** have taken the *Pedagogical Grammar* course online using previous versions of this work as their textbook. Their comments have also been very helpful in making this book user-friendly to online students. Many of the insightful suggestions made by **Ms. Andrea Vasconcellos** have been fully integrated into this final version of the book. Last but not least, I would like to acknowledge the invaluable help that **Ms. Joan Gill** provided by teaching me and modeling for me how to do the indexes of "Key Terms to Know." It is a valuable skill that will save me time and money in the future.

```
I N W B V J K C D R S P O
S K W L A S D K F N S Q I
W B W B N P O F R Q O W P
N R M U O T P E V E R B P
W E G H A U K I N A P O R
I V N W B V J K C N R S P
D D L A S D K F N U L A J
F A Q O W P I E B O A M U
P E W N C A P I W N G H A
N A P O R N W B V J K C D
A D J E C T I V E O A N S
D K F N W L A J W K E F R
```

HISTORICAL AND
THEORETICAL OVERVIEW

Chapter 1

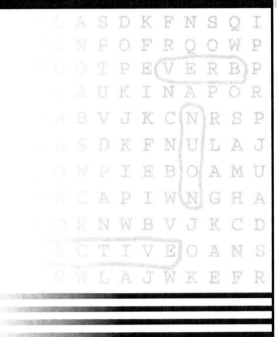

The Organization and Definition of Syntactic Concepts

A Preview, an Overview, and a Review

1.0 INTRODUCTION

This chapter serves as a preview, an overview, and a review. It is a preview because the concepts discussed here will be pursued in greater details in subsequent chapters. It is an overview because all the various chapters are summarized in this one. The advantage of such an approach is that it gives students the opportunity to encounter grammatical concepts at least once before combing through them at a later date. An overview of syntactic concepts with illustrative sentences is far superior to a catalogue of terms in a glossary. This chapter is also a review because it re-familiarizes students with some of the basic morphological and grammatical terms to which they were exposed when they took Introduction to Linguistics. Academic calendars are such that there is often a gap of one or several semesters between an introductory course in linguistics and a full-blown syntax or pedagogical grammar course. In the meantime, attrition takes its toll and students forget a great deal of useful information that they need for more advanced courses. So, this chapter reacquaints students with terms that they learned previously but may have forgotten. Finally, this chapter is meant to introduce students to practical ways in which contemporary grammatical analyses are done. Once pre-service teachers are familiar with this framework, and understand how linguistic units are organized, they will be in a position to show how grammar is relevant to many aspects of their students' academic pursuits. Moreover, they will feel confident as teachers in explaining points of grammar to their own students.

1.1 Definitions of Linguistics

It is not an easy task to define any academic field of study. Linguistics is no exception. For the sake of maximum clarity, I have highlighted five major areas that linguistics focuses on. First and foremost, linguistics is defined as the scientific study of the internal structure/organization of languages. However, this definition is not sufficient because linguistics is also the scientific study of language use in society. In the past fifty years, linguistic investigation has been expanded to include the scientific study of the processes involved in language perception and production and the scientific study of the processes involved in language acquisition by humans and machines. Since the nineteenth century, linguists have been interested in the scientific study of the processes involved in language change and reconstruction.

Lyons (1970:11) defines the term "scientific" simply as a description that is carried out systematically on the basis of objectively verifiable observations and within the framework of some general theory appropriate to the data. More will be said about the scientific nature of linguistics in the upcoming sections. In his now classic paper, *Linguistics among the Sciences,* Yngve (1986) claims that linguistics is a science because it meets all three criteria of physical sciences. The subject matter of all such sciences is observable and testable. Furthermore, their results are falsifiable. According to Yngve, descriptive linguistics is a science on par with physics, biology, and chemistry because it works on observable data; and its findings are testable and falsifiable. By the latter, he means that linguistic experiments done in one part of the world can be reproduced in another part of the world with the same results. Furthermore, he states that noted linguists, from Bloomfield and Hockett, all the way to Chomsky, have compared linguistics to physics, chemistry, biology, and mathematics. Linguists have borrowed heavily from the methodological frameworks used in these sciences to inform contemporary linguistic investigations.

1.1.2 The Core Components of Descriptive Linguistics

Yngve (1986:263) relies strongly on the notion of language as an integrated "**system**" to explain why linguistics is a science: "Physics works centrally with this concept of system; so does chemistry. In the biological sciences, dynamic system concepts are widely applied all the way from biochemistry and physiology to evolutionary theory, population biology, and ecology." The notion of language as a system has led descriptive linguists to divide language and linguistics into five interrelated areas, as shown in the diagram below:

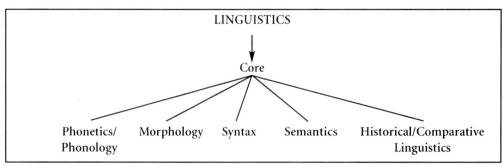

Table 1 *Core Areas of Linguistics*

Each one of the core areas listed here is a major area of specialization. Within each core area there are several types of micro-specializations. Needless to say, the description in the sections below outlines only the key concepts in each core area.

Phonetics and **phonology** focus primarily on the study of sound features, segments, and syllable structures. Syntax and phonetics/phonology interact indirectly through morphology. **Morphology** is the study of the structure and functions of morphemes, and deals with word formation processes. These are the processes that lead to the creation of words upon which **syntax** depends to construct phrases and sentences. Words that are created through these morphological processes are then filed into the **mental lexicon** according to their **parts of speech.** In making sentences, individual parts of speech are organized into **phrases** which are, in turn, combined into **clauses/sentences.** Sentences build on each other to make up larger units called "**paragraphs**" (for written texts), and "**utterances**" (for oral texts). Paragraphs and utterances are organized into yet a larger system called "**discourse.**" These aspects of utterances/sentences are studied mainly within the core areas of linguistics.

1.1.3 Descriptive Linguistics and Related Disciplines

All the leading linguists of the first half the 20th century wanted linguists to be solidly grounded in rigorous scientific methodology. However, the notion that linguistics should look only at mathematics, chemistry, biology, and physics for its methodology was not universally accepted. Yngve (1986:266) quotes Sapir who voiced skepticism at this approach:

> *It was perceptively sensed by Sapir when he foresaw lying in the future a really fruitful integration of linguistics and psychological studies. It is particularly important that linguists, who are often accused, and accused justly, of failure to look beyond the pretty patterns of their subject matter, should become aware of what sciences may mean for the interpretation of human conduct in general. Whether they like it or not, they must become increasingly concerned with the many anthropological, sociological, and psychological problems which invade the field of language.*

It seems that Sapir's advice was heeded. New sub-disciplines of linguistics have now emerged as a result of such interactions. Table 2 represents the main academic disciplines that interact with linguistics.

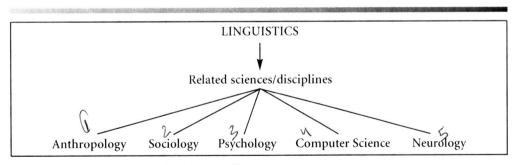

Table 2 *Linguistics and Related Disciplines*

The interaction between linguistics and anthropology has given birth to **anthropological linguistics (or linguistics anthropology,** as some prefer to call it). This new discipline studies the language used in specific communicative events: ceremonial speech, the language used in rites of passage and kinship terms. The combination of linguistics and sociology[1] has brought about the sub-discipline of **sociolinguistics.** It studies the correlations between linguistic variables and social variables. It also studies linguistic variations due to geography or social classes. Linguistics and psychology have teamed up to study language processing: both speech generation and speech perception. The discipline that has resulted from this teamwork is called **psycholinguistics.** Additionally, some psycholinguists focus on the factors involved in first and second language acquisition. For the past thirty years, linguistics and computer science have developed a warm relationship. The new discipline is called **computational linguistics.** It seeks to program computers with the ability to process, generate, and comprehend language the way humans do. Much will be said in subsequent discussions about this emerging partnership. Neurology has provided invaluable information to linguists in their quest for understanding the relationship between language and the brain. From this cooperation, the sub-discipline of **neurolinguistics** has emerged. It studies the relationship between language and the brain, and the processes involved in language production and perception. As a result of the work being done in this field, some linguists are now venturing into a new field of inquiry called **genetic linguistics.**

Aitchison (1992:30) provides the following rationale for dividing linguistics into core and interrelated areas. She notes that "the majority of professional linguists prefer to begin with those aspects of language which can most easily be detached from the social background. . . . They consider this to be the core of linguistic study, and expect to add on its interrelationships with society at a later stage. A knowledge of the linguistic resources of a language is often a prerequisite to an intelligent discussion of how these resources are used."

1.2 *Hierarchical Organization of Sentences*

Syntax is central in the study of grammar. It is often defined as the area of linguistics that studies word order, the function of words in sentences, and the rules and operations that specify the position of words in phrases and sentences. These definitions make the <word> and the <sentence> centerpieces of syntactic inquiry. Even though this is true, it is my experience that students gain more insight into syntactic analysis if they understand the overall architecture of speech and how the different parts of the system work harmoniously together. A comparison between linguistics on the one hand, and physics and chemistry on the other hand, may shed some light on how the system works. Chemistry and physics deal with "matter" reduced to one of its most basic components, the <atom>. This word is borrowed from Greek. It is made up of the prefix <*a-*> which means "not" and <*tomos*>, derived from a verb meaning "to cut." An <atom> in Greek refers to something so microscopic that it cannot be "cut" further into smaller pieces. Until recently, the atom was believed to be irreducible, or an indivisible component of "matter." Atoms organize into slightly bigger units that chemists and physicists call "molecules." A bottom-up approach to syntax claims that syntactic elements that make up sentences follow a similar organization. Irreducible elements of speech fuse into increasingly larger and larger units, from basic phonetic features all the way to discourse. The architecture below tries to capture the main details of the organization of linguistic elements in speech.

---

[1] Wardhaugh (2002:16–21) objects to this definition. He argues that sociolinguistics is its own discipline, not a random admixture of sociology and linguistics.

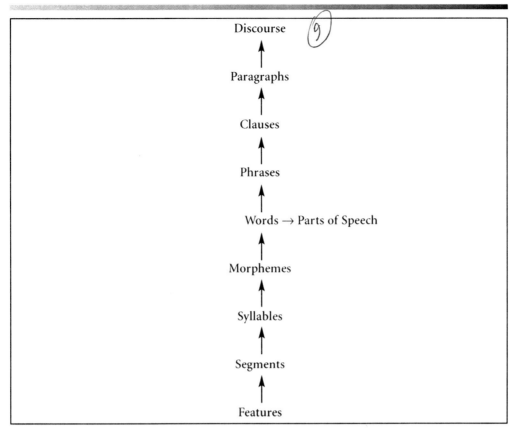

Table 3 *Overall Architecture of the Organization of Syntactic Elements*

Our focus in this book is from the morphemic level to the clausal level. Anything below or beyond these delineated areas is outside the scope of this book. The architecture presented here does not assign any special role to semantics because it permeates all levels of analysis from the morpheme upward.

1.2.1 Major and Minor Parts of Speech

There are concepts such as "parts of speech" that are indispensable in syntactic analysis. It is hard to understand grammar without first grasping the notion of parts of speech. Unfortunately, parts of speech analysis was the first casualty of the removal of grammar instruction from schools. It was out of fashion for several decades, but thanks to computational linguistics, it is back again. In computational linguistics jargon, parts of speech analysis is called "**tagging**" or "**parsing**." The label has changed, but the reality remains the same. The need to develop software which simulates human language abilities has made it clear that computational linguistics cannot be done without a thorough understanding of parts of speech. As might be expected, the eight or ten parts of speech inherited from Greek grammarians are woefully inadequate to meet the needs of automatic speech processing. Consequently, according to Jurafsky and Martin (2000:342, 412), computational linguists have introduced as many as 100 subcategories.

If parts of speech analysis is good for computational linguists in teaching machines how to understand, analyze, and process language, it must be good for teachers. It is my contention that if teachers know some of what computational linguists know, they can use the same information to improve their students' writing skills. Sadly, the reality at this time is that there are many future teachers who lack proficiency in basic grammatical concepts. Without an understanding of parts of speech and how they work, investments in grammatical instruction will continue to yield disappointing dividends. This is the reason why we will not proceed further until basic notions have been introduced and defined.

1.2.2 Major and Minor Classes

There are eight main parts of speech in English. Some grammar books add infinitives and participles to the list. However, this is unnecessary because they belong together in the verb class. Some grammarians argue that interjections or vocatives are parts of speech in English. However, this is also unnecessary because interjections in English do not take affixes the way (classical) Greek interjections do. Classical Greek had a suffix that was added to words to show that they were interjections. English lacks such a suffix. It is, therefore, superfluous to include interjections among the parts of speech of English.

Linguists divide parts of speech into two main categories: **major parts of speech** and **minor parts of speech.** The former is also referred to as **lexical category** or **open class words,** and the latter is known as **grammatical category** or **closed class words.** The label "open" class is meant to explain the fact that new nouns, verbs, adjectives, and adverbs are continually being created and added to the major parts of speech. The label "closed" class underscores the idea that no new conjunctions, prepositions, pronouns, and articles are being added to the list already in existence in English. These labels are applicable to the classification of lexical items in other languages.

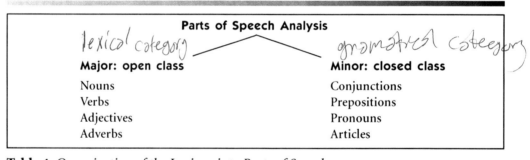

Parts of Speech Analysis

Major: open class	Minor: closed class
Nouns	Conjunctions
Verbs	Prepositions
Adjectives	Pronouns
Adverbs	Articles

Table 4 *Organization of the Lexicon into Parts of Speech*

Sections 1.3 through 1.6 in this chapter focus on the major parts of speech. Sections 1.7 to 1.10 are devoted to the minor parts of speech.

1.3 Focus on Nouns

Nouns were traditionally defined as words that "named a person, place, or thing." Later, "idea" was added to the list to cover "abstract concepts." Contemporary linguists consider this definition to be too simplistic. They are right. However, it is a good rule of thumb definition which can help identify and classify the majority of words in the lexicon. Consequently, it is a useful definition to know. Descriptive linguists rely on semantic, morphological, syntactic, and functional clues to identify and classify nouns. Some of the most important clues are shown in Table 5.

1.3.1 Main Semantic Features[2]

Any lexical item that has one or more of the following features is classified as a noun:

No.	List of Features	Examples
1.	[± abstract]	concrete *(table)* vs. abstract *(love)*
2.	[± common]	proper *(Larry)* vs. common *(people)*
3.	[± count]	mass *(hair)* vs. count *(coins)*
4.	[± Animate]	life *(bee)* vs. lifeless *(rock)*
5.	[± human]	human *(man)* vs. non-human *(lion)*
6.	[± divine]	spirit *(God)* vs. human *(woman)*

Table 5 *Summary of Semantic of Features of Nouns*

1.3.2 Morphological Characteristics

In addition to the semantic features listed above, words can be identified as nouns if they are morphologically marked for **gender.** This feature is not very important in English because most English words are genderless. However, for languages such as French and Spanish, gender is an important clue because all the nouns in the lexicon must be either masculine or feminine. In some languages such as Greek and German, nouns have an additional gender feature: the "**neuter.**"

A distinction is often made between biological gender and grammatical gender. Biological gender is part of the genetic endowment of [+animate] beings. However, grammatical gender is an arbitrary parameter that some languages add to the nouns in their lexicon. Only a small fraction of English words are grammatically encoded with gender. These words include <ship> and <earth> which are feminine (*Mother Earth*), and <child>/<infant> which are grammatically neuter.

The feature [+number] is assigned to nouns in many languages. Nouns are either **singular** or **plural.** The word <bird> is singular but <birds> is plural. There are languages such as ancient Hebrew that have the feature [+dual]. This feature appears on nouns that tend to occur in pairs such as the eyes, the ears, the legs, and the arms.

1.4 Focus on Verbs

The rule of thumb definition of verbs says that "verbs are words that describe an action, a state, or an experience." Often additional comments are made about the verb, namely, that it is the most important element in the sentence. Grammar books then proceed to give an endless list of various types of verbs. We will deal with these classifications later, but for now let us focus on the core characteristics of verbs.

1.4.1 Morphosyntactic Characteristics

Linguists use the umbrella term of **predicate** to include all **verbs.** English verbs fall into two major groups: **main verbs** and **auxiliary verbs.** This classification is based on the syntax and morphology of verbs. Auxiliary verbs are further subdivided between **modal**

---

[2] These are the most essential features that play important morphosyntactic roles in ascertaining the grammaticality of a sentence.

verbs and aspectual auxiliary verbs. The diagram below summarizes these various subclasses of verbs:

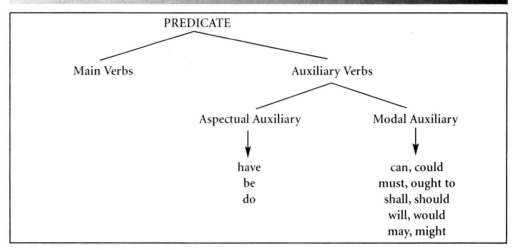

Table 6 *Classification of Verbs*

1.4.2 Tense Features

Tense is defined as "the time at which the action or state described by the verb takes place." It is an essential characteristic of verbs because all **finite** (conjugated) verbs must carry tense information. There are three tenses in English: **the present, the past,** and **the future.** The present and the past have tense suffixes. The future has a **grammaticalized** tense marker, <will>. This word did not originally fulfill a grammatical function, but over time its meaning changed from intention and volition to tense. As a result, <will> is now used by speakers of English to carry future meaning. The sentences below illustrate the use of these three tenses:

(1) *Negar loves linguistics.* (Present)

(2) *Negar loved linguistics.* (Past)

(3) *Negar **will** return to linguistics after she earns her degree in business.* (Future)

1.4.1 Aspect Features

The distinction between tense and **aspect** is one of the hardest to make. We will not attempt to explain it here except to say that aspect considers the actions or states described by the verb with regard to when they started, how they are progressing, how often they occur, how long they last, and how often they repeat themselves. English has three morphologically marked aspects: **the habitual, the perfect,** and **the progressive.** The habitual aspect has no special morpheme. The perfect is characterized by the morpheme <Have—EN>, and the progressive has the morpheme <BE—ING>. The sentences below illustrate the use of aspects in English:

(4) *Babies sleep all the time.* (Habitual)

(5) *The baby **is** sleep**ing**.* (Progressive)

(6) *The baby **has** eaten.* (Perfect)

1.4.4 Voice Features

Voice expresses what the subject is doing, what the subject is doing to itself, or what is being done to the subject. Traditional grammarians distinguish three voices which they define as follows: the **active voice** means that the subject is the "doer" of the action, **passive voice** means that the subject is affected by the action, and **middle voice** signals that the subject is doing something for his/her own benefit or to himself/herself. English has morphologically marked active and passive voices but it lacks a morphologically marked middle voice. Instead, it uses reflexive pronouns to express what a language such as Greek would express through the middle voice.

> (7) *Grandparents **spoil** their grandchildren.* (Active voice)
>
> (8) *Grandchildren **are spoiled by** grandparents.* (Passive voice)
>
> (9) *Grandparents **blame themselves** for spoiling their grandchildren.* (Middle voice)

English can also express the middle voice through "**ergative verbs.**[3]" The most important characteristic of ergative constructions is that the grammatical subject is not the doer of the action expressed by the verb. The doer of the action is left unstated, as in the example below:

> (10) *The chicken is **baking** in the oven.* (Ergative)

In this sentence <chicken> is the grammatical subject of the sentence. However, it is not the doer of the action. Somebody else is doing the action of "baking."

1.4.5 Mood Features

Mood indicates the speaker's attitude toward his/her utterance. If the speaker is confident and sure of his/her statement, the **declarative mood** (factual statement) is used. The **subjunctive mood** is used when the speaker expresses his/her desire or wish for something that has not happened yet. If a command or polite suggestion is intended, the speaker resorts to the **imperative mood.** If the realization of the action or state described is contingent upon circumstances beyond the speaker's control, he/she might use the **conditional mood.** The sentences below illustrate these four moods:

> (11) *Conscientious objectors hate wars.* (Declarative mood)
>
> (12) *If I become President, I will stop the war.* (Conditional mood)
>
> (13) ***Stop** all wars!* (Imperative mood)
>
> (14) *I pray that the war **stop.*** (Subjunctive mood)

The least used of these four moods is the subjunctive. Its main characteristic is that verbs in the subjunctive mood fail to agree in number with the third person singular. If this were not the case, <stop> in sentence (14) would end with an <s>.

---

[3] Here are some English verbs that are often used in ergative constructions: *to age, to begin, to bend, to break, to burst, to change, to close, to cool, to condense, to decrease, to develop, to drop, to empty, to end, to evaporate, to finish, to grow, to increase, to melt, to open, to shatter, to sink, to shrink, to slow, to spread, to start, to stop, to tear*, Celce-Murcia and Larsen-Freeman (1999:350–352).

1.4.6 Syntactic Features

In addition to the morphological features discussed above, verbs are also classified according to their syntactic behavior. There are four major classes of verbs, as listed and defined below:

1. **Transitive verbs:** these verbs are normally followed directly by a noun.

   (15) *Conscientious objectors hate war.*

2. **Intransitive verbs:** these verbs cannot be followed directly by a noun.

   (16) *The baby sleeps a lot.*

3. **Linking verbs:** these verbs are followed by an adjective.

   (17) *These students are brilliant.*

4. **Ditransitive verbs:** these verbs are followed by two nouns, one of which follows the verb directly, and another that does not follow it directly.

   (18) *The millionaire gave **a big gift to the university**.*

In (18) <a big gift> is the direct object and <the university> is the indirect object.[4]

1.5 Adjectives

Adjectives are defined as "words that describe, modify, or qualify a noun." One of the most important characteristics of adjectives is that where there is an adjective, there must necessarily be a noun. Nouns can occur in sentences without adjectives, but adjectives cannot occur without nouns.

No.	Types of Adjectives	Examples
1.	Nationality	an *American* tourist
2.	Material	a *leather* jacket
3.	Age	the *youngest* judge
4.	Size	an *enormous* blunder
5.	Shape	a *rectangular* building
6.	Color	a *red* car
7.	Quality	a *brilliant* student
8.	Quantity	*one hundred* songs

Table 7 *Semantic Classification of Adjectives*

1.5.1 Semantic classification of adjectives

Adjectives fall into several semantic categories, including but not limited to the following:

1.5.2 Morphological Features

Adjectival morphology is not as rich and complicated in English as it is in other languages. English adjectives do not agree in gender and number with the nouns they mod-

---

[4] Indirect objects are also called objects of a preposition. The reason for the latter label is that there is a preposition before the noun phrase. The two terms are synonymous.

ify as is the case in French, Spanish, and other languages. The only significant inflectional characteristics that are worth mentioning are the comparative suffix <-er> and the superlative suffix <-est> that appear on one-syllable and two-syllable words in English.

(19)   *Tallie is **taller** than all her classmates.*

(20)   *Emma is the **smartest** of her class.*

1.5.3 Syntactic Characteristics

Traditional grammarians gave the label "adjective" to words that modern linguists no longer classify as adjectives. For instance, demonstrative adjectives, possessive adjectives, and interrogative adjectives are now known as <**determiners**>.[5] Grammarians also distinguish between two types of adjectives according to their position in relation to the noun they modify. Adjectives that occur before the noun are called **attributive adjectives.** Those that occur after the noun are called **predicative adjectives.**

(21)   ***Poor** judgment was the cause of the accident.* (Attributive adjective)

(22)   *Mountain climbing is **fun** but **dangerous**.* (Predicative adjective)

1.6 Adverbs

In traditional grammar adverbs are defined as "words or groups of words that modify/ describe verbs, adjectives, and other adverbs." We will see later that this part-of-speech is ill-defined and that traditional grammarians dumped into this group many words that they found hard to classify.

1.6.1 Semantic Features

Adverbs are classified into five major semantic groups. **Manner adverbs** describe the manner in which an action described by the verb is carried out. **Place adverbs** describe the geographical location in which the situation/action occurs. **Time adverbs** tell about the time of events. **Modality adverbs** reflect the state of mind of the speaker and his/her degree of confidence with regard to the statements that he/she is making. Additionally, contemporary linguists have coined the phrase "**degree word**" to refer to a group of words that expresses degrees of intensity.

(23)   *The student rushed through the exam **quickly**.* (Manner adverb)

(24)   *Your syntax book is **here**.* (Place adverb)

(25)   *The mid-term is **tomorrow**.* (Time adverb)

(26)   *Sprinters run **extremely** fast.* (Degree word)

(27)   *The storm will **probably** miss us.* (Modality adverb)

1.6.2 Morphological characteristics of adverbs

Adverbs take three main suffixes: the comparative adverb has the suffix <-er>, the superlative takes the suffix <-est>, and the suffix <-ly> appears on most manner adverbs. There are also many other adverbs that do not have any specific affix. These adverbs are often confused with adjectives because they behave alike.

---

[5] We will see later that the class of determiners also include articles.

1.6.3 Syntactic characteristics

The main syntactic characteristic of adverbs is mobility. Adverbs as a class can occur in five different positions in the sentence. Because of this, any lexical item that seems to be mobile is often classified as an adverb.

(28) *The storm will **probably** miss us.*

(29) ***Probably,** the storm will miss us.*

(30) *The storm will miss us, **probably**.*

1.7 Focus on Minor Parts of Speech

In addition to the four major parts of speech, there are four minor parts of speech: conjunctions, prepositions, pronouns, and articles. As noted previously, the words that belong to these parts of speech are all closed class items.

1.7.1 Conjunctions

Conjunctions are a small set of words that help conjoin words, groups of words, or clauses. Traditionally, conjunctions are divided into four groups:

1. **Coordinating conjunctions:** the words *<for, and, nor, but, or, yet,* and, *so >* are the only words that belong to this subclass. They are known mnemonically as FANBOYS.

2. **Correlative conjunctions:** only a handful of words belong to this class. The most common are *<either . . . or>*, *<neither . . . nor>*, *<not only . . . but>*, *<whether . . . or>*, and *<both . . . and>*.

3. **Subordinating conjunctions:** this subclass contains a dozen or so words. Their main characteristic is that they introduce subordinate clauses. They include *<that>*, *<whether>*, *<because>*, *<while>*, *<when>*, *<after>*, and *<if>*.

4. **Conjunctive adverbs:** all other words that traditional grammarians did not know where to put were classified as "conjunctive adverbs." In this group are words such as *<moreover>*, *<in fact>*, *<furthermore>*, and *<notwithstanding>*.

The first two types of conjunctions conjoin words, groups of words, and sentences of the same syntactic type. The latter two conjoin two clauses, one of which is the main clause and the other the dependent clause. Clauses will be discussed in 5.8.

(31) *She baked a pie **and** prepared dinner for the guests.*
(Coordinating conjunction)

(32) *My dog is too quiet today. He is **either** upset **or** he is sick.*
(Correlative conjunction)

(33) *I wonder **when** the plane will finally arrive.* (Subordinating conjunction)

(34) *I was going to study mathematics. **However,** I fell in love with linguistics.*
(Conjunctive adverb)

1.8 Prepositions

Prepositions are small words that indicate a spatial or temporal relationship between two objects. Prepositions can be used metaphorically. Therefore, in some instances, the spatial or temporal ideas conveyed by prepositions need not be taken literally. English has a subset of verbs that always occur with words that look like prepositions. In the majority of such cases, the total meaning of the verb and the preposition cannot be calculated on the basis of the literal meanings of the individual words. Such verbs are called <phrasal verbs> and the prepositions that occur with such verbs are named <particles>. Additionally, English has a number of words that look like prepositions, but they function differently. These preposition look-alikes are called <particles>. The following sentences illustrate these three categories of words:

(35)   *The translator looked **up** every word in the dictionary.* (Phrasal verb)

(36a) *Pam ran **up** the bill.* (Phrasal verb, <up> is a particle)

(36b) *Pam ran **up** the hill.* (<up> is a preposition)

The word <up> looks like a preposition in all three sentences. But in two cases, it is not. In (35) it is part of the verb. In (36a) it is a particle. Particles can move to the right of the Noun Phrase (NP), as in <Pam ran the bill **up**> but prepositions cannot. In sentence (36b) if <up> moves to the right of <hill>, the sentence becomes ill-formed, as in <*Pam ran the hill up.> One important property of prepositions is that they are always followed by a noun or a pronoun. For this reason, a word may look like a preposition, but if it is not followed by one of these two parts of speech, then it is not a preposition.[6]

1.9 Pronouns

Pronouns are a small group of words that can be used to replace nouns. Grammarians have proposed the following classifications for English:

No.	Types of Pronouns	Examples
1.	Personal pronouns	SUBJECT: I, you, he, she, it, we, you, they OBJECT: me, you, him, her, it, us, you, them
2.	Emphatic pronouns	myself, yourself, himself, herself, itself, ourselves, yourselves, themselves
3.	Possessive pronouns	mine, your, his, hers, its, ours, yours, theirs
4.	Reflexive pronouns	myself, yourself, himself, herself, itself, ourselves, yourselves, themselves
5.	Reciprocal pronouns	each other, one another
6.	Relative pronouns	who, whom, that, which, when, where
7.	Demonstrative pronouns	this, that, these, those
8.	Interrogative pronouns	which, who, whom, where, what, how
9.	Indefinite pronouns	some, few, more, any

Table 8 *Classification of Pronouns*

English used to indicate morphological case on nouns. However, this morphological characteristic has disappeared, except on pronouns. The pronominal forms "who, whom, whose" are the remnant of the Old English case system that has now gone extinct.

---

[6] Except in cases of preposition stranding.

1.10 Articles

English has only two articles: the definite <the> and the indefinite <a> with its allomorph <an>. The primary characteristic of articles is that they must occur with a noun. They cannot occur by themselves. Consequently, where there is an article, there also must be a noun. Modern linguists have included articles in a larger syntactic category called <**determiner**>. This new class includes a wide variety of lexical items that occur with nouns, that is, demonstrative adjectives, interrogative adjectives, possessive adjectives, and nouns indicating possession:

(37)   *The book is expensive.* (Article)

(38)   *This book is expensive.* (Demonstrative adjective)

(39)   *Which book is expensive?* (Interrogative adjective)

(40)   *My book is expensive.* (Possessive adjective)

(41)   *Paul's book is expensive.* (Possessive noun)

All the highlighted words in these sentences are classified now as "determiners."

1.11 Focus on Phrases

According to the architecture presented in Table 1, words are assembled into slightly larger syntactic units that linguists call <**phrases**>. A phrase is defined as "a word or a group of words that form a coherent syntactic unit." It is important to keep in mind that a phrase can consist of a single word or of a long string of words, as in the examples below:

(42)   *It is snowing.*

(43)   *That my friend's car was stolen in broad daylight is incredible.*

The word <*it*> in (42) is a phrase; so is <*that my friend's car was stolen in broad daylight.*>

The eight parts speech discussed previously are merged into five **phrasal categories.** Of these five categories, four are headed by a major part-of-speech to form what is also called **lexical category.** Only the prepositional phrase is headed by a minor part-of-speech. The five phrasal categories are the following:

No.	Types of Phrases
1.	The Noun Phrase (NP)
2.	The Verb Phrase (VP)
3.	The Adjective Phrase (AdjP)
4.	The Adverb Phrase (AdvP)
5.	The Prepositional Phrase (PP)

Table 9 *Phrases Categories*

Ancient grammarians were aware of the "phrase" as a higher level of organization but they did not consider it crucial to grammatical analysis. However, generative grammarians consider the notion of "phrase" to be so important that they have made it the cornerstone of their linguistic investigations. Radford (1986:60) does not exaggerate when he states that "constituents and categories, phrases, have the status of theoretical constructs—i.e., elements without which it is not obvious how we could provide a principled explanation of linguistic phenomena such as coordination." Given the crucial role that phrases play in contemporary grammatical analysis, linguists have invented ways to test whether a group of words functions as a phrase or not.

1.11.1 Identifying Phrases

Three main tests help discover phrases.[7] They are:

1. the movement test

2. the substitution test

3. the deletion test

Following is a brief explanation of how these tests work.

1.11.2 The Movement Test

The movement test can be formulated as follows:

Movement Test

> Any word or group of words that can move from one location in the sentence to another location without causing the derived sentence to be ungrammatical is a phrase.

Let us apply this test to the following sentences:

(44) *Conscientious objectors hate **the death penalty.***

(45) ***The death penalty** is hated by **conscientious objectors.***

Based on the movement test, we conclude that <the death penalty> is a phrase because it has moved from its original position without yielding an ungrammatical sentence. The same reasoning leads us to posit that <conscientious objectors> is also a phrase. This test works very well except in (47) below:

(46) *The friends with whom I went hunting are from Colorado.*

(47) *The friends I went hunting with are from Colorado.*

Prescriptive grammarians frown on the sentences such as (47) because the preposition "with" has been separated from "the friends." Even though they may not be able to justify their dislike, their objection can be explained as a violation of the movement test for determining "phrasehood." We will return to this in the chapter on Prepositions and Prepositional Phrases.

1.11.3 The Substitution Test

The substitution test consists of replacing a word or group of words by another word called a <**pro-form**>. Pro-forms include all pronouns and words such as <*here*>, <*there*>, <*too*>, <*also*>, <*where*>, <*when*>, <*what*>, <*how*>, and <*so do I*>.

---

[7] There are actually four main tests. The "Coordination Test" will be introduced in Chapter 6.

The Substitution Test

Any word or group of words that can be replaced by a pro-form without resulting into an ungrammatical sentence is a phrase.

Let us apply the substitution test to Sentence (48) to see if <conscientious objectors> and <the death penalty> are phrases.

(48) ***They*** *hate the death penalty.*

(49) *Conscientious objectors hate **it**.*

The resulting sentences are well-formed. We conclude therefore that the groups of words <conscientious objectors> and <the death penalty> are phrases. The pronoun <it> replaces <the death penalty>; the pronoun <they> replaces <conscientious objectors>.

Different pro-forms help identify different types of phrases. For example, all pronouns and the pro-form <what> help identify NPs, the pro-forms <when>, <how>, <here>, <there>, and <where> help identify PPs and AdvPs. The pro-form <how> relates to AdvPs and AdjPs. Finally, the pro-forms <me too>, <I too>, <me also>, <I also>, and <so do I> help identify verb phrases.

(50) *Conscientious objectors hate the death penalty.*

(51) *Conscientious objectors hate **what?***

(52) *Teenagers drive very fast?*

(53) *Teenagers drive **how?***

(54) *Mary loves her children, and I love my children.*

(55) *Mary loves her children, **so do I**.*

The <what> in (51) replaces the noun phrase "the death penalty" found in (50). Similarly, <how> in (53) replaces the adverb phrase "very fast" in (52). Finally, <so do I> of (55) replaces the whole verb phrase "love my children" of sentence (54).

1.11.4 The Deletion Test

The first two tests work well for all phrases except for the verb phrase. To identify verb phrases, the deletion test is often used. It is formulated as follows:

The Deletion Test

Any word or group of words that can be deleted without resulting in an ungrammatical sentence is a phrase.

Let us see how this test applies to verb phrases. Consider the sentences below:

(56) *Conscientious objectors **hate the death penalty.***

(57) *I, too.*

(58) *So do I.*

Sentence (57) is well-formed, even though some might object to it as being pedantic. The pro-form <too> is used here to show that the whole verb phrase <hate the death penalty> has been deleted. Since (57) is well-formed, we conclude that <hate the death penalty> is a phrase.

Now let us consider two other sentences:

>   (59) *Sue likes anchovies on her pizza and Patty likes mushrooms on her pizza.*

>   (60) *Sue likes anchovies on her pizza and Patty, mushrooms.*

In (60) the portion of the second clause containing "likes" and "on her pizza" is deleted because they are identical with those in the first clause. The claim is that <likes> can be deleted because it is a verb phrase. The words <on her pizza> can also be deleted because they constitute a prepositional phrase.

1.11.5 Phrase Structure Rules

Generative transformational grammar, the model used in this book, claims that one aspect of grammatical competence can be represented by mathematical-looking formulas of the type shown in Table 10 below. These formulas fulfill two main purposes. First, they are like templates that help assess the grammaticality of the sentences that will be formulated. For this reason, these rules are said to have **predictive power.** Their second role is that they can be used to judge if a sentence that has been produced corresponds to the well-formedness conditions stated by the phrase structure rules. Because the rules can fulfill this function also, they are said to have **descriptive power.**

$$S \rightarrow NP \; AUX \; VP$$
$$NP \rightarrow (Det) \; (AdjP) \; N \; (PP)$$
$$VP \rightarrow V \; (NP) \; (PP) \; (AdvP) \; (AdjP)$$
$$AUX \rightarrow Tense \; (Have\text{-}EN) \; (Be\text{-}ING)$$

$$Tense \rightarrow \begin{Bmatrix} Present \\ Future \\ Past \end{Bmatrix}$$

$$PP \rightarrow P \; NP$$
$$AdjP \rightarrow Adj \; (PP)$$
$$AdvP \rightarrow Adv$$

Table 10 *Simplified Phrase Structure Rules (PSR)*

The phrase structure rules presented here are very basic. More expanded versions will be discussed later in the book.

1.12 Definition of Clause/Sentence

The **clause** is a syntactic notion, whereas the sentence is a semantic/functional notion. However, in most grammar books the two terms are used interchangeably. A clause/sentence is defined as "a group of words that has a subject (expressed or unexpressed) and a tensed (conjugated) or untensed (not conjugated) verb." Sentences fall into three major categories: **simple sentences, compound sentences,** and **complex sentences.** There is a fairly simple formula that one can use to calculate the number of clauses in a sentence. **There is a correlation between the number of main verbs[8] in a sentence and the number of clauses.** If a sentence has one main verb, it will have one

---

[8] Main verbs exclude the aspectual auxiliary verbs "have," "be" and "do" and the modal auxiliary verbs "can," "may," "must," "shall" and "will."

clause. If it has two, three, four main verbs, it will have two, three, four clauses. Let us first examine the properties of simple and compound sentences.

1.12.1 Simple and Compound Sentences

A simple sentence is a sentence that "can stand by itself." Implicit in this definition is that such a sentence does not need another sentence to make its meaning complete. A compound sentence is a juxtaposition of two or more simple sentences tied together by a coordinating conjunction or by a correlative conjunction. The sentences below illustrate a simple sentence, and a case of a compound sentence made up of two simple sentences joined together by a coordinating conjunction:

(61) *Conscientious objectors hate the death penalty.*

(62) *Conscientious objectors hate the death penalty;* **and** *they refuse to serve in the military.*

Sentence (61) is a simple sentence. The totality of its meaning is self-contained. Sentence (62) is made up of two simple sentences which express similar ideas. Each one of the two sentences can stand on its own.

1.12.2 Complex Sentences

In contrast to simple sentences that can stand alone, or to compound sentences which consist of two independent simple sentences that can stand alone, complex sentences are defined as sentences that "contain" other sentences "that cannot stand by themselves." The individual sentences in a complex sentence always need to lean on each other to express a complete thought. Complex sentences are analyzed in terms of clauses. They are divided into two types of clauses: a **main/independent clause** and a **subordinate/dependent clause**. Here are four important syntactic characteristics of subordinate clauses:

1.   They are clauses that cannot stand alone.

2.   They are clauses that are very often introduced by a subordinating conjunction.

3.   They are dominated by a phrasal category.

4.   They include the subordinating conjunction, if there is one.

Let us illustrate these four characteristics with (63) below:

(63) *Everybody knows that conscientious objectors* **hate** *war.*

(64) *I hope they are coming to the party.*

Following the formula alluded to in 1.12, we know that sentences (63) and (64) contain two clauses each because they each have two main verbs. The main verbs of sentence (63) are <knows> and <hate> while those of sentence (64) are <hope> and <come>. The portion <that conscientious objectors hate war> of (63) is the subordinate clause. This clause meets the first requirement because <that conscientious objectors hate war> cannot stand alone. It is also a subordinate clause because it is introduced by the subordinating conjunction <that>. The presence of a subordinating conjunction is not a prerequisite for a clause to qualify as a subordinate clause, as is seen in sentence (64). Finally, (63) meets the third requirement because the <that conscientious objectors hate war> is dominated by a VP. One should always keep in mind that a label such as "independent clause" is a misnomer. Even though grammarians have labeled <Everybody knows> "an independent clause," this clause is "independent" only syntactically, but not semantically. In (65) below, <Everybody knows> is syntactically independent in the sense the sentence is grammatically well-formed. However, semantically <Everybody knows> does not express a complete idea. So, the clause is not semantically "independent." If such a sentence were made, invariably, somebody would ask: <Everybody knows what?>.

Since the verb plays a major role in clausal structure, some linguists base their classifications of subordinate clauses on the morphological characteristics of verbs. This verb-centered approach yields the following categories:

Tensed subordinate clause: the verb is morphologically marked for tense.

> (65) *Everybody knows that conscientious objectors **hate** war.*

To-infinitive subordinate clause: the subordinate clause contains a verb in the infinitive form.

> (66) *Concerned mothers urged Congress **to ban** violent toys.*

Bare infinitive subordinate clause: the subordinate clause contains a verb in the bare infinitive form.

> (67) *Concerned mothers made toy manufacturers **appear** in person before Congress.*

Participial subordinate clause: the subordinate clause contains a verb whose form is in the present participial or past participial form.

> (68) *The senators heard toy manufacturers **contradicting** themselves.*

> (69) *The senators watched toy manufacturers **humiliated** by their inconsistencies.*

Wh-subordinate clause: the subordinate clause is introduced by a Wh word:

> (70) *The senators wondered **whether toy manufacturers should be fined.***

A diagram summary of the different types of sentences and clauses will help give a visual display of the preceding analysis:

More will be said about compound sentences and subordinate clauses in Chapters 12 and 13.

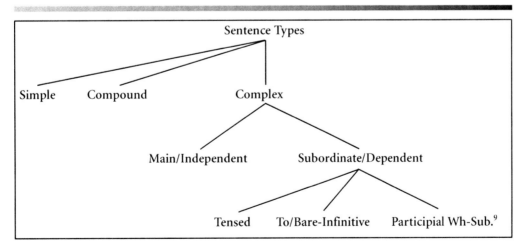

Table 11 *Functional Descriptors*

[9] These clauses can also be introduced by conjunctive adverbs, to be discussed in 12.5.4 and 13.3.

1.12.3 Subordinate Clauses in the Noun Phrase

Some subordinate clauses occur within the subject noun phrase or the object noun phrase. Such clauses are called "relative clauses" because the pronominal antecedent relates the clause to the lexical NP as seen in the sentences below:

(71) **The place where** I find peace and tranquility is in the mountains.

(72) The American **president whom** I admire the most is Lincoln.

The relative pronoun <where> has as its antecedent the lexical NP <the place>. Similarly, the antecedent of <whom> is <the American president>. The pronoun agrees with its lexical antecedent in semantic features.

1.13 Formal vs. Functional Analyses

Many grammar books do not make a clear distinction between **formal analysis** and **functional analysis.** However, this distinction is very important in the identification and classification of parts of speech. Formal analysis focuses on the formal characteristics of a word that help identify it. Morphological and syntactic clues are considered formal characteristics. Functional characteristics rely on semantics, or the role that a word plays in a particular sentence to help identify and classify it according to its part-of-speech. The two do not always coincide, as illustrated by the three sentences below:

(73) I did my **best.**

(74) He works **best** alone.

(75) He is the **best.**

According to formal characteristics, the word <best> is an adjective. However, in (73) it is not an adjective, but a noun. We know this because any lexical item that is preceded by a determiner is a noun. In (74) <best> is an adverb because it modifies the verb <works>. Finally, in (75) <best> is not only an adjective, but also a superlative adjective. We arrive at this conclusion because it modifies the pronoun <He>. In (75) the presence of <the> is misleading. It would mislead the unsuspecting analyst into thinking that <best> is a noun. However, this is not true. These examples reinforce the view that a syntactic analysis must take into account both formal and functional characteristics of words.

1.14 Minimal Accuracy Threshold in Grammatical Analysis

A grammatical analysis is deemed accurate if it brings insights from both functional analysis and formal analysis to bear on the grammatical element under investigation. I have given the acronym MAT Condition (Minimal Accuracy Threshold) to this accuracy threshold and formalized it as follows:

MAT Condition = Functional Descriptors + Formal Descriptor

Minimally, two descriptors are necessary to satisfy the MAT Condition. A grammatical analysis that omits one of the two factors falls short of the accuracy threshold and becomes unsatisfactory because it lacks precision. The level of accuracy and sophistication of any grammatical analysis is directly proportionate with the number of accurate descriptors used. Ideally, more than two descriptors should be used but in practice elementary analyses such as the ones proposed in this book are acceptable if only two descriptors are used. Customarily, the first descriptor indicates the grammatical function of the word, phrase, or construction under consideration. The second descriptor focuses on formal characteristics such as the part-of-speech, the phrasal category, and the type of syntactic construction. In (76) each word can be described accurately by using only two descriptors:

(76)   *The students left the room hurriedly.*

The word <the> is a definite article. The two descriptors combine to give an accurate grammatical picture of <the>. However, if we limit ourselves by saying that <the> is only an "article," the analysis is not entirely satisfactory because it gives only information about the part-of-speech of <the> while ignoring its grammatical function. Such an analysis is only partially accurate because we know that <the> is not the only article in English. As a result, the analysis does not sufficiently discriminate between the articles <the> and <a/an>. However, minimal accuracy is achieved if both functional and formal descriptors are used to label <the>. In so doing, the analysis moves from being overly generic to being very specific. In grammatical analyses, specific descriptions are preferred to generic ones. Saying that <the> is a definite article satisfies the MAT Condition. Table 12 summarizes the main descriptors for the words in (76):

The remaining chapters will provide definitions and examples of the functional descriptors found in Tables 12 and 13. The "+" sign in a part-of-speech column means that the functional descriptor is associated with that specific part-of-speech. The classification below is by no means exhaustive.

No.	Word	Functional Analysis	Formal Analysis	Complete Grammatical Analysis
1.	the	definite	article	definite article
2.	students	subject	noun	subject noun[10]
3.	left	transitive	verb	transitive verb
4.	the	definite	article	definite article
5.	room	direct object	noun	direct object
6.	hurriedly	manner	adverb	manner adverb

Table 12 *Minimal Accuracy Threshold*

Table 13 (on the following page) reveals some of the weaknesses of the traditional system of classifying words both formally (that is according to their parts of speech) and functionally (according to their function in the sentence). A case in point is the functional classification of prepositions. According to this table, prepositions fulfill only a locative function. However, as will be discussed in 6.2.5, prepositions fulfill a variety of other functions in the sentence, including but not limited to the following: accompaniment/comitative, beneficiary, instrument, source, goal, and path as illustrated by the examples below:

(77)   Tallie is playing *with* Chloe. (Comitative function)

(78)   Joni paints *with* her teeth. (Instrumental function)

---

[10] Usually the grammatical functions "subject" and "object" entail that the word is a noun. However, this is not always the case. For instance in the sentence "to err is human," <to err> is the subject but it is not a noun. Consequently, it is not redundant to provide formal information about the subject or object.

No.	Functional Descriptors	Noun	Verb	Adjective	Adverb	Pronoun	Conjunction	Preposition[11]	Article
1.	Subject, Nominative	+				+			
2.	Direct Object, Accusative	+				+			
3.	Indirect Object, Dative	+				+			
4.	Transitive		+						
5.	Intransitive		+						
6.	Ditransitive		+						
7.	Stative, Copular, Linking		+						
8.	Demonstrative			+		+			
9.	Possessive			+		+			
10.	Indefinite			+		+			+
11.	Definite			+		+			+
12.	Reciprocal					+			
13.	Reflexive					+			
14.	Relative					+			
15.	Locative				+			+	
16.	Temporal				+				
17.	Manner				+				
18.	Coordinating						+		
19.	Subordinating						+		
20.	Conjunctive				+				
21.	Correlative						+		
22.	Modal		+						
23.	Auxiliary		+						
24.	Attributive			+					
25.	Predicative			+					
26.	Prenominal			+					
27.	Postnominal			+					
28.	Numeral			+					
29.	Ordinal			+					
30.	Flat				+				

Table 13 *Functional Descriptors*

[11] Traditional Grammar does not offer a lot of possibilities in classifying prepositions according to their syntactic function. However, this situation has changed a lot since the advent of Thematic Role Analysis as described in Section 6.2.5.

(79) Men are *from* Mars and women *from* Venus. (Source function)

(80) Our friends are flying *to* Ghana. (Goal function)

(81) Jeff went to Casablanca *through* Paris. (Path function)

(82) Parents work hard *for* their children. (Beneficiary function)

Jurafsky and Martin (2000:343) observe that contemporary linguists have been forced to create many additional functional categories because the categories proposed by traditional grammar are too restrictive. They note that as many as 100 subcategories have been added to the classification of verbs whereas traditional grammar had only two categories: transitive and intransitive.

1.15 Conclusion

The ability to identify, name, and classify parts of speech is an important first step in the process of developing grammatical awareness. Greek grammarians did not develop significant insights into the grammatical structure of their language until they "discovered" its parts of speech. Similarly, it is virtually impossible to understand grammar without first understanding the semantic, morphological, syntactic, and functional characteristics of the elements that make up phrases and sentences. The goal of this chapter has been to provide rule-of-thumb definitions. These definitions will be expanded as we examine more and more syntactic structures.

Key Terms to Know

These are the key terms that you should be able to use and define after reading this chapter. Do not be intimidated by this list. You will encounter the same words in subsequent chapters. By the time you finish the book, you will know these terms very well.

1. active voice: 1.4.4
2. adjective: 1.2.2, 1.4.6, 1.5, 1.5.1, 1.5.2, 1.5.3, 1.6, 1.6.2, 1.10, 1.11, 1.13, 1.14
3. anthropological linguistics or linguistics anthropology: 1.1.3
4. aspect: 1.0, 1.1.2, 1.1.3, 1.4.1, 1.4.3, 1.11.5
5. attributive adjective: 1.5.3
6. clause: 1.1.2, 1.2, 1.7.2, 1.11.4, 1.12, 1.12.2, 1.12.3
7. complex sentence: 1.12, 1.12.1, 1.12.2
8. compound sentence: 1.12, 1.12.1, 1.12.2
9. computational linguistics: 1.1.3, 1.2.1
10. conditional mood: 1.4.5
11. coordinating conjunction: 1.7.1, 1.12.1
12. descriptor: 1.12.2, 1.14
13. discourse: 1.1.2, 1.2
14. ditransitive verb: 1.4.6, 1.14
15. ergative verb: 1.4.4
16. feminine: 1.3.2
17. formal analysis: 1.13, 1.14
18. formal descriptor: 1.14
19. functional analysis: 1.13, 1.14
20. functional descriptor: 1.12, 1.14
21. gender: 1.3.2, 1.5.2
22. grammatical category: 1.2.2
23. habitual aspect: 1.4.3
24. historical linguistics: 1.1
25. imperative mood: 1.4.5
26. indicative/declarative mood: 1.4.5
27. infinitive: 1.2.2, 1.12.2
28. interjections: 1.2.2
29. intransitive verb: 1.4.6: 1.14
30. lexical category: 1.2.2, 1.11
31. linguistics: 1.0, 1.1, 1.1.2, 1.1.3, 1.7.2
32. linking verb: 1.4.6, 1.14

EXERCISE 1—ON THE NATURE OF LINGUISTICS

1. This is the first day of the fall semester. You meet your roommate for the first time and strike up a conversation with him/her. You tell him/her that your major is linguistics because you want to teach Language Arts or English as a Second/Foreign language in the Peace Corps. With a puzzled look, your new roommate asks you: "What is linguistics?" How would you define it for him/her?

2. Now that you have defined linguistics for your roommate, proceed to tell him/her the core areas of linguistics.

3. After your somewhat lengthy definition, your new roommate tells you that his/her major is computer science. Tell her/him why linguistics is a bedfellow with computer science. Now that you have drawn your roommate's attention, proceed to tell him/her the other academic disciplines that linguistics interacts with.

EXERCISE 2—MAJOR PARTS OF SPEECH IDENTIFICATION

Examine the text below and answer the relevant questions:

The Gettysburg Address

by Abraham Lincoln

"Fourscore and seven years ago our fathers brought forth on this continent a new nation, conceived in liberty and dedicated to the proposition that all men are created equal. Now we are engaged in a great civil war, testing whether that nation or any nation so conceived and so dedicated can long endure. We are met on a great battlefield of that war. We have come to dedicate a portion of that field as a final resting-place for those who here gave their lives that that nation might live. It is altogether fitting and proper that we should do this.

But in a larger sense, we cannot dedicate, we cannot consecrate, we cannot hallow this ground. The brave men, living and dead, who struggled here have consecrated it far above our poor power to add or detract. The world will little note nor long remember what we say here, but it can never forget what they did here. It is for us the living rather to be dedicated here to the unfinished work which they who fought here have thus far so nobly advanced. It is rather for us to be here dedicated to the great task remaining before us—that from these honored dead we take increased devotion to that cause for which they gave the last full measure of devotion—that we here highly resolve that these dead shall not have died in vain, that this nation under God shall have a new birth of freedom, and that government of the people, by the people, for the people shall not perish from the earth."

Fill in the table with five words that belong to the parts of speech specified in the table below. **Note:** There may not be five words to fill all fields. Also, do not repeat the same word.

No.	Nouns	Verbs	Auxiliaries	Adjectives	Adverbs
1.					
2.					
3.					
4.					
5.					

EXERCISE 3—MINOR PARTS OF SPEECH IDENTIFICATION

Examine the previous text and fill in the table below with the relevant part-of-speech. Do not repeat the same word. **Note:** There may not be enough words to fill all fields.

No.	Articles	Conjunctions	Prepositions	Pronouns
1.				
2.				
3.				
4.				
5.				

EXERCISE 4—MINIMAL ACCURACY THRESHOLD ANALYSIS

Use **two** descriptors, a functional descriptor and a formal descriptor, to analyze each of the highlighted words in the text below. Refer back to section 1.14 if necessary to do this assignment.

The Gettysburg Address

by Abraham Lincoln (excerpt)

. . . **But** (1) in a larger sense, we cannot dedicate, we **cannot** (2) consecrate, we cannot hallow **this** (3) ground. The brave men, living and dead, who struggled **here** (4) have consecrated it far above our **poor** (5) power to add or **detract** (6). The world **will** (7) little note nor long remember what we say here, but it can never forget what they did here. It is for **us** (8) the **living** (9) rather to be dedicated here to the unfinished work which they **who** (10) fought here have thus far so **nobly** (11) advanced. It is rather for us to be here dedicated to the great task **remaining** (12) before us— that from these **honored** (13) dead we take increased devotion to that cause for which they gave the **last** (14) full measure of devotion—that **we** (15) here highly resolve that these dead shall not have died in vain, that this nation under **God** (16) shall have a new **birth** (17) of freedom, and that government of the people, **by** (18) the people, for the people shall not **perish** (19) from **the** (20) earth."

The first one has been done for you to give you an example.

No.	Word	Functional Descriptor	Formal Descriptor
1.	but	coordinating	conjunction
2.	cannot		
3.	this		
4.	here		
5.	poor		
6.	detract		
7.	will		
8.	us		
9.	living		
10.	who		
11.	nobly		
12.	remaining		
13.	honored		
14.	last		
15.	we		
16.	God		
17.	birth		
18.	by		
19.	perish		
20.	the		

EXERCISE 5—CLASSIFICATION OF SENTENCES

Three types of clauses are generally found in languages: **simple clauses, compound clauses,** and **complex clauses.** The latter consists of a **main clause** and a **subordinate clause.** Examine the highlighted sentences/clauses below and classify them according to their clause type. **Note** that there may be multiple layers of embedding in some sentences.

The Gettysburg Address

by Abraham Lincoln

"*Fourscore and seven years ago our fathers brought forth on this continent a new nation,* conceived in liberty and dedicated to the proposition that all men are created equal. Now we are engaged in a great civil war, testing whether that nation or any nation so conceived and so dedicated can long endure. *We are met on a great battle-field of that war. We have come to dedicate a portion of that field as a final resting-place for those who here gave their lives that that nation might live. It is altogether fitting and proper that we should do this. . . .*"

1. How would you classify the sentence, "*Fourscore and seven years ago our fathers brought forth on this continent a new nation*"? Choose one of the following options:

    a. Simple sentence

    b. Compound sentence

    c. Complex sentence

    Provide a short justification for your answer:

2. How would you classify the sentence, "*We are met on a great battlefield of that war*"? Choose one of the following options:

    a. Simple sentence

    b. Compound sentence

    c. Complex sentence

    Provide a short justification for your answer:

3. How would you classify the sentence, "*We have come to dedicate a portion of that field as a final resting-place for those who here gave their lives that that nation might live*"? Choose one of the following options:

    a. Simple sentence

    b. Compound sentence

    c. Complex sentence

    Provide a short justification for your answer:

4. How would you classify the sentence, "*It is altogether fitting and proper that we should do this*"? Choose one of the following options:

    a. Simple sentence

    b. Compound sentence

    c. Complex sentence

    Provide a short justification for your answer:

Chapter 2

A Brief History of the Study of Grammar

2.0 INTRODUCTION

Many grammar textbooks begin their study without giving students enough information about the history and evolution of grammatical concepts. Catchy phrases such as "the Chomskyan revolution," "modern syntax," "prescriptive grammar," "descriptive grammar," and "traditional grammar" are used here and there without sufficient explanation. I have sought to avoid these pitfalls by devoting this chapter and the next to such issues. I retrace the steps in the study of grammar from its humble beginnings in Greece in 5th Century B.C. to its vibrant developments in America since the end of the Second World War.

Knowledge is cumulative. In the history of ideas, it is hard to know precisely when one methodological framework stopped and where another one began. In actuality, linguistic theories blend into each other seamlessly. The timeline proposed in this chapter serves only a pedagogical interest. It highlights important landmarks in the evolution of linguistics that students might find useful to know. For reasons that will become clear in the next chapter, we have taken the liberty here to divide the history of linguistics into two major periods: the pre-Chomskyan era and the Chomskyan era. Chomsky (2000:3) seems to agree with the timeline outline in this chapter. He states that

> The study of language is one of the oldest branches of systematic inquiry, tracing back to classical India and Greece, with a rich and fruitful history of achievement. From a different point of view, it is quite young. The major research enterprises of today took shape only 40 years ago, when some of leading ideas of the tradition were

revived and reconstructed, opening the way to what has proven to be a very productive inquiry.

2.1 It All Began with Writing

Human beings have spoken longer than they have analyzed. Historical evidence suggests that prior to the development of writing systems, people did not have a metalinguistic awareness of the language(s) they spoke. **Metalanguage** is defined as the language used to talk about language or to describe language. Thus, metalinguistic knowledge is only a by-product of literacy (Fromkin et al 2003:546–7):

15000 B.C.	Petroglyphs: cave drawings
4000 B.C.	The invention of Sumerian cuneiforms
3000 B.C.	The invention of Egyptian Hieroglyphs
1500 B.C.	The invention of the syllabary by Phoenicians
1000 B.C.	The development of alphabetic writing by Greeks

Table 1 *Time Line of the Development of Writing*

The Greek started writing their language around 1000 B.C. Until then, Greek was only an oral language. Even when Greek became a written language, metalinguistic terminology to describe it did not develop until 500 years later. Plato and his students are widely credited with coining words to describe the Greek language.

2.2 Syntactic Traditions

Before the 5th Century B.C. there was no syntactic consciousness among the Greeks. It was not until Plato (429/7–347 B.C.) that such a consciousness developed. He is credited with having formally distinguished **vowels** from **consonants.** This "discovery" led him to find the **syllable.** It is widely believed that Plato is the first in the Western linguistic tradition to have distinguished **nouns** from **verbs** and **adjectives.** His student Aristotle (384–322 B.C.) continued in his master's footsteps and coined the labels for **conjunctions** and functional terms such as **subject** and **predicate.**

The most important ancient Greek grammarian was Dionysius Thrax (120–90 B.C.) of Alexandria (Egypt, Africa). Most linguists credit him and Philetas of Cos with having laid the foundation for subsequent linguistic analysis. He wrote the first descriptive grammar of Greek. Disterheft (2003:24) notes that "subsequent grammars written for other languages relied on it until the twelfth century A.D. Dionysius distinguished eight parts of speech, a number that remained standard until the twentieth century."

2.2.1 The Legacy of Greek Grammar on Latin

Greek was the international lingua franca from the 4th Century B.C. to around the 2nd Century A.D. Even though the Romans conquered the Greeks and their former colonies, they continued to use Greek for centuries before they finally switched to Latin (Koffi 1997:186–88). Most Latin scholars were thoroughly educated in Greek. When they decided to describe Latin, they borrowed their linguistic metalanguage from the Greeks. Kristeva (1981:120–21) shows that Varron, the author of *De Lingua Latina* (47–45 B.C.), translated rather literally Greek linguistic terms and applied them to Latin.[1]

[1] *De Lingua Latina* is seen by many Latin scholars to be the best grammar of Latin of its time. Varron dedicated it to Cicero.

2.2.2 Scholasticism and Indigenous Grammars

The scholasticism movement that started around the 9th and ended in the 14th Century has its roots in the Monastic Movement that began in Egypt among Coptic Christians in the 4th Century A.D. When the movement reached Europe in the 4th and 5th Centuries, it underwent some changes. Unlike North African monks, European monks did not move to desert places in solitude. Instead, they formed communities of like-minded individuals. They devoted themselves to the following activities:

1. the copying of the Bible

2. the study of Holy Scriptures

3. the study of Church Fathers

4. the study of Rhetoric

5. the writing of Grammar of local European languages

6. the training of young monks

As a result, Walker, Williston, et al. (1985:323) argue that monasteries were at the vanguard of the intellectual awakening in most European countries. Knowledge gained in the monasteries was little by little transferred to urban cathedrals where lay people were taught to read and write in the various European languages. It was during this era that the grammars of languages such as English and French were first written.

Major European universities such as Sorbonne in France, Cambridge and Oxford in England, and Leipzig in Germany were closely associated with churches. The language of instruction in all these institutions of higher education was Latin. However, the desire for some non-conformist clergymen to see the native languages of Europe play a major role in religious life led to a flurry of Bible translation activities in the second phase of the Scholastic Era. Bible translation activities often went hand in hand with the writing of grammars, syllabaries and primers.

2.2.3 Humanism and the Study of Grammar (15th to 17th Century)

The fall of Constantinople in 1453 is seen by many as a watershed event. It marked the end of the Scholastic Era and ushered in the Age of Humanism. Humanism is defined as a devotion to the study of the humanities, that is, the study of classical literatures and cultures. With the fall of Constantinople, Eastern Christian scholars fled the Byzantine Empire (the name given to the Roman Empire in the East) with precious religious documents written in Hebrew and Greek. However, scholars in the West knew only Latin, for the most part. Soon Hebrew and Greek became academic subjects at the major European institutions of higher education. These events had a major impact on the study of language. Disterheft (2003:26) writes that because of their exposure to the new structures and forms found in these languages, linguists started to think in terms of language universals rather than confining their remarks to Latin.

The flurry of Bible translation that started at the close of the Scholastic Age gained momentum during the Renaissance and the Reformation. By the end of the 16th Century the Bible had been translated into all the major European languages. Some clergymen taught laypeople to read Scriptures in their mother tongue at the risk of their lives. Many scholars believe that the "subversive" activity of translating Scriptures into the native tongues of Europeans marked the first giant step towards the Reformation. Martin Luther, who is regarded by many as the "father" of the German language, is credited with the following statement: "You cannot affect succeeding generations if you do not provide the Bible in the vernacular of the people."

2.2.4 The Era of Comparative Linguistics

Another important development in linguistics during this era was the great interest in comparative linguistics. Interest in learning other languages, dead or living, was the main characteristic of this period. Consequently many books were written which compared aspects of different languages, highlighting the differences and the common features. As remarkable as these achievements were, European grammarians who wrote the grammar of their own languages still used Latin as the model. Baker (1978:21) writes:

> "The examples that we have given of grammatical statements couched within this traditional framework have been from Latin. Many grammars based on the same framework were written for languages all over the world by European scholars, administrators, missionaries, and travelers. Most of the grammars, whether they were grammars of African, American Indian, or Asian languages, were organized in much the same fashion as were the Latin grammars of their day."

2.2.5 The Era of Reconstruction (18th to 19th Century)

On September 27th, 1786, Sir William Jones gave a remarkable paper in which he claimed that Sanskrit, an ancient language in India, was genetically related to Greek, Latin, and English. Jones based his claim on regular sound correspondences that he was able to trace among languages in Europe and languages in India. This led scholars to coin the phrase **"Indo-European"** to name a large family of languages that are related genetically. This "discovery" fuelled the interest of scholars who spent a great deal of time comparing European languages and Indian languages.[2] Franz Bopp (1791–1867) added Persian and German to the languages related to Sanskrit. Rasmus Rask (1787–1832) later found that Armenian and Lithuanian were also related to Sanskrit. As a result, an impressive methodology was invented to account for how languages change. Scholars such as Jacob Grimm and K. Verner (1864–1893) came up with rules that accounted for the regularity of sound changes between Sanskrit and European languages. This work has led to a massive linguistic reconstruction effort. Joseph Greenberg and his former students at Stanford have classified all the languages spoken in the world today into 13 mega language families:

1. the Indo-European family

2. the Caucasian family

3. the Altaic family

4. the Finno-Uralic family

5. the Dravidian family

6. the Austro-Asiatic family

7. the Sino-Tibetan family

8. the Austronesian family

9. the Indo-Pacific family

10. the Afroasiatic family

11. the Niger-Congo family

[2] Mounin (1974:162) argues that comparative linguistics borrowed some of its terminology and scientific methodology from biology, anatomy, and paleontology.

12. the Nilo-Saharan family

13. the Khoisan family

The methodology developed for the purposes of historical reconstruction proved invaluable for the cataclysmic changes that would take place in the study of languages in the 20th Century. Statistical methods were used by historical linguists to help reconstruct proto-languages.

2.2.6 Structuralism (Late 19th Century to the first half of 20th Century)

The intense reconstruction efforts of the early 19th Century began to solidify the scientific methodology used by linguists. Gradually, the emphasis shifted from reconstruction to the description of unwritten languages of the Americas and Africa. Ferdinand de Saussure (1857–1913) is often mentioned as the person who helped change the focus of linguistics from reconstruction to description. According to Aitchison (1992:24), he is the one who first suggested that language was an integrated structure. She contends that before him "nobody had seriously examined the relationship of each element to all others." Saussure used the metaphor of a game of chess to underscore his point: "chess is a game in which each item is defined by its relationship to all others. His insistence that language is a carefully built **structure** of interwoven elements initiated the era of structural linguistics."

Saussure may have provided the ideas that led to structuralism. However, the rigorous scientific methodology for the description of unwritten languages came from American linguists. Faced with the rapid disappearance of Native American languages, linguists had to design reliable and systematic methods for the description of these languages. The publication of *Language* in 1933 by Leonard Bloomfield (1887–1949) marked the beginning of "scientific" linguistics. Lyons (1970:29) observes that Bloomfield did more than anyone else to make linguistics autonomous and "scientific." Bloomfield and his associates held dear the followings axioms:

1. A scientific methodology must be based on **"discovery procedures."** The procedures were a set of strict guidelines that one followed to discover the phonemes, morphemes, and the syntactic patterns of unwritten languages. These procedures are now summarized in a beautiful flowchart in *Language Files*, p. 91.

2. **Primacy of spoken language over written language:** the linguists of Bloomfield's generation distinguished themselves from those of the previous generations by taking the theoretical and radical position that speech is primary and written language is secondary. Up until the Structuralist Era, grammarians had preferred written language as the basis for writing grammars. Robdy and Winterowd (2005:3) note that Dionysius Thrax and other Greeks used the works of Homer as the basis of their grammars. The Romans used the works of Cicero and Virgil in writing their grammars of Latin. English grammars followed the same pattern. The writings of established authors and the speech patterns of the educated class became the norm on which grammatical opinions were based.

3. **The distinction between descriptive grammar and prescriptive grammar:** Structural linguists made a clear distinction between these two approaches to grammar. Prescriptive grammar is the kind of grammar that legislates the speech patterns or the writings of the educated class. Bloomfield (1933:8) held

prescriptive grammar in utmost contempt as can be seen from this excerpt from his book:

They [eighteenth century scholars] stated grammatical features of language in philosophical terms and took no account of the structural difference between languages, but obscured it by forcing their descriptions into the scheme of Latin grammar. . . . This failure to distinguish between actual speech and the use of writing distorted also their notions about the history of language. They saw that in medieval and modern times highly cultivated persons wrote (and even spoke) good Latin, while the less educated or careless made many mistakes: failing to see that this Latin-writing was an artificial and academic exercise, they concluded that language was preserved by usage of educated and careful people and changed by the corruptions of the vulgar. In the case of modern languages like English, they believed accordingly, that the speech forms of books and of upper-class conversation represented an older and purer level, from which the vulgarisms of the common people had branched off as corruptions by a process of linguistic decay. The grammarians felt free, therefore, to prescribe fanciful rules which they derived from considerations of logic.

Lyons (1970:37) writes that the "Bloomfieldians" and various other "schools" were so opposed to prescriptive grammar that "they made it a point of principle not to venture any judgment about the grammaticality, or correctness, of sentences, unless these sentences had been attested in the usage of native speakers and included in the corpus of material that formed the basis of the grammatical description." In rejecting prescriptive grammar, linguists were not bashful about their preference of spoken language over written language.

4. **The proclamation of linguistic equality:** Structural linguists took it for granted that all languages were equal. Allusions to "primitive" languages were found in the writings of previous generations of linguists. However, American structural linguists broke away from this entrenched belief in European speculative linguistics. Bloomfield and like-minded linguists believed that "all human societies of which we have knowledge speak languages of roughly equal complexity; and the differences of grammatical structure that we do find among languages throughout the world are such that they cannot be correlated with the cultural development of the people speaking them and cannot be used as evidence for the construction of an evolutionary theory of human language," Lyons (1970:18).

5. **The exclusion of semantics:** Semantics is elusive, so structural linguists did not know how to integrate semantics into a "scientific" study of languages. Bloomfield (1933:139–40) gave the following excuse for not including semantics:

The situations which prompt people to utter speech include every object and happening in their universe. In order to give a scientifically accurate definition of meaning for every form of a language we should have to have a scientifically accurate knowledge of everything in the speakers' world. . . . The statement of meaning is therefore the weak point in language-study, and will remain so until human knowledge advances very far beyond its present state.

In spite of the structuralists' neglect of semantics, they laid the foundation for a fruitful analysis of semantics by introducing the notion of **componential analysis.** At its core, componential analysis assumes that every word is made of a bundle of features that contribute to its overall meaning. Thus, it was believed that the sum total of the features helps determine the complete meaning of the word. Wasow (2003:304) sees the structuralists' contribution as follows:

> "... treating categories as bundles of features makes it possible to represent a large number of grammatical categories quite compactly, since every different combination of features and values is a different category. . . . It does make it possible to capture generalizations across categories of words and phrases, as well as characterizing categories at more or less fine-grained levels."

In the early days of Generative Grammar, semantics was deemed to play only a marginal role in syntax. Chomsky (1965:226)[3] did not substantively change his view of semantics, but he showed considerable willingness to allow it to assume more important roles. Beginning with the Extended Standard Theory, semantics was incorporated into syntax.

2.2.7 The Legacy of Structural Linguistics

Commenting on Bloomfield's legacy, Aitchison (1992:24–25) writes that "Bloomfield had immense influence—far more than the European linguists working during this period—the so-called Bloomfieldian era lasted more than twenty years. During this time, large numbers of linguists concentrated on writing descriptive grammars of unwritten languages . . . The Bloomfieldians laid down a valuable background of linguistic methodology for future generations." Other prominent linguists associated with structural linguistics are Franz Boaz (1858–1942), Edward Sapir (1884–1939), Benjamin Wolf (1897–1941), Zellig Harris (1909–1992), Roman Jacobson (1896–1982), to mention only these.

2.3 The Dawn of Generative Transformational Grammar

Aitchison (1992:25) begins her description of linguistics in the mid-20th Century with this remarkable statement: "In 1957, linguistics took a new turn. Noam Chomsky, then aged twenty-nine, a teacher at the Massachusetts Institute of Technology, published a book called *Syntactic Structures*. Although containing fewer than 120 pages, this little book started a revolution in linguistics. Chomsky is, arguably, the most influential linguist of the century. Certainly, he is the linguist whose reputation has spread furthest outside of linguistics. He has, in the opinion of many, transformed linguistics from a relatively obscure discipline of interest mainly to PhD students and future missionaries into a major social science of direct relevance to psychologists, sociologists, anthropologists, philosophers, and others." Jackendoff (2002:68) claims that Chomsky's influence extends even to biology. Pinker (1994:23) adds that Chomsky is currently among the ten most cited writers in all of the humanities. Jurafsky and Martin (2000:348) note that Chomsky's influence on computational linguistics is undeniable. Some computational linguistic operations have even been named after him!

2.3.1 Innovation

The most important innovations that Chomsky brought to linguistics are formalism and a set of new concepts. The formal apparatus will be discussed in the next chapter. In the present one, we introduce the important terms indispensable for understanding contemporary linguistics.

---

[3] See Chomsky's footnote 15 on p. 226.

2.3.2 Competence and Performance

The terms most associated with generative grammar (Chomsky's brand of linguistics) are "competence" and "performance". I will define them simply as follows: **Competence**[4] is the ideal knowledge that members of a speech community have of their language. It allows them to generate all the sentences they want to produce, and to understand all the sentences that other members of the same speech community use to communicate with them. **Performance,** on the other hand, is the everyday use of competence to express one's ideas and/or to understand ideas expressed by others. Competence is perfect; performance is imperfect. Competence is ideal; performance is not ideal. Some linguists, especially sociolinguists, have scoffed at the idea of an undifferentiated competence. They note that such a concept is hard to reconcile with sociolinguistic realities which point to speech variations in all language communities. To his detractors, Chomsky has said repeatedly[5] that due to the complexity of language, a certain amount of idealization is necessary to describe it scientifically. He argues on page 3 that "linguistic theory is concerned primarily with an ideal speaker-listener, in a completely homogeneous speech-community, who knows its language perfectly and is unaffected by such grammatically irrelevant conditions as memory limitations, distractions, shifts of attention and interest, and errors (random or characteristic) in applying his knowledge in actual performance." More recently, he has argued that idealization "is the procedure we follow in attempting to discover reality, the real principles of nature" (Chomsky 2000:49, 123).

2.3.3 Grammaticality Judgment

In the idealized world of linguistic analysis, linguists catch a glimpse of competence by analyzing the sentences that speakers produce. Speakers are called upon to use their intuition and give their opinion about sentences to native speakers. Their judgment allows linguists to elicit three types of responses:

1. The sentence is grammatical, that is, it conforms to the mental grammar that all the speakers of the language will normally produce;

2. The sentence is ungrammatical, that is, no adult member of the speech community is likely to produce such a sentence;

3. The sentence is acceptable but some people may not produce it.

The grammaticality judgment that linguists seek in order to make some claims about the rules of a language has nothing to do with prescriptive grammar (Chomsky 1965:11). The intuition that helps native speakers and proficient speakers to form grammaticality judgment is not an easy thing to explain. Chomsky observes on page 151 that explaining all the knowledge that speakers rely on to accept or reject sentences requires a very high level of theoretical sophistication.

2.3.4 Universal Grammar

Chomsky's main criticism of structural linguistics is that even though it provided a wealth of information about individual languages, it was unable to make claims concerning language universals (Chomsky 1965:5). From the very beginning, Chomsky has made it clear that his overall agenda in studying language is to find out what is common about all human languages and how the human mind works in processing language. This aspect

---

[4] In his most recent writings, Chomsky has replaced "competence" by "I-language." He notes that "I" stands for "internal, individual, intentional," (Chomsky 2000:78).

[5] See Chomsky (1965:3) and also Chomsky (1995:9).

of Chomsky's approach is known as **Universal Grammar (UG).** In order to distinguish between what qualifies as language universal and what qualifies as language specific, Chomsky has introduced two technical terms: **"principles"** and **"parameters."** Culicover (1997:4) provides, perhaps, the most intelligible definitions of the two: "The Principles and Parameters view is that much of this knowledge [of language] is not learned, but an intrinsic part of the human mind. If some knowledge of language is built into the human mind, it must be built into all human minds, and must therefore be universal. . . . The universal knowledge concerns the *principles* that determine the basic architecture of any linguistic system, and the *parameters* that govern the range of variation that this architecture may display." The belief about linguistic universals has led Chomsky to propose theories that are putatively applicable to all human languages.

Universal Grammar is a central notion in Generative Linguistics. For Chomsky (1965:35) it seems to be the single issue that would determine progress in linguistics. He argues forcefully that "real progress in linguistics consists in the discovery that certain features of given languages can be reduced to universal properties of language, and explained in terms of these deeper aspects of linguistic form." Chomsky (2000:79) is not oblivious of the differences between languages. But for him, these differences are inconsequential. Instead, he focuses on what is invariant among all human languages:

> *It may be that the computational system [of language] itself is (virtually) invariant, fixed by innate biological endowment, variation among languages and language types being limited to certain options in the lexicon; quite restricted options. Slight changes in an intricate system may yield what appear to differ drastically from one another, though they differ only in rather marginal ways, it appears.*

On page 118 he argues that "a rational Martian scientist would probably find the variation rather superficial, concluding that there is one human language with minor variants." Thus, generative grammar pursues two different but interrelated goals. Baker (1989:14) describes these two goals as follows:

> *Generative grammar thus consists of two related enterprises. One of these is concerned with discovering the rules of particular languages—for instance, English, Chinese, and Arabic. The other is concerned with uncovering the genetically determined principles that make their effects felt in all languages. Just as we speak of English grammar, Chinese grammar, and Arabic grammar when we are talking about the rules of these individual languages, so we can use the term* universal grammar *when we are talking about the genetically determined principles.*

2.3.5 Linguistic Creativity and Recursion

The concepts of creativity and recursion are intertwined. Both seek to explain how the human mind generates and comprehends language. Linguistic **creativity** is defined as the ability that all human beings have to generate and comprehend an infinite number of sentences that they have never produced before or heard before by using a finite number of rules that they subconsciously know. Lyons (1970:21) explains the effects of creativity as follows: "He [native speaker] is generally unaware of applying any grammatical rules or systematic principles of formation when he constructs either new sentences or sentences he has previously encountered. And yet the sentences that he utters will generally be accepted by other native speakers of the language as correct and will be understood by them." **Recursion,** on the other hand, is defined as a rule that allows a syntactic category to generate another syntactic category of its own kind. Pinker (1999:8–9) states that "a recursive grammar can generate sentences of any length, and thus can generate an infinite number of sentences. So a human being possessing a recursive grammar can express and understand an infinite number of distinct thoughts, limited in practice only by stamina and mortality. The idea that the creativity inherent in language can be explained by grammar of combinatorial rules is usually associated with the linguist Noam Chomsky." Freeman and Freeman (2004:226) illustrate recursion as follows: "the rules for NP and PP are recursive because NPs can include PPs and PPs must include NPs. Recursive structural rules are those for which the output of one rule forms the input for the other."

2.3.6 Ambiguity and the Two Levels of Structure

For Disterheft (2003:8) the most important innovation that Chomsky has brought to linguistics is his recognition of two different levels: **the surface structure** and **the deep structure.** She defines the two structures as follows: "the surface structure is what you are familiar with from speech and writing; the deep structure is an abstract level that forms the basic sentence type from which the nonbasic and surface-level utterances are derived." Chomsky was able to demonstrate convincingly that these two levels exist by appealing to the notion of **ambiguity.** He used the by-now famous sentence:[6]

   (1)   *Flying planes can be dangerous.*

to show that sentences may have two different deep structure forms even though their surface structure is identical. It is the differences in deep structure that account for the differences in meaning. Sentences whose ambiguity comes from two separate deep structures are said to be syntactically or structurally ambiguous. **Syntactic/structural ambiguity** contrasts with **semantic/lexical ambiguity.** In the latter, the differences in meaning of the surface structure sentence does not come from a difference in the deep structure but rather from the fact that the same word has multiple meanings, as in the sentence below:

   (2)   *I saw the cardinal.*

The sentence is ambiguous because the word <cardinal> is ambiguous. Among other things, it can mean an official in the hierarchy of the Catholic Church, and it is also the name given to a specific species of birds. Usually, but not always, the larger context of the discourse helps to disambiguate the sentence. Ravin and Leacock (2002:1) argue that up to 40 percent of English words are lexically/semantically ambiguous:

> *The study of polysemy, or the 'multiple meanings' of words has a long history in the philosophy of language, linguistics, psychology, and literature. The sheer number of senses listed by some sources as being available to us usually comes as a surprise: Out of approximately 60,000 entries in Webster's Seventh Dictionary, 21,488, or almost 40 percent, have two or more senses. Moreover, the most commonly used words tend to be the most polysemous. The verb run, for example, has 29 senses in Webster's, further divided into nearly 125 subsenses. Although rarely a problem in language use, except as a source of humor and puns, polysemy poses a problem in semantic theory and in semantic applications, such as translation or lexicography.*

2.3.7 Innateness Hypothesis and the Language Acquisition Device

The dominant psychological theory during the era of structuralism was **behaviorism.** Structural linguists appealed to it to account for a wide variety of linguistic behavior. It was used to explain why people talk to each other. More importantly, it was used to explain how children acquire their first language and how non-native speakers acquire a second or third language. In Chapter 2 of his book, Bloomfield applies behaviorism,

---

[6] Aspects of the Theory of Syntax, p. 21.

especially **stimulus-response,** to explain a normal communication exchange that takes place between two people. He argues that communication consists of three main parts:

1. Practical events preceding the act of speech;

2. Speech;

3. Practical events following the act of speech.

Behaviorism and stimulus-response cannot be entirely dismissed as not playing any role in human communication. However, the theory came under fire when it was used to account for child language acquisition (Bloomfield 1933:29–32). Chomsky (1965:25, 27, 32–3, 51) attacked it vehemently, demonstrating through his famous "argument from the poverty of stimulus"[7] that behaviorism cannot account for child language acquisition. A battery of "wug-tests" designed by the MIT psycholinguist Steven Pinker (1999:296) has completely laid to rest the behaviorist account of first language acquisition. He defines his "wug-test" as follows: "A test of linguistic productivity in which a person is given a novel word and encouraged to use it in some inflected form: `Here is a wug. Now there are two of them; there are two . . .'" Instead of the behaviorist account of language acquisition, Chomsky proposes two interrelated concepts: the **Innateness Hypothesis** and the **Language Acquisition Device (LAD).** He defines the former as follows:

> *To learn a language, then, the child must have a method for devising an appropriate grammar, given primary linguistic data. As a precondition for language learning, he must possess, first, a linguistic theory that specifies the form of the grammar of a possible human language, and, second, a strategy for selecting a grammar of the appropriate form that is compatible with the primary linguistic data. As a long-range task for general linguistics, we might set the problem of developing an account of this innate theory that provides the basis for language learning. . . . To say that the assumption about innate capacity is extremely strong is, of course, not to say that it is incorrect, (p. 25, 32).*

As for the Language Acquisition Device (LAD), Chomsky (1965:47) hypothesizes that it "has certain analytical data-processing mechanisms or inductive principles of a very elementary sort, for example, certain principles of association, weak principles of generalization . . . taxonomic principles of segmentation and classification, . . ." The commonalities found in how children acquire human languages have reinforced both the Innateness Hypothesis and the Language Acquisition Device. Quite a bit of research effort has gone into investigating these claims. It is now assumed that parametric setting is responsible for the acquisition of specific languages. However, up until a certain age, a child is prone to acquire any human language that he/she is exposed to. Guasti (2002:17–20) explains it as follows: "The hypothesis that language capacity is innate and richly structured explains why language acquisition is possible, despite all limitations and variations in the learning conditions . . . Under the principles-and-parameters model, children are innately endowed with principles and parameters, because both are given by UG (Universal Grammar). . . . UG is the human genetic endowment that is responsible for the course of language acquisition. Parameters define the range of variation that is possible in language, and together, principles and parameters define the notion of possible human language."

---

[7] The "argument from the poverty of stimulus" is sometimes referred to as "the logical problem in language acquisition." The fact that every human who does not suffer from cognitive impairment can acquire his/her first language is baffling to linguists. It is baffling to linguists that children acquire their L1 with little apparent effort or explicit instruction. The input that they receive is imperfect. However, somehow, from this imperfect input they abstract the rules of their L1.

So far, no part of the brain has been identified as being responsible for first language acquisition. Rumor has it that scientists working with people suffering from SLI (Specified Language Impairment) have identified some gene responsible for the impairment. Even so, no gene has yet been located as the gene that is directly associated with language acquisition (Pinker 1999:46). However, Chomsky's Language Acquisition Device has proven very helpful in explaining why past a certain age, language acquisition becomes extremely difficult. Available evidence suggests that the LAD is time-sensitive. Past puberty, the acquisition of language becomes problematic. This has led to another hypothesis known as the **Critical Period[8] Hypothesis.** Both the LAD and the Critical Period Hypothesis were unexpectedly confirmed in 1970 in California. A young girl with a scientific alias of "Genie" was found completely deprived of language input. Her parents confined her to her room and had not spoken to her since her birth. When she was found at the age of 13 her language and cognitive developments were severely compromised. In spite of intense therapy, Genie remained severely impaired linguistically (Russ 1993).

2.4 Conclusion

For many centuries after its inception, grammar has been part of philosophy. Greek philosophers argued about the origin and nature of language. This conception of language lasted until the end of the 15th Century. From then on, the study of grammar became dependent on literature since the usage of celebrated authors helped decide which forms were correct and which ones were not. However, all this changed with the advent of comparative and structural linguistics. In the late 19th Century, linguistics became its own discipline with its own methods of investigation. The umbilical cord of dependency that linked linguistics to literature and to philosophy was forever cut. Since the advent of the Chomskyan revolution in the second half of the 20th Century, linguistics has forged new alliances with the hard sciences in its quest for answers. Chomsky (2000:77) argues that "the place to look for answers is where they are likely to be found: in the hard sciences, where richness and depth of understanding provide some hope of gaining insights into these questions." For this reason, linguists have adopted a formal and rigorous scientific methodology in their study of grammar. Chapter 4 will focus on the formal apparatus of this new approach in the study of grammar.

---

[8] Lately, the phrase "Critical Periods," the plural instead of the singular, has been proposed because puberty does not affect all the areas of language structure the same way. Phonetics and phonology seem to be more strongly affected by the age of the learner than syntax, morphology, and semantics.

Key Terms to Know

These are the key terms that you should be able to use and define after reading this chapter:

1. ambiguity: 2.3.6
2. Behaviorism: 2.3.7
3. competence: 2.3.2
4. componential analysis: 2.2.6
5. descriptive grammar: 2.0, 2.2, 2.2.6, 2.2.7
6. discovery procedure: 2.2.6
7. grammaticality judgment: 2.3.3
8. Indo-European: 2.2.5
9. Innateness Hypothesis: 2.3.7
10. Language Acquisition Device (LAD): 2.3.7
11. lingua franca: 2.2.1
12. linguistic equality: 2.2.6
13. linguistic reconstruction: 2.2.5
14. performance: 2.3.2
15. prescriptive grammar: 2.0, 2.2.6, 2.3.3
16. principles and parameters: 2.3.4
17. proto-language: 2.2.5
18. semantic/lexical ambiguity: 2.3.6
19. stimulus-response: 2.3.7
20. structural/syntactic ambiguity: 2.3.6
21. structuralism: 2.2.6, 2.3.7
22. structure: 2.2.3, 2.2.6, 2.3, 2.3.6, 2.3.7
23. The Critical Period Hypothesis: 2.3.7
24. Traditional grammar: 2.0, 2.2.4
25. Universal Grammar: 2.3.4, 2.3.7

EXERCISE 1—PRIMACY OF SPEECH OVER WRITING

Until the beginning of the 20th Century most grammar books were based on the writings of well known authors. This practice was severely criticized by structural linguists (and by almost all contemporary linguists). Is this criticism justified? Why or why not?

EXERCISE 2—THE REJECTION OF SEMANTICS

In their goal of making the study of language scientific, structural linguists rejected semantics. What are the pros and cons of this decision?

EXERCISE 3—AMBIGUITY

The sentences in this exercise are all ambiguous. Some are **semantically/lexically** ambiguous while others are **syntactically/structurally** ambiguous. Write *SEA* by the sentence if it is semantically ambiguous, and *SYA* if it is syntactically ambiguous.

    A.   Decide the possible meanings associated with each sentence.[9]

    1.   Very smart boys and girls attend Ivy League schools.

    2.   The shower was awesome.

    3.   They can fish here.

    4.   He was knocked over by the punch.[10]

[9] There is nothing wrong with you if you do not perceive all the ambiguities. Chomsky (1965:21) explains that when presented with an ambiguous sentence "the listener will interpret it immediately in a unique way, and will fail to detect the ambiguity. In fact, he may reject the second interpretation, when this is pointed out to him, as forced or unnatural (independently of which interpretation he originally selected under contextual pressure)."

[10] Sentences "4" to "9" are taken from Fromkin et al. (2003:224). Sentences "10" to "12" are taken from Loebeck (2000:19).

5. The proprietor of the fish is the sole owner.

6. The police were urged to stop drinking.

7. He saw that gasoline can explode.

8. Dick finally decided on the boat.

9. We laughed at the colorful ball.

10. Squad helps dog bite victims.

11.   Doctor testifies in horse suit.

12.   Enraged cow injures farmer with ax.

Chapter 3

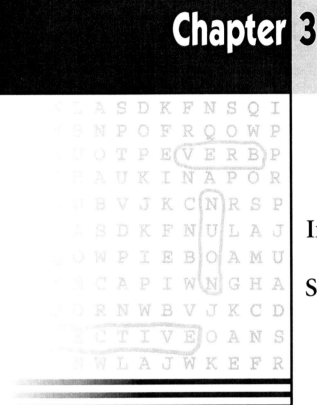

Innate Grammar vs. School Grammar

3.0 INTRODUCTION

The repeated assaults of structural and generative linguists on the failings of traditional and prescriptive grammars have led many in the education community to doubt the usefulness of grammar instruction in school. So, from the second half of the 20th Century until now, there has been a "lost generation" of English as a Second/Foreign Language, and Language Arts teachers. These language professionals have very little knowledge of grammar. Disterheft (2003:22–3) laments this situation as follows:

> For over fifty years, the National Council of Teachers of English (NCTE) has discouraged teaching grammar overtly in primary and secondary schools because most research shows that teaching parts of speech and basic sentence structure does not improve students' writing. And so, the reasoning goes, why teach a topic if it does not directly improve writing? The fallacious logic underpinning this attitude becomes obvious if we apply it to other fields. Should we refrain from teaching art, geography, mathematics, and so on if they don't likewise directly improving writing skills? ... Most state departments of education require very little knowledge of English language and linguistics in order to teach English skills at the primary and secondary levels. ... No teacher would ever be certified to teach subject areas [science and mathematics] at any level with only two college-level courses as background. In fact, most states require that a teacher have a major or minor in a subject in order to teach it. In order to teach mathematics or science, even at an elementary level, the teacher must have a knowledge of underlying theory that far exceeds the level of instruction. Yet as far as grammar goes, some English teachers' knowledge of

the topic comes directly from the textbook they use in their classroom. It's no wonder that teachers avoid grammar and that knowledge of it has, for the most part, fallen into such a state of disrepair."

However, Kolln and Funk (2006:xv) are optimistic because they see a new trend gradually emerging. In the preface of their book, they write this: "We're happy that our profession's attitude towards the study of grammar has also changed since 1982, a time when the study of grammar in language arts classrooms throughout the country was marginalized at best, if not completely absent." Some educators are slowly coming to the realization that banishing grammar instruction from the curriculum was a mistake. It is good news that grammar is resurfacing; but we, in the language profession, should do everything not to squander this opportunity. We should, for instance, avoid the mistakes of the past when grammar instruction was no more than the robotic memorization of parts of speech. That approach was woefully inadequate because it failed to translate grammar instruction into academic gains. The approach to grammar instruction advocated in this book will raise teachers' grammatical awareness and show them how grammar can be used to improve students' writing and analytical skills. However, before getting there, we must first review the different types of "grammars" often encountered in the linguistic literature. We must also clarify the long-standing misunderstanding between linguists and educators.

3.1 *Misunderstanding between Linguists and Educators*

Contemporary linguistics burst on the scene with an agenda and a methodology that were radically different from previous studies of language. The death threats on Native American languages led American linguists to design a "scientific" methodology to codify these languages. Contrary to previous language studies that relied on written sources, structural linguistics depended entirely on spoken language. Bloomfield (1933:21), the leading linguist of his time, was openly hostile to analysis based on written text. He went so far as to state that "writing is not language, but merely a way of recording language by means of visible marks."

The convincing scientific arguments marshaled by linguists to defend their position against language studies based on written texts led educators to conclude erroneously that grammar instruction was unnecessary. This was a misguided conclusion that stemmed from a misunderstanding of the claims of theoretical linguistics. Saying that speakers of a language are verbally competent in their native language is quite different from saying that they can use it competently in academics. Oral language is innate and subconscious, but the language needed to succeed academically must be learned consciously. This is where the crux of the misunderstanding lies. Educators were looking to linguists for ways to teach grammar meaningfully, not realizing that linguists did not have classroom applications in mind in their theorizing about the nature of innate grammar. The misunderstanding between the two groups can be summarized by the diagram below:

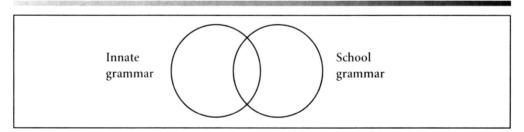

Table 1 *Relationship between Innate Grammar and School Grammar*

The overlapping area is not very significant. This shows that theoretical linguistics itself cannot be part of the solution. What educators need is applied linguistics. Pinker (1999:52) recounts a story worth repeating here to highlight the difference between theoretical and applied linguistics. There was a family in California whose child suffered from a linguistic impairment. They read about Chomsky's work in a popular science magazine. They called him at his MIT office and suggested that their daughter's condition might be of interest to him. Here is Pinker's comment about Chomsky's reaction: "Chomsky is a paper-and-pencil theoretician who wouldn't know Jabba the Hutt from the Cookie Monster, so he suggested that the parents bring their child to the laboratory of the psycholinguist Ursula Bellugi in La Jolla." This incident illustrates the situation between educators and linguists. Educators know that the traditional way of teaching grammar is not working. They hear about linguistics. They are crying out for help. But theoretical linguistics can't help because its theoretical claims are not directly applicable to education. Contemporary linguistics needs to be specially packaged for the classroom. Unfortunately, according to Gee (2003:647) this has yet to be done. He notes that "linguistics has had much less impact on education, and teachers know much less about language and linguistics, than the current state of our knowledge about language in education, or the current dilemmas of our schools, would seem to merit." The focus of this book is to repackage the findings of theoretical syntax for classroom use by teachers and their students.

3.2 Applied Linguistics and School Grammar

Applied linguistics repackages the claims of theoretical linguistics for use in everyday life. Education-minded linguists have coined the acronym CALP (Cognitive Academic Language Proficiency) to refer to the type of English competence needed for academic success. This linguistic knowledge is often contrasted with BICS (Basic Interpersonal Communication Skills), (Marshall 2002:194–6). According to them, the best approach to achieving competence in CALP is through pedagogical grammar (also known as teaching grammar). **Pedagogical grammar** is an eclectic method of teaching grammar whose various components can be summarized by the following equation:

Pedagogical Grammar = Traditional Grammar + Prescriptive Grammar + Sociolinguistics + Descriptive Grammar

Table 2 *The Components of Pedagogical Grammar*

Pedagogical grammar can be defined in two ways. On the one hand, it is the conscious grammatical knowledge that the teacher needs to teach grammar. On the other, it is the conscious grammatical knowledge that the learner needs to know to succeed academically. Our focus in this book is the grammatical awareness of the teacher. It is believed that if teachers are competent in contemporary understanding of grammar, they will be able to use their knowledge meaningfully to meet their students' academic needs. Consequently, we will concentrate on the first definition of pedagogical grammar.

3.3 The Contribution of Traditional Grammar to Pedagogical Grammar

The main contribution that traditional grammar brings to pedagogical grammar is in the area of the **metalanguage.** Metalanguage is the language used to talk about language.

Linguists use different terms to refer to elements in a sentence. Consider the labels that are applied to the words in (1):

(1)   *Linguists speculate about the nature of innate grammar.*

The words <linguists>, <nature>, and <grammar> are classified by traditional linguists as nouns. The word <speculate> is a verb. The words <about> and <of> are known as prepositions. The word <the> is an article. Additionally, <linguists> is known as the subject of the sentence while <the nature of innate grammar> is the complement of the preposition <about>. The word <innate> functions as an attributive adjective. The word <speculate> is called a main verb.[1] These metalinguistic terms were inherited from traditional grammar but they are still in use. Wasow (2003:300) reminds us that "the traditional categories of noun, verb, etc. (inherited from the grammatical studies of ancient Greece) are still quite generally employed, supplemented by a number of other categories, some of them idiosyncratic to particular theories." Language Arts teachers and English teachers cannot understand modern linguistics if they do not have a firm grasp of the traditional metalinguistic **jargon.** Jargon is a sociolinguistic term which describes the terms and expressions specific to a profession. It would be absurd to belong to a profession and not know its jargon. It is unthinkable for a chemist not to know the technical terms of chemistry. It would be intolerable for a medical doctor not to know the jargon of medicine. It would also be unthinkable for a computer scientist not to know the appropriate terms for computer science. Similarly, language teachers should master the grammatical terminology that has been in use for more than two thousand years. There is simply no excuse for not knowing the jargon used in the language profession!

3.4 The Contribution of Prescriptive Grammar to Pedagogical Grammar

Prescriptive grammar is the kind of grammar that seeks to tell native speakers how they should speak or write their own language. It prescribes rules of correct usage. Discussions of prescriptive grammar in English never fail to mention Bishop Robert Lowth. He is the one who single-handedly forbade the use of double negatives in English. Commentators usually explain the rise of prescriptive grammar in European languages by the influence of humanism, the fear of language decay, and the appeal to logic.

Humanism, 15th to 17th Century, has been defined as an intellectual era characterized by an unmatched love for classical literature. The works of Greek and Latin authors were studied for their great rhetorical value. When European writers began writing in their own languages, they too, for the most part, used the same lofty language and elevated grammar that they had studied in classical literature.

The 18th Century was nicknamed the "Age of Reason." It was a time when logical explanations were given to natural and supernatural phenomena. This tendency to rationalize everything was also applied to language. Bishop Lowth's prohibition of double negation was based on mathematical logic. Disterheft (2003:31) explains Bishop Lowth's reasoning as follows: "two negatives in English destroy one another, or are equivalent of an affirmative."

The eighteenth century was strongly influenced by historical linguistics. After Sir William Jones' discovery that Sanskrit was related to Greek and other European languages, there was a real interest in finding the pristine, unadulterated "language". It was wrongly believed that the proto-language was purer and nobler. An offshoot of this idea was the

---

[1] These terms are used here only for the purpose of illustration. They will be defined in subsequent chapters.

belief that linguistic change inevitably resulted in language decay. For this reason, they thought that the language used by previous generations, especially the aspect of language used by classical writers, was the best. In the England of the eighteenth century, the King James Version of the Bible of 1611 came to be regarded as a masterpiece of literary genius because it preserved the old ways of speaking and writing.

Contrary to what one might think, there are not many things wrong with prescriptive grammar. There are only two problems that I see with prescriptive grammar. Firstly, its proponents were/are unable to distinguish clearly between the demands of **Cognitive Academic Language Proficiency (CALP)** and the demands of **Basic Interpersonal Communication Skills (BICS)**. Instead, prescriptive grammarians continue to legislate indiscriminately irrespective of the mode of communication used. Secondly, prescriptivists state the rules of grammar so rigidly that they do not take into account changes in linguistic habits. Fortunately, the grip of prescriptive linguistics on grammatical anathemas such as the prohibition of split infinitives and preposition stranding is being loosened slowly. Now, it is not unusual to read sentences such as the following in print:

> (2) *"The big guns" said they couldn't, claiming they had agreed **to** never again **work** in insurance outside the big firm.*

This sentence is taken from a book. Here we see a split infinitive in use. The infinitive marker <to> is separated from the verb <work> by <never again>.

> (3) *"When he met **somebody** he was interested **in,** he studied him in the most profound way."*

The second sentence illustrates preposition stranding. Here the preposition <in> has been stranded from its noun <somebody>. This sentence comes from the same book but by a different author.[2]

3.5 The Contribution of Sociolinguistics to Pedagogical Grammar

Prescriptive grammar is as much a sociolinguistic concept as it is a type of grammar. Its advent created a sociolinguistic divide between language users all over Europe. Those who wrote and spoke according to the stipulations of prescriptive grammar were highly esteemed whereas those who did not were frowned upon. Fromkin et al. (2003:15) observe that "in the renaissance, a new middle class emerged who wanted their children to speak the dialect of the upper classes. This desire led to the publication of many prescriptive grammars." The effects of prescriptive grammar are still felt today. For this reason grammar teachers cannot and should not ignore its verdicts and the consequences attached to flouting its rules. Insights into the place of prescriptive grammar in education can be gained if we analyze it from the viewpoint of the Game Theory.

3.5.1 The Game Theory and Pedagogical Grammar

The Game Theory is a mathematical and statistical method that has been applied to economic forecasting and gambling behavior. It has also been applied in political science for conflict resolutions. It was first applied to sociolinguistics by Laitin in 1992 in his book, *"Language Repertoire and State Construction in Africa."* In it, he sees language as a capital, an asset, and a portfolio, not just a medium of communication. Thus, in a multidialectal language environment, for all the citizenry to be socio-economically mobile, they

---

[2] These examples are from Marion, Ed. 2000. The first quote is from an essay by Ed Marion and the second by Donald Honig.

must be competent in at least two different dialects: their own sociolect (BICS) and the standard dialect (CALP). A **sociolect** is defined as the spoken dialect that a subgroup in society uses for their daily communication. The **standard dialect,** on the other hand, is the written or spoken language used in formal or official settings. Citizens whose language repertoire consists only of their sociolect have less chance for socio-economic mobility. This is particularly true if their sociolect is relatively distant from the standard academic dialect. The Game Theory proposes the following formula to represent the ideal linguistic portfolio:

$$
\text{Language Repertoire} = \left\{ \begin{array}{ccccc} 1 & + & 1 & = & 2 \\ 1 & + & 0 & = & 1 \end{array} \right\}
$$

Table 3 *Ideal Linguistic Portfolio in Multidialectal Society*

It is a sociolinguistic truism that dialects exist in any language. It is also a truism that in any given society, some dialects have more prestige than others. The more socially prestigious dialect is often considered the standard dialect of education. No amount of complaining is likely to change this situation. Game theoretic linguists liken this sociolinguistic condition to the human condition. Since the Universal Declaration of Human Rights, all human beings are equal before the law. However, all human beings do not have the same prestige in life. Similarly, even before the Universal Declaration of Linguistic Rights of Barcelona in 1996,[3] structural linguists had declared that all languages and dialects were equal. However, all languages and dialects do not have the same prestige. This candid and commonsensical assessment of the role of language in society should urge schools to do everything within their power to teach the standard dialect in order to assure that their students obtain the ideal linguistic portfolio diagrammed above.

3.5.2 A Game Theoretical Approach to Prescriptive Grammar

Prescriptive grammar is a set of linguistic dos and don'ts passed down from generation to generation. Professional linguists often ridicule the pronouncements of prescriptive grammar. However, in bashing it we do a disservice to schools because we all know full well that academic writing expects conformity to Standard English. So long as prescriptive grammar does not intrude on people's sociolect, there is no reason to worry about it. Aspects of prescriptive grammar have their place in the school curriculum. Sociolinguists distinguish between a **sociolinguistic indicator** and a **sociolinguistic marker.** An indicator is a sociolinguistic variable that provides nonjudgmental information about the speaker. A marker, on the other hand, brings up all kinds of negative evaluations of the speaker. The teacher should see to it that students avoid grammatical items that are considered sociolinguistic markers by members of the academic community, just as they see to it that their students avoid gender-specific language.

3.5.3 Pedagogical Grammar, Bidialectalism, and Diglossia

From a Game Theoretical view, pedagogical grammar should aim at bidialectal competency for all students. **Bidialectalism** is defined simply as the ability to use and under-

---

[3] For more information about the Universal Declaration of Linguistic Rights, visit the following website: www.uji.es/serveis/slt/triam/triam15.html.

stand two or more dialects of the same language. For the proponents of the Game Theory, academic success and sociolinguistic mobility depend to a large extent on one's ability to acquire the standard dialect in addition to the dialect of the language that one has acquired innately.

Dialects that are markedly different from the Standard English used in academic circles are considered to be near-**diglossia.** According to Ferguson's original definition, a diaglossic situation exists when the written version or the formal dialect of the language is so far removed from the spoken dialect that mutual intelligibility between the two is significantly impaired. Such a situation exists in the Arabic world, in Germany, in Haiti, and in Switzerland.[4] It is said that dialects of German are so different from each other that a Swiss German might have .difficulties understanding the speech of a person from Germany, and vice versa. Though the term "diglossia" has not been used in reference to English in the United States, Wardhaugh (2002:94) raises this possibility. For all practical purposes, academic English stands in a diaglossic relationship with many dialects of American English.

A typical American classroom is a conglomerate of different dialects, some of which are closer to the standard dialect than others. Teachers should be familiar enough with the sociolects of their students so as to compare and contrast their home dialects with the demands of the standard academic dialect. The grammatical tools that are necessary for this analysis will be discussed throughout this book. From this perspective, school grammar is no more or no less than dialectal adjustment. Baker (1989:25) explains the proper role of school grammar as follows: "To a large extent, then, school grammars for native English speakers have the aim of improving their speech and writing by eliminating[5] or modifying any rules that differ from those found in the prestigious `standard' dialect or that differ from the small collection of rules borrowed from Latin several centuries ago."

3.6 The Contribution of Descriptive Grammar to Pedagogical Grammar

The last piece in the equation proposed in 3.2 is descriptive grammar. Descriptive grammar is an umbrella term to describe both **context-free grammar** and **functional grammar.** Wasow (2003:300–2) defines a context-free grammar as a formal grammar that uses universal phrase structure rules and other formal mechanisms to generate sentences. Generative Transformation Grammar is a context-free grammar. This approach to grammar is particularly useful in helping students to become better writers. By teaching students how transformations manipulate sentence structure and meaning, they can use this knowledge to improve their writing skills. Syntactic transformations distinguish between ordinary writers and excellent writers. Knowing how to move an element from its location in the deep structure to a different location in the surface structure, and knowing the rules that go along with such an operation can give tremendous power to an argument, as can be seen by the two sentences below:

(4) *We hope fondly—we pray fervently—that this mighty scourge of war pass away speedily.*

(5) *Fondly do we hope—fervently do we pray—that this mighty scourge of war speedily pass away.*

---

[4] If we use Fishman's definition, diglossia exists in all previously colonized countries. But we are using diglossia here as originally intended by Ferguson.

[5] The focus of a linguistically well-adjusted teacher is not to eliminate the student's dialect. The objective is simply to help the student learn a new dialect of English so that he/she can be fully bi-dialectal.

The impact of the two sentences is not the same. The first is ordinary, the second is more poignant. The difference between the two statements lies only in the fact that (4) follows the canonical SVO sentence pattern, whereas (5) uses movement rules, a subject-auxiliary inversion rule, and Do-support to achieve a stronger stylistic effect.

Knowledge of **functional grammar** is also needed for teaching grammar meaningfully. This is an approach to grammar in which both formal and functional analyses matter. Formal grammars de-emphasize the meaning/function of linguistic elements in the sentence, but functional grammars take both form and function into account. "In functional linguistic analysis," argues Valin (2003:324), "forms are analyzed with respect to the communicative functions they serve, and functions are investigated with respect to formal devices that are used to accomplish them. Both forms and functions are analyzed, not just functions. The interplay between form and function in language is very complex and is the prime focus of functional linguistics." Functional grammar will be used to explain why the same lexical item may be analyzed differently depending on its function in the sentence. For example, the word <best> is used in the three sentences below. It is the same lexical item, but its grammatical function changes in each sentence:

(6) *Children are encouraged to do their best at school.*

(7) *Computers work best when they are defragmented.*

(8) *Deanna's best friend is her cat.*

The behavior of <best> in these three sentences underscores the need for pedagogical grammar to include functional grammar. In (6) <best> is a noun. In (7), it functions as an adverb. However, in (8) <best> is an adjective. All this may be confusing now. But, it will make sense after Chapters 6, 9, and 10.

3.7 New Perspective on the Teaching of Grammar

There is sufficient evidence that the traditional approach of teaching grammar which consisted mostly in teaching metalinguistic skills is no longer adequate. Over the past few decades, a consensus has emerged that grammar must be taught differently. The ingredients of the new school grammar were discussed in the previous sections. The remaining sections are devoted to the investigation of how *Traditional Grammar + Prescriptive Grammar + Sociolinguistics + Descriptive Grammar* can be used in the classroom to improve students' reading and writing skills. Voices have risen here and there to show the way. In a recent article, the *English Journal* asked the following question to teachers: "What is Your Most Compelling Reason for Teaching Grammar?"[6] Here is a sampling of the reasons given. The aggregate of the responses corresponds to the approach advocated in this book:

1. "I teach grammar for two reasons. The first is that grammar instruction gives students a metalanguage, language about language. Having this, students can learn a great deal more about how to communicate clearly than they can without it. The second reason is that students are interested in language—its changes and variations—and they feel gratified to learn how it works and what it can do . . . The English language despite its complexity and flexibility, is simple when we understand it through patterns: With just a handful of sentence patterns, with expandable and shrinkable noun phrases and verb phrases, we can accomplish the most extraordinary of human capabilities: communicate" (Amy Benjamin 2006:19).

[6] From *English Journal*, Volume 95, No. 5, May 2006. Copyright © 2006 National Council of Teachers of English. Reprinted with permission.

2.	"I believe it is the responsibility of English teachers to give students every opportunity to learn the vocabulary, the language of literacy. In every other class in their schedule, they learn that discipline's special vocabulary: the language of mathematics, of history, of biology, of soccer. . . . By the time they graduate from high school, students have the right to a fully developed vocabulary of literacy, along with an understanding of the social and political power of language. Learning grammar means bringing to conscious level the language expertise students know subconsciously, the miraculous system that was almost fully developed when they started kindergarten" (Martha Kolln 2006:19).

3.	"I teach grammar to ensure that all my students, not only those with English teachers for mothers and pedants for fathers, will graduate knowing how to write without grammatical error. Wonderful ideas aren't enough; students need to be able to present their ideas with clarity and precision. Correctness matters. . . . Grammatical correctness is like apparel. Before writers are judged for the content of their work, they are judged for their grammar. I want my students to have an influence on society. That is why I teach grammar. In my classroom, I do not dedicate weeks of concentrated study of grammar. Rather, I take five minutes daily to present sentences that feature grammatical errors. My tenth graders and I make the corrections, reminding ourselves of the rules that explain the corrections: parallel structure, subject-verb agreement, unclear pronoun references, split infinitives, and so forth. These short, focused grammar lessons reinforce what students know but have forgotten and fill in gaps in prior instruction" (Carol Jago 2006:19–20).

4.	"So often grammar is taught from the perspective of deficit. Students, particularly those who speak a dialect, are considered wrong, and so there is a strong temptation to drill students in the rules of correctness in the hopes of transforming them. But the promise of upward mobility is not a compelling reason to teach grammar. It is, in fact, disrespectful. We should teach grammar to help students gain flexibility in their use of language. Just as we wear different clothing for different occasions, we `wear' language to suit a particular audience and purpose. . . . Grammar becomes a highly compelling subject for students when they can use their own language and play with it, recast it in the other modes for other audiences than their immediate peers and family. . . . What happens when a phrase moves from one part of the sentence to another? How is meaning affected when we add direct address? What happens when we code-switch? How would we code-switch any given phrase? We teach grammar, then, not as a means of taming wayward students, but as a means of developing linguistic flexibility and power" (Nancy Patterson 2006:19–20).

5.	"No English teacher needs a reason to teach reading or writing or literature or vocabulary. These activities are axiomatic to our function; they define our task. But how can we discuss with students their reading or their writing or literature without providing them the conventional vocabulary for doing so: noun, verb, adjective . . . sentence. . . . Active, passive. . . . Past, present, future. . . . How can we fulfill our function and perform our task without providing students a grammar? We cannot; our profession compels us—by definition" (James Penha 2006:20).

6.	"When should we teach grammar? If what is meant by 'teaching grammar' is labeling parts of speech, diagramming sentences, underlining subjects, and double-underlining predicates, we'd say as loudly as often as we could: "Never!" . . . When should we teach grammar? We should teach grammar when it's needed to help kids do something that matters, and then we should teach it in a way that maximizes the utility of what we are teaching and minimizes the amount of time spent on memorizing terms or filling in blanks. . . . It may be that some terms will be useful in that effort, but you don't have to identify an introductory adverbial clause or recognize a subordinating conjunction to write with power and grace" (Jeffery D. Wilhelm 2006:20).

7. When I read the question 'What is your most compelling reason for teaching grammar?' my first thoughts were, 'But I don't. I don't teach grammar. Well, I don't teach grammar as a separate subject. . . . Instead of teaching grammar in isolation, I teach—and advocate teaching—selected aspects of grammar that can help writers add variety to sentence structures, . . . and can empower writers to use accepted mainstream conventions in such matters as subject-verb agreement, pronoun reference, and punctuation" (Constance Weaver 2006:19).

8. "I teach grammar to help teachers discover how much students already know. No longer do teachers see students as struggling, making errors, leaving off endings. . . . In this context, I offer teachers research-based techniques for teaching Standard English: contrastive analysis and code-switching. Students compare and contrast the grammar of home speech to the grammar of school for the purpose of adding Standard English to their linguistic repertoires. Students then can code-switch to choose the language style to fit the setting" (Rebecca S. Wheeler 2006:21).

It is obvious from the preceding responses that teachers are in search for an approach to school grammar that purposefully improves reading and writing skills. The Pedagogical Grammar approach as schematized in Table 2 of section 3.2, meets these needs because it has all the necessary ingredients.

3.7.1 Speaking vs. Writing

Contemporary linguists take for granted that elementary school-aged children have innate competency in Basic Interpersonal Communication Skills. Consequently, schools should focus their resources on developing Cognitive Academic Language Proficiency skills. The new approach to teaching grammar is better suited for this task. Teachers who use the new approach can teach grammar from a bidialectal perspective as outlined in 3.5 through 3.5.3. The Game Theory can assist in developing the grammatical skills that students need to succeed academically. Unlike oral proficiency that emerges naturally, writing abilities are hard to nurture because, as noted by Pinker (1994:401), the language used for writing is somewhat different from the language used for speaking:

> *Expository writing requires language to express far more complex trains of thought than it was biologically designed to do. Inconsistencies caused by limitations of short-term memory and planning, unnoticed in conversation, are not as tolerable when preserved on a page that is to be perused more leisurely. . . . Overcoming one's natural egocentrism and trying to anticipate the knowledge state of a generic reader at every stage of the exposition is one of the most important tasks in writing well. All this makes writing a difficult craft that must be mastered through practice, instruction, feedback, and—probably most important—intensive exposure to good examples.*

The new perspectives on teaching grammar seek to develop the following subskills in students:

1. awareness of prescriptive rules

2. proficiency with sentence-level phenomena

3. proficiency with inter-sentential cohesion

4. proficiency with different registers

These are not the only subskills needed to write successfully. However, they are the most basic ones that proficient writers weave seamlessly together in creating their texts. Grammatical instruction that correlates highly with writing proficiency is extremely challenging, as noted by Adger et al. (2007:113):

> Teaching students to write is seen as one of the most important functions of schools. But teaching writing is hard work. Students bring a range of language skills to this task. For speakers of vernacular dialects, there are special factors for teachers to consider in writing instruction largely because of the contrasts between the language of speaking and the language of writing are greater for them than for speakers of standard varieties.

3.7.2 Awareness of Prescriptive Rules

Proficiency in Cognitive Academic Language Proficiency calls for an awareness of different types of rules in writing. Williams (2007:15) distinguishes between three such rules which he labels "Real Rules," "Social Rules," and "Invented Rules". For him, "Real Rules" are "what make[s] English: articles must precede nouns: *the book,* not *book the.* Speakers born into English don't think about these rules at all when they write, and violate them only when they are tired or distracted." Since "Real Rules" are innate, no grammar teacher needs to worry about "Real Rules" because students do not violate them. They are part of students' internal grammar. These rules are exactly the same for spoken and written English. Children born into English-speaking families know these rules even before they enter kindergarten. Pedagogical Grammar does not address "Real Rules."

The remaining rules are "Social Rules" and "Invented Rules." Available data indicate that even college students struggle with these rules in their writings. In his article, *The Seven Deadly Sins of Student Writers,* Yagoda (2006:B13) attributes poor writing skills to the lack of proficiency in these two types of rules.

Yagoda begins his article by categorizing college students' mistakes into two groups. The first deals with style and the second with "usages that do not follow the accepted rules of standard English." The latter classification corresponds to Williams' "Social Rules" which he defines as rules that "distinguish Standard English from nonstandard: *He doesn't have any money* versus *He don't have no money.* Schooled writers observe these rules as naturally as they observe "Real Rules" and think about them only when they notice others violating them." Table 4 (see page 64) lists some common "Social Rules."

Williams makes it clear that "Social Rules" must be adhered to in academic writing. This is not the case for "Invented Rules" which he defines as a handful of rules invented by some grammarians that "they think we *should* observe. These are the rules that the grammar police enforce and that too many educated writers obsess over. Most date from the last half of the eighteenth century." Descriptive linguists have attacked all prescriptive rules but their most virulent attacks have been reserved for "Invented Rules." Pinker (1994:374) refers to them as "silly" and "dumb" rules. Table 5 (see page 64) includes some of the most common "Invented Rules."

No.	Categorizations	Illustrations[7]
1.	Letter Metathesis	aks a question
2.	<-g> deletion	workin'
3.	1st Person BE Contraction	ain't
4.	Double Negation	I can't get no satisfaction
5.	Failure of Subject-Verb Agreement in the Present Tense with 3rd Person Singular Subject	he don't
6.	Mistaking a Pronoun for a Determiner	them boys
7.	Failure of Subject-Verb Agreement in the Past Tense with 1st Person Plural Subject	we was
8.	Use of an accusative case instead of a nominative case	*Me* and Jennifer are going to the mall

Table 4 *Social Rules*

No.	Categorizations	Examples
1.	Passive Avoidance	The bill *was voted down*
2.	Back-formation	Let me *caveat* that ...
3.	Hopefully Fronting	*Hopefully,* it won't rain.
4.	Split Infinitive	To *boldly* go where no man has gone before.
5.	Preposition Stranding	Who did you agree *with*?
6.	Violation of Number Agreement with Indefinite pronouns	"Everyone should return to *their* seats."
7.	Case Agreement with "who" and "whom"	*Who* do you trust?
8.	Case Agreement with "I" and "me"	Mary is taller than *me*.
9.	Avoidance of Sentence Initial "and" or "but."	*But* I did not see any merit in his argument.
10.	Avoidance of Sentence Initial "because," and "since"	*Because* I'm your mother.
11.	Avoidance of "which" as a relative pronoun	The action *which* Congress has taken resulted in hardship.
12.	Singular Agreement with "any" and "none"	*None* of the reasons *is* sufficient to end that project.
13.	Never use *like* for *as* or *as if.*	These operations failed *like* the earlier ones.
14.	Don't use *hopefully* to mean "*I hope.*"	*Hopefully,* it will not rain.
15.	Don't use *finalize* to mean "*finish*" or "*complete*"	Let's *finalize* this paper before the deadline.
16.	Don't use *impact* as a verb	The survey *impacted* our strategy.
17.	Don't modify absolute words such as "*perfect,*" "*unique,*" "*final,*" or "*complete*" with "*very,*" "*more,*" "*quite,*"	The people of the United States, in order to form a more *perfect* union ...

Table 5 *Invented Rules*

[7] Most of the Illustrative examples in Tables 4 and 5 are taken from Pinker (1994:370–403) and Williams (2007:16–30).

No matter how silly these rules may seem to linguists, prescriptive teachers still adhere to them. Pinker (1994:374) does not hide his opposition to prescriptive rules. But he concedes that writers must submit to the dictums of these silly rules for the following reasons:

> *Once introduced, a prescriptive rule is very hard to eradicate, no matter how ridiculous. Inside the educational and writing establishments, the rules survive by the same dynamic that perpetuate ritual genital mutilation and college fraternity hazing: I had to go through it and am none the worse, so why should you have it any easier. Anyone daring to overturn a rule by example must always worry that readers will think he or she is ignorant of the rule, rather than challenging it . . . Perhaps most importantly, since prescriptive rules are so psychologically unnatural that only those with access to the right schooling can abide by them, they serve as shibboleths, differentiating the elite from the rabble.*

Williams (2007:16) advises writers to observe rules thoughtfully. He never advocates mindless obedience, nor does he encourage brazen disrespect. He even cautions against selective observance. He proposes a middle-of-the road approach which he offers in a form of an advice, "If you want to avoid being accused of 'lacking standards,' but refuse to submit to whatever 'rule' someone can dredge up from ninth-grade English, you have to know more about these invented rules than the rule-mongers do." This piece of advice is unlikely to be heeded because, unless a whole catalog of prescriptive rules is put in front of students, it is unlikely that they will know all these rules. The best course action would consist in helping students match their register with the type of writing assignment.

3.8 Register and Writing

The term "register" is a sociolinguistic concept used to describe different levels of speech that a person may use depending on the context of communication. It is often used synonymously with "style." Numerous attempts have been made to classify registers but, to date there is no classificatory consensus. The following levels are the most recurrent. Fromkin et al. (2007:437–8) divide registers broadly into two main categories: **formal** and **informal** registers. The formal register has been divided further into three distinct but overlapping styles. The same goes for the informal register.

3.8.1 Formality Continuum

The classification of formal registers into **ceremonial register, formal register,** and **academic register** is based on insights derived from ethnography of communication. There is a noticeable difference in formality between Resolution 1368 passed by the United Nations' Security Council in the aftermath of September 11th, 2001, and any State of the Union Address. Both texts are formal but the United Nations' resolutions, or resolutions passed by the US Congress are far more formal than any State of the Union speech. Resolution 1368, condemning international terrorism, consists of a single sentence of 240 words. Furthermore, the resolution concludes with the formulaic fragment "*[the Security Council] decides to remain seized of the matter.*" Such a concluding phrase is found only in highly ceremonial speeches. There is also a noticeable difference in formality between a State of the Union address and an article that appears in a refereed journal. These examples underscore the need to establish a hierarchy of formality. The most formal of all formal registers would be the ceremonial register, and the least formal along this continuum would be the article in a refereed journal. These three registers in the formality continuum correspond to Burch's (2003:81) definition of formal style. She defines such a style as one "designed to inform and to maintain a distance between the writer/speaker and the reader/hearer. . . . It refrains from using ellipsis and doesn't even stoop to contractions. Its sentences tend to be long and complex. It is usually characterized by third person and frequently by words of many syllables derived from Latin." Clouse (2007:137) concurs with this evaluation of formal registers. She adds that this formal register "*requires strict adherence to all the rules of grammar* [emphasis added]. It includes technical language and long sentences and avoids personal pronouns *I* and *you,* and contractions such as *don't* and *aren't*. The tone is impersonal, humorless, and unemotional."

Articles that appear in a refereed journal are generally written in a register that Faigley (2007:290) has labeled **"academic register."** His use of this term is synonymous with what Clouse (2007:137) has referred to as "popular" register. The latter is defined as "the level of diction common in many magazines, newspapers, and books. If you are using popular diction, you need to adhere to grammar rules, but you can usually use contractions and *I* and *you*. You can express emotion and humor. Your tone will usually be relaxed, and you can let your personality show through. A popular level of diction is suitable for most college essays written in your English class." In her article *From Usage to Grammar: The Mind's Response to Repetition*" that appeared in *Language,* Bybee uses "*I*" to refer to herself.[8] She also uses various contractions. Clearly, her style is academic without being overbearingly formal.

The distinction between various levels of formal register is important in this new approach to teaching grammar. Students should calibrate their writing style to fit the writing assignments. It also helps in determining which of the prescriptive rules to adhere to and which ones to flout. It will be argued in Chapter 15 that "Invented Rules" pronouncements against passive constructions, split infinitives, case agreement, and the like can be ignored in academic writing.

3.8.2 Informality Continuum

For students to be competent in the academic register, they must not only pay attention to formal register but also differentiate between different layers of informal register. The purpose of such an exercise is to know what to avoid when writing for school or for publication. Fromkin et al (2007:438) define informal style as a register in which "the rules of contraction are used more often, the syntactic rules of negation and agreement may be altered, and many words are used that do not occur in formal style. . . . Informal talk is not anarchy and even informal registers are rule-governed, but the rules of deletion, contraction, and word choice are different from those of formal language." Clouse (2007:137) goes one step further and states that informal diction is not acceptable for college papers . . . but it is often suitable for friendly letters, e-mails, and personal journals."

The style of discourse that Fromkin et al. and Clouse label "informal register" has been referred to by others as **colloquial register.** Burch (2003:80–81 calls it **casual register.** Burch singles out the omission of the subordinating conjunction "that" as a sign of a colloquial register. Another form of informal register is called **intimate style.** Even though there may be no syntactic differences between colloquial register and intimate register, the two can be distinguished by the choice of lexical items. Words such as "*honey, sweetheart, mom, dad,*" and nicknames belong to the intimate style and are usually not appropriate in academic writing. When I was working on this chapter, a colleague barged into my office with a book review written by one of his college students. The student wrote

---

[8] *Language,* Volume 82, Number 4, 2006.

the following conclusion: "*This is a fascinating little book. It was so good that I could not put it down. I nearly peed in my pants because I wanted to get to the end before going to the bathroom.*" This last sentence is sociolinguistically not appropriate for a book review!

Further down on the continuum of informality, one finds a style called **slang.** This register develops around some lexical items whose meanings are known only by the insiders of a subculture. This register is common among gang members, groups belonging to various subcultures within the larger community. Slang terms are transient and only a small fraction of them make it into the mainstream vocabulary. Pinker (1994:400) notes that the following words started as slang but are now accepted as mainstream words: "*clever, fun, sham, banter, mob, stingy, bully, junkie, jazz.*" He explains the life cycle of slang as follows "most slang lexicons are preciously guarded by their subcultures as membership badges. . . . When the most passé terms get cast off and handed down to the mainstream, they often fill expressive gaps in the language beautifully." Unless one is quoting a slang term, vocabulary items associated with slang register are not usually accepted in academic writing.

3.8.3 Focus on Academic Register

Native speakers, regardless of their level of education, control a fair amount of informal, casual, intimate, and slang registers. These registers are acquired effortlessly in the process of acquiring their first language. However, this is not the case for the various shades of formal register. The latter is acquired only after a long time of apprenticeship and tutoring. Furthermore, there is generally a high correlation between one's mastery of formal registers and one's level of formal education. This point is underscored by Fromkin et al. (2007:438) as follows: "Most speakers of a language speak one way with friends, another on a job interview or presenting a report in class, another talking to small children, another with their parents, and so on." Proficiency with different registers is a necessary condition for successful writing, because, as noted by Wardhaugh (2006:52) "each register helps you to express your identity at a specific time or place, i.e., how you seek to present yourself to others." The register one uses to write sends multiple messages to the reader. As noted by Jago earlier, "Before writers are judged for the content of their work, they are judged for their grammar." It is therefore very important that grammatical accuracy match the level of register used.

The purpose of writing in academia is to convince the reader of one's knowledge about a particular subject, viewpoint, analysis, or finding. Consequently, every effort should be made to ensure that the strength of the argument is not diminished by a mismatch between the level register and adherence to proper grammatical rules. Lunsford and Ruszkiewicz (2007:383) give the following piece of advice to novice writers: "What level of formality is most appropriate? In the United States, a fairly informal style is often acceptable, even appreciated. Many cultures, however, tend to value formality. If you're in doubt, therefore, it's probably wise to err on the side of formality, especially in communicating with elders or with those in authority."

Academic writing can be seen as "communicating with those in authority." Consequently, the appropriate academic register should be used. The academic world is currently very fragmented. Therefore, there is no consensus about what constitutes an appropriate academic register. The best possible model one can follow is to conform to the style acceptable to the leading journals in one's academic field. For linguists, the style used in *Language,* the Journal of the Linguistic Society of America, should be seen as the norm.

Many in the humanities follow the guidelines of the MLA, while those the social sciences adhere to the recommendations of the APA. Irrespective of one's area of specialization, writers are advised not to stray too far from standard grammar:

> *So what should be done about usage? Unlike some academics in the 1960s, I am not saying that instruction in standard English grammar and composition are tools to perpetuate an oppressive white patriarchal capitalist status quo and that The People should be liberated to write however they please. . . . It is just common sense that people should be given every encouragement and opportunity to learn the dialect that has become the standard in their society and to employ it in many formal settings, Pinker (1994:399, 400).*

3.9 Research Findings on Grammar and Writing

The leitmotiv of those who are lukewarm or opposed to the teaching of grammar in school is that the teaching of grammar does not improve students' writing ability. This was alluded to in the lengthy quote at the beginning of this chapter. This finding is so counter-intuitive that its premises have to be vigorously challenged. The test items that led to this conclusion have to be re-examined. The grammatical elements on which students are tested have to be re-evaluated. The grammatical approach used prior to testing must be made known for better scrutiny. Such pronouncements are met with skepticism by many practicing linguists. Unfortunately, this finding has been embraced by the advocates of "progressive education," and now, the whole debate has been turned into a cultural or political war. Gee (2003:649) reports that forty Massachusetts linguists signed a petition against "the state's new whole language-inspired English standards in July 1996." The consensus among linguists is that the findings of contemporary linguistics about first language acquisition cannot inform educational practice. Conversational language is different from academic language. The former is innate, while the latter is not. Therefore, it is not fitting to apply the findings of the former to the latter without discernment. The best approach for teaching grammar that can benefit writing would be one that raises students' and teachers' levels of grammatical awareness. This is the view taken in this book. By helping students discover the various patterns of sentence formation and the operations that move, delete, add, or substitute one lexical category for another, they become critically aware of the requirements of academic English. Once teachers are grammatically informed, they will use their creative genius to help improve their students' proficiency in academic English. Teachers are creative with language, and the new approach to teaching grammar discussed in this chapter can unleash their creativity in the classroom.

3.10 Conclusion

Teachers need to know pedagogical grammar to help their students succeed academically. This knowledge should be broad enough to include aspects of traditional grammar, prescriptive grammar, sociolinguistics, and descriptive grammar. The combination of all these perspectives on grammar will provide the teacher with the necessary background knowledge to teach writing more efficiently. Fifty years of booting grammar out of school has led to disastrous results. Linguistics is partly to blame because it downgraded prescriptive grammar without providing teachers with a suitable alternative. Now, a formula such as the one proposed in Table 2 gives teachers a broader view of grammar and a new approach of teaching grammar that is compatible with the academic register.

Key Terms to Know

These are the key terms that you should be able to use and define after reading this chapter:

1. academic register: 3.8.1, 3.8.2, 3.8.3, 3.10

2. BICS: 3.2, 3.4, 3.5.1

3. bidialectalism: 3.5.3

4. CALP: 3.2, 3.4, 3.5.1

5. casual register: 3.8.2

6. ceremonial register: 3.8.1

7. colloquial register: 3.8.2

8. context-free grammar: 3.6

9. descriptive grammar: 3.2, 3.6, 3.7, 3.10

10. diglossia: 3.5.3

11. formal register: 3.8., 3.8.1

12. formality continuum: 3.8.1

13. functional grammar: 3.6

14. informal register: 3.8.1

15. informality continuum: 3.8.2

16. innate grammar: 3.1, 3.3

17. intimate register: 3.8.2

18. Jargon: 3.3

19. metalanguage: 3.3, 3.7

20. pedagogical grammar: 3.2, 3.3, 3.4, 3.5, 3.5.1, 3.5.3, 3.6, 3.7, 3.7.2, 3.10

21. prescriptive grammar: 3.0, 3.2, 3.4, 3.5, 3.5.2, 3.7, 3.10

22. register: 3.7.1, 3.8

23. school grammar: 3.1, 3.2, 3.5.3, 3.7

24. sociolect: 3.5.1, 3.5.2, 3.5.3

25. sociolinguistic index: 3.5.2

26. sociolinguistic marker: 3.5.2

27. standard dialect: 3.5.1, 3.5.3

28. traditional grammar: 3.0, 3.2, 3.3, 3.7, 3.10

EXERCISE 1—PRESCRIPTIVE GRAMMAR[9]

Prescriptive grammarians frown upon aspects of the sentences below. For each sentence, decide if it is sociolinguistically an **indicator,** a **marker,** or a **stereotype.** Wardhaugh (2006:145) define these three terms as follows: "*An indicator is a linguistic variable to which little or no social import is attached. Only a linguistically trained observer is aware of indicators. . . . On the other hand, a marker does carry with it social significance. In fact, markers may be potent carriers of social information. People are aware of markers, and the distribution of markers is clearly related to social groupings and to styles of speaking. . . . A stereotype is a popular, and therefore, conscious characterization of speech of a particular group.*" Decide what rule of prescriptive grammar has been violated. Rephrase each sentence according to the demands of academic English.

1. Who did you go to the movie with?

2. The person who you were talking to was my chemistry teacher.

3. I don't want to play no more.

4. You should have heard the language that them boys were using!

5. I should have test drove this car before buying it.

6. Let me tell you! You was wrong! Wrong as wrong can be!

7. We hope to truly eliminate the estate tax forever.

[9] These are actual sentences produced by native speakers. None of them was made up.

8.   Becoming increasingly cloudy, the temperature today will be in the teens.

9.   I was exhausted, completely pooped! I lied the baby down in his crib and went right back to sleep.

10.   One day, we were at the mall. I thought I had brought my purse. I looked everywhere. Purse, where are you? So, in the end my sister had to borrow me some money to buy a dress.

11.   In a war, there's a lot of casualties. That's the nature of war!

12.   Can you itch my back for me, please?

13.   The Vikings won the Green Bay Packers.

14.   You should have went to see the game. It was lots of fun!

15.   My sisters are taller than me.

16.   Mary and me attended the same college.

Chapter 4

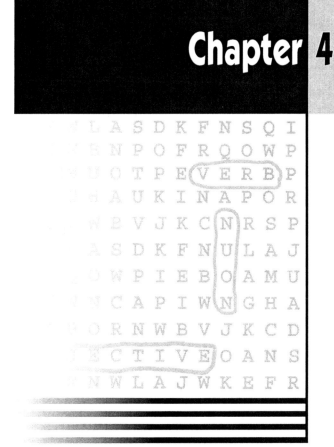

The Formal Apparatus of Generative Grammar

4.0 THE RATIONALE BEHIND THE FORMULAS

It was argued in 1.1 and 1.1.2 that linguistics is a hybrid science; it is situated somewhere between the "hard" sciences and the social sciences. This is a privileged position that allows it to be in a fruitful dialogue with other sciences. Pinker (1999:52) notes that at some major research universities, linguists collaborate with molecular biologists, neurologists, and computer scientists. Linguistic analysis is strongly influenced by the methodology of the "hard" sciences. Mathematics (a dreadful word for many students in the humanities) and formal logic provide the main staple of linguistic analysis. Chomsky (1965:62) summarizes the relationship between mathematics and linguistics as follows: "In brief, mathematical study of formal properties of grammars, is very likely, an area of great potential. It has already provided some insight into questions of empirical interest and will perhaps some day provide much deeper insights." Linguistics has taken advantage of its relationship with the hard sciences to develop a set of formulas that are uncommon to many fields in the humanities. On the surface, these formulas are austere and forbidding. However, with practice one finds them very useful.

4.1 Methodological Axioms

There are some important axioms that all of us who study languages "scientifically" subscribe to. Radford (1986:25–6) defines them formally as follows:

1. **Observational adequacy**

   A grammar of a language is *observationally adequate* if it correctly predicts which sentences are (and are not) syntactically, semantically and phonologically well-formed in the language.

2. **Descriptive adequacy**

   A grammar of a language is *descriptively adequate* if it correctly predicts which sentences are (and are not) syntactically, semantically and phonologically well-formed in the language, *and also* correctly describes the syntactic, semantic and phonological structure of the sentences in the language in such a way as to provide a principled account of the native speaker's intuitions about this structure.

3. **Explanatory adequacy**

   A grammar attains *explanatory adequacy* if it correctly predicts which sentences are and are not well-formed in the language, correctly describes their structure, *and also* does so in terms of a highly restricted set of optimally simple, universal, maximally general principles which represent psychologically plausible natural principles of mental computation, and are 'learnable' by the child in a limited period of time, and given access to limited data.

4. **Justification of analysis**

   "Secondly, there is a stress in syntactic theory on the justification of analysis. This means that syntacticians seek to demonstrate that their analyses work well and especially work better than the obvious alternatives." Borsley (1991:6)

5. **The Occam Razor principle**

   As the saying goes, there are many ways to get to Rome. However, some ways of getting there are faster and more efficient. Similarly, in linguistics, there are many ways of analyzing the same linguistic form. However, some analyses are better than others. In general, linguistics subscribe to the Occam Razor principle:

   "Widely accepted as a principle of science ever since the 12th century, it means that if two theories account for a phenomenon equally well, that theory which is simpler is better."

4.1.1 Methodological Rigor

In their quest for scientific rigor in syntactic analysis, linguists have refined their methodologies and added more constraints. Linguistics is an empirical science. For this reason, it uses the same kind of methodology commonly used in other sciences. Radford (1986:21, 25) summarizes this methodology as follows:

1. Collect a set of data relevant to the phenomenon being studied.

2. Hypothesize a set of principles (i.e., rules) which account for the data.

3. Test the hypothesis rule(s) against further data.

It is expected that if a scientific methodology is followed, syntactic analysis will achieve its goals. Baker (1978:5, 8) states that:

"[The overall goal is to] formulate explicitly a set of rules which mirror the effects of the native speaker's unconscious system of rules. . . . There is a further requirement that we will try to satisfy: the set of rules in a grammar must be revealing, rather than unnecessarily complex. The rules should be as general as possible, so that they do not make the language appear to be more complicated than it actually is."

Linguistic data are organized in such a way that they can be easily analyzed. The goal here is to allow the researcher to make generalizations about linguistic behavior based on available data.

4.1.2 Theorizing about Universal Principles

Chomsky and other theoretical linguists have an even bigger goal in mind. This goal extends beyond the confines of linguistics per se and reaches into other areas of intellectual inquiry. Borsley (1991:1, 4) describes this as follows: "[syntax] is also a potential source of insight into the human mind, one point to note about Chomsky's conception of a language is that it makes syntactic theory a branch of psychology, and especially cognitive psychology, the psychology of the systems of knowledge and belief." Chomsky (2000) is devoted entirely to the exploration of the inner workings of language and the brain.

4.1.3 Scientific Neutrality

Linguistic analysis is done with impartiality. Prior to contemporary linguistics, previous generations of language experts laced their findings with biases of all kinds. Some languages and their speakers were deemed primitive or simple because their languages lacked this or that feature found in the "civilized" languages of Europe. Blatant claims of linguistic superiority have no place in contemporary linguistics. All linguists subscribe to the view that all languages, written or spoken, are linguistically equal. Consequently, there is no inferior language or dialect. Naïve views such as "French is appropriate for the sciences, whereas Greek, Latin, Italian, and English are betters for the letters" are no longer part of the description of language (Chomsky 1965:6–8).

4.2 The Forerunners of Scientific Linguistics

Chomsky was a student of Zellig Harris, whose methodology Lyons (1970:34) regards as the most ambitious and the most rigorous attempt at establishing discovery procedures. So, in a sense, Chomsky is a by-product of American structural linguistics. However, for Lyons (1970:43, 45), what distinguishes generative linguistics from structural linguistics is the application of mathematics to the description of languages: "Chomsky's most original, and probably most enduring, contribution to linguistics is the mathematical rigor and precision with which he formalized the properties of alternative systems of grammatical description." He argues that Chomsky's "notion of constituent structure, or phrase structure, is comparable to the notion of bracketing in mathematics or symbolic logic" (p. 61). In this chapter we will review the formalisms and conventions that contemporary linguists use in their analysis of grammar.

4.2.1 Presentation of the Model

The original Generative Transformational Grammar apparatus is generally summarized graphically by the following diagram:

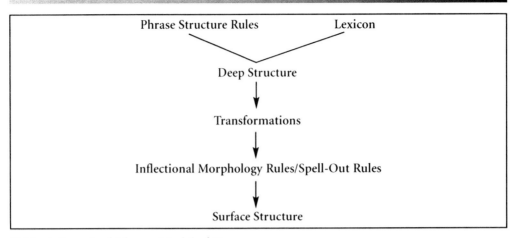

Table 1 *Standard Theory Model of Grammar*

Jackendoff (2002:109–110), and Riemsdjik and Williams (1986:172–3) present various other architectures which show the developments within Generative Grammar. The architecture of the Minimalist Program discussed in 4.4 and shown in Table 5 looks markedly different from the previous four. However, in this introductory text we will not concern ourselves with the fine points that distinguish the different theories. Instead, we will only highlight the aspects of the theories that help raise the teachers' grammatical awareness.

The traditional architecture presented in Table 1 will inform the analysis presented in the remainder of the book. Linguists claim that this model is **psycholinguistically real.** In linguistic circles, such a claim means that the model explains adequately how language is processed by human beings. Baker (1989:13) remarks that this is one of the goals of Generative Grammar: "... in the middle and late 1950s, a new movement arose within linguistics; it came to be called generative grammar. . . . The most striking change was its strong psychological orientation, centered around the conviction that the study of language was essentially a study of one aspect of the human mind." Chomsky (1965:8) states it as follows: "Any interesting generative grammar will be dealing, for the most part, with mental processes that are far beyond the level of actual or even potential consciousness." Additionally, I will argue based on available neurological information that the model seems to be also neurolinguistically real.

4.2.2 Explanation of the Architecture

All the architectures of Generative Grammar except for the Minimalist Program have three important components:

1.   the base and the deep structure

2.   the transformational component

3.   the surface structure

The base consists of two sub-components: the **categorial component** and the **Lexicon,** as represented by the diagram below. The phrase structure rules and the lexicon feed information into the deep structure:

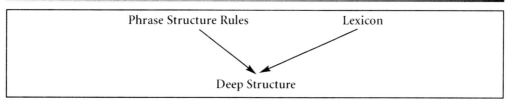

Table 2 *Architecture of the Base Component*

The phrase structure rules are found in the categorial component, while lexical items are located in the Lexicon. Neurolinguistic evidence seems to support the division of the base into two. **Neurolinguistics** was defined earlier as the branch of linguistics that studies the relationship between language comprehension and production and the brain. It seems that **phrase structure rules** (PSR rules) may be found in Broca's area, while the Lexicon may be located in Wernicke's area of the brain. Let us focus on the phrase structure rules first before dealing with the Lexicon and the deep structure.

4.2.3 The Categorial Component

The categorial component of the base houses all the mathematical formulas and syntactic and lexical categories that human beings rely on to make sentences. A very simplified model of phrase structure rules is presented in the table below:

Phrase Structure (PS) Rules
S → NP   AUX   VP
AUX → Tense
NP → Det   N
VP → V   NP

Table 3 *A Skeletal Version of PS Rules*

Formulas such as those contained in Table 3 are known as **"rewrite rules."** The arrow "→" stands for "is rewritten as." Phrase structure rules are the formal mathematical-looking apparatus that many consider to be Chomsky's most important innovation in the study of grammar. Expanded versions of the phrase structure rules will be presented and discussed at appropriate times throughout the rest of the book.

In the categorial component we find symbols for the following **syntactic categories:**[1]

1. **S** for "sentence"

2. **NP** for "noun phrase"

3. **VP** for "verb phrase"

4. **AdjP** for "adjective phrase"

5. **AdvP** for "adverb phrase"

6. **PP** for "preposition phrase"

7. **AUX** for auxiliaries

---

[1] This is a partial list. More syntactic categories will be introduced as we proceed.

This component also includes symbols for **lexical categories.** Lexical categories are synonymous with **parts of speech** (POS):

1.   **N** for "noun"
2.   **V** for "verb"
3.   **Adj** for "adjective"
4.   **Adv** for "adverb"
5.   **P** for "preposition"
6.   **Conj.** for "conjunction"
7.   **Det.** for "article"
8.   **Pro** for "pronoun"

Chomsky (1965:73) assumes that the phrase structure rules and symbols such as S, NP, VP, N, V and AUX are **grammatical universals.** This claim is accepted by practicing linguists all over the world.

Phrase structure (PS) rules serve a dual purpose. They have **predictive power** and **descriptive power.** They predict that sentences in a given language conform to its PS rules, i.e., S → NP AUX VP. Additionally, PS rules help describe all sentences. Any sentence that deviates from the PS rule of a specific language will be ungrammatical. Most software programs that have a grammar check are built on the assumption that every sentence begins with an S symbol. This is the reason why sentences are underlined green when they do not satisfy the requirements of the built-in phrase structure rules.

4.2.4 The Mental Lexicon

The mental Lexicon is similar to conventional dictionaries. A typical dictionary entry lists a certain amount of information concerning the word in question. Theoretical linguists speculate that the mental Lexicon is just like commercial dictionaries, but a million times more complex and more detailed. One major difference is that the words (also called "lexemes") in the mental lexicon are not listed alphabetically (Chomsky 1965:142). Experts are not at all sure how the words are listed in the brain of speakers. Aitchison (1994) offers several compelling and competing models.[2] One view that I subscribe to is that of the Multiple Listing Hypothesis. According to this view, words may be listed in many ways such as by semantic domains, by their semantic relationships with other words, by phonological structure, or by their morphological structure. The information in the mental lexicon can be represented schematically as follows:

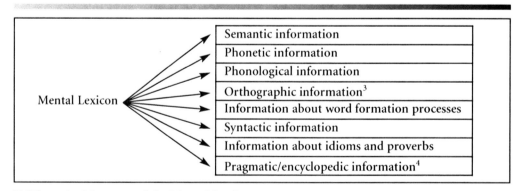

Table 4 *Architecture of the Mental Lexicon*

---

[2] Aitchison, Jean. 1994. *Words in the Mind: An Introduction to the Mental Lexicon.* 2nd edition. Cambridge, Massachusetts: Blackwell Publishers, Inc.

[3] Orthographic information is found only in the mental Lexicon of literate people.

[4] Pinker (1994:227) estimates that human common sense comprises at least ten million facts.

Phrase structure rules and the mental Lexicon interact through what is called **lexical insertion rules.** While the phrase structure rules provide the structure of the sentences, lexical insertion rules insert lexical items where they are supposed to go. For this to happen, syntactic and semantic information are crucial. If lexical insertion were done randomly, the phrase structure rules could generate sentences such as the ones below:

(1)   *My uncle is reading his book.*

(2)   *?My dog is reading his book.*

(3)   *?The corpse is reading his book.*

(4)   *?The toddler is reading his book.*

Only metaphorically can (2) and (3) be acceptable even though they satisfy the phrase structure rules for English sentence formation. The examples show that phrase structure rules are too powerful. Not only do they generate well-formed sentences such as (1) but they can also produce sentences such as (2) and (3).[5] To curb this extraordinary power, Chomsky introduced the notions of **subcategorization** and **selectional restriction.** Through subcategorization rules, the verb dictates which nouns it can take as its subject and which nouns it can take as its object. Chomsky (1965:93) argues that "a verb is positively specified with respect to the contextual feature associated with the context in which it occurs." Selectional restriction provides information about semantic features that make it possible for a given word to occur in a specified syntactic environment. Sentence (2) is unacceptable because the verb <read> must have a subject that is a human being. However, being a human being is not the only criterion. The subject of <read> must also be an animate human being. But clearly, to be an animate human being is still not the final criterion. Sentence (4) is dubious because even though <toddler> is [+animate], because generally people at this age cannot read. It seems then that <read> requires that its subject be of a reading age. Notions such as <human being>, <animate> and <appropriate age> are called **semantic features.** Thus, the syntactic information in the mental lexicon includes parts of speech and subcategorization information. Furthermore, it refers to semantic features in the form of selectional restriction.

4.2.5 The Deep Structure

Information from the mental lexicon fills in the slots created by the phrase structure rules. The convergence and merger of information from these two sub-components of the base constitute the **deep structure** of the sentence. The deep structure is thus a gold mine of information about the sentence. In earlier formulations of the deep structure, Chomsky (1965:136) made it the sole provider of information on the interpretation of sentences. However, in the Extended Standard Theory and in subsequent theories, the surface structure has been given some interpretive power. Even with this semantic power sharing arrangement, most of the semantic information carried by sentences is still found in the deep structure.

English sentences in the deep structure follow the canonical word order; that is, they are all SVO (Subject-Verb-Object). Additionally, there are no negative sentences, no interrogative sentences, no passive constructions, no imperatives. All sentences in the deep structure are in their most basic affirmative forms. A sentence such as <*do my students love syntax?*> can be represented as follows in the deep structure:

(5)   Deep structure: *My student plural present love syntax*

---

[5] Phrase structure rules can even generate weirder sentences such as Chomsky's famous, "Colorless green ideas sleep furiously" (Chomsky 1965:149).

Deep structures can be extremely abstract. However, linguists prefer a deep structure that is closer to the threshold of consciousness. Kempton (1986:160) lists seven important characteristics of the deep structure:

1. The output of phrase structure rules

2. The input to the set of transformational rules (which state the relationship between this level and the surface string of elements making up the sentence)

3. The level at which relations such as subject and object are defined

4. The level at which lexical items are inserted

5. The level at which the so-called selectional restrictions are stated

6. The level at which ambiguity in sentences is captured by assigning a different deep structure corresponding to each interpretation a sentence has

7. The level of deep structure was said to be the input to the semantic component

In this book we will avoid very abstract deep structures. Instead, we will focus on deep structures that are relatively close to the surface structure.

4.2.6 Tree Diagramming

All well-formed sentences in all languages conform to three essential criteria which are:

1. hierarchy

2. categoriality

3. linearity

What is meant by **hierarchy** is that sentences display a hierarchical order. In other words smaller elements are grouped together into larger units which in turn are grouped into even larger units, until they form highest possible unit, the sentence. This is demonstrated by the phrase structure rules in Table 4, where the symbol "**S**" stands for "sentence".[6] The criterion of **categoriality** means that every lexical item used in a sentence belongs to a syntactic category, to a lexical category, and then to a phrasal category. Lastly, sentences are characterized by **linearity.** This means that when the sentence is produced, the lexical items follow each other in a linear fashion.

Generative grammar tries to capture these important properties of sentences by what is commonly called a **tree diagram.** Three other methods exist for representing sentence structure graphically. The oldest one is called the Reed and Kellog system. Kolln and Funk (2006:52) indicate that it dates back to the 19th century. Linguists hardly ever use it anymore. Bloomfield (1933) invented the Immediate Constituent Analysis method. This method was later replaced by what has come to be known as labeled-bracketing. It, too, has been superseded by the method of the **tree diagram,** also known as the **phrase structure tree.** Harris and his student Chomsky are said to have invented this popular method of representing sentences graphically. Tree diagramming is a widely used tool because it is the most effective way to represent sentence structures visually. Freeman and Freeman (2004:233) note that "in fact, some students who may have difficulty reading about syntactic structure find that they can grasp many of the concepts more easily when they see them in a diagram. The diagram captures linear order, grouping of words into

---

[6] More recent syntactic theories prefer to represent the sentence as Inflectional Phrase (IP), but we will use the more traditional label "S". As much as possible, we will use terms that are more widespread than the more recent theory dependent terms.

constituents, and labels for morphological categories of words. Such diagrams help students understand the structure of sentences and phrases." Tree diagrams are a visual representation of basic aspects of the deep structure.

4.2.7 Tree Diagramming Conventions

There are a few important conventions that need to be kept in mind when diagramming sentences:

1.   **The line crossing constraint:** In diagramming trees, association lines should not cross. Kaplan (1995:215) formulates this constraint simply as follows: "branches are not allowed to cross each other."

2.   **Constraint against functional categories:** Chomsky (1965:68–9) discourages adding functional information in tree diagrams. Even though it is done in the name of clarity, Chomsky argues that such an approach is mistaken and confuses categorial function with functional notions by assigning categorial status to both. The representation of functional information in tree diagrams has always been a bone of contention between my students and me because I follow standard generative grammar practice, while some textbooks do not.

4.2.8 Tree Diagram Terminology

Linguists have coined a special jargon to name various aspects of tree diagrams, as seen in the diagram below:

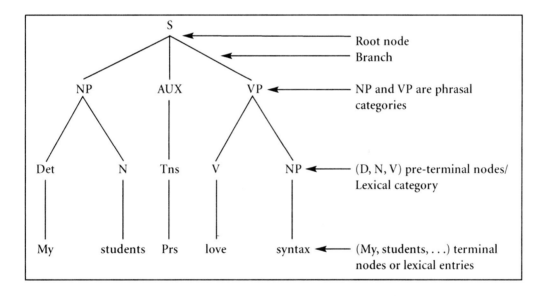

Linguists also use a number of family metaphors to refer to sets of relationships between the nodes on the tree. For instance, the **"S"** node is called the **mother.** A node is a mother if it immediately dominates another node. Here "S" is a mother because it dominates NP and VP. Note also that NP and VP are mothers to Det—N and V—N, respectively. Nodes that are dominated by the same mother are **daughters** to the dominating node. Naturally, two nodes that are dominated by the same mother are **sisters.** As you might expect, Det—N and V—N are the **granddaughters** of **"S"** (Radford 1986:84).

4.3 *Notational Conventions in Generative Grammar*

Some conventions have become standard in linguistics irrespective of the theoretical framework. The following conventions are commonly found in linguistic articles and textbooks:

1. **Ungrammaticality Convention:** The asterisk "*" in front of a sentence indicates that such a sentence is ill-formed.

    (6) * *I apple pie love.*

2. **Acceptability Convention:** A question mark "?" in front of a sentence shows that there is something dubious about the sentence which makes its overall acceptability uncertain.

    (7) ? *The toddler is reading his book.*

3. **The Angle Bracket Convention:** It is represented by "{ }." It is also called the brace convention. This convention indicates an **"either ... or"** possibility in the selection of the elements. However, all the elements must occur as seen in the example below:

    $$VP \rightarrow V \quad NP \quad \left\{ \begin{array}{c} NP \\ PP \\ AdjP \end{array} \right\}$$

    This rule can be expanded as follows:

    $$VP \rightarrow V \quad NP \quad NP$$
    $$VP \rightarrow V \quad NP \quad PP$$
    $$VP \rightarrow V \quad NP \quad AdjP$$

4. **The Parentheses Convention:** This convention is represented as "( )." The parentheses designate an optional element that may or may not occur. Baker (1978:50) explains this convention as follows: "If two phrase structure rules are identical except that one contains a symbol or a sequence of symbols that the other does not, we abbreviate the two rules as one by writing out the longer rule and enclosing in parentheses the symbols or sequence of symbols that is missing in the shorter rule."

    $$NP \rightarrow Det \ Adj \ N$$
    $$NP \rightarrow Det \ N$$

    The rule is abbreviated as follows with the parentheses convention:

    $$NP \rightarrow Det \ (Adj) \ N$$

When the parentheses convention is used, the number of options is calculated as follows: 2^n, where "n" represents the number of parentheses. In the example above, since there is only one parenthesis, the number of options is 2^1. This means that there are 2 options because $2 \times 1 = 2$.

The angle bracket convention and the parentheses convention are collectively known as **abbreviatory conventions.** Both can be used to collapse various phrase structure rules, as in the example below:

$$VP \rightarrow V \; (\left\{ \begin{array}{c} NP \\ PP \\ AdjP \end{array} \right\})$$

This phrase structure rule can be written as four separate rules:

1. $VP \rightarrow V \; NP$
2. $VP \rightarrow V \; PP$
3. $VP \rightarrow V \; AdjP$
4. $VP \rightarrow V$

5. **The Trace Convention:** The symbol "_____" indicates a **trace** or **place holder.** If it is a trace, then it shows that an element that used to occupy that position has been moved. If it is a place holder, it means that an element must occur in that position. The latter possibility can be illustrated by the **subcategorization** formula below:

$$Eat, V \; [\;_____ \; (NP)]$$

This formula is interpreted as follows: the verb <eat> occurs in the place holder between the two braces. When it does, it may or may not occur with a noun phrase (NP).

6. **The Triangle Convention:** Linguists use a triangle "Δ"in a tree diagram if they do not wish to go into details about a specific aspect of the diagram.

7. **The Deletion Convention:** The symbol "Ø" is used in a tree diagram to indicate that an element has been deleted.

4.4 New Theoretical Releases

Since Chomsky's 1957 book, *Syntactic Theories,* there have been numerous developments in syntax. The theories and approaches are too many to mention here. Chomsky himself has significantly refined generative grammar. Here are the different names of the subsequent refinements of Generative Grammar:

1. the Standard Theory (1968)

2. the Extended Standard Theory (1972)

3. the Revised Extended Standard Theory (1975)

4. Government-Binding Theory (1981)

5. the Minimalist Program (1993)

The first major overhaul of Chomsky's original proposals came to be known as the "Standard Theory." The next three releases are revisions and expansions of the Standard Theory. In spite of terminological and conceptual changes, the theoretical foundation remained essentially the same. However, with the Minimalist Program, Chomsky has drastically changed the overall architecture of the theory. Jackendoff (2002:110) diagrams it as follows:

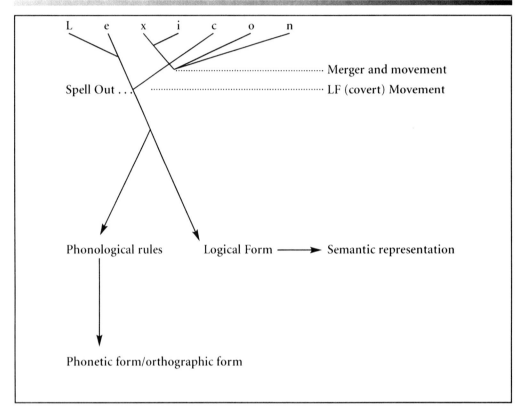

Table 5 *Architecture of the Minimalist Program—1993*

Reading *The Minimalist Program* (MP), one gets the impression that this approach is not yet fully formulated. Chomsky (1995:173, 220, 242, 249) repeatedly underlines the fact that the MP is a work in progress. Chomsky (2000) provides some justification for this approach and refines some concepts. Even so, Culicover (1997:347)[7] believes that it will take time before the MP becomes widely used. For our purpose, the most significant change is the elimination of the transformational component. As we will see throughout the book, and especially in Chapter 15, I believe that the transformational component in the previous models is a powerful tool for teaching writing. For this reason, insights from the MP will be used only if they shed new light on the analysis. Otherwise, information used in this book is based on the previous models of Generative Grammar, that is, the approaches used between 1968 and 1981.

---

[7] Some in the linguistic community are growing weary of the different changes. Jackendoff (2002:74) laments the fact that, because of the constant tweaking of generative grammar, the initial excitement that it brought to other disciplines is all but gone. In footnote 8, Jackendoff explains the divorce between linguistics and psychology. At the Linguistic Society of America annual meeting in Boston, MA, (2003), Jackendoff reiterated this same complaint in his presidential address. Therefore, in my opinion, one must wait until the dust is completely settled on the MP to see if it is applicable to writing.

4.5 *Transformations*

No better definition of transformation can be found than the one that Chomsky (1965:136) provides. He states that "one major function of the transformational rules is to convert an abstract deep structure that expresses the content of sentences into a fairly concrete surface structure that indicates its form." Chomsky (1965:125–33) also distinguishes three types of transformations:[8]

1. obligatory transformations

2. optional transformations

3. stylistic transformations

As one might expect, generative grammar pays little or no attention to stylistic transformations. As noted earlier, since the advent of structural linguistics written language has been de-emphasized. However, as we will see here and especially in Chapter 15, stylistic transformations should matter a great deal to classroom teachers because they provide the necessary ingredients for improving students' writing skills.

Understanding how transformations operate is crucial to most contemporary approaches to linguistics. Transformations are so important that Klammer et al. (2004:253) use this hyperbole to describe them: "Without transformations that enable us to combine sentences . . . , our ability to communicate would be severely hampered."

4.5.1 The Transformational Component

The transformational component is usually summarized by the following architecture:

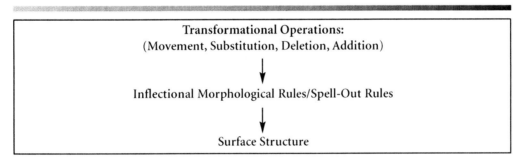

Table 6 *Skeletal Architecture of the Derivational Apparatus*

The transformational component contains four different types of operations:

1. movement rules

2. addition rules

3. substitution rules

4. deletion rules

One of the most important constraints imposed on the transformational component is that all of its operations should be "meaning-preserving." **Constraints** are so important in contemporary syntax that Baker (2003:273) sees them as "the most interesting and significant discovery of all." He goes on to state that "when the various rules of syntax are

---

[8] In the Minimalist Program, the transformational component has been done away with, (Chomsky 2000:13). However, we keep it because the notion of transformation has great pedagogical value for teaching grammar and composition.

stated in their simplest and most general forms, they typically 'over-generate,' producing a number of ungrammatical sentences along with the grammatical ones. Therefore, syntacticians have proposed a system of constraints that prevent these rules from running wild." The **meaning-preserving constraint** insures that no matter what operation(s) takes place in generating the surface structure, the meaning of the sentence found in the deep structure remains essentially the same as the one found in the surface structure.

4.5.2 Movement Operation and Constraints

In earlier approaches of generative grammar, the four operations in the transformational component were given equal importance. However, in subsequent approaches, especially in the approach known as Government-Binding (1981), **movement rules** were deemed to be the most important. In this book, for the sake of a comprehensive coverage of the whole framework, we will discuss all four operations. It should be noted, however, that in the thirty or so transformations commonly encountered in writing and in speech, movement operations are used more extensively.

Movement rules help move constituents from their original position in the deep structure to another position in the sentence. As a result of movement transformation, the sentence in the surface structure is structurally different from what it was in the deep structure, as seen in the examples below:

(8)   *Tallie likes this book a lot.*

(9)   *This book, Tallie likes—a lot.*

Sentence (8) is the base sentence because it reflects closely the SVO pattern found in the deep structure form of all English sentences, while (9) is the result of the application of a transformational rule. We see that <this book> has moved from its original position in (8) to an initial position in (9) after a movement transformation has been applied.

Each one of the four operations has constraints that contribute to the overall goal of meaning preservation. The most important constraint on the movement rule has been formulated as follows:

Movement Constraint: Move α (where alpha is a category variable, i.e., designates any random category you care to choose)[9]. *(Radford 1986:203)*

A subset of this constraint is the **Constituency Condition.** It is formulated as follows:

Constituency Condition: Movement is allowed when the element(s) that is moved is **a constituent/phrase.**

What constitutes a "phrase" will be discussed in later chapters. For the time being, let us only say that this constraint works very well in the majority of cases involving movement. However, it fails to account for **preposition stranding** that we hear in the speech of many Midwesterners, as illustrated by (10) and (11):

(10)   *I was talking to Kim.*

(11)   *It was Kim that I was talking to—.*

---

[9] The α-movement rule is too broad, but it makes sense. This is the logic behind it: "But Chomsky's reasoning is essentially along the following lines. If we know that languages have rules moving constituents from one position into another in a sentence, then we ought to expect (as the simplest hypothesis) that in principle, languages allow you to move any constituent anywhere, and if in practice this is not the case, then there must be a set of universal or language-specific principles which determine why it's not possible to move certain constituents into certain other positions. The task of Universal Grammar is then to discover what these conditions are that 'block' certain types of movement in language, that determine how movement rules apply, and so forth." (Radford:1986:204)

A preposition is said to have been stranded when the NP moves out of the PP, leaving the preposition behind. In (11) <Kim> moves out of the whole PP, i.e., <to Kim> and leaves <to> stranded all by itself.

4.5.2.1 Addition Operation and Constraints

Chomsky (1965:132) imposes a stringent condition on addition transformation. This constraint is formulated as follows:

> **Addition Constraint:** Transformations cannot introduce meaning-bearing elements.

This constraint allows transformations to add only what is often referred to as **"dummy"** elements, that is, words that do not have a dictionary meaning on their own. Words such as <do>, <it>, <there>, <so>, <too>, and <by> are added to make the transformation possible. Addition transformations can be illustrated by the following examples:

> (12) *Annie can sing and Mary can sing.*

> (13) *Annie can sing and Mary can, too.*

Sentence (13) is obviously derived from (12). The word <too> that appears in the surface structure is not part of the deep structure. It is added somewhere during the derivation. Other details are left out because they do not matter at this point. We will re-analyze these two sentences later and add some of the missing pieces.

4.5.2.2 Substitution Operation and Constraints

Substitution rules allow the transformational component to substitute some elements in the deep structure with other elements, under some very stringent conditions stipulated as follows:

> **Structure-Preserving Constraint:** A category can only be substituted for another category of the same type. *Radford (1986:204)*

This constraint is rather broad. So, it is refined into two sub-constraints when pronouns are involved:

> **Indexing Rule**[10]: Assign every NP in a sentence an index (where the index is a random integer). *Radford (1986:366)*

> **Matching Condition:** If two NPs are assigned the same integer, they must "match" in features (e.g., number, gender, person, etc.) *Radford (1986:366)*

These three constraints are very important. We will return to them in later chapters. For now, let us take a quick look at how they work:

> (14) *Alicia[1] is bulimic; so she[1] hates herself[1].*

In this sentence, <Alicia> has the same integer as <she> and <herself>. Since the integers match, we assume that <she> and <herself> refer back to <Alicia>. Sentence (14) is derived from (15) below.

> (15) *Alicia[1] is bulimic; so Alicia[1] hates Alicia[1].*

Nobody produces a sentence like (15) in English. The second <Alicia> and the third <Alicia> are replaced by the pronouns <she> and <herself> through a substitution operation. Since (14) is well-formed, it means that the Structure-Preserving Constraint is satisfied. It also means that <Alicia>, <she>, and <herself> belong to the same category.

---

[10] Other Substitution constraints will be discussed in Chapter 14.

4.5.2.3 Deletion Operation and Constraints

There are two main constraints on deletion. The first, the Deletion Constraint, is very powerful but useful. The second, the Recoverability Constraint, allows lexical items to be deleted under strict guidelines. Both constraints are stated as follows:

Deletion Constraint: "Only elements which do not have semantic content can be deleted." (Radford 1986:266)

Recoverability Constraints: Lexical item (s) (= real word(s)) can be deleted only if their meaning is recoverable.

Let us return to (12) and (13) discussed previously. In this section, they will be (16) and (17), respectively:

(16) *Annie can sing^1 and Mary can sing^1.*

(17) *Annie can sing and Mary can, too.*

In the base form represented by (16), we see that the two occurrences of the word <sing> have the same integer. The deletion constraint would prevent the erasure of <sing>. However, the recoverability condition would permit it for the second occurrence of <sing> because it is co-indexed with the first <sing>. Thus, the deletion operation can apply to erase the second <sing>.[11] The two constraints on deletion prevent transformation operations from deleting content words randomly.

4.6 Cyclical Application of Transformational Rules

Chomsky (1965:134) observes that transformational rules apply in an orderly fashion. The sequence in which the rules apply depends on the type and the complexity of the sentence. The sequential application of rules is known as derivation. Let us illustrate this by the example below:

(18) *Many students don't take linguistics.*

Before we embark on the full derivation[12] of (18), it is important to remember that no questions, no commands, no exclamations, no negation, no passive constructions, and no pronominalization are found in the deep structure. In other words, all sentences in the deep structure are affirmative sentences with a subject-verb-object (SVO) word order. With this in mind, let us see the derivational steps involved in producing (18) above:

Deep structure:	many student plural present take linguistics
1. Negative Insertion:	many student plural present **NOT** take linguistics
2. DO-Support addition:	many student plural present **DO NOT** take linguistics
3. NOT-Contraction:	many student plural present **DON'T** take linguistics
4. Affix Hopping:[13]	many student plural DON'T **present** take linguistics
5. Spell-Out Rule:[14]	many students **DON'T** take linguistics
Surface Structure:	Many students don't take linguistics.

---

[11] We will have to wait until later to give a full account of all the mechanisms involved in producing these sentences.

[12] Many points of the derivation will be ignored for now. Full justification will be provided in later discussions where and when it is most appropriate to do so.

[13] The Affix Hopping transformation applies generally to tense markers on verbs. It applies only once in any given derivation.

[14] The Spell-Out Rule subsumes a number of rules including, but not limited to, agreement rules and other inflectional morphology rules.

It is generally argued that no matter what rules should apply in the derivation, inflectional morphology rules apply right before the syntactic surface structure. We will see later that the sequence in which the derivation occurs will depend on the mode of communication used: writing, speaking, and reading aloud. Generative transformational linguists focus on obligatory transformations. Negation, questions, and passive constructions are the flagship examples used to illustrate the order of application of transformational rules. We will follow the same well-established linguistic tradition here.

4.6.1 Illustration of Yes/No Transformations

Yes/No questions are characterized by the fact that they require an answer which is "yes" or "no." Let us illustrate the different derivations involved in producing a Yes/No question by analyzing (19) and (20):

(19) *Brad past buy the car.*

(20) *Did Brad buy the car?*

Sentence (19) is the deep structure from which (20) is derived. Here is the full derivation involving both sentences. A full explanation of the addition of <DO> is not possible at this point.

Deep structure:	Brad past buy the car
1. Yes/No Question:	Q Brad past buy the car
2. Do-Support addition:	Q Brad past **DO** buy the car
3. Subject-Auxiliary Inversion:	Q past DO Brad—buy the car
4. Affix Hopping:	Q DO **past** Brad buy the car
5. Spell-Out Rule:	Q did Brad buy the car
Surface structure:	Did Brad buy the car?

In deriving Yes/No questions, one must follow a strict order as in the example here, or else the final result will be wrong. More complex transformations involving questions will be delayed until later.

4.6.2 Illustration of Passive Transformations

In the early stages of generative grammar, passive sentences were used to illustrate how many different transformational operations can apply to the same deep structure. This way of analyzing passive sentences is out of date, but we will use it to illustrate the point. Let us consider (21) and (22) below:

(21) *The police arrested the criminal.*

(22) *The criminal was arrested by the police.*

---

[15] A slightly different solution will be discussed in Chapter 7.

Sentence (22) is allegedly derived from (21) by applying the following transformations:[15]

Deep structure:		the police past arrest the criminal
1.	Movement rule 1:	—past arrest the criminal **the police**
2.	Movement rule 2:	**the criminal** past arrest—the police
3.	<Be – en> addition:	the criminal past <**Be-EN**> arrest the police
4.	<By> addition:	the criminal past <Be-EN> arrest **by** the police
5.	Affix Hopping rule:	the criminal Be past arrest **EN** by the police
6.	Spell-Out Rule:	the criminal was arrested by the police
	Surface structure:	The criminal was arrested by the police.

Movement rules 1 and 2 are called **permutation.**[16] We will discuss the status of <Be-EN> later; suffice it to say now that <Be-EN> and <by> are inserted during the derivational process. The Addition Constraint is satisfied because these are dummy elements that do not add meaning.[17] The rule of Affix Hopping moves <-EN> and attaches it at the end of the main verb <arrest>. It also moves <past> and attaches it to <Be>. It is only after these rules have been applied that Spell-Out Rules can apply. One Spell-Out rule is responsible for changing the past participial ending <-EN> to <-ED>. This is the reason why the surface structure form of the verb <arrest> is <arrested> and not *<arresten>.

The negation example, the Yes/No example, and the passive voice example all show that transformational rules occur in a certain order. This must be kept in mind when deriving a surface structure from the deep structure.

4.7 The Surface Structure

Grammar books do not usually specify which type of surface structure they are alluding to when they use the phrase "surface structure." However, there are three types of surface structures:

1. the spoken surface structure

2. the written surface structure

3. the reading aloud structure

The sequencing of transformation rules will vary, depending on the mode of communication used. Let us use Yes/No question discussed in 4.6.1 to illustrate it. The new elements in the derivation appear in bold.

[16] We have separated the two movement rules because movement rules apply one at a time. Bickford (1999:210) explains it as follows: "There is one very important restriction on movement rules: a rule can move only one constituent at a time. Movement rules in languages around the world do not move more than one constituent at a time."

[17] Some would argue that, even though transformations do not appear to change propositional meaning, some can change the ideological meaning of a sentence. The arguments in favor of this claim are beyond the scope of this book. Let us note simply that this restriction has been loosened somewhat. Now transformations are allowed to change meaning slightly, but not a whole lot. It is argued that contrastive emphasis changes the meaning a little bit. For this reason, it has been argued that a transformation that affects meaning must precede any other that does not affect meaning (Bickford 1999:211).

4.7.1 The Spoken Surface Structure

If the sentence is meant to be spoken aloud, the sequencing of transformations is represented by the following architecture:

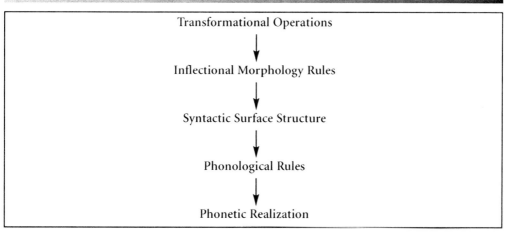

Transformational Operations

↓

Inflectional Morphology Rules

↓

Syntactic Surface Structure

↓

Phonological Rules

↓

Phonetic Realization

Table 7 *Skeletal Architecture of Spoken Language*

Deep structure: Brad past buy the car

1. Yes/No Question: Q Brad past buy the car

2. Do-Support addition: Q Brad past **DO** buy the car

3. Subject-Auxiliary Inversion: Q past DO Brad buy the car

4. Affix Hopping: Q DO **past** Brad buy the car

5. Inflectional Morphology Rules: Q did Brad buy the car

6. **Application of Phonological Rules: A number of rules apply**

7. **Phonetic Surface Structure:**   [dɪd bræd bɑɪ ðə kʰɑr][18]

Chomsky (1965:143) has this order in mind when he argues that "the phonological component consists of a sequence of rules that apply to a surface structure 'from the bottom up' in the tree diagram representing it." The syntactic surface structure <did Brad buy the car?> serves as the input for the phonological underlying structure. Various phonological rules apply to this structure to derive the correct pronunciation of the word, phrase, or sentence.

4.7.2 The Written Surface Structure

If the sentence is to be written down, Spelling Rules apply to the output of inflectional morphology rules. Disterheft (2003:214) defines these rules as "a set of pronunciation rules that operate to produce the correct forms of both regular and irregular verbs. They also add capitalization, punctuation, sentence intonation, and so on." The full

---

[18] This is a phonetic transcription of the sentence. This is just an illustration. Since phonetics and phonology are not the concern of this book, this is all we will say. Linguists use square brackets "[ ]" to represent words phonetically.

derivational apparatus of written surface structures can be represented by the architecture below:

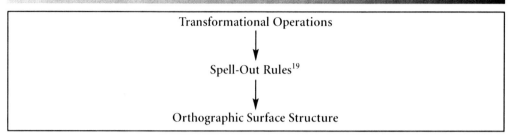

Table 8 *Skeletal Architecture of Written Language*

Deep structure:	Brad past buy the car
1. Yes/No Question:	Q Brad past buy the car
2. Do-Support addition:	Q Brad past **DO** buy the car
3. Subject-Auxiliary inversion:	Q past DO Brad buy the car
4. Affix Hopping:	Q DO **past** Brad buy the car
5. **Spell-Out Rule:**	Q did Brad buy the car
6. **Orthographic Surface structure:**	<Did Brad buy the car?>

From now on, the written surface structure is assumed. Linguists use "< >" to represent words orthographically. This convention will be used throughout the book.

4.7.3 Reading Aloud and Spoken Surface Structure

If the sentence is to be read out loud, graphophonological rules apply to the written text in the following fashion:

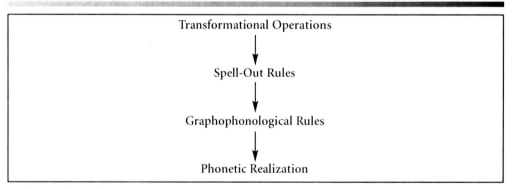

Table 9 *Skeletal Architecture of Reading Aloud*

---

[19] Textbooks that do not distinguish the mode of output use the general label of "Spell-Out Rules." Generally, it is assumed that such rules apply right after all inflectional morphology rules have applied. However, some linguists combine inflectional morphology rules and spell out rules into a single rule that they label "Inflectional Spell-Out Rule." Bickford (1999:204) uses the combination but Disterheft (2003:214–5) does not. Spell-Out rules are sometimes abbreviated as SO.

Deep structure: Brad past buy the car

1. Yes/No Question: Q Brad past buy the car
2. Do-Support addition: Q Brad past **DO** buy the car
3. Subject-Auxiliary Inversion: Q past DO Brad buy the car
4. Affix Hopping: Q DO **past** Brad buy the car
5. **Spell-Out Rules:** Q did Brad buy the car
6. **Application of Graphophonological Rules: A number of rules apply**
7. **Phonetic Surface Structure:** [dɪd bræd bɑɪ ðə kʰɑr]

These derivational stages underscore the fact that reading aloud involves a series of very complex cognitive operations.

4.7.4 Overview of Common Transformations

A question that students ask frequently is: "How many transformations are there in English?" It is hard to answer this question with any degree of accuracy because the number of transformations depends on whether one is speaking or writing. Since the focus of this book is on School Grammar, we will emphasize transformations used in writing. Chapter 15 goes into greater details about this point. For this reason, we will give only a preview and an overview of the types of transformations that will be discussed in the rest of the book. The goal here is not to show the derivational steps, but only to list the deep structure form of the sentence and its corresponding surface structure form(s). One important piece of information to keep in mind is that syntacticians assume that the canonical word order of any English sentence in the deep structure follows an SVO (Subject Verb Object) pattern. Any deviation from this pattern that results in a well-formed sentence is the result of an application of some transformation rules. The following are the labels given to the most common transformations in English syntax:

1. **Interrogative Yes/No Sentence**
   Deep Structure: Brad Sg. Past buy a car last year.
   Surface Structure: Did Brad buy a car last year?

2. **Interrogative Wh-Sentence** or **Wh-Movement**
   Deep Structure: Brad Sg. Past buy bought a car last year.
   Surface Structure: *When did Brad buy a car?*
   Surface Structure: *What did Brad buy last year?*
   Surface Structure: *Who bought a car last year?*
   Surface Structure: *Brad bought what last year?*

3. **Negation**
   Deep Structure: Brad Sg. Past buy a car last year.
   Surface Structure: Brad did *not* buy a car last year?

4. **Negation with Not-Contraction**
   Deep Structure: Brad Sg. Past buy a car last year.
   Surface Structure: Brad *didn't* buy a car last year?

5. **Passivization**
   Deep Structure: Brad Sg. Past buy a car last year.
   Surface Structure: *A car was bought by Brad last year.*

6. **Subject-Auxiliary Inversion**
   Deep Structure: Alex Sg. Pres. smile rarely at school.
   Surface Structure: Rarely *does Alex* smile at school.

7. **Adverbial Fronting**
   Deep Structure: Alex Sg. Pres. smile rarely at school.
   Surface Structure: *Rarely* does Alex smile at school.

8. **Particle Shift Movement**
   Deep Structure: Valerie Sg. Past bring up the matter again.
   Surface Structure: Valerie brought the matter *up* again.

9. **Prepositional Phrase Fronting/Preposing**
   Deep Structure: Cindy Sg. Past race up to the finish line.
   Surface Structure: *Up to the finish* Cindy raced.

10. **Split Infinitive**
    Deep Structure: She Sg. Past not[20] decide to marry him.
    Surface Structure: She decided to *not* marry him.

11. **Adjectival Fronting**
    Deep Structure: Adele Sg. Pres be lucky. Adele, Sg. Past find a job.
    Surface Structure: *Lucky* is Adele. She[21] found a job.

12. **Topicalization**
    Deep Structure: My passion Sg. Pres be linguistics.
    Surface Structure: *Linguistics* is my passion.

13. **Left Dislocation**
    Deep Structure: I Sg. Past dread trigonometry in high school.
    Surface Structure: *Trigonometry,* I dreaded *it* in high school.

14. **Extraposition**
    Deep Structure: That the professor Sg. Past lie about his resume Pres be dishonest.
    Surface Structure: *It is dishonest* that the professor lied on his resume.

15. **There-Insertion**
    Deep Structure: Injustice Sg Pres. be everywhere.
    Surface Structure: *There* is injustice everywhere.

16. **Pronominalization**
    Base Sentence: Noam Chomsky Sg. Pres be a controversial MIT linguistics professor.
    Surface Structure: *He* is a controversial MIT linguistics professor.

17. **Indirect Object Movement**
    Deep Structure: Jeff Sg. Past write a letter to the dean to complain.
    Surface Structure: Jeff wrote *the dean* a letter to complain.

18. **Ellipsis**
    Deep Structure: Jeremy Sg. Pres can swim and Tallie Sg Pres can swim.
    Surface Structure: Jeremy can swim and Tallie can, *too.*

---

[20] More will be said about the position of "NOT" in English sentences in 10.6.2.

[21] The details of pronominalization will be discussed in Chapter 14. Do not worry about it now.

19. **Gapping**

Deep Structure: Jeffery Sg Past major in economics and Kurtika Sg Past major in education.

Surface Structure: Jeffery majored in economics and Kurtika—in education.

20. **Relativization**

Deep Structure: The professor, Sg. [the professor Sg.] Past write a book Fut. give a keynote address.

Surface Structure: The professor *who* wrote a book will give a keynote address.

21. **Cleft-Sentence Formation**

Deep Structure: Bob Sg. Past find the puppy in apartment.

Surface Structure: *What* Bob found in the apartment *was* the puppy.

22. **Clicization**

Deep Structure: Bob Sg. Past find the puppy in apartment.

Surface Structure: *It is/it was* a puppy that Bob found in the apartment.

23. **Complementizer Deletion**

Deep Structure: The criminal Sg. Past think that the criminal Past not Be-EN arrest.

Surface Structure: The criminal thought—he would not be arrested.

24. **Relative Clause Reduction**

Deep Structure: The police Sg. Past see a car that Past Be-ING go over 120 miles per hour.

Surface Structure: The police saw a car—going over 120 miles per hour.

25. **Main Verb Fronting**

Deep Structure: You Sg Pres. must surrender or you Sg Fut. die.

Surface Structure: *Surrender,* you must or *die,* you will.

From the deep structure, one follows several steps before arriving at the surface structure. These steps are called derivations. Again, the number of derivational steps is not pre-ordained. All depends on the assumptions that one makes about the deep structure of a sentence and the type of sentence that one has to deal with. However, in this book and in similar books, for written surface structure sentences, it is assumed that the Affix Hopping and the Spell-Out steps will apply last before one reaches the surface structure. The details of the derivations that mediate between the deep structure and the surface structure have been overlooked in the examples above. However, this chapter has laid the foundation upon which such an analysis can be based. Finally, it must be stressed once again that now transformations do not carry the weight that they once did. The reasons for this will be discussed in several places in the book. The decision to focus on transformations in this book is not theoretical but practical and pedagogical. In my opinion a transformation-based approach to grammar has a better chance to impact students' writing positively than non-transformational one.

4.8 The Debate over the Psychological Reality of Transformations

Some linguists have cast doubt on the psycholinguistic reality of transformations. Psycholinguists have been unable to find behavioral evidence for the psychological reality of the intermediate stages of transformational derivations. However, Pinker (1994:219–20), a noted psycholinguist from MIT, claims that transformations are psycholinguistically real: "Since the early 1960s, when Chomsky proposed transformations that convert deep structure to surface structures, psychologists have used laboratory techniques to try to detect some kind of fingerprint of the transformation. After a few false alarms the search was abandoned, and for several decades the psychology textbooks dismissed transformations as having no 'psychological reality.' But laboratory techniques have become more sophisticated, and the detection of something like a transformational operation in people's minds and brains is one of the most interesting recent findings in the psychology of language." He goes on to explain that EGG records provide evidence in support of transformations.

4.9 *Conclusion*

The concept of a transformational component mediating between the deep structure and the surface structure has had a strong appeal in contemporary linguistics because it is logical. The four transformational operations (addition, deletion, movement, and substitution) and their constraints are powerful tools in the hands of teachers. They can use transformations to explain why sentences may be structurally different and yet convey the same meaning. Furthermore, teachers can use transformations in teaching writing. By learning how and when to move some elements of the sentence, delete some, substitute one element for another, or add other elements, students can apply this knowledge to a variety of writing tasks.

Key Terms to Know

These are the key terms that you should be able to use and define after reading this chapter:

1. acceptability convention: 4.3
2. addition operation: 4.5.1, 4.5.2.1, 4.6, 4.6.1, 4.6.2, 4.7.1, 4.7.2, 4.7.3, 4.9
3. angle bracket/braces convention: 4.3
4. categorial component: 4.2.2, 4.2.3
5. categoriality: 4.2.6
6. constraints on addition: 4.5.2.1
7. constraints on deletion: 4.5.2.3
8. constraints on movement: 4.5.2
9. constraints on substitution: 4.5.2.2
10. cyclical application of rules: 4.6
11. deep structure: 4.2.1, 4.2.2, 4.2.5, 4.2.6, 4.5, 4.5.1, 4.5.2, 4.5.2.2, 4.6, 4.6.1, 4.6.2, 4.7.1, 4.7.2, 4.7.3, 4.8, 4.9
12. deletion convention: 4.3
13. deletion operation: 4.5.1, 4.5.2.3, 4.7.3
14. derivation of negation: 4.7.3
15. derivation of passive sentences: 4.6.2
16. derivation of Yes/No questions: 4.6.1
17. derivation: 4.6, 4.6.1, 4.6.2, 4.7, 4.7.2, 4.7.3, 4.8
18. descriptive power: 4.2.3
19. grammatical universal: 4.2.3
20. grammaticality convention: 4.3
21. hierarchy: 4.2.6
22. indexing rule: 4.5.2.2
23. lexical insertion rules: 4.2.4
24. linearity: 4.2.6
25. matching convention: 4.5.2.2
26. meaning-preserving constraint: 4.5.1, 4.5.2.3
27. mental lexicon: 4.2.4, 4.2.5
28. movement operation: 4.5.1
29. parentheses convention: 4.3
30. permutation: 4.6.2
31. phrase structure rule: 4.2.1, 4.2.2, 4.2.3, 4.2.4, 4.2.5, 4.3

EXERCISE 1

1.   What is Chomsky's ultimate goal behind the study of grammar/syntax?

2.   Can this goal be useful to classroom teachers? Explain why or why not.

EXERCISE 2—ABBREVIATORY CONVENTIONS

The following phrase structure rule uses abbreviatory conventions. Write out all the phrase structure rules that the main rule abbreviates. **Hint:** There are 24 possible phrase structure rules.

$$S \rightarrow \quad NP \quad AUX \quad VP$$

$$NP \rightarrow \quad (Det) \quad (Adj) \quad N \quad (PP)$$

$$VP \rightarrow \quad V \quad \left\{ \begin{array}{c} NP \\ PP \\ AdjP \end{array} \right\}$$

EXERCISE 3—DEEP STRUCTURES AND TRANSFORMATIONS

A.   The deep structure of each sentence has been provided.

B.   Now, it is your turn to provide a full derivation which helps to arrive at the surface structure.

(1)

Deep structure: Janet Pres keep Janet Poss car keys where

Surface structure: Where does Janet keep her car keys?

(2)

Deep structure: George Pres brag about George all the time.

Surface structure: George brags about himself all the time.

(3)

Deep structure: Red tape Past frustrate the administration

Surface structure: The administration was frustrated by red tape.

EXERCISE 4—TREE DIAGRAMMING

Diagram the following sentences. Keep in mind that some of them may be syntactically/ structurally ambiguous.

1. They can fish here.

2. The new student is from southern California.

3. The politician spoke convincingly at the rally.

```
I N W B V J K C D R S P O
S K W L A S D K F N S Q I
W B W B N P O F R Q O W P
N R M U O T P E V E R B P
W E G H A U K I N A P O R
I V N W B V J K C N R S P
D D L A S D K F N U L A J
F A Q O W P I E B O A M U
P E W N C A P I W N G H A
N A P O R N W B V J K C D
A D J E C T I V E O A N S
D K F N W L A J W K E F R
```

MAJOR PARTS OF SPEECH

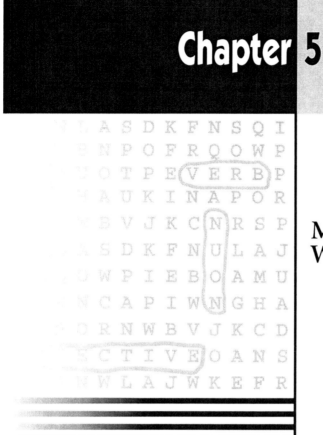

Chapter 5

Morphology and Word Formation Processes in Grammatical Analysis

5.0 INTRODUCTION

There is no impenetrable firewall between morphology and syntax when it comes to parts of speech identification. For the trained eye, the endings of a word give it away very easily. Just by examining the forms of a word it is possible to classify it according to its syntactic category. Consequently, morphology is a reliable tool in parts of speech tagging. In addition to morphology, word formation processes give useful hints in identifying and classifying words. Computational linguistics has now demonstrated that being able to parse words correctly is crucial in developing grammatical awareness. Thus, the importance of parts of speech identification can hardly be overestimated. Without such a knowledge base, it is impossible to understand or to teach grammar. Anyone who aspires to teach Language Arts must be able to rely on morphological clues to parse words and classify them according to their parts of speech. The primary goal of this chapter is to gather in a single chapter all the clues that one would need to build competence in this area. For this reason, the chapter has been divided into two main parts. The first part deals with morphological issues that are useful in parts-of-speech tagging. The second part focuses on the various processes that languages (especially English) use to create new words.

5.1 Affixation

Affixation is a morphological process which consists of adding an **affix** or affixes to a root or a stem to provide grammatical information, or to create new words. An affix is a bound morpheme. A **morpheme** is defined as the smallest linguistic unit capable of meaning and/or function. Linguists distinguish between two main types of morphemes: free morphemes and bound morphemes. A **free morpheme** is a morpheme that can stand by itself. Free morphemes are called **root**. They are listed in conventional dictionaries. **Bound morphemes,** on the other hand, cannot stand on their own. They must always be attached to a root. Let us illustrate the distinction between the two with the word <unhappiness>. The word <happy> is a free morpheme. However, the morphemes <un-> and <-ness> cannot occur on their own. They must be attached to the root/stem. English has over a hundred bound morphemes which are either classified according to their structure or to their function. Sections 5.2 through 5.2.3 deal with the distribution pattern of affixes while sections 5.3 to 5.4 focus on the functions of affixes.

5.1.1 Structural Morphology and Affixation

Structural morphology deals with the internal structure of affixes and their position in the word. Linguists have identified five types of affixes that I diagram as follows:

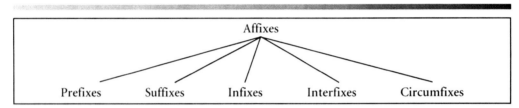

Table 1 *Affixation Patterns in World Languages*

Prefixes and suffixes are the most common affixation pattern in English and in world languages. We will save them for a more in-depth discussion later in this chapter. Let us now deal briefly with infixes/interfixes and circumfixes. Fromkin et al. (2003:80) observe that there is only one productive **infix** in the English language. It is the morpheme <-fuck-> that is used by some people as an expletive in a fit of anger.

Discussions of English affixation usually omit **interfixes.** However, they do exist. Davis (1988:317) describes a class of morphemes in Hausa (a West African language) to which he gives the label "interfix." He defines it as follows: "interfixes are empty morphemes placed between a stem and a suffix. . . . They do not add any meaning to the word; they usually begin with a vowel followed by one or two consonants. . . ." Based on this description, it can be argued that English also has interfixes. The morphemes <-o-> and <-i-> in the words <psychologist> and <infanticide> are **interfixes.** In the first word, the affix <-o-> is used to help form an English word from two Greek roots <psyche> and <logos>. The affix <-o-> is inserted between the two roots.[1] Similarly, the affix <-i-> is inserted between <infant> and the Latin suffix <-cide> which means "death." Whenever this Latin suffix is used to form English words, the affixation of <-i-> becomes necessary. Morphological parsing is made easier if other morphemes are taken to be interfixes. Words such as <talkative>, <affirmative>, <declarative> can be parsed without difficulty if <-at-> is taken as an interfix.

[1] In some cases readjustments are made. However, let us ignore details that are not pertinent to this explanation.

Circumfixes, also known as **discontinuous morphemes,** are two separate affixes or a grammaticalized word and an affix that function as a single morpheme. An element can be inserted between the two. **Grammaticalized words** are words such as <have> or <will> which have a dictionary meaning but are also used as morphemes. Let us illustrate this by the French negation morpheme <ne—pas>. The place holder between <ne> and <pas> shows that an element can intervene between the two as in the sentence below:

Je n'   aime pas   l'   astrologie
I   negation love   negation the astrology
I hate astrology

The sequence <ne—pas> is analyzed as one single morpheme even though an element can be sandwiched between the two constitutive parts.

Kaplan (1995:75) claims that English also has discontinuous morphemes. This claim is not accepted by the vast majority of linguists. However, his insights are worth mentioning here. Kaplan argues that if the perfect, the passive, and the progressive are considered, it is possible to postulate that English has three circumfixes. The discontinuous morpheme for the perfect is <Have—EN>, the one for the passive is <Be—EN>, and the one for the progressive is <Be—ING>, as illustrated by the three sentences below:

(1)   *Charlie **has** <u>work**ed**</u> as a missionary all his life.*

(2)   *The villain **was** <u>arres**ted**</u> by the police.*

(3)   *The students **are** <u>work**ing**</u> hard in syntax.*

The elements in bold are discontinuous morphemes. The underlined words represent the items that have been inserted between the morphemes. A more detailed discussion of the perfect, the passive, and the progressive will come in Chapter 7. Other discontinuous morphemes in English include comparative and superlative adjectives and adverbs such as <as ... as>, <more ... than>, <less ... than>, <-er ... than>, <-est ... than> discussed in Chapters 9 and 10 and correlative conjunctions such as <either ... or>, <neither ... nor>, and <not only ... but> in Chapter 12.

5.1.2 Structural Morphology: Prefixes and Suffixes

English has a vast amount of prefixes and suffixes many of which are of Greek or Latin origin. Knowing the meaning of these affixes can increase students' vocabulary power exponentially. In some schools, premed and medical students are encouraged to take a morphology class so as to help them remember technical medical vocabulary.

Most English words have only one prefix or one suffix. However, there are words that have both a prefix and a suffix as illustrated by the word <unhappiness>. The root <happy> has both the prefix <un-> and the suffix <-ness>. It is possible for a root to have two prefixes in English as seen in the word <disenfranchise>. Here <dis-> and <en-> are both prefixes. But English does not allow more than two prefixes in a single word. The word <disenfranchisement> shows that words with two suffixes are quite common. However, words formed with three derivational suffixes are rare. Almost nonexistent are four derivational suffixes added to the same root. There is no English word that has five derivational suffixes. Thus, the structural morphology rule of English can be formulated as follows:

$$\text{English Word} \rightarrow (\text{Prefix})^2 + \text{Root} + (\text{Suffix})^4$$

Even the word <antidisestablishmentarianism> that many consider to be the longest word in English conforms to this formula. It has two prefixes <anti-> and <dis->. It has four derivational suffixes <ment-> <ari-> <an-> and <ism->.[2]

5.1.3 Graphic Representation of Words

Just like sentences, words too have been represented by tree diagrams so as to reveal clearly their internal structures. The technical name for dividing up words into their different parts is called **parsing.** There are two ways to parse a word: a **linear parsing** and a **hierarchical parsing/**or word diagram. Linear parsing is obtained by inserting the symbol "+" between the affix(es) and the root. Hierarchical parsing is represented by a tree diagram. Hierarchical parsing is preferred because it shows clearly the hierarchical scaffolding of the word. Let us illustrate both types of parsing with the word <unhappiness>:

Example 1: Linear Parsing

<unhappiness> = <un+happy+ness>

Example 2: Hierarchical Parsing

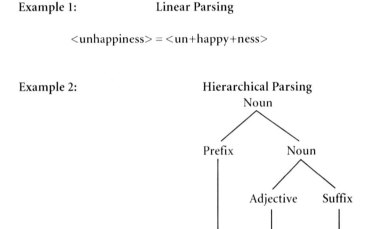

The hierarchical parsing of <unhappiness> shows clearly that it is formed as follows: the prefix <un-> is attached to the nominal stem <happiness> which is also formed by adding the suffix <-ness> to the adjectival root <happy>. Notice, however, that the same word can be given a slightly different interpretation depending on the meaning that one wishes to assign to it. It could be diagrammed as follows:

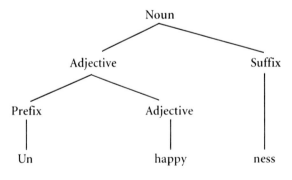

---

[2] Fromkin et al. (2003:71) indicates that *Webster's Seventh International Dictionary* has the word <pneumonoultramicro-scopicsilicovolcanokoniosis>, a disease of the lung, as the longest word in English. However, notice that this word is a compilation of compounds, not of affixes.

This diagram makes a slightly different claim than the one above. Here, the assumption is that <unhappiness> is formed by adding the suffix <-ness> to the adjectival stem <unhappy>. Then from there, the prefix <un-> was adjoined to the adjectival root <happy>. These two diagrams show that the word <unhappiness> is structurally ambiguous.

When it comes to diagramming words, linguists do not seem to have any preference. The ambiguity found in <unhappiness> can also be represented by linear parsing as <[un+happy]+ness> or <un+[happi+ness]>. Computational linguists prefer linear parsing. For pedagogical purposes, many textbooks prefer hierarchical parsing. The tree diagram representation of words has an advantage over the linear representation because it includes the labels for morphological categories (prefix, suffix, stem) and the labels for parts of speech (noun, verb, adjective, adverb, preposition, etc.).

5.2 Functional Morphology

Functional morphology studies the function of affixes in the grammar. Affixes have two main functions. They are either **inflectional morphemes** or **derivational morphemes**. Traditionally, inflectional morphemes are said to add only grammatical information whereas derivational morphemes usually change the part of speech of the word to which they are attached.

5.2.1 Inflectional Morphology

Compared with most languages, English is relatively impoverished in inflectional morphemes. It has only 8 or 10 inflectional morphemes depending on how one counts them. Linguists who list 10 affixes do so because <-er> and <-est> have different functions. Those who mention only 8 inflectional affixes consider the form, not the function. In this book, it is assumed that English has 10 inflectional morphemes as shown in the table below:

No.	Morphemes	Meaning/Function	Examples
1.	{-s}[3]	Regular verbs present tense marker	he does, talks, finishes
2.	{-s}	Regular plural noun marker	tomatoes, books, buses
3.	{-'s}	Possessive marker for nouns	Bob's, Scott's, Hoss
4.	{-ed}	Regular verbs past tense	he walked, seized, dreaded
5.	{-en}	Regular past participle marker[4]	eaten
6.	{-ing}	Progressive verb aspect marker	reading
7.	{-er}	Comparative adjective marker	faster
8.	{-est}	Superlative adjective marker	fastest
9.	{-er}	Comparative adverb marker	faster
10.	{-est}	Superlative adverb marker	fastest

Table 2 *English Inflectional Morphemes*

[3] Pinker (1999:35) argues that English has an affective suffix <-s> as in Pops, Moms, Fats, Pats, and Wills. This affective suffix is found in the phrase "Pops and Moms store."

[4] Theoretical linguistics takes <-EN> to be the canonical marker of the past participle even though regular verbs take <-ED> in the past participle.

5.2.2 Regular and Irregular Inflections

In all languages, affixation is both **regular** and **irregular.** Regular affixation is obtained when the form of the word that undergoes affixation, or the affix itself, can be predicted. Most affixation processes are regular. For instance, in English, plural nouns take the suffix <-s>, most verbs in the past tense take the suffix <-ed>, most comparative adjectives take the suffix <-er>, and most manner adverbs are formed by adding the suffix <-ly> to the adjectival root. These are all examples of regular morphological affixation.

There are also instances where affixation yields an irregular form. For instance, the plural of <woman> is not <*womans>; nor is the past tense of <run> <*runned>. It is a fact of linguistic life that high frequency words tend to be irregular. Pinker (1999:16, 42, 123–4) claims that there are about 150 to 180 irregular verbs in English. In English for instance, the ten most common verbs are irregular, (Pinker 1999: 123–4):

Ranking	Top Ten Verbs	Occurrences in a million words of text
1	to be	39,175
2	to have	12,458
3	to do	4,367
4	to say	2,765
5	to make	2,312
6	to go	1,844
7	to take	1,575
8	to come	1,561
9	to see	1,513
10	to get	1,486

Table 3 *Top Ten Verbs in English*

5.2.3 Classification of Irregular Affixation

There are many types of irregular affixations. There are also different scales of morphological irregularities. At one extreme are words that are only mildly irregular; at the other are words that are so irregular, their derived forms are unrecognizable from their original root. The most common cases of irregularity are the following:

1. allomorphy
2. internal vowel change
3. irregular affixation in loan words
4. zero-forms
5. suppletion

5.2.3.1 Allomorphy

Allomorphy deals with morphemes whose spellings and/or pronunciations change predictably based on their environment. For instance, the plural suffix in English is normally <-s>. However, sometimes it surfaces as <-es> or even as <-en>. Both <-es> and <-en> are said to be allomorphs of <-s>. The <-es> spelling is predictable. We find it in words that end with the graphemes <o>, <s>, <x> or <sh>. However, the plural suffix <-en> is not predictable. We find it in words such as <child> vs. <children>, <ox> vs. <oxen>, <brother> vs. <brethren>[5].

---

[5] The word <brethren> is used almost exclusively in a religious sense.

5.2.3.2 Irregularity due to Internal Vowel Change

Some irregular words still bear a close resemblance to the original root from which they are derived. The most noticeable change is the vowels. Otherwise, the consonants remain the same. Thus, we find words such as <*womans> vs. <women>, <*runned> vs. <ran>, <*singed> vs. <sang>, <*mouse> vs. <mice>, <*gooses> vs. <geese> etc. The irregularities in these words are attributable to historical processes whose explanation will take us on a rabbit trail.

5.2.3.3 Irregular Affixation in Loan Words

English has borrowed an impressive amount of words from a variety of languages. Generally, these loan words are made to conform to English inflectional morphology patterns. However, there are Latin and Greek-based nouns whose plurals are irregular. The reason for this is that English did not only borrow the singular form, it also borrowed the plural as well. Words in this group include the following:

No.	Singular	Plural	Status of the Plural in Contemporary English
1.	focus	foci	foci is often avoided
2.	alumnus	alumni	alumni is in use
3.	cactus	cacti	cactuses is in use
4.	fungus	fungi	funguses is in use
5.	locus	loci	loci is often avoided
6.	nucleus	nuclei	nuclei is in use
7.	stimulus	stimuli	stimuli is in use
8.	syllabus	syllabi	syllabi is in use
9.	symposium	symposia	symposiums is in use
10.	datum	data	datum is hardly used
11.	agendum	agenda	agendum is hardly used
12.	corpus	corpora	corpora and corpuses are in use
13.	medium	media	medium is hardly used in this sense
14.	maximum	maxima	maxima is hardly used
15.	curriculum	curricula	curricula is in use
16.	memorandum	memoranda	memorandums and memoranda are in use
17.	millennium	millennia	millennia is in use
18.	referendum	referenda	referendums is in use
19.	podium	podia	podiums is in use
20.	aquarium	aquaria	aquariums is in use
21.	stadium	stadia	stadiums is in use
22.	criterion	criteria	criterion is hardly in use
23.	appendix	appendices	appendix and appendices are in use
24.	index	indices	index and indices are in use
25.	matrix	matrices	matrix and matrices are in use
26.	automaton	automata	automata is in use
27.	phenomenon	phenomena	phenomena is in use

Table 4 *Irregular Plurals of Latin Words*

These Latin and Greek based words create difficulties at times, especially when the singular is not commonly in use. When <data> and <agenda> are used, should the verb in the present tense take a singular or a plural inflection?

(5)   *The data supports/support my claim.*

(6)   *The agenda for today is/are the election of a new chair.*

The spellchecker in most software programs accept both possibilities. Teachers may want to draw their students' attention on plural forms that are correct but not commonly in use. Pinker (1999:54) refers to people who use them as pedantic, "people with an attitude."

5.2.3.4 Irregularity due to Zero-forms

Some words are invariable in the singular or in the plural. Pinker (1999:52) observes that these words refer generally to gregarious animals that are hunted, gathered, or farmed. The list of nouns that belongs to this group includes <deer>, <sheep>, <fish>[6], <cod>, <flounder>, <herring>, <salmon>, <shrimp>, <swine>, <antelope>, <bison>, <elk>, <moose>, <grouse>, and <quail>. This type of irregularity is known as **zero-form.** Some words also fall into this category. The verbs <hit>, <cast>, <bet>, <quit> are invariable in the past tense because they do not take the morpheme <-ed>. Pinker (1999:42) claims that there 28 verbs in English which have zero-form in the past tense. A group of manner adverbs called "flat adverbs" have zero-form also. Even though they are manner adverbs, they do not take the characteristic suffix <-ly>. Lobeck (2000:178–9) and Kolln and Funk (2006:273) list <late>, <fast>, <hard>,<long>, <high>, <low>, <deep>, <near> as flat adverbs. More will be said about these adverbs in a later chapter.

5.2.3.5 Irregularity due to Suppletion

The extreme cases of irregularity are referred to in morphology as **suppletion.** Suppletive forms are words that are so irregular that the inflected form has absolutely no phonetic similarity with the root. Moreover, it is impossible to look such words up in a dictionary if one does not know the original root. The various conjugations of the verb <to be> are good illustrations of suppletion. In the present tense <to be> is conjugated <I am, you/they are, he/she is>. In the past tense, we have <I/he/she was, you/they were>. There is absolutely no phonetic similarity between the root <to be> and all its various forms in the present and in the past tense. The past tense of <to go> is <went>. The two forms do not bear any phonetic similarity. The suppletive forms of <good> are <better> and <best>; those of <bad> are <worse> and <worst>. The suppletive forms of <far> are <further> and <furthest>.

5.2.3.6 Sociolinguistics and Irregular Inflections

Sociolinguists note that the morphological component of languages, especially, the inflectional morphology component, demands more conformity than any other aspect of language (Wardaugh 2002:5–7). Failure to use irregular morphology correctly leads to all kinds of negative evaluations of the speaker or writer. Teachers who have non-native speakers in their classroom should see to it that mistakes related to irregular inflectional morphology are attended to early-on for fear that they might fossilize. **Fossilization** occurs when a form is learned improperly and becomes so entrenched that no amount of instruction can replace the wrong form with the correct one.

---

[6] The plural "fishes" refers to different species of fish.

5.3 Derivational Morphology

Derivational affixes are morphemes that usually[7] change the part of speech of the word to which they are added. Derivational morphemes are by far the largest group of morphemes in English. Both derivational prefixes and suffixes exist in English. However, the most frequent ones are derivational suffixes.

5.3.1 Derivational Prefixes

There are very few derivational prefixes in English. They generally convert adjectives or nouns into verbs as in the examples below:

<en->	as in	<en+dear>, <en+courage>, <en+title>, <en+grain>
<in->	as in	<in+sure>, <in+dent>
<be->	as in	<be + little>, <be+witch>, <be+friend>, <be+guile>

The prefix <en-> has an allomorph <em-> when it is added to roots that begin with the bilabial sounds /p, b, m/. Thus, we have <embellish>. This word is a borrowing from French where <belle> (pretty) is the feminine form of <beau> (handsome).

5.3.2 Derivational Suffixes

There are more than a hundred derivational suffixes in English. The availability of such a diversified list of suffixes allows English to create as many words as it wants. No wonder English has the largest vocabulary of any language known to humankind. Fromkin et al (2003:86–87) illustrate the multiplicity of derivational suffixes with the examples below:

Verb-to-Noun Derivation

A noun is created based on an existing verbal root.

No.	Derivational Suffix	Original Verb → Derived Nominal Form
1.	<-al>	to acquit → acquittal
2.	<-ance>	to clear → clearance
3.	<-(a)tion>	to create → creation
4.	<-or>	to create → creator
5.	<-ence>	to deter → deterrence
6.	<-er>	to sing → singer
7.	<-ment>	to ship → shipment
8.	<-ing>	to dance → dancing
9.	<-dom>	to bore → boredom
10.	<-edge>	to know → knowledge
11.	<-ist>	to pacify → pacifist

Table 5 *Verb-to-Noun Derivation*

---

[7] The key here is the word "usually." There are a few cases where a derivational suffix does not change the part of speech. The suffix <-ship> does not change the part of speech of the word to which it is added. The words <friend> and <friendship> are both nouns. The suffix <-ish> also does not change the part of speech. The words <red> and <reddish> are both adjectives.

Noun-to-Verb Derivation

A verb is created based on an existing nominal root.

No.	Derivational Suffix	Original Noun → Derived Verbal Form
1.	<-(i)fy>	deity → to deify
2.	<-ize>	moral → to moralize
3.	<-ate>	vaccine → to vaccinate
4.	<-ish>	brand → to brandish
5.	<-en>	haste → to hasten

Table 6 *Noun-to-Verb Derivation*

Noun-to-Adjective Derivation

An adjective is created based on an existing nominal root.

No.	Derivational Suffix	Original Noun → Derived Adjectival Stem
1	<-al>	economy → economical
2	<-ate>	affection → affectionate
3	<-(e)ous>	danger → dangerous
4	<-ary>	discipline → disciplinary
5	<-ic>	alcohol → alcoholic
6	<-ful>	fruit → fruitful
7	<-ist>	legal → legalist
8	<-ly>	friend → friendly
9	<-ish>	boy → boyish
10	<-(i)an>	America → American
11	<-ive>	offense → offensive

Table 7 *Noun-to-Adjective Derivation*

Adjective/Noun-to-Adverb Derivation

An adverb is created based on an existing adjectival or nominal root.

No.	Derivational Suffix	Original Noun/ Adjective → Derived Adverbial Stem
1.	<-ly>	quick → quickly
2.	<-wise>	clock → clockwise
3.	<-ward>	back → backward

Table 8 *Adjective-to-Adverb Derivation*

Adjective-to-Noun Derivation

A noun is created based on an existing adjectival root.

No.	Derivational Suffix	Original Adjective → Derived Nominal Form
1	<-ness>	tall → tallness
2	<-ce>	brilliant → brilliance
3	<-ity>	human → humanity

Table 9 *Adjective-to-Noun Derivation*

Verb-to-Adjective Derivation

An Adjective is created based on an existing verbal root.

No.	Derivational Suffix	Original Noun/Adjective → Derived Adverbial Stem
1	<-able>	read → readable
2	<-ive>	create → creative
3	<-ory>	migrate → migratory

Table 10 *Verb-to-Adjective Derivation*

5.3.3 Complex Derivational Processes

Some words are formed using two different derivational processes: a prefixation and a suffixation. Words formed by this complex process are rare in English. The most common words formed this way have the following structure:

$$\boxed{\text{Word} = <\text{en}> + \text{adjective} + <\text{en}>}$$

Examples of words belonging to this class are: <en+light+en>, <em+bold+en>, <en+live+en>. Other words are formed by the following structure:

$$\boxed{\text{Word} = \left\{ \begin{array}{c} <\text{e}> \\ <\text{a}> \\ <\text{in}> \end{array} \right\} + \text{adjective} + <\text{ate}>}$$

The following illustrate these derivationally complex words:

<elucidate>, verb	→ from the adjective <lucid>
<effeminate>, verb	→ from the adjective <feminine>
<emasculate>, verb	→ from the adjective <masculine>
<aggravate>, verb	→ from the adjective <grave>
<incorporate>, verb	→ from the noun <corpora>

Additionally, words that have been formed by this way can take other derivational suffixes that turn them into nouns as shown here:

<enlighten>, verb	→ <enlightenment>, noun
<enrich>, verb	→ <enrichment>, noun
<enable>, verb	→ <enablement>, noun
<empower>, verb	→ <empowerment>, noun
<emasculate>, verb	→ <emasculation>, noun

5.3.4 Lexical Gap and False Etymology

More often than not, languages play a bad joke on users. Words that should normally exist are found to be non-existent. This is called **lexical gap**. For instance, the word <rebut> exists. So, one should expect <prebut> to exist. But it does not exist yet. Another way by which languages fool unsuspecting users is through false etymology. **False etymology**[8] refers to words whose definitions are misleading because they do not mean what they should. Fromkin et al. (2003:91, 112) provide the following examples of words wrongly defined by students:

---

[8] The equivalent of false etymology in Second Language Acquisition is called "false friend." These are words that exist in both L1 and L2 but have different meanings.

No.	Word	Student's definition
1.	deciduous	"able to make up one's mind"
2.	longevity	"being very tall"
3.	fortuitous	"being well protected"
4.	gubernatorial	"to do with peanuts"
5.	bibliography	"holy geography"
6.	adamant	"pertaining to original sin"
7.	diatribe	"food for the whole clan"
8.	polyglot	"more than one glot"
9.	gullible	"to do with birds"
10.	homogeneous	"devoted to homelife"
11.	stalemate	"husband or wife no longer interested"
12.	effusive	"able to be merged"
13.	tenet	"a group of ten singers"
14.	dermatology	"a study of derms"
15.	ingenious	"not very smart"
16.	finesse	"a female fish"
17.	inflammable	"that cannot catch on fire"

Table 11 *False Etymology*

5.4 *The Mental Lexicon*

It has been found that a typical high school graduate knows about 60,000 words. These thousands of words in his/her mind are all created by a dozen or so word formation processes. One of the most amazing discoveries of the second half of the twentieth century in linguistics is that all languages rely on similar processes to augment their vocabulary. In addition to the process of derivation discussed in the previous sections, English uses the following word formation processes[9]:

1. compounding

2. acronym

3. blending

4. coining

5. clipping or abbreviation

6. back-formation or conversion

7. reduplication

8. eponym

9. borrowing

[9] There is a marginal process which creates sentence-like words. This process has not been named yet. I refer to it as "proverbial words." Some examples of this process include phrases such as <honey do list>, and <Johnny come lately>.

10. echoism

11. political correctness

Though these processes are available to all languages, not all languages use all of them equally. Some languages use some processes more heavily than others. For instance, West African languages use more reduplications than English. English, on the other hand, uses more compounds than French. It seems that unwritten languages hardly ever use acronyms. These word formation processes will be defined and illustrated in sections 5.4 through 5.4.10.

5.4.1 Compounding

Compounding is the process whereby two roots or stems are joined together to create a new word. A **root** is often defined as an indivisible part of the word. **A stem,** on the other hand, is defined as a root plus an affix. The word <girl> is a root, but <girls> is a stem because it has the affix <-s>. Some linguists use root and stem interchangeably but a difference between these two terms is made in this book. The roots <girl> and <friend> can be combined to form a new word <girlfriend>. **Compounding** is one of the most productive word formation processes in English. All the different parts of speech (except the articles <a/an> and <the>) can be combined in various ways to create new words. The examples below are only a small sample of compounding in English:

No.	Classification of Compounds	Examples
1.	Noun + Noun	textbook, suitcase
2.	Noun + Adjective	headstrong, busybody
3.	Verb + Verb	sleepwalk
4.	Verb + Preposition	sit-in
5.	Adjective + Noun	sickbed
6.	Adjective + Adjective	bittersweet
7.	Adjective + Preposition	early-on
8.	Preposition + Noun	in-law, inmate, alongside
9.	Preposition + Verb	outlive, underscore

Table 12 *Letter Pronounced Separately*

5.4.2 Acronyms

Acronyms are formed by taking the initial letters of individual words and putting them together to form a new word. There are three types of acronyms depending on how they are pronounced and/or spelled. In the first group, the letters that make up the acronym are pronounced individually as in the table following:

No.	Acronym	IPA Pronunciation
1.	FBI	[ɛf bi aɪ]]
2.	CIA	[si aɪ e]
3.	UN	[juː ɛn]
4.	POW	[pi o dʌblə juː]]
5.	MRI	[ɛm ar aɪ]]
6.	IRS	[aɪ ar ɛs]
7.	RSVP	[ar ɛs vi pi]
8.	PET	[pi i ti]
9.	FYO	[ɛf waɪ o]
10.	RN	[ar ɛn]
11.	AFL-CIO	[e ɛf ɛl si aɪ o]
12.	WHO	[dʌblə juː etʃ o]
13.	IMF	[aɪ ɛm ɛf]
14.	VA	[vi e]

Table 13 *Letter Pronounced Separately*

The second group of acronyms is pronounced just like ordinary words:

No.	Acronym	IPA Pronunciation
1.	NATO	[neto]
2.	AIDS	[edz]
3.	UNESCO	[junɛsko]
4.	UNICEF	[junisɛf]

Table 14 *Acronyms Pronounced as Words*

Acronyms stand out in spelling because all the letters are capitalized. However, there is a third group of acronyms that are spelled without capitalization. These include acronyms such as <radar> (radio detecting and ranging), <laser> (light amplification by stimulated emission), <scuba> (self-contained underwater breathing apparatus), and <zip> (zone improvement plan). These acronyms are so well integrated into the lexicon that few people think of them as acronyms.

Acronyms are also widely used in contemporary linguistics. The following acronyms are used in syntax:

SVO   = Subject-Verb-Object
NP   = Noun Phrase
VP   = Verb Phrase
PP   = Prepositional Phrase
AP   = Adjective Phrase. However, some linguists use AdjP
AdvP = Adverbial Phrase
GB   = Government-Binding, etc.

5.4.3 Blending

Blending is a word formation process whereby parts or the entirety of two roots may be combined to produce a new word. The word <smog> is formed by fusing <smoke> and <fog> together. The same is true for the words <motel> which combines <motor> and <hotel>. The words <urinalysis> (urine + analysis), <cranapple> (cranberry + apple), <brunch> (breakfast + lunch), <spork> (spoon + fork), <frigidaire> (frigid + air), <gogurt> (go + yogurt), <happenstance> (happen +instance), <simulcast> (simultaneous + broadcast), <infomercial> (information + commercial), etc. follow this process.

5.4.4 Coining

Coining is a process that creates brand new words from scratch. Words created by this process are not based on previously existing roots. The pharmaceutical industry, the internet, and other industries continually flood the market with new products. They usually coin new labels for these products. The most successful ones become household terms that eventually find their way into our conventional dictionaries. The most cited examples of this are <google>, <yahoo>, <xerox>, <kodak> , <nylon>, and <viagara>. Some of these words have become verbs, such as <to google> and <to xerox>. The word <kodak> is so much part of our way of speaking that it has led to the coining of the expression <kodak moment>.

5.4.5 Clipping or Abbreviation

Clipping, also known as **abbreviation,** uses only the first part of the word to represent the whole word. The word <exam> is created by eliminating the part with the strikethrough <exam~~ination~~>. The words <profe~~ssor~~>, <profe~~ssional~~>, <memo~~randum~~>, <ad~~vertisement~~>, <vet~~eran~~>, <con~~vict~~>, <fan~~atical~~>, <prom~~otion~~>, <dis~~cotheque~~>, <retro~~grade~~>, <deli~~catessen~~>, <fax~~simile~~>, <Pam~~ela~~>, <Chris~~topher~~>, <~~tele~~phone> are all the product of clipping.

There is another word formation process akin to clipping that linguists find hard to classify. In some respects it behaves like clipping, but in others it doesn't. The words created by this process are called **hypochoristic** terms, or **pet names.** Bloomfield (1933:157) treats them differently from normal clippings even though he admits that they are closely related. He argues that proper names such as <Tom>, <Will>, <Ed>, <Pat>, <Dan>, and <Mike> are formed through clipping, but <Bob> for <Robert> and <Ned> for <Edward> are not clippings but hypochoristic terms. Hypochoristic terms may be structurally different from the words from which they derived. For instance, it is hard to explain structurally how <Bob> is derived from <Robert>, <Ned> from <Edward>, <Dick> for <Richard>, and <Bill> for <William>. Hypochoristic clippings are quite frequent in English. They are so frequent that there is a diminutive suffix <-ie> or <-y> that is added to words to create their hypochoristic equivalents, as in the examples below:

No.	Full Name	Hypochoristic Equivalent
1.	William	Billy or Willie
2.	Frances	Frankie
3.	Susan	Susie
4.	Margaret	Maggie
5.	John	Johnny
6.	Thomas	Tommy

Table 15 *Hypochoristic Terms*

The mode of communication most conducive to clipping is BICS (Basic Interpersonal Communication Skills). Some types of clippings like <pro>, <fan>, <con>, etc. represent the form of language appropriate for communication between friends and acquaintances. However, some other clippings have become acceptable in CALP (Cognitive Academic Language Proficiency). Words such as <exam>, <memo>, <ad>, <fax>, <deli>, etc. are used in formal speech. It is the teacher's responsibility to tell his/her students which clippings belong to BICS and which are acceptable in CALP.

Contemporary syntax uses the following clippings:

S	= sentence
Aux	= auxiliary
N	= noun
V	= verb
Adj.	= adjective
Adv.	= adverb
P	= preposition
Art.	= article
Det	= determiner
Conj	= conjunction
Pro	= pronoun
Tns	= Tense

5.4.6 Back-formation or Conversion

In English, **back-formation** helps create verbs out of existing nouns. Stageberg and Oaks (2000:132) note that the verbs <to edit>, <to peddle>, <to beg>, and <to swindle> were created from the nouns <editor>, <peddler>, <beggar>, and <swindler> respectively. In these examples, the new verbs are created by deleting the endings <-or>, <-er>, and <-ar> from the nominal stem. In an article entitled "*Just Listen to Us,*" Arnaud (2003:13–14) complains bitterly about this tendency in contemporary English. She makes the following statement:

Just about any noun can become a verb these days. No one will even question our use of it, either. Maybe this started with the very first time someone uttered, "Let's party" instead of "Let's have a party." The noun "party" instantly became the verb "party." Similarly, a "bird" is also a noun, but an acquaintance of mine recently told me he was "birding" (as birdwatching). I recently received a letter from a company that informed me it was "transitioning" as opposed to "making a transition." (The old noun-to-verb trick again.) People "bike" these days, but when I grew up we referred to riding our bikes. Perhaps we're always looking for ways to shorten our speech—take less time saying what we have to say. The 1990s ushered in the phrase, "Let's do lunch," but that is certainly no quicker than saying "Let's eat lunch." I opened a note from a friend the other day that read, "Let's coffee."

She goes on to list <to tantrum>, <to seizure>, <to journal>, among others. In some cases, conversion is also formed by moving the stress slightly as seen in the following pairs: <a díscount> vs. <to discóunt> and <an ímport> vs. <to impórt>. This is a very economical way that languages all over the world have at their disposal to increase their vocabulary. This is certainly true for the tone languages of Africa and Asia. Aanrud's complaint about noun-to-verb conversion is misguided. As noted in Bauer (1983:226–230), English is availing itself of a productive word formation process that it has used in the past to create the words in the table following:

No.	Original Nominal Stem	Verb Created through Conversion
1.	a head	to head
2.	a hammer	to hammer
3.	a bridge	to bridge
4.	a mail	to mail
5.	a badger	to badger
6.	a mushroom	to mushroom
7.	a balloon	to balloon
8.	a scale	to scale
9.	a vacation	to vacation
10.	a discount	to discount
11.	an import	to import
12.	a walk	to walk
13.	a swim	to swim
14.	a ski	to ski
15.	a candidate	to candidate
16.	a caveat	to caveat
17.	a nuance	to nuance
18.	a dialogue	to dialogue
19.	a parent	to parent
20.	an input	to input
21.	an access	to access
22.	a showcase	to showcase
23.	an intrigue	to intrigue
24.	a host	to host
25.	a chair	to chair
26.	a progress	to progress
27.	a contact	to contact
28.	a bird	to bird
29.	a journal	to journal
30.	a party	to party
31.	a tantrum	to tantrum

Table 16 *Noun-to-Verb Conversion*

5.4.7 Reduplication

Reduplication is not very **productive** in English. A word formation process is said to be productive when it can be used freely to form new words or when it has a high frequency of occurrence in the language. Stageberg and Oaks (2000:134–5) list the following words to illustrate the process of **reduplication:** <pooh-pooh>, <hanky-panky>, <ticktock>,

<singsong>, <boogie-woogie>, <dilly-dally>, <knick-knack>, <ding-dong>, <wishy-washy>, <hocus-pocus>, <flipflop>, <nitty-gritty>, <wiggle-waggle>, <super-duper>, and <lovey-dovey>. Bloomfield (1933:156–7) gives <snip-snap>, <zigzag>, <riff-raff>, <jim-jams>, <fiddle-faddle>, <teeny-tiny>, <hodge-podge>, and <hugger-mugger> as examples of reduplication in English. Teachers may want to draw their students' attention to the fact that reduplication belongs to a very familiar and even intimate register. Consequently, its use in academic forums may be frowned upon.

Reduplication may not be productive in English, but it is the word formation process whereby many African and Asia Pacific languages create new words. Linguists distinguish between two types of reduplication: **partial reduplication** and **complete reduplication.** Partial reduplication usually reduplicates the first syllable of the word. Complete reduplication just repeats the same word twice. This explanation may give the false impression that reduplication is straightforward and uncomplicated. Nothing is further from the truth. Some instances of reduplication are very complicated because they involve complex morphological and phonological processes.

5.4.8 Eponym or Antonomasia

Eponym is a process whereby a famous proper name (of a person or a place) is entered into the dictionary as an ordinary word. It is claimed that the word <sandwich> came from a British nobleman who was so busy hunting that he did not have time to sit down for a meal. He took two slices of bread, put a piece of meat between them, and ate it for his lunch while hunting. Over time, this practice became popular and Earl Sandwich's name was given to this type of meal. Similarly, <cashmere> sweater came from a region of India known for its expertise in weaving. Political commentators, journalists, and historians like to name eras after well-known figures. Thus, we often encounter words such as <jeffersonian>, <newtonian>, <abrahamic>, <hooverville>, <reagonomics>, etc. Phrases such as <average Joe>, <smart Alick>, <a Perry Mason moment>, <don Juan> are eponymic constructions.

The use of certain eponyms in academia is a sign of intellectual maturity. If a student uses the names of the proponents of leading theories in his/her field of study or if a student uses words such as <freudian>, <darwinism> <saussurean>, <bloomfieldian>, <chomskyan>, <whorfian>, etc. in academic writing, it shows that that student is knowledgeable.

5.4.9 Borrowing

English has an open-arm policy when it comes to **borrowing** words from other languages. The list of loan words in English is astronomical. The core vocabulary is Germanic because English belongs to the Proto-Germanic language family. However, some argue that as much as 40% percent of English vocabulary comes from Romance languages: French, Spanish, and Latin. French loan words are many because of nearly 300 years of French linguistic imperialism. From the 18th century onward, English has borrowed hundreds of scientific terms from Latin and Greek. Presently, the contact situation between English and Spanish has led to the infusion of hundreds of Spanish words in English. Borrowing is a natural phenomenon which is the logical result of population contacts. Stageberg and Oaks (2000:128) list the following languages as having contributed words to English:

No.	English Words	Source Language	Meaning in Source Language
1.	chauffeur	French	stoker of train engine, driver
2.	campus	Latin	field, plain
3.	guru	Hindi	spiritual leader
4.	sheikh	Arabic	old man, chief
5.	alligator	Spanish	the lizard
6.	window	Old Norse	wind eye
7.	agnostic	Greek	unknowable
8.	bazaar	Farsi	market
9.	chow mien	Chinese	fried noodles
10.	tsunami	Japanese	big wave
11.	macho	Spanish	masculinity
12.	safari	Swahili	trip
13.	orangutan	Indonesian	forest people

Table 17 *Source Languages of English Borrowing*

We will see later that some borrowings are problematic for language use in an academic setting.

Languages may also increase their vocabulary through **calquing.** Calques are usually phrases that are taken from another language. However, instead of borrowing the actual words, the target language uses its own terms to translate the foreign reality. It is hard to find examples of calques in English. However, French uses quite a number of them. Here are two examples of English words that have been calqued into French. The concept of <hot dog> is foreign to French. French Canadians calqued it as <chien chaud> which means literally "hot dog." Similarly, the phrase <to burn a CD> was initially calqued into French as <brûler un CD> (to burn a CD) before being changed to <graver un CD>. Both terms are used interchangeably. It is my understanding that <to burn a CD> has also been calqued into Korean.

5.4.10 Political Correctness

Most discussions overlook political correctness as a word formation process. However, it deserves to be included because it too contributes to create new words and phrases that eventually find their way into conventional dictionaries. **Political correctness** consists of replacing a term deemed to be demeaning or unpopular with one that is neutral or upbeat. This phenomenon has grown exponentially since the 1990s. The acceptance of gender neutral language in academia and in the press has heightened awareness of politically incorrect forms. Thus, the following politically correct forms are used to replace their former equivalents: <firefighter> → <fireman>, <senior citizen> → <old person>, <peacekeeping> → <war>, <Native Americans> → <Indians>, <African American Vernacular English> → <Black English>, <collateral damage> → <war casualty>, <revenue enhancement> → <tax increase>, <chemical dependency> → <drug addiction>, <driving while under the influence (DWI)> → <drunk driving>, <correctional facility> → <prison>, <inmate> → <prisoner>, <ethnic cleansing> → <genocide>, etc.

5.4.11 Echoism

Stageberg and Oaks (2000:129) define **echoism** as follows: "echoism is the formation of words whose sound suggests their meaning." There are two main types of echoisms: onomatopoeias and idiophones. The definition given here applies more closely to onomatopoeias than to idiophones. In European languages, **onomatopoeias** play a marginal role. They are often found in colorful and expressive language such as <bang bang bang, he shot the criminal>. Onomatopoeias are also used to imitate the natural sound that animals make. For instance, <meow> stands for the cat, <moo> for the cow, <cockle doodle do> for the rooster, etc. They are also used to represent other sounds in the environment. Thus, <ding dong> represents the noise a bell makes, <zoom> stands for the noise made by a fast moving vehicle, <clink> is the noise made by glasses, etc. Echoism belongs to the colloquial register and is used sparingly in formal registers. For this reason, many African Bible translators refrained from using **idiophones** even though they are used extensively in everyday language as adjectives or adverbs. Some researchers have catalogued as many 3,000 idiophones in some languages.

5.5 Word Formation Processes, the Lexicon, and Spell-Out Rules

Morphology is messy. It is not completely clear why some forms find their way into the lexicon unchanged while others undergo changes before being accepted into the lexicon. In some instances, words that should or could exist are not found in the lexicon. Nobody really knows why this is so. However, Scalise (1986:31, 63) has proposed a model which seems to capture the essence of how words finally end up in conventional dictionaries.

List of Morphemes	WFR	Readjustment Rules[10]	Filter	Dictionary
1. friend				
2. boy hood				
3. recite al			[+idiosincrasies]	
4. ignore ation			X [-LI]	
5. mountain al	X			

Table 18 *Universal Derivational Apparatus*

The diagram can be interpreted as follows: the word <friend> is a free morpheme, that is, a word that is indivisible into parts. It is not formed by any word formation rule. Therefore, it goes directly into the lexicon. The word <boyhood>, on the other hand, is a morphologically derived word. It is composed of the free morpheme <boy> and the suffix <-hood>. The combination goes directly into the lexicon without modification. However, this is not the case for the word <recital> which is formed by adding the suffix <-al> to the root <recite>. However, the combination <*reciteal> is not a real word. To make its way into the dictionary, it has to transit through the orthographic filter. There

---

[10] There are two types of Readjustment rules: Allomorphy Rules and Truncation Rules, Scalise (1986:58, 63–4). We will not go into the details of this component because it is very technical.

are spelling rules to insure that the word enters into the lexicon only if it conforms to the spelling conventions of the language. The word <*ignoration> is blocked from entering the lexicon because <ignore> cannot accept the suffix {-ation}. This suffix is very productive in English. It is therefore hard to explain why <adoration> which is derived from <adore> is a well-formed word but <*ignoration> cannot be derived from <ignore>. This is an example of lexical gap. As for <*mountainal> it is blocked right away because the noun <mountain> cannot be turned into an adjective by adding the suffix <-al>. Presumably Scaliese' derivational apparatus is universal. All languages have a similar mechanism that allows well-formed words into the lexicon or blocks ill-formed words from entering the lexicon. In written languages, these rules are stated explicitly in the form of orthographic (spelling) rules.

5.6 *The Role of Morphology in Linguistics Analysis*

The example of <*mountainal> reveals something very interesting about languages. This word is ill-formed because the affix <-al> is added only to a limited number of nouns to create new adjectives. The list of English nouns that can be turned into adjectives by adding the suffix <-al> is not very long. The following words are the ones that come readily to mind: <parent> → <parental>, <government> → <governmental>, <family> → <familial>, <music> → <musical>, <function> → <functional>. The fact that some suffixes are selective as to the part of speech they go with shows that we can discover the part of speech of derived words by inspecting the kind of affix they take. Lobeck (2005:5) expresses this as follows: "Morphological affixation gives us clues about the syntactic category as a noun, adjective, verb, and so on, . . . we rely on affixation in identifying syntactic categories." Affixation also gives us information about grammatical relations. We see this clearly by examining the various forms of the relative pronoun <who>. The form <who> points to a relative pronoun that functions as subject, <whose> indicates possession, and <whom> signals that the relative pronoun is an object.

There is a special sub-branch of linguistics that studies the kind of grammatical information that languages use to encode grammatical information through affixation. This sub-discipline is called **morphosyntax.** English used to depend a lot on morphosyntactic information to communicate grammatical relations. However, over time it lost much of this ability. As a result, word order became rigid. However, word order is relatively less rigid in Greek, Latin, and other languages which have a rich case system. **Case** is the name given to affixes that indicate grammatical relations/functions. The table below shows the most common grammatical functions carried by affixation. Some languages, including Swedish and Russian have many more cases than the ones listed here. The table gives both the technical terminology and the commonly used one.

No.	Technical Terminology	Commonly used Terminology	Illustrative Examples
1.	Nominative	Subject	**Paul** is studying
2.	Accusative	Direct object	Paul loves **mangos**
3.	Dative	Indirect object	Paul gives mangos to **pigs**
4.	Genitive	Possession	**Paul's** car broke down
5.	Vocative	Exclamation	**Paul,** watch out!

Table 19 *Case System*

English used to be a case language. But contemporary English has lost its case. This has led Pinker (1999:78–9) to comment that "for the past thousand years, syntax has been shouldering the load formerly borne by morphology." Because of this, flexibility in word order has all but disappeared in contemporary English.

5.7 Classification of Words in the Mental Lexicon

Morphological information has allowed language experts to classify the words in the mental lexicon (or conventional dictionaries) into two major groups. Each group has words that are subcategorized in various ways. The diagram below summarizes the classifications that will be used in the rest of the book:

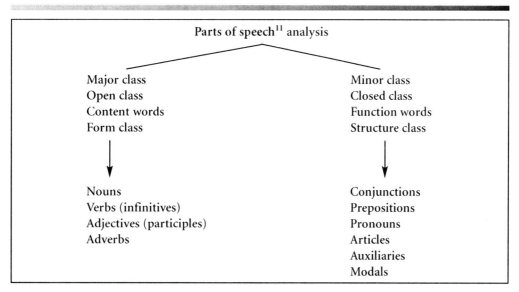

Table 20 *Classification of Words*

The labels in each of the two major subcategories mean roughly the same thing. They are used interchangeably. The first three sets are most commonly found in the linguistic literature.

5.98 Conclusion

All the words of all languages are created by a dozen different word formation processes. Some of the words created by these processes enter the lexicon without undergoing modifications. Others go through mild processes of alteration. Still others are modified so radically that they bear no phonetic or orthographic resemblance with the original root from which they are derived. Affixation, the name of the process which adds bound morphemes to roots, can be summarized by the following diagram:

[11] Parts of speech are also known as "Lexical category" or "Word class."

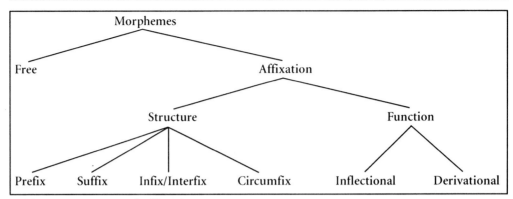

Table 21 *Summary of Affixation*

The model of generative transformational grammar that is used in this book subscribes to the split morphology hypothesis. According to this hypothesis, the morphology of languages is divided into two. Derivational morphology takes place in the Lexicon where word formation rules are located. Inflectional morphology, on the other hand, is found between the transformational component and the surface structure as mentioned in Table 1 in 4.2.1. Inflectional morphology rules are said to be late rules because they apply after transformational rules have had the chance to be applied.

Key Terms to Know

These are the key terms that you should be able to use and define after reading this chapter:

1. abbreviation: 5.4, 5.4.5
2. acronym: 5.4, 5.4.2
3. affixation: 5.1, 5.4, 5.6, 5.9
4. antonomasia: 5.4, 5.4.8
5. back formation/conversion: 5.4, 5.4.6
6. blending: 5.4, 5.4.3
7. borrowing: 5.4, 5.4.9
8. bound morpheme: 5.1, 5.9
9. calquing: 5.4.8
10. case: 5.6
11. circumfix: 5.1.1, 5.9
12. clipping: 5.4, 5.4.5
13. coining: 5.4, 5.4.4
14. conversion: 5.4, 5.4.6
15. compounding: 5.4, 5.4.1
16. derivation: 5.2, 5.3, 5.3.1, 5.3.2, 5.3.3, 5.4, 5.5, 5.9
17. echoism: 5.4, 5.4.10
18. eponym: 5.4, 5.4.8
19. false etymology: 5.3.4
20. fossilization: 5.2.3.6
21. free morpheme: 5.1, 5.5
22. hypochoristic/pet name: 5.4.5
23. idiophone: 5.4.11
24. infix: 5.1.1, 5.9
25. inflection: 5.2, 5.2.1, 5.2.2, 5.2.3.3, 5.2.3.6, 5.9
26. interfix: 5.1.1, 5.9
27. internal vowel change: 5.2.3.2
28. irregular inflection: 5.2.2, 5.2.3.6
29. lexical gap: 5.3.4, 5.5
30. morphosyntax: 5.6
31. onomatopoeia: 5.4.11
32. parsing: 5.1.1, 5.1.3

EXERCISE 1—LINEAR PARSING

Use the symbol "+" to indicate the root and affix boundaries in the words below. Label each affix that you find, that is, say whether it is a prefix or a suffix.

1. womanizer
2. liquefy
3. comprehensible
4. biological
5. endearment
6. unbiased
7. children
8. mistreatment
9. speedometer
10. dysfunctional
11. impeachable
12. fingerprints

EXERCISE 2—AFFIXATION

Examine the italicized words below and determine the nature of the affix: derivational or inflectional. Additionally, determine if the affixation process is regular, irregular, internal vowel change, loanword, suppletion, or zero-form. In some cases, more than one label may apply. The first one has been done for you as a model.

Women : Irregular Inflectional Plural Suffix with internal vowel change

1. *Befriended*
2. She *quit* yesterday.
3. *Compliance*
4. They were *shaken* by the accident.
5. *Endearment*
6. *Alumni*
7. They have a lot of *homework.*
8. *Sandwiches*
9. You *are*
10. He *sang*
11. They have *been* sick.
12. This baby has tons of *hair.*
13. This house is infested with *mice.*

Chapter 5—Morphology and Word Formation Processes in Grammatical Analysis **133**

EXERCISE 3—WORD DIAGRAM

Draw a word diagram that reflects the hierarchical structure of the words below.

1. Endearment

2. went (as in she **went** home)

3. prioritize

4. friendliness

5. fastest

6. informative

7. airsickness

8. internationalization

9. worse

10. enlightenment

EXERCISE 4—WORD FORMATION PROCESS

Each of the italicized words in the list below has been created by one of the eleven word formation processes discussed in the textbook. Name the word formation process that helped create each of the words below. If the word is a clipping/abbreviation or an acronym, provide the full form: [**Hint:** some words are formed by more than one process].

1. *bra*

2. *itsy bitsy* spider

3. *infomercial*

4. *Premed*

5. She went to the dealership to *winterize* her car.

6. The *tech* department at the university is huge.

7. *Aristotelian*

8. *Gogurt*

9. *to candidate*

10. Everybody yearns to be a *Good Samaritan* once in life.

Chapter 6

Nouns and the Noun Phrase

6.0 INTRODUCTION

According to Robertson (1934:246) the label that Greek grammarians found for the part of speech that we now refer to as a <noun> is *to onoma*. The same stem is found in the word *onomatopoeia*. Admittedly, this label was given to nouns because they describe the reality that they name, just as onomatopoeias are deemed to have a non-arbitrary relationship with the reality that they represent. Latin grammarians gave the label of *nomen* to the same part of speech in their language. Nouns are one of the most important parts of speech found in every language. Cross-linguistic studies have revealed some important characteristics about nouns.

1. The words that children utter when they begin to make one-word sentences in every language are nouns.

2. Nouns are also more easily borrowed from language to language.

3. Languages have more nouns in their lexicon than any other parts of speech. Consequently, given a text of any length, there are more nouns than any other lexical item.

Despite their frequency and wide range of distribution, nouns are not as easy to identify as one might think. For this reason, linguists have designed a number of tests to detect nouns among other parts of speech. These tests are language neutral, that is, they can be used to categorize parts of speech in any human language. The process of identifying parts of speech is often referred to as **parts of speech tagging.**

6.1 Classificatory Instinct

It seems like human beings are born with the urge to classify and sub-classify the things they see in their natural environment. There is no society known to humankind where people do not categorize existential reality. Pinker (1997:12) argues that "an intelligent being cannot treat every object it sees as a unique entity unlike anything else in the universe. It has to put objects in categories so that it may apply its hard-worn knowledge about similar objects, encountered in the past, to the object at hand." This need for classification was extended to language more than two thousand years ago. It is often noted that this categorization of Greek words into parts of speech is the foundation of grammatical analysis in the Western linguistic tradition.

6.1.1 Fuzziness

That many college students have a deficit in their knowledge of grammar is well known. However, less known is their inability to identify and classify the words of sentences according to their parts of speech. At the beginning of my teaching career I was amazed at the number of students who could not determine the part of speech of the word <airsickness>. Year after year, in my introduction to linguistics class, my students have classified it as an adjective or an adverb. Usually after much deliberation, somebody will come upon the right answer and classify it as a noun. However, when pressed for justification, they would say, "I just took a wild guess." This lack of proficiency in the most elementary grammatical notions is a serious handicap, because, as Pinker (1999:270) argues, "to understand mental categories is to understand much of human reasoning." Without a firm grasp of the parts of speech and the tools used to categorize them, the teaching of grammar may not prove to be effective because understanding higher level concepts depends on the mastery of these basic notions.

6.1.2 The Rationale and Reliability of Tests

Tests are useful diagnostic tools that help discriminate between candidates that look like or behave similarly. Medical pathologists run all kinds of tests in order to correctly diagnose pathogens. Scientists in a wide variety of fields run tests for purposes of identification. Similarly, linguists run a battery of tests that allow them to formally distinguish the various elements that occur in speech or writing. Understanding the nature of these tests and being able to use them effectively is a critical step towards developing grammatical awareness.

There are different types of tests. Some are quick and easy; others are sophisticated and more involved. In the medical profession, if one is suspected of having strep throat, for instance, the doctor may do a quick five-minute test in the office. If the results are positive, a proper course of treatment is prescribed. If the results are inconclusive, the practitioner does not conclude right away that there is no strep throat. Instead, he or she may require a more sophisticated test in a lab. In medicine, as in other branches of science, there are instances when, in spite of multiple tests, the results are inconclusive. This analogy applies to linguistics as well. When linguists want to determine the nature of a linguistic element, they subject it to a quick test. If the result is inconclusive, more sophisticated testing is needed. In linguistics, as in medicine, there are cases where the different tests are inconclusive or even contradictory. A case in point is the status of the word <can> in the sentence below:

(1)   *They saw that gasoline **can** explode.*

The part of speech of the word <can> in this sentence is difficult to establish. This is because the word <can> is ambiguous. If it is the metal container, then <can> is a noun. However, if it is not, then <can> is a modal verb. Jurafsky and Martin (2000:299) allude to this difficulty in part of speech tagging in computational linguistics. They ask: "How hard is the tagging problem? Most words in English are unambiguous; i.e., they have only a single tag. But many of the most common words of English are ambiguous. . . . In fact DeRose (1988) reports that while only 11.5% of English word types in the Brown Corpus are ambiguous, over 40% of the Brown[1] tokens are ambiguous."

There are four serious difficulties in classifying words (Pinker 1999:270–3). The most formidable obstacle is finding "a set of membership conditions." Secondly, the members of a category are not equal. Some meet most of the conditions for being admitted into the category while others may meet only a portion of the conditions. Thirdly, it is hard to delineate clearly the boundary between categories. Additionally, Clark (2003:44) points out that when it comes to the classification of words, there is inconsistency. The classification of nouns and verbs is based on meaning whereas that of adjectives and adverbs is based on function. This lack of clear boundary leads to the fourth problem, namely, the existence of words that overlap two or more categories. Linguists have not given up testing for the elements of language because of these difficulties, just as the wider scientific community has not given up testing altogether because of inconclusive results. To minimize the amount of errors in parts of speech classification, linguists have designed a battery of tests that consists of the following:

1. the semantic test

2. the morphological test

3. the syntactic test

4. the functional test

Taken together, these four tests give results that are usually very conclusive. The presentation in this chapter will follow the order of these tests.

6.1.3 Testing for Nouns

To qualify as a noun, a lexical item must pass the four types of test listed above. Under each one of these headings, there are several mini-tests that are used, as we will see shortly.

6.2 Semantic Quick Test for Nouns

Presumably every literate person has in his/her linguistic toolkit a ready-made semantic test for identifying nouns. The semantic test comes readily to mind because, presumably, it is the first test that human infants acquire in classifying the words of speech:

> How might a child assign words into categories like noun and verb? Clearly, their meanings help. In all languages, words for objects and people are nouns or noun phrases, words for actions and change of state are verbs. Similarly, words for kinds of paths and places are prepositions, and words for qualities tend to be adjectives. Recall that children's first words refer to objects, actions, directions, and qualities. This is convenient. If children are willing to guess that words for objects are nouns, words for actions are verbs, and so on, they would have a leg up on the rule-learning problem (Pinker 1994:284).

[1]The Brown Corpus is a databank of English sentence tokens used in computational analysis.

In most educational systems, the use of the semantic test is learned and reinforced in the early grades. According to this test, nouns name "people, places, things, or ideas." Not surprisingly, this test works very well in most cases. However, as with any quick test, it has its drawbacks. Rodby and Winterowd (2005:95) remark that "[it] leads us into a quagmire from which we can never escape." The quagmire to which they allude is discussed by Kaplan (1995:112). He wonders if the traditional definition of noun is really applicable to words such as <rodeo>, <party>, <development>, <destruction>, and <arrival>. He contends that these words are "without doubt action words, not person, places, or things." Clark (2003:44) contends that the traditional definition of nouns is not applicable to words such as <appetite> and <impossibility> because these two words do not name persons, places, or things. She argues that expanding the traditional definition to include "qualities and ideas" is not a good solution either because one never knows when the definition is complete. To avoid this problem, linguists now use five universal semantic features to tag nouns.

6.2.1 Semantic Features Tests for Nouns

Structural linguists believed that linguistic elements, just like matter in the physical world, are made up of indivisible elements called atoms. In linguistics, these atomic elements are labeled **features.** Phoneticians and phonologists of the 19th century were the first among language experts to use this notion to study sounds as bundles of features. This approach was so effective that semanticists and grammarians have also applied it to the study of meaning and grammar. The meaning of words and their syntactic properties were analyzed in terms of the binary feature <+> or <->. The symbol <+> indicates that the feature is present; while <-> means that feature is absent. Chomsky (1965:82) sees a great value in using these features in syntactic analyses because they "contribute to the general unity of grammatical theory." In tagging words, linguists rely on five important features. These features are [± Count], [± Abstract], [± Common], [± Animate] and [± Human].[2] Of these five semantic features, only [± Count] and [± Common] are directly pertinent for tagging a word as a noun. The other features will not be considered in this chapter. However, their importance to syntactic analyses will be apparent in subsequent chapters.

6.2.2 The Feature [±Count] Noun

Any lexical item that has the feature [**±Count**] is most likely a noun. The expression "most likely" is used in conjunction with each of the upcoming tests so as not to give the impression that a single test can lead to conclusive parts of speech identification. In English the distinction between [±Count] nouns is very important for the choice of determiners. If a noun is [+Count], it means that it can be preceded by **cardinal** and **ordinal** numbers. However, [-Count] nouns cannot be preceded by these numbers nor can they be pluralized. The table following classifies English words according to the feature [±Count].

---

[2]Chomsky (1965:82) refers to these as syntactic features. However, most linguists refer to them as semantic features.

No.	Components of [± Count] Nouns	Examples
1.	Numerals	one, two, three, ... billion.
2.	Ordinals	first, second, third, ... billionth.
3.	Fractions	half, a third, one fourth.
4.	Percentages	ten percent, twenty percent, fifty percent.
5.	Multipliers	once, twice, three times.
6.	Collectives	the team, the family, the committee, the government, the audience, the clergy, the band, the orchestra, the student body, the faculty, the staff.
7.	Partitives	a herd of, a pride of, a school of, a truckload of, a gallon of, a pair of, a mountain of, two pieces of, a slice of, one of the, ten out of, the remainder of, the rest of.
8.	Quantifiers	many, much, few, little, some, each, no, none, several, all, both, neither, etc.

Table 1 *The Components of [± Count] Nouns*

Nouns to which the feature [-Count] is assigned are also knows as **mass nouns.** Languages select arbitrarily which nouns are [-Count] and which are [+Count]. Thus, in English <rice>, <water>, <hair>, <oil>, <gold>, <iron>, <milk>, <information>[3] are mass nouns but some of these same words are not mass nouns in French or Spanish.

All the nouns that have the feature [+Count] also have the feature [± Number]. This feature helps determine whether a noun is **singular, plural,** or **dual.** The feature "dual" is used with nouns that come in pairs such as the eyes, the ears, the legs, etc. Even though the feature [± Number] can help tag a word as a noun in English, it is not very reliable, especially in languages where there is agreement between nouns and adjectives. It can lead to a misidentification of adjectives as nouns. This observation also applies to the feature [± Gender]. It is useful in many languages because it can help identify a lexical item as a noun. **Gender** can be biological in the case of the distinction between **male** or **female** in the class of animate beings. It can also be grammatical: **masculine, feminine,** and **neuter.** In English, any lexical item that encodes gender is most likely a noun. However, this statement is not true for all languages. In French, Spanish, and Greek adjectives and verbal forms have gender. So, the use of [± Gender] as a part of speech tagging device is not valid for all languages.

English is relatively poor in gender differentiation. It makes only a biological gender distinction between males and females. This distinction is also carried over in the pronominal system in a very limited fashion. English scrupulously distinguishes between the masculine <he, him, his, himself> and the feminine <she, her, hers, herself>. Other languages have a more extensive gender system. Spanish and French, for instance, have a grammatical gender system in which all the nouns in the lexicon are divided between masculine and feminine. In English, with the exception of words that end in <-man> or <-ette>, most words are not listed in the lexicon according to their grammatical gender.

---

[3]There are exceptions. We find the phrase "the waters of . . ." in a number of biblical texts. The plural <hairs> means something slightly different.

The few commonly used words that are marked for grammatical gender are the following: <country>, <ship>, <spinster>, <widow>, <widower>, <bachelor>, <pretty>, and <handsome>. With the rise of political correctness, gender neutral language is preferred. It is not clear what will remain of English grammatical gender in the future.

6.2.3 Collective Nouns

As shown in Table 1, collective nouns are a subset of the feature [±Count]. This subgroup deserves a special mention because of the agreement problems that they create in writing. It is often not clear whether the verb should agree with its subject in number if the latter is a collective noun. In many instances agreement with the plural is as acceptable as agreement with the singular, as in the two sentences below:

(2)   *The team decided that **they** should avoid distractions before the playoffs.*

(3)   *The team decided that **it** should avoid distractions before the playoffs.*

There are a few instances where agreement with the plural seems to be preferable to agreement with the singular:

(4)   *The jury has found him guilty on all counts except one. On the charge of voluntary manslaughter, **they are** equally divided.*

(5)   *The jury has found him guilty on all counts except one. On the charge of voluntary manslaughter, **it is** equally divided.*

It is not clear why most people prefer (2) and (4) to (3) and (5). Pragmatic considerations and frequency of use seem to play a role here. Sentences (2) and (4) are more commonly found in news reports than (3) and (5).

Pragmatic considerations are also responsible for why most native speakers prefer (6), (7), (8) and (9) to their counterparts (10), (11), (12) and (13).

(6)   *A number of students **have** dropped the course.*

(7)   *Ten dollars **is** a lot of money.*

(8)   *A majority of votes **is** needed to win.*

(9)   *None of those firefighters **enjoy** hearing the alarm go off.*

(10)   *?A number of students **has** dropped the course.*

(11)   *?Ten dollars **are** a lot of money.*

(12)   *?A majority of votes **are** needed to win.*

(13)   *?None of those firefighters **enjoys** hearing the alarm go off.*

It should be noted here that the grammar check in *Microsoft Word 2003* and *2007* accepts all these sentences as well formed. It suggests <have> for (10). However, this suggestion is clearly based on frequency of use not on any grammatical rule. The claim that the noun closer to the verb controls agreement works only for (6) but fails to account for why most people reject (10), (11), (12) or (13).

Bock et al. (2006:64) show that subject verb agreement patterns with collective nouns vary greatly between American English and British English. They quote from the style manuals of the British Broadcasting Company (BBC) and the Associated Press to illustrate the differences between these two dialects of English:

> *A familiar but still striking difference between British and American English is the realization of verb agreement with collective-head subject noun phrases. The difference is maintained in the usage of speakers and enforced by pronouncements from language watchdogs in British and American communities. The BBC News Style guide notes that 'It is the policy of BBC Radio News that collective nouns should be plural, as in* The Government have decided.' *In American English, the Associated Press Stylebook says 'Nouns that denote a unit take singular verbs and pronouns:* class, committee, crowd, family, group, herd, jury, orchestra, team. *Some usage examples:* The committee is meeting to set its agenda. The jury reached its verdict.

They go on to provide numerous examples where Americans and British speakers differ on their agreement patterns. Following these examples, they observe that "many of the British examples strike American speakers as completely unacceptable. In a test performed on students from the United States and Britain, samples of British-style collective agreement were corrected by American students 95% of the time, compared to 29 percent by British students." However, the situation is not as clear-cut as these percentages suggest. In an article by Bollag (2006:A29) in *The Chronicle of Higher Education*, we read the following within the same paragraph: "*The faculty have* spoken. *The board has* created a huge mess on campus and *they* need to stop it. Let the healing begin." (Italics added)

6.2.4 The Feature [± Common] Noun

Any lexical item that has the feature [±Common] is most likely a noun. The feature [-Common] refers to all **proper nouns.** Syntactically, [-Common] nouns are not usually preceded by the articles <a> and <the>. They almost never occur with fractions, multipliers, and percentages. Morphologically, they do not take the plural suffix <-s> except when used as collective nouns, as in (14).

(14)   **The** *Stewarts are leaving the state.*

Here, <the Stewarts> stands for all the members of the Stewart family. There are also rare cases such as sentence (15) when a proper noun is used with an indefinite article:

(15)   **A** *Karen called and wanted to see you in person.*

In this case the indefinite article <a> means "a certain Karen." Such usages are rather rare in English.

6.2.5 Thematic[4] Role Test

Generative linguists introduced the concept of **thematic roles** to describe the roles that certain linguistic items play in sentence interpretation. It is generally accepted that verbs and prepositions assign thematic roles to nouns in the deep structure. Once assigned, these roles are not affected by transformations. For this reason, many consider them to be reliable clues for identifying nouns. Any lexical item that receives one of the following thematic roles is most likely a noun. In the examples following, thematic roles are italicized.

[4]Thematic roles are also called "semantic roles" by some linguists.

No.	Thematic Role	Definition	Examples
1.	Agent	The volitional causer of an event	*The students* passed the exam.
2.	Accompaniment/ Commitative	Two agents involved in an event	Tallie is playing with *Chloe*
3.	Experiencer/ Patient	The experiencer of an event	*Jeremy* had surgery a year ago.
4.	Theme	The participant most directly affected by the event	The students passed *the exam.*
5.	Force	The non-volitional causer of an event	The *tornado* destroyed their house.
6.	Instrument	An instrument used in an event	Joni paints with *her teeth.*
7.	Beneficiary	The beneficiary of an event	Parents work hard for *their children.*
8.	Source	The origin of an object or a person	Men are from *Mars* and women are from *Venus.*
9.	Goal	The destination of an object or a person	Our friends are flying to *Ghana.*
10.	Location	The place where an object or a person is found	Melissa and Brit used to live in *Kazakhstan.*
11.	Path	The path followed by a person or an object	Jeff went to Casablanca through *Paris.*
12.	Possessor	One who has something	*Chomsky's* theory of Universal Grammar

Table 2 *Thematic Roles*

The semantic tests that we have discussed so far can be summarized by the table below:

Test	Noun	Verb	Adjective	Adverb	Proposition	Conjunction	Pronoun	Article
[±Count]	+	−	−	−	−	−	+	−
[±Common]	+	−	−	−	−	−	+	−
[±Thematic Role]	+	−	−	−	−	−	+	−

Table 3 *Semantic Tests for English Nouns*

Pronouns will be discussed much later. However, before we get there, it is important to note the striking similarities between nouns and pronouns.

6.3 Morphological Tests

Morphology was covered in the previous chapter. There, we learned about the Split Morphology Hypothesis which claims that morphology operates at two distinct levels.

Derivational morphology helps create new words while inflectional morphology provides grammatical information. Both types of morphology are very useful in parts of speech tagging.

6.3.1 Inflectional Morphology Test for Nouns

Inflectional morphology provides useful information in identifying nouns in English. Any lexical item that takes the plural suffix <-s> or the genitive (possession) suffix <-'s> is most likely a noun. The inflectional morphology test for nouns is summarized by Table 4:

Test	Noun	Verb	Adjective	Adverb	Proposition	Conjunction	Pronoun	Article
Plural <-s>	+	–	–	–	–	–	+	–
Genitive <-'s>	+	–	–	–	–	–	+	–

Table 4 *Inflectional Morphology Test for English Nouns*

6.3.2 Derivational Morphology Test for Nouns

In addition to the inflectional morphology tests discussed above, derivational morphology can boost the confidence of teachers that a lexical item is indeed a noun. There are derivational suffixes that attach themselves to roots **only** to form nouns. Some of these suffixes appear in the table below:

No.	Nominal Suffixes	Illustrations
1.	<-al>	acquittal
2.	<-ance>	acceptance
3.	<-ary>	grainary
4.	<-(a)(t)-ion>	transportation
5.	<-dom>	freedom
6.	<-ence>	confidence
7.	<-er>	writer
8.	<-eer>	auctioneer
9.	<-eria>	cafeteria
10.	<-ery>	eatery
11.	<-ity>	enormity
12.	<-ment>	enjoyment
13.	<-ness>	happiness
14.	<-or>	actor
15.	<-(or)ium>	auditorium
16.	<-ory>	observatory
17.	<-ship>	friendship
18.	<-ure>	pleasure

Table 5 *Derivational Morpheme Test for Nouns*

Thus, any English word that has any of these suffixes is most likely a noun.

6.4 The Notion of Phrasehood in Parts of Speech Tagging

The evidence offered by semantic and morphological tests for tagging nouns is solid. However, scientific linguistics is not fully satisfied with these results because they have loopholes. To strengthen parts of speech identification, linguists rely heavily on additional syntactic tests. The notion of "phrasehood" becomes very important in applying syntactic tests. For this reason, we must first define the concept of phrase before proceeding. A **phrase** is defined simply as a word or a group of words that functions as a coherent syntactic unit. Linguists claim that there are five types of phrases in all the languages of the world:

1.   the Noun Phrase (NP)

2.   the Verb Phrase (VP)

3.   the Adjective Phrase (AdjP)

4.   the Adverb Phrase (AdvP)

5.   the Prepositional Phrase (PP)

Closely related to the concept of phrase is the notion of syntactic head. The **head** is the most important lexical item around which all the other elements of the phrase gravitate. All the five phrases listed above have heads. As might be expected, the head of the NP is the noun, that of the VP is the verb, the head of the AdjP is the adjective, that of the AdvP is the adverb, and PPs are headed by prepositions. Generally, in head-first languages such as English, the head occurs first in the phrase followed by its satellites. This is the reason why the head constituent occurs first in phrase structure rules. In their efforts to use syntactic means for parts of speech tagging, linguists have developed three main tests for determining if a group of words that occurs together functions as a phrase. The focus of this chapter is on noun phrases. Upcoming chapters will provide tests for identifying the other phrases.

6.4.1 The Pronominalization Test

Any word or group of words that can be replaced by a pronoun qualifies as noun phrase. Let us illustrate this by the following examples:

(16)   *Curt bought a brand new car.*

The group of words "a brand new car" is a noun phrase because it can be replaced by the pronouns <what> or <it>:

(17)   *Curt bought what?*

(18)   *Curt bought it.*

The pronoun <who> can replace <Curt>. Therefore, <Curt> is a noun phrase.

(19)   *Who bought a brand new car?*

The pronominalization test shows that the sentence <Curt bought a brand new car> has two noun phrases <Curt> and <a brand new car>.

6.4.2 The Movement Test

According to the movement test, if a word or a group of words are moved from their original location to elsewhere in the sentence, and if the result is a grammatical sentence, then the constituent that is moved is a phrase. Let us illustrate this with the previous sentence:

> (20) *Curt bought a brand new car.*

> (21) *A brand new car was bought by Curt.*

Since (21) is well-formed, we conclude that <a brand new car> is a noun phrase and <Curt> is also a noun phrase.

6.4.3 The Coordination Test

Any word or group of words that can be coordinated with another word or group of words of the same type is a phrase if the result of the coordination is a well-formed sentence. This can be illustrated by (22) below:

> (22) *Curt bought a brand new car and a boat.*

The fact that the sentence is well-formed means that <a brand new car> and <a boat> are syntactic elements of the same type. Moreover, <a brand new car> is a noun phrase, and <a boat> is also a phrase.

6.5 The Structure of English Noun Phrases

An analysis of the sentence < Curt bought a brand new car > that has been used to establish the "phrasehood" of noun phrases shows that there are different types of noun phrases. Some are made up of only one lexical item. It was argued previously that <Curt> is a noun phrase. We also saw that <a brand new car> is a noun phrase. Sentence (24) below shows us that a noun phrase can contain several elements. There is no limit to the number of elements that can occur in a noun phrase. For instance, we can make (23) (a repetition of (20)) longer by adding <for his wife>:

> (23) *Curt bought a brand new car.*

> (24) *Curt bought a brand new car for his wife.*

Here we see that the noun phrase <a brand new car> is followed by <for his wife>. Based on information of this nature, linguists have determined that an English noun phrase may contain elements that precede the head noun and elements that follow it. Thus, noun phrases may have up to three main parts, as seen in the formula below:

> **Structure of NP** = Premodifier—**Head Noun**—Postmodifier

The presence of premodifiers of nouns seems to contradict the claim made earlier, namely that noun phrases are headed by nouns. Even though English is a head-first language, noun phrases constitute an exception to this generalization. However, in many West African languages, noun phrases are actually headed by nouns as discussed in 6.4. The fact that English and some European languages behave differently in this respect does not invalidate this worldwide syntactic phenomenon. English noun phrases may start with various types of lexical elements to which linguists have given the label of **premodifier.** Elements that may occur before the noun are the following:

No.	Premodifiers	Illustration
1.	Indefinite articles	a, an, some
2.	Definite articles	the
3.	Demonstratives	this, that, these, those
4.	Interrogative words	what, which, whose
5.	Possessives	my, your, his, her, our, their
6.	Possessive NPs	Pam's, Jonathan's, Phil's, Tracy's
7.	Quantifiers: (quantity terms and partitives)	some, all, several, a herd of
8.	Numerals (ordinals, cardinals, percentages, multipliers)	one, first, half, ten percent, once
9.	Adjective	most adjectives can occur as premodifiers

Table 6 *Premodifier of Nouns*

The observations about noun pre-modifiers have been translated into a phrase structure rule which is formulated as follows:

$$NP \rightarrow (Det)\ (AdjP)\ \mathbf{N}$$

All the noun premodifiers except for adjectives[5] are called **determiners (Det).** However, from the point of view of syntax, there are two main groups of determiners. Some determiners can co-occur with other determiners but others cannot. The determiners in the first group are represented by the following phrase structure rule:

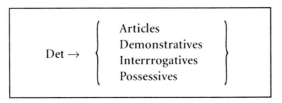

The prohibition against co-occurrence accounts for the ungrammaticality of the following sentences:

(25) *The this grammar book makes sense.*

(26) *Your which grammar book makes sense.*

(27) *My the grammar book makes sense.*

(28) *A Dale's grammar book makes sense.*

From the examples above, we conclude that the combination of an article and a demonstrative, an article and an interrogative word, and article and a possessive word, etc. cannot premodify the same head noun. However, **numeral (Num)** and **cardinals (Card)** premodifiers can co-occur with other premodifiers as seen in the sentences below:

---

[5]Premodifying and postmodifying adjectives will be the subject of an entire chapter. Therefore, the discussions in this section will exclude adjectives.

(29) *The first three presidents are Harvard graduates.*

(30) *These first three presidents are Harvard graduates.*

(31) *Our first three presidents are Harvard graduates.*

The first group of noun premodifiers that cannot co-occur are called **primary determiners.** In contemporary linguistics, genitive constructions such as *<my sister's>* in the sentence *<My sister's* fiancé cancelled the wedding> fall under the category of determiners. Some linguists label them **"possessive NP"** which is abbreviated as **Poss NP.** Unlike true determiners, Poss NP can co-occur with some primary determiners. The second group of noun premodifers is given the umbrella term of **quantifiers (Q).** However, Lobeck (2000:96) makes a useful distinction between quantifiers. She assigns the label of **numerals (Num)** to cardinals, ordinals, multipliers, fractions, and percentages. She keeps the term quantifiers for indeterminate expressions of quantity such as <all>, <both>, <several>, <many>, <much>, etc. She also includes collectives and partitives among quantifiers. Jurafsky and Martin (2000:336) go one step further and make a distinction between numerals and cardinals. Taking all this information into account, I have conflated the phrase structure rules found in Jurafsky and Martin (2000:336) and the one proposed by Lobeck (2000:95) as a single rule to account for English nouns and their premodifiers:

$$NP \rightarrow (Q) \ (Det) \ (Poss \ NP) \ (Num) \ (AdjP) \ N$$

Lobeck (2000:95) puts (Det) and (Poss NP) between braces because normally proper nouns cannot be preceded by a determiner in English. However, this is not necessary here because there are numerous instances where a determiner can precede a common noun as in *<my sister's fiancé>*. Here <my> is a determiner, and *<sister's>* is a Poss NP.

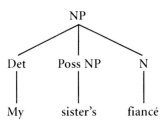

To show that *<sister's fiancé>* forms another coherent sub-unit, one can diagram the same NP as follows:

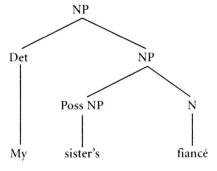

There are important theoretical considerations whether one uses the first diagram or the second diagram. Since our primary goal is the application of syntactic concepts to teaching, we will not concern ourselves with the pros and cons of either position. Suffice it to say that both represent the components of the NP accurately. The second tree diagram which follows the X-bar theory of syntax is more accurate because it represents the inner structure of the NP more clearly. However, the drawback of such tree diagrams is that they tend to take more paper space. For this reason, in most cases we will prefer a simpler tree diagram that shows all the constituents of the NP rather than a tree diagram that shows the inner organization of the phrase more accurately.

The phrase structure rule for NP will be expanded as additional information becomes available. The premodifiers and the head noun in the following <all our first three presidents> can be diagrammed as follows:

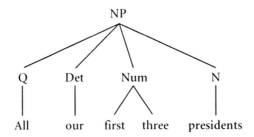

The claim that this phrase structure rule makes is that in English, if all the different classes of premodifiers are to co-occur in a single NP, the most likely order is the one in the tree diagram. This same NP will be diagrammed again in 9.4.6 using the X-bar theory. However, for now let's focus our attention on identifying and labeling accurately the elements found in noun phrases.

6.5.1 Partitive Quantifiers

A subset of quantifiers is called **partitives.** English partitives are characterized by the following structure:

$$\text{Partitive} \rightarrow \left\{ \begin{array}{l} \text{NP}^1 \text{ of NP}^2 \\ \text{Q of NP}^2 \\ \text{Num of NP}^2 \end{array} \right\}$$

NP^1, Q, and Num are the premodifiers. NP^2 is the head noun. It is generally marked with the feature [+Common]. Below are some of the most common partitives. The highlighted portion is the premodifier of the partitive construction (See Table 7).

The status of partitives in theoretical linguistics is a matter of debate. As far back as 1931, Curme, p. 113 argued that the word <of> in partitives is not a preposition. Recently Baker (1989:129–135) has taken a similar position. In diagramming NP^1 of NP^2 which are partitive constructions, Bickford (1998:64–65) proposes a phrasal category called **quantifier phrase (QP)**. There is now compelling evidence from the literature on first and second language acquisition that partitive constructions are acquired or learned as indivisible chunks known as **patterns.** Dulay et al. (1982:232–3) define patterns as "utterances that are only partially unanalyzed. They include an open slot for a word or phrase

No.	Partitive Quantifiers
1.	*some of* the students
2.	*many of* the students
3.	*three of* the students
4.	*all of* the students
5.	*several of* the students
6.	*a lot of* students
7.	*a gang of* students
8.	*a bunch of* hooligans
9.	*an army of* protesters
10.	*a wave of* violence
11.	*a group of* students
12.	*a litany of* complaints
13.	*a deck of* cards
14.	*a piece of* evidence
15.	*a school of* fish
16.	*a gallon of* gas
17.	*a yard of* linen
18.	*a pair of* scissors
19.	*a herd of* buffalo
20.	*a pride of* lions
21.	*a mountain of* evidence

Table 7 *Partitive Premodifiers*

such as *That's _____.* or *Do you want_____?*" They also observe that the unanalyzed portions of patterns are "of extraordinarily high frequency." Learning them and using them is comparable to learning long vocabulary words. According to this view, partitive quantifiers can be construed as ready-made constructions with empty slots that the speaker fills with a small set of available data. The noun phrase <a group of demonstrators> is made up of a QP consisting of the determiner <a>, the open slot filled by the noun <group>, and the genitive marker <of>. Based on this insight, I propose the following phrase structure rule for English partitive constructions:

$$
\text{Partitive NP} \rightarrow \quad \text{QP} \quad \text{N}
$$

$$
\text{QP} \rightarrow (\left\{ \begin{array}{c} a \\ the \end{array} \right\}) \quad \text{N} \quad \text{of}
$$

From this perspective, the noun phrase <*a group of demonstrators*> can be represented by the following tree diagram:

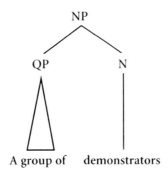

This interpretation of partitive constructions is plausible not only from the point of language acquisition but also from the point of analysis. It is the whole QP that modifies the head noun, not a portion of it, as assumed in analyses such as Baker's (1989: 129–135).[6] If one wishes to break down the QP further, it could be represented as follows:

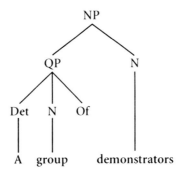

In addition to quantifier phrases such as <*a group of demonstrators*>, English has complex quantity phrases whose representation in tree diagrams is often problematic. How should one represent <fewer than>, <more than>, and <as many as> in a tree diagram? How can the NP portion of (32) be represented in a tree diagram?

(32) **Fewer than** *twenty demonstrators came.*

Opinions vary depending on how one sees <fewer than>. Some take <fewer> to be an adjective but others take it to be a quantifier phrase just like <a group of>. How one interprets this group of words will determine how it is represented in a tree diagram. Let us give both alternatives here:

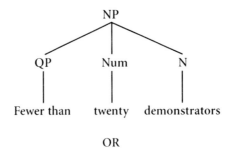

OR

[6]Baker (1989:129–135) has also argued that <of> is not a preposition. In diagramming NP with QP, Baker introduces a category that he labels Of-P.

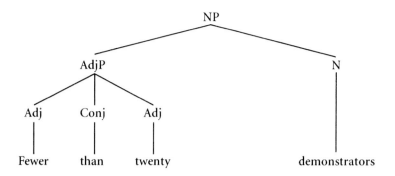

For now, let's say that these two tree diagrams are both correct. We will see later in Chapter 9 that both tree diagrams make different claims about how these structures are processed by speakers of English. We will not say more about it until we have introduced the chapters on adjectives and coordinating conjunctions.

6.5.2 Partitive Usage and Register

Some partitives are used as hyperboles to exaggerate or emphasize the quantity involved in a description. In informal and colloquial speech, all kinds of partitives are used. However, in academic writing where hyperbolic statements are toned down, the use of certain partitives may be frowned upon. Therefore, students should be made aware of the issue of register in the use of partitives. Celce-Murcia and Larsen-Freeman (1999:336) advise against partitives such as *<lots of, plenty of, heaps of, oodles, truckloads of, tons of>* because they do not belong in the register of Cognitive Academic Language Proficiency (CALP).

6.5.3 English Noun Postmodifiers

English nouns can also be followed by lexical elements such as <for his wife> in (24) discussed previously. Groups of words such as <for his wife> and others like it are called noun **post-modifiers**. A list of the most common post-modifiers of English nouns is given here only for illustration. Post-modifiers will not be discussed at this point because the elements necessary for such a discussion are not all in place yet.

No.	Postmodifiers	Illustration
1.	Adjectives	<Tell me something *exciting* about your trip to Malaysia.>
2.	PP	<The girl *in the back* wants to see you after class.>
3.	VP	<The team *to beat* is UCLA.>
4.	S	<Linguists *who can explain linguistics in simple terms* are not many.>

Table 8 *Postmodifier of Nouns*

The phrase structure rule of noun phrases becomes very complex when postmodifiers are included. By including the information in the table above, the rule can now be expanded as follows:

$$NP^7 \rightarrow (QP)\ (Det)\ (Poss\ NP)\ (Num)\ (AdjP)\ \mathbf{N}\ (AdjP)^8\ (PP)\ (S)$$

[7]Normally, determiners do not precede proper nouns. Thus, this formula must be understood to apply to NPs whose head noun is [+common].

[8]Refer to 9.5.3 for the small set of English adjectives that follow the head noun.

The NP portion of the sentence <*the girl in the back* wants to see you after class...> can be diagrammed as follows:

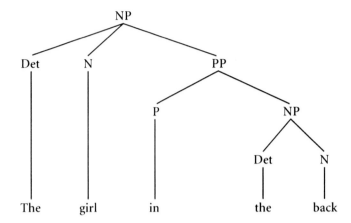

More will be said later on about noun postmodifers in upcoming chapters. For now, let us limit ourselves only to the PP <in the back>. In this case, the PP functions as an adjective because it modifies the head noun <the girl>.

6.5.4 NP^1 of NP^2 as Noun Postmodifiers

In 6.5.1 we saw that English partitive constructions have an NP^1 of NP^2 structure. However, there are other types of NP^1 of NP^2 constructions that are not partitives. Phrases such as <a man of his word>, <the practice of medicine>, <a labor of love>, <a coat of many colors> etc. are called **attributive genitives.** These NP^1 of NP^2 constructions are structurally different from the one discussed previously. For one, they do not express any idea of part-to-whole relationship as partitives do. Secondly, unlike partitives which function as head noun premodifiers, attributive genitives are head noun postmodifiers. Thus, the surface structure similarities mask the deep structure differences between the two constructions. In attributive genitives, <of-NP^2> functions as an adjective that modifies < NP^1>, the head noun. Following Baker (1989: 129–135), it can be argued that NP^1 of NP^2 constructions of this type have the following phrase structure rule:

$$NP \rightarrow NP^1 \quad PP$$
$$PP \rightarrow P \quad NP^2$$

The tree diagram of <*a coat of many colors*> is representative of the deep structure form of these constructions:

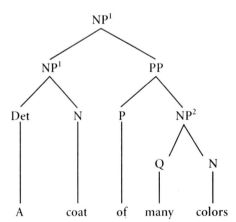

Here the postmodifier <many colors> is not a quantifier but rather an NP linked to the previous NP[1] by the genitive marker <of>. Therefore, its grammatical category is not Q but rather NP. Cumes (1931:77–88) identifies three important semantic functions of attributive genitives. They denote origin as in the phrase <prince of Egypt>, they express possession <the father of the bride>, and they describe some characteristics <the sweetness of victory>. In all of these cases the "PP" is a noun postmodifier that functions as an adjective. Labeling <of many colors> a PP is a misnomer because, as will be discussed in Chapter 11, this so-called PP does not behave like "real" prepositional phrases. So, the label <PP> is used here for lack of a better category.

6.5.5 Summary of Syntactic Tests

The information gathered up to this point allows us to propose a battery of syntactic tests to identify nouns. Any lexical item whose premodifier has the syntactic feature <+>, as shown in the table below, is most likely a noun.

Test	Q	Card	Num	Demonstrative	Possessive	Poss. NP	Of-P	Article
Noun	+	+	+	+	+	+	+	+
Verb	–	–	–	–	–	–	–	–
Adjective	–	–	–	–	–	–	–	–
Adverb	–	–	–	–	–	–	–	–
Conjunction	–	–	–	–	–	–	–	–
Preposition	–	–	–	–	–	–	–	–
Pronoun	–	–	–	–	–	–	–	–

Table 9 *Summary of Syntactic Tests*

The syntactic tests outlined in this table work for all languages. Beginning and intermediate students of classical Greek, for instance, are encouraged to master the cases of definite articles because their inflection is the surest way for determining the declension of nouns. A **declension** is all the morphological information that a noun takes.

6.6 *Functional Test*

The semantic, morphological, and syntactic tests provide excellent clues for identifying nouns. However, sometimes these tests fail, or they do not capture the full range of lexical elements that qualify as nouns. Let us illustrate this with the following sentence:

(33)   *When the going[1] gets tough[1], the tough[2] get going[2].*

The first <going[1]> is a noun but the second < going[2]> is a verb. We know that <going[1]> is a noun because it passes the determiner test. It has <the> in front of it. It was argued in 6.5 that any lexical item that has a determiner is most likely a noun. The first <tough[1]> is an adjective but the second <tough[2]> is a noun for the same reason as in <going[1]>. Functional tests can help tag words correctly even if in the lexicon they do not normally belong to that part of speech. Grammarians have known for a long time that some lexical items that are not strictly speaking nouns often behave or function as nouns in sentences. The label **nominal** has been given to such lexical items. Almost all the parts of speech can qualify as nouns in one form or another. Let us examine other sentences along the same line of reasoning:

(34) *This professor uses a lot of **buts** in her speech.*

(35) *His **quitting** surprised the faculty.*

(36) ***To plagiarize** is a major academic offense.*

(37) ***Big** is better.*

(38) *Life has its **ups and downs.***

The portions of the sentences that are in bold are all nominals. In sentence (34) <but> is normally a conjunction, in (35) and (36) <quitting> and <to plagiarize> are verbs, <big> in (37) is an adjective, and "ups and downs" in (38) are prepositions. The clause (sentence) <*that linguists argue about terminology*> in (39) below is also a nominal. Sentences such as (35) and (36) have led linguists to reformulate the phrase structure rule for English noun phrases as follows:

$$
\begin{aligned}
NP &\rightarrow CP \\
CP &\rightarrow Comp\ S
\end{aligned}
$$

Kaplan (1995:261) notes that the NPs in Table 10 are complex complementizers phrases:

No.	Complementizer Phrases
1.	the proof that
2.	the notion that
3.	the claim that
4.	the proposal that
5.	the fear that
6.	the hypothesis that

Table 10 *NPs as Complementizer Phrases*

The group of words <*That linguists argue all the time about terminology*> is an NP. This NP is also a sentence.

(39) ***That linguists argue all the time about terminology** is nothing new.*

When this new phrase structure rule is added to those discussed previously, we come up with the following phrase structure rules for NP in English:

$$
NP \rightarrow \left\{ \begin{array}{l} (QP)\ (Det)\ (Poss\ NP)\ (Num)\ (AdjP)\ \mathbf{N}\ (AdjP)\ (PP)\ (S) \\[1em] CP \end{array} \right\}
$$

The phrase structure of noun phrases will be expanded again later to make room for relative clauses and different types of subordinate clauses. Instances where NP can be rewritten as NP → CP will not be discussed until Chapters 13, 14, and 15.

6.7 Grammatical Functions

Cross-linguistic study of nouns has revealed that they assume six important functions in sentences. **Grammatical functions** are also called **grammatical relations.** These are listed in the table below:

No.	Grammatical Functions	Illustrations
1.	Subject	*To plagiarize* is a major academic offense.
2.	Subject Complement	Deanna's mother is *a librarian.*
3.	Direct Object	This professor uses *a lot of buts* in her speech.
4.	Indirect object	A baseball player gave an autographed ball *to Jeremy.*
5.	Object complement	They elected her *chair* unanimously.
6.	Object of a preposition	The union speaks for *the faculty.*

Table 11 *Grammatical Functions*

So, any lexical item that is found fulfilling any one of these functions is most likely a noun or a nominal. The table below summarizes the **functional** tests for nouns:

Test	Subject	Subject Complement	Direct Object	Indirect Object	Object Complement	Object of a Preposition
Noun	+	+	+	+	+	+
Verb	+	+	+	+	+	+
Adjective	+	+	+	+	+	+
Adverb	+	+	+	+	+	+
Conjunction	+	+	+	+	+	+
Preposition	+	+	+	+	+	+
Pronoun	+	+	+	+	+	+

Table 12 *Summary of Functional Tests*

The <+> symbol across all these categories indicates that all parts of speech can function as nominals.

6.8 Conclusion

Nouns are important in all languages. They occur most often and they are also the first lexical items that children acquire when learning to speak. Consequently, teachers and other language professionals should feel confident in identifying them. The rule of thumb definition that most people have of nouns usually goes a long way in helping to label words as nouns. In many instances, a noun will indeed name a person, a thing, a place, or an idea. However, since these rudimentary semantic features are not foolproof, language professionals might consider adding a few ready-made morphological tests to their repertoire. The features of case, number, and gender are reliable and can be used to enhance the identification of nouns. Furthermore, distributional/syntactic tests can help identify nouns very easily. Knowing that any lexical item preceded by a determiner, a quantifier, a Poss NP, a preposition, and an adjective is most likely a noun is a powerful tool that one can use to build one's metalinguistic competence. The assurance of knowing that any lexical item that functions as the subject or the object in a sentence is most likely a noun (or a nominal) gives teachers and other language professionals the confidence needed to examine any text and classify any word as a noun without second guessing themselves.

Key Terms to Know

These are the key terms that you should be able to use and define after reading this chapter:

1. [± Common]: 6.2.1, 6.2.4, 6.2.5, 6.5.1
2. [± Count]: 6.2
3. [± Gender]: 6.2.2, 6.8
4. [± Number]: 6.2.2, 6.2.3
5. article: 6.2.4, 6.2.5, 6.5, 6.5.5
6. attributive genitive: 6.5.4
7. cardinal number: 6.2.2, 6.5
8. collective: 6.2.2, 6.2.3, 6.2.4, 6.5
9. declension: 6.5.5
10. demonstrative: 6.5, 6.5.5
11. feature: 6.2.1, 6.2.2, 6.2.3, 6.2.4, 6.5.1, 6.5.5, 6.5.8
12. female: 6.2.2
13. feminine: 6.2.2
14. gender : 6.2.2
15. grammatical function: 6.7
16. grammatical relation: 6.7
17. head noun: 6.4, 6.5, 6.5.1
18. interrogative: 6.5
19. male: 6.2.2
20. masculine: 6.2.2
21. mass noun: 6.2.2
22. neuter: 6.2.2
23. nominal: 6.3.2, 6.6, 6.7, 6.8
24. noun phrase: 6.2, 6.2.3, 6.4, 6.4.1, 6.4.2, 6.4.3, 6.5
25. noun: 6.0, 6.1.2, 6.1.4, 6.2.1, 6.2.2, 6.2.3, 6.2.4, 6.2.5, 6.3.1, 6.3.2, 6.4, 6.4.1, 6.5, 6.5.1, 6.5.3, 6.5.4, 6.5.5, 6.6, 6.7, 6.8
26. numeral: 6.2.2, 6.5
27. ordinal number: 6.2, 6.5
28. partitive: 6.2.2
29. phrase: 6.4
30. possessive NP: 6.5
31. possessive: 6.5

EXERCISE 1—PARTS OF SPEECH ANALYSIS

Find **10 nouns or nominals** in the text below. In each case use **two** of the tests below to justify your findings.

1.   semantic evidence

2.   morphological evidence

3.   syntactic evidence

4.   functional evidence

The Gettysburg Address

by Abraham Lincoln—Part 2

". . . But in a larger sense, we cannot dedicate, we cannot consecrate, we cannot hallow this ground. The brave men, living and dead who struggled here have consecrated it far above our poor power to add or detract. The world will little note nor long remember what we say here, but it can never forget what they did here. It is for us the living rather to be dedicated here to the unfinished work which they who fought here have thus far so nobly advanced. It is rather for us to be here dedicated to the great task remaining before us—that from these honored dead we take increased devotion to that cause for which they gave the last full measure of devotion—that we here highly resolve that these dead shall not have died in vain, that this nation under God shall have a new birth of freedom, and that government of the people, by the people, for the people shall not perish from the earth."

No.	Words	Test 1	Test 2
1.			
2.			
3.			
4.			
5.			
6.			
7.			
8.			
9.			
10.			

EXERCISE 2—TREE DIAGRAM OF NPS

Diagram the NPs found in the following incomplete sentences.

1.   A politician of great oratory skills

2.   A bunch of sophomores on their way to Florida for spring break

3.   That friend of yours

4.   More than ten feet from side to side

EXERCISE 3—UNDERSTANDING GRAMMATICAL TERMINOLOGY

Make English sentences based on the grammatical information provided below:

1.   Make a sentence in which there is a noun. Underline the noun.

2.   Make a sentence in which there is a non-count noun. Underline the non-count noun.

3.   Make a sentence in which there is a plural noun. Underline the plural noun.

4.   Make a sentence in which there is a masculine noun. Underline the masculine noun.

5.   Make a sentence in which there is a feminine noun. Underline the feminine noun.

6.   Make a sentence in which there is a collective noun. Underline the collective noun.

7.   Make a sentence in which there is an indefinite article. Underline the indefinite article.

8.   Make a sentence in which there is a definite article. Underline the definite article.

9.   Make a sentence in which the determiner is a possessive word. Underline the possessive determiner.

10. Make a sentence in which the determiner is a quantifier. Underline the quantifier determiner.

11. Make a sentence in which the noun fulfills the thematic role of agent. Underline the agent thematic role.

12. Make a sentence in which the noun fulfills the thematic role of accompaniment/commitative. Underline the accompaniment/commitative thematic role.

13. Make a sentence in which the noun fulfills the thematic role of experiencer/patient. Underline the experiencer/patient thematic role.

14. Make a sentence in which the noun fulfills the thematic role of source. Underline the source thematic role.

15. Make a sentence in which the noun fulfills the thematic role of instrument. Underline the instrument thematic role.

16. Make a sentence in which the noun fulfills the thematic role of force. Underline the force thematic role.

17. Make a sentence in which the noun fulfills the thematic role of beneficiary. Underline the beneficiary thematic role.

Chapter 7

AUX, Auxiliary Verbs, Tense, Aspect, and Mood

7.0 INTRODUCTION

The concept of an auxiliary verb is foreign to Greek grammatical categories. Consequently, the term cannot be traced back to ancient Greek grammarians but rather to Latin grammarians. The word <auxiliary> is a Latin word which means "help." For this reason, some people have tried to replace it with the synonymous phrase **"helping verb."** This change of label is futile because it is not the word "auxiliary" that is the problem. The term is used quite freely in the medical field. Everybody knows what an auxiliary nurse does. Therefore, it is not the term that needs changing. What we need is to define what the "help" is all about. In order for the concept of auxiliary or helping verb to be well understood by students, they need to know what kind of help these verbs provide. For this reason, I define an auxiliary verb as a verb that helps the main verb (MV) in fulfilling the following duties:

1. Auxiliary verbs carry tense information on behalf of the main verb.

2. Auxiliary verbs carry aspect information on behalf of the main verb.

3. Auxiliary verbs carry mood information on behalf of the main verb.

4. Auxiliary verbs help negate information on behalf of the main verb.

5. Auxiliary verbs help ask questions on behalf of the main verb.

The best analogy for explaining the relationship between auxiliary verbs and main verbs is found in the nurse-physician relationship. Physicians are very important in the medical establishment. However, for all their training and their expertise, they depend on nurses to perform many essential functions. Physicians cannot operate without nurses. Similarly, nurses, for sure, cannot work independently of physicians. They need each other for the best possible patient care. In sentences, main verbs need auxiliary verbs to help them fulfill certain functions that they cannot carry on alone.

7.1 *The Semantic Characteristics of AUX*

The standard phrase structure rule that has been proposed for generating sentences is as follows:

$$S \rightarrow NP \quad AUX \quad VP$$

Admittedly, all well-formed sentences in all languages conform to this formula. This means that the syntactic category **"auxiliary"** which is abbreviated as AUX is on par with both NP and VP. This observation is not trivial. It lies at the heart of modern linguistics understanding of auxiliary. The contemporary usage is somewhat different from the traditional one. Modern linguists distinguish between "big" AUX (all in capital letters) and "small" Aux (only the initial letter is capitalized). Big AUX is a syntactic category similar to NP, VP, AdjP, AdvP, and PP. Small Aux, on the other hand, includes only auxiliary verbs. If AUX is a syntactic category, we do expect it to have phrase structure rules. The following rule has been formulated to account for English AUX:

$$AUX^{1} \rightarrow Tense \ (Modal) \ (Have—EN) \ (Be—ING) \ (Be—EN) + [MV]^{2}$$

A more comprehensive rule of AUX will be proposed later. For now, let us content ourselves with this rule. The abbreviation <MV> stands for "main verb". English AUX contains both non-lexical and lexical elements. The non-lexical components of AUX are **Agreement, Tense, Aspect, Mood,** and **Voice.** The lexical elements comprise a closed class of verbs known as auxiliary verbs.

In modern linguistics, the syntactic category AUX is deemed to be universal. However, this does not mean that in all languages there are verbs that can be identified as auxiliary verbs. For instance, classical Greek does not have auxiliary verbs per se. However, the same functions carried by Latin auxiliary verbs were carried in Greek by morphemes. Even in English, some elements of AUX such as the progressive and the perfective aspects are expressed only through morphological inflection. In some other languages, the information carried by auxiliary verbs can be conveyed by adverbs or other lexical categories.

There are two approaches to dealing with auxiliary verbs in contemporary syntax. Some linguists connect Aux directly to VP. Such is the view now taken by Fromkin et al. (2007:147) in the eighth edition of *An Introduction to Language.* They propose the following phrase structure rule for verb phrases:

$$VP \rightarrow Aux \ VP$$

---

[1] There are several nuances in the formulation of the phrase structure rule for AUX. The position taken here assumes that tense is obligatory. Celece-Murcia (1999:645) proposes a comprehensive rule that differs from this one only in a few minute details.

[2] The main verb "MV" is placed between brackets because it is not normally part of AUX. However, it is part of this phrase structure rule because it is closely connected to AUX.

In the seventh edition (2003:150) of the same book, we find the following formula:

$$S \rightarrow NP\ Aux\ VP$$

These two proposals make significantly different claims. The claim that Aux is part of the verb phrase (VP → Aux VP) is not accepted by all linguists. Finegan (2004:160–170) and many other linguists argue that auxiliary verbs are different from main verbs. Therefore, they favor the phrase structure rule NP Aux VP where Aux and VP are two different syntactic categories. The reasoning behind considering auxiliary verbs as forming a separate category goes back to ancient Latin grammarians and to mainstream generative grammar. It has been known since Varron (see 2.2.1) that a small group of verbs do not behave like the rest of the verbs in the lexicon. Such verbs indicate tense, aspect, and modality. Furthermore, auxiliary verbs form a closed class. Very rarely is a new auxiliary verb added to the verbs in this group. For this reason, some linguists maintain that auxiliary verbs have separate grammatical status even though they are verbs. Other linguists, especially those who work within the theory of syntax known as the X-bar Theory, lump auxiliary verbs together with main verbs as part of a larger group of verbs called "predicate." Proponents of this theory include auxiliary verbs in the verb phrase. There are good arguments on both sides to include or to exclude auxiliary verbs from the verb phrase. The decision to put auxiliary verbs under AUX in this book is motivated by the fact that a deliberate choice has been made to follow mainstream generative grammar as closely as possible.

7.2 The Non-lexical Components of AUX

The concepts of tense, aspect, mood, and voice are expressed by means of affixation in English. These inflectional morphemes add information to the main verb. They constitute what some linguists refer to as non-lexical components of AUX. This term is used in contrast to lexical auxiliary verbs such as <will>, <have>, <be>, <may>, <can>, <shall>, and <must>.

7.2.1 AUX and Agreement

One of the most important non-lexical components of AUX is agreement. It transfers the semantic features of number and person of the head noun or pronoun onto the main verb or the auxiliary verb. It also transfers the tense information under AUX onto the main verb or the auxiliary verb. Tree diagrams and derivations often omit this subcomponent of AUX. However, since the Government-Binding (GB) theory (to be discussed in Chapter 13), a closer attention has been given to Agreement (AGR) within AUX. Some linguists have started to represent Agreement in tree diagrams as INFL which stands for "inflection." In this book, Agreement will not be represented directly in tree diagrams. Instead, the morphological information carried by AGR will be subsumed under the inflectional morphology rule that applies right before the Spell-Out rule. When this rule applies, all the necessary inflectional rules will take place at once.

The essential ingredients of Agreement can be summarized as follows:

1. In English, there is a number and person agreement between the head noun and the verb or the auxiliary verbs <Have>, <Be>, and <Do>. If the head noun is singular, the verb with which it agrees is singular. Alternatively, if it is plural, the verb is plural.

2. Tense suffixes are added to the main verb or to the auxiliary verb to indicate that it has been inflected for tense.

These observations can be exemplified by the sentences below:

(1) *My daughter is playing with her dolls.*

(2) *The girls are playing with their dolls.*

(3) *My daughter played with her dolls all afternoon.*

(4) *The girls were playing with their dolls.*

Sentences (1) and (2) exemplify agreement in number between the head noun and the verb in the present tense. The focus in (3) and (4) is agreement in tense with the main verb or the auxiliary verb. Here too, agreement in number is in effect. Fromkin et al. (2007:147) succinctly summarize all this information as follows:

> *In addition to specifying the time reference of the sentence, Aux specifies the agreement features of the subject. For example, if the subject is* we, *Aux contains the feature first-person plural; if the subject is* he *or* she, *Aux contains the features third-person singular. Thus, another function of the syntactic rules is to use Aux as a 'matchmaker' between the subject and the verb. When the subject and the verb bear the same features, Aux makes a match; when they have incompatible features, Aux cannot make a match and the sentence is ungrammatical.*

7.2.2 AUX and Tense

Tense is to time what the mind is to the brain. Both tense and the mind are abstract realities whose concrete counterparts are time and the brain. The brain is a tangible organ of the body but the mind is an abstract faculty. Similarly, time is a concrete reality that is measurable, but tense is only a grammatical concept. All human beings are conscious of time, but not all languages express tense grammatically. Classical Hebrew and many African languages do not have morphological tense. Instead, tense is indicated by means of adverbial markers such as <yesterday> for the past, <today> for the present, and <tomorrow> for the future. These temporal divisions are indicated in English and many European languages by inflectional morphemes. In Generative Grammar, tense is thought of as a syntactic category for which the following phrase structure rule has been proposed:

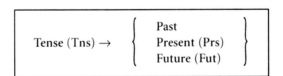

Some linguists recognize the past and the present as the only two tenses in English. For this reason, they do not indicate the future in the deep structure and on tree diagrams. They contend that the future tense marker <will> is not a true tense marker but only a modal verb. Cumes (1931:362–3) explains this objection as follows:

> *In spite of the great importance of a pure future, English has not yet developed such a form. Our future tense is made up of modal auxiliaries which are not only used as future but are sometimes employed elsewhere in their old modal meanings. . . . The use of* will[3] *. . . as a pure future developed out of its modal meaning of wish, desire.*

---

[3] The italics appear in the original.

The idea of desire was overshadowed by the conception of future occurrence, pure futurity, which is often implied in the idea of desire.

Though this may have been the case hundreds of years ago, this modal verb has now grammaticalized as the marker of the future tense. Consequently, one should not hold onto historical reality to exclude <will> from being a tense marker in contemporary North American English (NAE). Thus, in this work, <will> is considered a future tense marker as is seen in the tree diagram below:

(5)   *Jenny will visit her father in California.*

Deep structure: *Jenny **Fut.** visit her father in California*

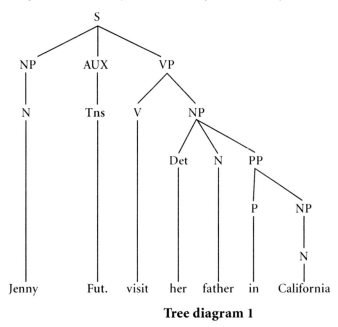

Tree diagram 1

Those who do not consider <will> to be a future tense marker omit it from their tree diagrams (Disterheft 2003:107, diagram 24). They assume that during the derivation, the inflectional morphology component will ensure that <will/shall> is inserted. However, the approach advocated here does not take this route. Instead, it claims that the future is present right in the deep structure. This approach is consistent with how the future tense is derived in languages such as French and Spanish that have an inflectional suffix for the future. It is also consistent with how the past and the present are derived in English. In diagramming sentences with the past or present tense, the features [+past] and [+present] are inserted under Tense (Tns).

7.2.3 AUX and Aspect

Tense and aspect always go together. They are like the two sides of a coin: head and tail. A coin is useless if it has a head but lacks a tail. It is also useless if it has a tail without a head. These twin notions of tense and aspect are so intertwined that it is hard to separate them successfully. It is nearly impossible to come across a definition of aspect which does not somehow refer to tense. The similarities between them tend to overshadow their differences. Yet the two are grammatically different. The dividing lines between the two are often blurred beyond recognition. All this has led to a great amount of debates among linguists. As a result, students are confused. Labov (1998:367) highlights the problem as follows:

> Of all linguistic categories, the concept of aspect is the hardest to understand, and linguists disagree more about aspect than anything else. The meaning of tense is easier to comprehend for it situates an event at a point in time. Aspect communicates the shape of the event in time: Did it happen all at once (punctual), at many separate times (iterative or habitual), or was it spread out in time (durative)? Was it just beginning (inceptive) or was it finished and done with (perfective)? These are not clear and distinct ideas, but rather (as the term "aspect" implies) they represent ways of looking at things. Aspect is seldom found in a pure form; it is often combined with questions of causation (is the event relevant to the present?) and reality (was it really so?). Finally, it is often combined with tense, so that we speak of a "tense-aspect system." Given all these complications, it isn't surprising that there is so little agreement on the meaning of general English aspects. There are almost as many theories to explain the contrast of (4) "They hit people" and (5) "They have hit people" as there are linguists to argue them.

This labovian quote does more than highlight the difficulties that the notion of aspect evokes. It also provides us with a partial list of the different types of aspects. The table below lists the most common aspects:

No.	Classification of Aspects	Definitions
1.	Simple	it is the unmarked form of the verb.[4]
2.	Habitual	describes an event or state that occurs or lasts over a long period of time. It also makes statements about unchanged truths.
3.	Iterative	describes an event or state that repeats itself over a period of time.
4.	Inceptive or inchoative	describes the beginning of an event or a state.
5.	Punctual	describes an event or state that occurs or lasts for a specific period of time.
6.	Progressive	describes an ongoing event or state.
7.	Continuative	describes an event or state that started at one point but continues on.
8.	Resultative	describes the results of an event or a state that has taken place already
9.	Perfective	describes or refers to an event or a state that has some relevance to another event or time.
10.	Durative	describes the relationship of duration of actions or states in relation to one another.

Table 1 *Classification of Aspects*

In many languages aspectual information is encoded by morphemes. When such an affix is missing, languages use lexical items to convey the same information. For instance, English does not have an inceptive morpheme. To compensate for it, it uses verbs such as

---

[4] Some authors include the simple aspect in their presentation but others do not. However, it is worth mentioning here because labels such as "simple present," "simple past," and "simple future" are still used in many grammar books.

<begin> or <start>. English has the suffix <-ing> to signal the progressive aspect but it lacks a morpheme for the continuative aspect. Instead, it uses the lexical items <keep>, <continue>, or the adverb <still> as in (6) and (7) below:

(6) *It is raining.*

(7) *It keeps raining.*

Sometimes, English uses both the progressive and the continuative aspects in the same sentence as a way of emphasizing the progressive and continuative aspects:

(8) *It is still raining.*

7.2.3.1 Phrase Structure Rule and Morphosyntax of Aspects

The standard phrase structure rule for the subcomponent Aspect is given as follows:

> **Aspect** → (Have—EN) (Be—ING) MV

This formula brings into focus the two morphologically marked aspects in English, namely the **perfective** and the **progressive aspects.**

According to Funk and Kolln (2006:70) the term "perfect" comes from Latin grammar where "it refers to action that is completed before the present moment." Morphologically and syntactically, the English perfective aspect is characterized by the presence of a discontinuous morpheme which is made up of the verb <have> and the suffix <-EN>. The suffix <-EN> is in capital letters because it is a standard linguistic convention. It has various allomorphs, including <-ed>, internal vowel change, suppletion, and zero morphemes. During the transformational process, a rule of **"Affix Hopping"** applies before the application of inflectional morphology rules. The latter converts the affix <-EN> into its proper orthographic or phonetic forms. Let us illustrate the process with (9) below:

(9) *Kim has completed her program.*

The deep structure of this sentence is <Kim [3rd pers. Sing. Fem.]Pres. Have—EN complete Kim Poss program>. The derivations are as follows:

Deep structure:	Kim [3rd pers. Sing. Fem.] Pres Have—EN complete Kim Poss program
Indexing/Matching:	Kim¹ [3rd pers. Sing. Fem.] Pres Have—EN complete Kim¹ Poss Program
Pronominalization:	Kim [3rd pers. Sing.] Pres Have—EN complete her Program
Affix Hopping:	Kim [3rd pers. Sing.] Have Pres—complete+EN her program
Spelling-Out Rule:	Kim has completed her program
Surface structure:	*Kim has completed her program*

The rule of Affix Hopping moves <-EN> out of the (Have—EN) complex and affixes it to the main verb <complete>. Once this process has taken place, the inflectional morphology rule of agreement (AGR) applies to change <have> into <has> since the subject <Kim> is third person singular. The spelling rules of English insure that <-EN> becomes <-ed>.

Sentences with the perfective aspect are diagramed as below:

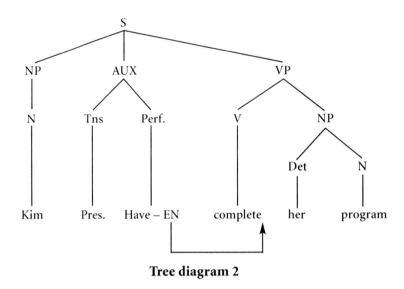

Tree diagram 2

The arrows are meant to show the Affix Hopping process. They are normally not part of tree diagrams.

The discontinuous morpheme <Be-ING> is used to signal the progressive aspect. The suffix <-ING> has the particularity of being the only English suffix without an allomorph. It is also characterized by a morphosyntactic rule of Affix Hopping. The derivational steps and the tree diagram of the progressive are similar to that of the perfective as is illustrated by this example:

(10) *Kim is completing her program.*

The deep structure of this sentence is <Kim [3rd pers. Sing.] Pres. Be—ING complete Kim Poss program>. The overall derivational process is as follows:

Deep structure:	Kim [3rd pers. Sing. Fem.] Pres Be—ING complete her program
Indexing/Matching:	Kim[1] [3rd pers. Sing. Fem.] Pres Be—ING complete Kim[1] Poss Program
Pronominalization:	Kim [3rd pers. Sing. Fem.] Pres Be—ING complete her Program
Affix Hopping:	Kim [3rd pers. Sing.] Be Pres—complete+ING her program
Spell-Out Rule:	Kim is completing her program
Surface structure:	*Kim is completing her program*

The rule of Affix Hopping moves <-ING> out of the discontinuous morpheme complex <Be—ING> attaches it to the end of the main verb <complete>. The standard tree diagram of the progressive aspect is as follows:

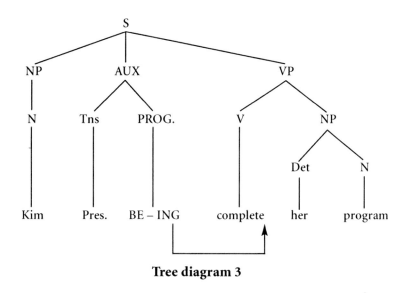

Tree diagram 3

7.2.3.2 Tense-Aspect Combinations

The two main English aspects discussed above combine with each other into the perfect progressive. Additionally, they each combine with <Tense> in a number of ways. If the simple aspect is added to the mix, the various combinations yield 12 different patterns as reflected in Table 2 below:

No.	Tense-Aspect Combination	Examples
1.	Simple Present	Kim *studies* hard
2.	Simple Past	Kim *studied* hard
3.	Simple Future	Kim *will study* hard
4.	Present Progressive	Kim *is studying* hard
5.	Past Progressive	Kim *was studying* hard
6.	Future Progressive	Kim *will be studying* hard
7.	Present Perfect	Kim *has studied* hard
8.	Past Perfect	Kim *had studied* hard
9.	Future Perfect	Kim *will have studied* hard
10.	Present Perfect Progressive	Kim *has been studying* hard
11.	Past Perfect Progressive	Kim *had been studying* hard
12.	Future Perfect Progressive	Kim *will have been studying* hard

Table 2 *Tense-Aspect Combination*

Most students have difficulties labeling tense-aspect combinations. However, labels such as <future perfect progressive> or <past perfect> are often used in grammar books. The way to interpret tense-aspect combinations is as follows. By convention, the first label refers to tense. The second and third labels (if there is a third one) refer to aspect. The perfective aspect is characterized by the discontinuous morpheme <Have—EN>. The progressive aspect has the structure <Be—ING>. In reading tense-aspect combination, we proceed from left to right as indicated by the diagram below:

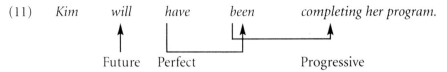

(11)   *Kim   will   have   been   completing her program.*

Future   Perfect   Progressive

Sentences in which tense-aspect combinations occur are diagrammed as follows:

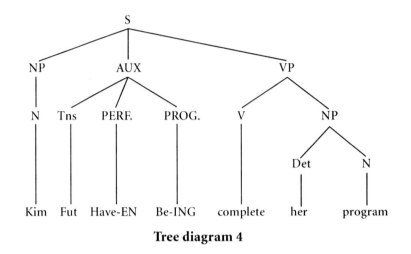

Tree diagram 4

Here, all three subcomponents of AUX occur side by side in the tree diagram in their proper syntactic order. The derivational process is as follows:

Deep structure:	Kim [3rd pers. Sing. Fem.] Fut. Have—EN Be—ING complete Kim Poss program
Indexing/Matching:	Kim[1] [3rd pers. Sing. Fem.] Fut. Have—EN complete Kim[1] Poss Program
Pronominalization:	Kim [3rd pers. Sing. Fem.] Fut. Have—EN complete her Program
Affix Hopping:	Kim [3rd pers. Sing.] Fut. Have ___ Be+**EN** complete+ING her program
Spelling-Out Rule:	Kim will have been completing her program
Surface structure:	*Kim will have been completing her program*

The rule of Affix Hopping applies to move <-EN> onto the lexical auxiliary <Be>. The progressive suffix <-ING> moves to the main verb <complete>. As a result, we have the form <Have Be+**EN** complete+**ING**>. The derivational rules apply in an ordered sequence. However, for the purpose of this course, let's just focus on the last two rules in the derivation. The Affix Hopping rule must apply before the Spelling-Out Rule. The output of these two rules leads to the syntactic surface structure. Syntactic rules are said to apply **cyclically.** This is an important notion in generative syntax.[5]

---

[5] Of course, the latest version of Generative Grammar does away with transformations. So, cyclical application of rules becomes a moot point. However, many introductory textbooks such as this one have not yet followed the approach outlined in *The Minimalist Program.*

7.2.3.3 The Meaning of Tense-Aspect Combinations

The purpose in this section is not to catalogue all the meanings of the different tense-aspect combinations. Such an exercise is beyond the scope of this presentation. My goal is simply to highlight the difficulties involved in interpreting some of the combinations. Kaplan (1995:197) expresses these difficulties as follows: "a difficulty in analyzing tense and aspect in English is the rather chaotic match of form to meaning. Rather than having one form equaling one meaning, the tense-aspect area contains several different forms which express one meaning, and several different meanings expressed by a single form. To muddy the picture further, some of the meanings expressed by 'basically' tense or aspect have nothing to do with tense or aspect." The examples below illustrate this lack of one-to-one correspondence between tense-aspect combinations and meaning:

(12) *I have lived here for six months.*

(13) *I have been living since spring.*

(14) *I moved here in spring.*

The verbs and auxiliaries in (12) are in the present perfect, those in (13) are in the present perfect progressive, and the verb in (14) is in the simple past. Despite their differences in tense-aspect combinations, they all express a present reality, namely that the subject of the sentences is still living in the place where he/she moved six months ago. These examples and others like them should make teachers not rely too much on the tense-aspect combinations in interpreting sentence meaning. They should take other elements of the sentence into account, especially adverbial modifiers. When it comes to interpreting tense-aspect combinations, it seems that language users rely more on pragmatics than on verbal morphology. **Pragmatics** is a branch of linguistics that specializes in the interpretation of utterances. It relies both on linguistic and extralinguistic information to make sense of linguistic inputs. Kaplan (1995:203) notes that the perfect has four main uses in English:

1. The "Continuative" use to indicate a situation that has endured from a time in the past up to the present as in *"We have lived here since 1989."*

2. The "Existential" use to indicate the existence of past events as in *"This bed has been slept in by George Washington."*

3. The "Resultative" use to indicate that the effects of a past event continue to the present moment as in *"I need a ride; my car has broken down."*

4. The "Hot News" use to report brand new information as in "The *students have occupied the President's office!"*

7.2.4 Mood

Mood indicates the speakers' attitude toward their utterances. If they are certain about their statements, they use a **declarative** mood. If they want to issue a command, they might use the **imperative** mood. If they wish to express a desire, they employ the **subjunctive** mood. If they hedge about their statement, or if the fulfillment of what they are saying is dependent on a situation beyond their control, they fall back on the **conditional** mood. In many languages, these moods are not all expressed through morphological affixation. When languages lack the morphemes to express mood, they may rely on verbs, adverbs, or other complex constructions to express it. Irrespective of how mood is expressed, traditional grammarians and contemporary linguists claim that all languages have at least four types of moods:

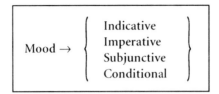

Mood combines with tense as shown in the table below. The symbol <-> indicates that the combination is not possible in English.

Tense	Indicative Mood	Imperative Mood	Subjunctive Mood	Conditional Mood
Past	+	–	+	+
Present	+	+	+	+
Future	+	–	–	+

Table 3 *Mood and Tense Combination*

The indicative mood and the conditional mood are the only ones that occur in all three tenses. The former is also the most frequent mood in all languages. Generative grammarians take it to be the basic mood from which all others are derived.

7.2.4.1 The Imperative Mood

From the indicative mood, languages generate the imperative mood by deleting the deep structure subject. We will illustrate how it works. However, before we get to it, a proper context must be set up. Suppose a boy named <Colton> is supposed to finish his homework. But instead, he is playing videogames. His mother comes into his room and yells at him: "Finish your homework!" The deep structure of this sentence looks something like this:

(15)   *Colton[2nd pers. Sing.] Imp finish Colton Poss homework.*

To derive (15) the following transformations take place:

Deep structure:	Colton[2nd pers. Sing.] Imp finish Colton Poss homework.
Indexing/Matching:	Colton[1] [2nd pers. Sing.] Imp finish Colton[1] Poss homework
Pronominalization:	Colton[1] [2nd pers. Sing.] Imp finish your homework
Subject deletion:	_____ Imp. finish your homework
Spell-Out Rule:[6]	finish your homework
Surface structure:	Finish your homework

It is hard to believe that a simple sentence such as <finish your homework> calls for so many derivational steps. It is cases such as this that have led Chomsky (2000:10) to propose the Minimalist Program, a new approach that does away with transformations.

---

[6]Affix Hopping does not apply in this case because there is inflectional morpheme for the imperative mood.

7.2.4.2 The Subjunctive Mood

The subjunctive mood is so rarely used in English that on a few occasions, my interlocutors have felt the need to correct my sentences by adding an <-s> to the verb form that I have left uninflected because of the subjunctive mood. If I were to make the sentence <it is important that our president pay attention to looming threats>, somebody may correct me indirectly by adding <-s> to <pay> thinking the verb needs an <-s>. However, this sentence is perfectly well formed. The verb <to pay> does not require an <-s> because it is in the subjunctive mood. The subjunctive, unlike the indicative, does not take third person singular subject-verb agreement in the present tense. In languages such as Spanish or French where the subjunctive still exists, it expresses wishes. Thus, if the verb of the main clause is <*vouloir*> (to want in French) or <*querer*> (to want in Spanish), and the subject of the main is different from the subject of the subordinate clause, the verb in the subordinate clause takes the subjunctive mood.[7]

7.2.4.3 The Conditional Mood

The conditional mood in French and Spanish is expressed through inflectional affixation. However, in English there are no morphemes for the conditional. For this reason, the conditional is a syntactic construction. It is characterized by an <if-clause> and a main clause, as seen in (16):

(16) *If it snows more than a foot, we will cancel class.*

The conditional clause is <if it snows more than a foot>. There is a complex system of tense and conditional mood interaction as illustrated by (17) and (18) below. However, a detailed analysis of the processes involved will be delayed until the discussions on subordinate clauses in Chapter 13:

(17) *If it **snowed** more than a foot, we **would** cancel class.*

(18) *If it **had snowed** more than a foot, we **would have** cancelled class.*

7.3 Voice

Voice is usually defined in relation to the subject of the verb. For some reasons, very few authors actually indicate that voice is a subcomponent of AUX. Jurafsky and Martin (2000:344) are the exceptions. Voice has three elements:

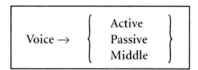

The **active voice** is universal. But a large number of languages in Africa, except for Malagasy, lack the **passive voice.** English has both the active and the passive voices but lacks the **middle voice.** Greek has all three voices.

---

[7]There are many more environments where the subjunctive is required but we will be content with only this example.

7.3.1 The Active and Passive Voices

The traditional definition of the active voice is that the subject is the doer of the action expressed by the verb. Sentence (19) below is in the active voice because both <Mike and Terri> are the "doers" of the action expressed by the verb <buy>:

(19) *Mike and Terri bought a new home.*

The same information can be communicated slightly differently by using the passive voice as in (20):

(20) *A new home was bought by Mike and Terri.*

Both sentences (19) and (20) express the same propositional content. Sentence (20) is said to be in the passive voice because the doer of the action is de-emphasized or relegated to a secondary role in the discourse. In this sentence, presumably, the emphasis is on the <new home>, not on <Mike and Terri>. For this reason, it is alleged that the meaning expressed by active and passive sentences is not one hundred percent identical. Pragmatic considerations and ideological motivations may lie behind the choice of the active voice over the passive voice, or vice versa.

7.3.2 Controversy over the Generation of Passive Constructions

There are two schools of thoughts about passive constructions. Early generative linguistic approaches generated all passive constructions from their active counterparts. However, enthusiasm about such an approach has subsided considerably because it has been found that there are passive constructions in English that do not have active counterparts. For instance, <to be born> occurs only in the passive. It is very clumsy to derive a sentence such as <Tallie was born in July> from <Somebody bore Tallie in July>. Celce-Murcia and Larsen-Freeman (1999:346–347) list other cases where deriving passive constructions from an alleged active counterparts is implausible. Because of this difficulty, some linguists generate passives by means of phrase structure rule in AUX. The following phrase structure rule has been proposed:

$$\textbf{Passive} \rightarrow \text{Be—EN}$$

Thus, the phrase structure rule for AUX that generate passives can now be expanded as follows:

$$\textbf{AUX} \rightarrow \text{Tense (Modal) (Have—EN) (Be—ING)} \textbf{ (Be—EN)} + [\textbf{MV}]$$

We see from this formula that voice, tense, and aspect can combine in twelve possible ways to produce sentences in the passive voice as shown in the following table:

No.	Tense-Voice-Aspect Combination	Illustrative Sentences
1.	Present Passive	A new house *is built.*
2.	Past Passive	A new house *was built.*
3.	Future Passive	A new house *will be built.*
4.	Present Perfect Passive	A new house *has been built.*
5.	Past Perfect Passive	A new house *had been built.*
6.	Future Perfect Passive	A new house *will have been built.*
7.	Present Progressive Passive	A new house *is being built.*
8.	Past Progressive Passive	A new house *was being built.*
9.	Future Progressive Passive	A new house *will be being built.*
10.	Present Perfect Progressive Passive	A new house *has been being built.*
11.	Past Perfect Progressive Passive	A new house *had been being built.*
12.	Future Perfect Progressive Passive	A new house *will have been being built.*

Table 4 *Voice and Tense-Aspect Combinations*

Generally in parsing, the active voice is considered the "default" voice and is not necessarily specified.

7.3.3 The Use of Passive Constructions in CALP

Disterheft (2003:33) remarks that "most writers know that they are not supposed to use the passive voice." Language Arts teachers warn their students against using the passive in their compositions. This resistance towards the passive voice is puzzling because it is commonly used in textbooks, academic journals, administrative, and legal language. Of course, excessive use of any one syntactic feature contributes to poor style. However, a balanced use of passive constructions is a sign of stylistic maturity. Textbook authors and authors of journal articles use the passive voice to avoid drawing excessive attention to themselves. Journalists use the passive voice to protect their sources. Lawmakers and administrators use passive constructions regularly in formulating legal and administrative dos and don'ts. A moderate use of the passive and the communicative contexts that make its use preferable should be taught explicitly to students. Celce-Murcia and Larsen-Freeman (1999:354) indicate that "where the focus is on the outcome or what happened, such as with scientific or journalistic writing, passives are more frequent than with fictional and conversational English." Since this is the case, teachers should take pragmatics into account in teaching writing. Some genres are more appropriate for the active voice while for others the passive voice seems to be the recommended choice.

7.3.4 The Middle Voice

The middle voice is the least common voice of all. It is generally defined as a construction in which the subject acts on itself, on its behalf, or for its own self-interest. Languages that do not indicate the middle voice morphologically express the same thought in other ways. English, for example, uses the reflexive pronouns (<myself>, <yourself>, <himself>, <herself>, <ourselves>, <yourselves>, and <themselves>) to communicate what Greek expresses by the middle voice. Spanish and French use the clitic pronoun <se> with or without other pronouns to express the concept of the middle voice.

7.3.5 Voice and Ergativity

There is another aspect of the middle voice that has been labeled **ergative.** An ergative construction is one in which the grammatical subject is only a make-believe subject. It is grammatically present, it controls subject-verb agreement, but in reality, it is not the doer of the action. Let us illustrate it with the sentence below:

(21)   *This car drives smoothly.*

In this sentence, the subject of <drive> is <this car>. However, we know that a car cannot drive itself. An unexpressed agent is behind the scene. A number of languages express ergativity morphologically. However, English has no morphological means to communicate it. So, it uses a combination of syntax and semantics to communicate ergativity. Ergative constructions play a useful role in discourse. For one thing, they allow language users to avoid taking responsibility for their actions. In sentences such as <the chicken burnt>, <the negotiations fell through>, <the car broke down>, ergativity helps hide the identity of the agent. Pragmatics is very useful in interpreting ergative constructions. Many English verbs can be used as ergatives. More will be said about ergativity in Chapter 8.

7.4 The Lexical Components of AUX

The bulk of the preceding discussions dealt with the non-lexical components of AUX. From now till the end of the chapter our attention will be devoted to the lexical components of AUX, that is, to **auxiliary verbs.** These are the verbs that help the main verb (MV) fulfill the various semantic functions discussed in 7.1. It is important to stress again the two notational conventions that are often confusing to beginners, namely the distinction between AUX and Aux (see 7.1). AUX is a major component which houses both the non-lexical components and auxiliary verbs. The diagram below captures this distinction and also doubles as a summary of the preceding sections.

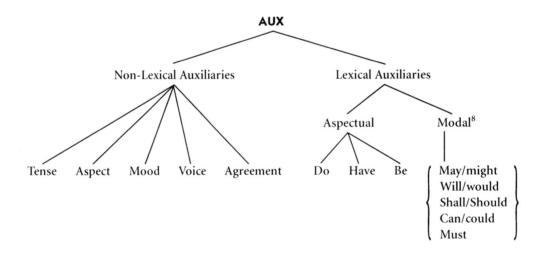

Linguists distinguish between three main groups of auxiliary verbs in English. The first group comprises <Have> and <Be>, the second <DO> and the third, all the modal verbs. The analyses that follow focus on this three-way distinction.

---

[8]This list does not include phrasal modals such as <Have to>, <Be about to>, <Ought to>, etc.

7.4.1 Aspectual Auxiliary Verbs

The first group of auxiliaries is sometimes referred to as **"aspectual" auxiliary verbs.** The rationale behind this label is that both <Have> and <Be> intervene in the syntactic construction of two important aspects. The discontinuous morpheme <Have—EN> contributes to the perfective aspect, while <Be—ING> helps the main verb carry the progressive aspect. Additionally, <Be—EN> contributes to the construction of passive voice as outlined in Table 4 previously.

7.4.2 The Auxiliary <Do>

The clumsy label of <Do-Support> is often given to the auxiliary <Do> for lack of a better term. Despite its clumsiness, <Do-support> is a very informative label. It conveys the idea that the auxiliary <Do> helps the main verb in asking Yes/No questions or in negating statements. The deep structure of English sentences does not contain questions, nor does it contain negation. To ask a Yes/No question or to negate a statement in English, <Do-support> is needed at some point in the derivation. Let us reintroduce the same sentences discussed in sections 3.7 and 3.8.1 as (22):

(22) *Many students don't take linguistics.*

The derivational steps used to produce <many students don't take linguistics> are as follows:

Deep structure:	many student plural Pres take linguistics
Negative Insertion:	many student plural Pres **NOT** take linguistics
DO-Support addition:	many student plural Pres **DO NOT** take linguistics
Affix Hopping:	many student plural **DO** Pres **NOT** take linguistics
NOT-Contraction:	many student plural **DON'T** Pres take linguistics
Spell-Out Rule:	many students **DON'T** take linguistics
Syntactic Surface Structure:	Many students don't take linguistics.

Similarly, <Do-Support> is needed to generate (23):

(23) *Did Brad buy the car?*

Deep structure:	Brad Past buy the car
Yes/No Question:	Q Brad Past buy the car
Do-Support:	Q Brad Past DO buy the car
Subject-Auxiliary Inversion:	Q Past DO Brad buy the car
Affix Hopping:	Q DO past Brad buy the car
Spell-Out Rule:	Q did Brad buy the car
Surface structure:	Did Brad buy the car?

<Do-Support> is also needed, as might be expected, in producing interro-negative sentences such as <Didn't Brad buy a new car?>. In this sentence, both negation and Yes/No question appear but <Do-support> applies only once. <Do-support> is also required in negative imperatives such as <Don't stick your tongue out in public>.

7.4.3 Modal Auxiliaries

English modal auxiliary verbs are: <can/could>, <shall/should>, <will/would>, <may/might>, and <must>. A detailed survey of the semantics of these auxiliary modals is beyond the scope of this chapter. Suffice it to say they express mood as defined in 7.2.4. The table below summarizes the main meanings associated with modal verbs.

No.	Modal Verb	Main Meaning
1.	Can/could	possibility, permission, polite request, low probability, potentiality
2.	Shall/should	obligation, suggestion, request, prediction with low degree probability, weak obligation
3.	Will/would	desire, suggestion, request, prediction with some degree of certainty, past habit, promise, command, future time
4.	May/might	possibility, permission, request, uncertainty, obligation
5.	Must	moral or physical necessity, strong suggestion, high probability, strong obligation

Table 5 *The Meaning of Modal Verbs*

It is important to note the striking semantic similarities between all these modal verbs. Given this, one wonders why English would use these five modals to express roughly the same meaning. One possible answer is that historically they were not semantically similar. For instance, a long time ago there was a distinction between <shall/should> and <will/would>. The form <shall/should> was used only in the first person singular or plural while <will/would> was used for the second and third persons singular and plural, (Cumes 1931: 362-66). However, in contemporary North American English, this distinction does not apply anymore. Furthermore, the use of <shall> as a future tense indicator has all but disappeared. However, the use of <should> remains strong. Similarly, the distinction between <can> and <may> in formulating requests is on the decline much to the consternation of my children's elementary school teachers. Celce-Murcia and Larsen-Freeman (1999:145) observe that "in North America there are many situations where there is a lack of clearly defined authority, and *can* tends to be more widely used than *may* and is often perceived as more polite than *may*," (italics in the original).

7.4.4 Phrasal Modals

It seems that each lexical modal in English has its phrasal equivalent as seen in the table below:

No.	Modal Verb	Phrasal Modal
1.	Can/could	be able to
2.	Shall/will	be going to, be about to
3.	May/might	be allowed to, be permitted to
4.	Must	have to, have got to
5.	Should	ought to, be supposed to
6.	Would	used to

Table 6 *Phrasal Modals*

Phrasal modals are sometimes called **"periphrastic" modals.**[9] However, here too, there are subtle changes in meaning between lexical modals and their alleged semantic counterparts. For one thing, most phrasal counterparts usually carry only one of the possible meanings of lexical modals. The examples below make this point rather clearly.

(24) *Kim could complete her program in a year.*

(25) *Kim was able to complete her program in a year.*

In (25) <was able to> does not convey the meanings of probability or of polite suggestion that could be associated with <could> in (24).

The tree diagram of (25) is as follows:

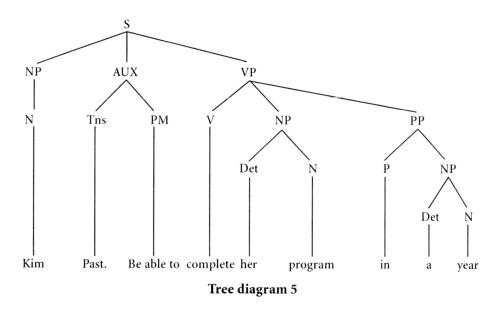

Tree diagram 5

Note that phrasal modals or periphrastic modals constitute an indivisible chunk under the node <PM>.

7.5 The Morphosyntactic Similarities and Differences among Auxiliaries

The three-way distinction made between lexical auxiliaries is based on their morphosyntactic behavior. The aspectual auxiliaries <Have> and <Be> agree with their subjects in number and tense. For <Have>, this means that if its subject is [+ Singular] and the tense in AUX [+Present], it becomes <has>. Otherwise, its form is <Have>. In the past tense, it has only one form <had>. The situation is rather different for <Be>. It agrees with its subject according to the following features: [± Plural] and [± Present]. This auxiliary verb has the distinctiveness of being the verb which has the most varied form in the English language. Children and English Language Learners have more problems conjugating <Be> than any other verb.

[9]The prefix <peri> comes from Greek. It means around. The phrase "periphrastic modal" can be translated loosely as "the long way around to express modality."

Additionally, when both <Have> and <Be> are used as auxiliaries, the rule of Affix Hopping causes the main verb to become a participle, as noted in the discussions on aspects and voices. In the sentence <Kim will have been completing her program>, the word <been> is said to be in the **past participle,** and <completing> has a **present participial form.** We will revisit these notions in Chapter 8.

The auxiliary verb <Do> shares much of the subject-verb agreement characteristics of <Have> and <Be>. However, the main difference with <Do> is that the main verb that follows it is in the bare infinitive form. In the sentence <Did Brad buy the car?>, the word <buy> is said to be a **bare infinitive.**

Unlike the aspectual auxiliaries <Have> and <Be>, or the auxiliary <Do>, modal auxiliaries are not inflected for subject-verb agreement. However, they, like <Do>, are followed by main verbs in the bare infinitive form.

7.5.1 The Controversy about the Tense of Modal Auxiliaries

The past tense of the auxiliary verbs <Have>, <Be>, and <Do> is uncontroversial. The past tenses of these verbs indicate that an action, a state, or an event has occurred. However, this is not the case for modal auxiliaries. Take the verb <can> for example. In (26) its corresponding form <could> indicates a past action:

(26) *Brandon can swim now. A year ago, he could not.*

(27) **Brandon can swim now. A year ago, he can not.*

Sentence (26) is well-formed but (27) is not. The only reason why (27) is ill-formed is because <can> does not agree with the adverbial phrase <a year ago> which denotes a past event. This evidence seems to suggest that the past tense form of <can> is <could>. However, such a conclusion cannot be made because there are other instances where <could> does not denote a past tense action. Take (28) for instance. Even though <could> is used, the past tense is not in force here because the adverbial phrase <next week> indicates an event that has not yet taken place:

(28) *Could Kaylee come to the birthday party next week?*

Instances such as these have led Larsen-Freeman (1999:139) and others to claim that modal auxiliaries are tense-less. However, such an assertion is too categorical and must be mitigated by discourse considerations. A less radical view would be to say that modals have tense but that their past tense morphology cannot always be interpreted as denoting a past action, event, or state. This is the view adopted in this book.

7.5.2 Tense-Aspect Combination with Modal Verbs

Tense and aspect combine with modal verbs to convey a complexity of meanings. Here again, it is the communicative situation, not the morphological characteristics of the modal verb, that determines the overall meaning of the combination. In accordance with the position taken in this book, we will parse modal verbs as having three tenses: present, past, and future.[10] Table 7 outlines the various possible combinations:

---

[10]When the modal verb is <will> or <shall>, it is the main verb with which it occurs that is parsed. The main verb is tagged morphologically as having the future tense.

No.	Tense-Modal-Voice-Aspect Combination	Illustrative Sentences
1.	Present modal	Kim *can* study tonight.
2.	Past Modal	Kim *could* study tonight.
3.	Present Modal Perfect	Kim *may have studied* tonight.
4.	Past Modal Perfect	Kim *might have studied* tonight.
5.	Past Modal Perfect Passive	A new house *should have been built.*
6.	Past Modal Perfect Progressive Passive	A new house could have been *being built.*

Table 7 *Modals and Tense-Aspect Combinations*

Constructions involving past-modal-perfect-progressive passive as in <*a new house could have been being built* > or present-modal perfect-progressive passive as in < *a new house may have been being built* >, though theoretically possible, are actually rare in written or spoken English. Since speakers and writers know that these constructions are cognitively taxing to process, they do not exploit these combinatorial possibilities. They usually find less convoluted ways to express themselves.

7.5.3 Teaching the Use of Modal Auxiliaries

Pragmatics is indispensable in interpreting modality. As noted earlier, English, unlike French and Spanish, does not have morphemes to signal power differential between interlocutors. To convey the same thought, English resorts to modal auxiliaries. It happens that the "past" tense of modal auxiliaries is deemed more respectful than their equivalent forms in "present" tense (Larsen-Freeman, 1999:145). The past tenses of modal auxiliaries occur more often in academic writing than the present tense also because they make statements less forcefully. Since academic writing tends to avoid categorical and presumptuous claims, the past tense seems more appropriate.

7.6 Functional Analysis of Auxiliary Verbs

The auxiliary verbs <Have>, <Be>, and <Do> can also function as main verbs. This is generally the case when they occur as the only verbs in the sentence:

(29) *My sister is silly.*

(30) *I did my homework.*

(31) *I have a headache.*

If <Have>, <Be>, and <Do> are used as main verbs, it means they can also take auxiliaries:

(32) *My sister is being silly.*

(33) *I did do my homework.*

(34) *I have had a headache before.*

In these sentences <is> is the auxiliary for <being>, <did> for <do>, and <have> for <had>, respectively.

7.6.1 Semi-Auxiliaries

If some auxiliary verbs can become main verbs, it means that some main verbs can also function as auxiliaries. The label of **semi-auxiliary** is given to any main verb that functions sometimes as an auxiliary verb. The verbs <dare> and <need> function sometimes as modal auxiliaries and sometimes as main verbs. If they are main verbs, they agree with their subjects in number and person, as shown in the examples below:

(35) *Jeremy needs a haircut.*

(36) *The dean dares the disgruntled professor to sue him.*

In these two sentences, the suffix <-s> on <need> and <dare> indicates that they are both main verbs. However, when they are used as modal auxiliaries, there is no subject-verb agreement in the present tense:

(37) *Jeremy need not have a haircut.*

(38) *The disgruntled professor dare not sue the dean.*

In these two sentences, <need> and <dare> do not take the suffix <-s>. This is clear evidence that the two verbs are functioning as modal auxiliaries. As observed in 7.4.3, with modal auxiliaries there is no subject-verb agreement in the present tense.

Cumes (1931:386) adds <keep> to the list of main verbs that can function auxiliary verbs. However, even though <keep> has also acquired a meaning as a marker of the continuative aspect, it behaves much like a main verb in many respects. For this reason, in my opinion, it is not a semi-auxiliary verb.

7.7 Conclusion

The traditional and the contemporary notions of auxiliary overlap. However, there are differences between the two. Traditionally, the term <auxiliary> is used exclusively in relation to auxiliary verbs. However, today, the term is understood more broadly. This chapter has explained and highlighted the differences and the similarities between the two. It has also provided a principled account of the different types of auxiliary verbs and their semantic, morphological, and syntactic behaviors. This is a prelude to the discussions in the next chapter which focus on the various characteristics of main verbs in English. We will also see later in 13.4.4 that the syntactic category AUX has been expanded to include elements that were not traditionally part of Aux.

Key Terms to Know

These are the key terms that you should be able to use and define after reading this chapter:

1. active voice: 7.3, 7.3.1, 7.3.2
2. affix hopping: 7.2.3.1, 7.5
3. agreement: 7.1, 7.2, 7.2.1, 7.2.3.1, 7.3.2, 7.3.5, 7.4, 7.5, 7.6.1
4. aspect: 7.0, 7.1, 7.2, 7.2.2, 7.2.3, 7.2.3.1, 7.3.2, 7.3.5, 7.4.1, 7.5, 7.5.2
5. aspectual auxiliaries: 7.4.1
6. auxiliary : 7.0, 7.1, 7.2, 7.2.1, 7.2.3, 7.4, 7.4.1, 7.4.2, 7.5, 7.5.1, 7.6, 7.6.1, 7.7
7. bare infinitive: 7.5
8. big AUX: 7.1, 7.2.1, 7.2.2, 7.2.3, 7.4, 7.5
9. conditional mood: 7.2.4, 7.2.4.2
10. continuative aspect: 7.2.3, 7.6.1
11. Do-support: 7.4.2
12. ergative/ergativity: 7.3.5
13. future tense: 7.2.2, 7.4.3
14. imperative mood: 7.2.4, 7.2.4.1
15. inceptive aspect: 7.2.3
16. indicative/declarative mood: 7.2.4, 7.2.4.1
17. iterative aspect: 7.2.3
18. middle voice: 7.3, 7.3.4, 7.3.5
19. modal auxiliary: 7.4.3, 7.5.3
20. mood: 7.0, 7.1, 7.2, 7.2.4, 7.2.4.1, 7.2.4.2, 7.2.4.3, 7.4, 7.4.3
21. passive voice: 7.3, 7.3.1, 7.3.3, 7.4.1
22. past participle: 7.5
23. past tense: 7.5, 7.5.1, 7.5.3
24. perfective aspect: 7.1, 7.2.3, 7.2.3.1, 7.3.2, 7.4.1
25. phrasal/periphrastic modal: 7.4.4
26. pragmatics: 7.2.3.3, 7.3.3, 7.3.5, 7.5.3
27. present participle: 7.5
28. present tense: 7.2.1, 7.2.2, 7.2.4.2, 7.5.3, 7.6.1
29. progressive aspect: 7.2.3, 7.2.3.1, 7.4.1
30. punctual aspect: 7.2.3
31. semi-auxiliary: 7.6.1

EXERCISE 1—TREE DIAGRAMS

Draw a tree diagram of the following sentences:

1.   The faculty boycotted the meeting.

2.   The university might increase tuition next year.

3.   The student should have received a B for her efforts.

4.   The politician must have seen the handwriting on the wall.

EXERCISE 2—AUXILIARY VERBS IDENTIFICATION

Fill in the table below with the required information.

The Gettysburg Address

by Abraham Lincoln

"Fourscore and seven years ago our fathers brought forth on this continent a new nation, conceived in liberty and dedicated to the proposition that all men are created equal. Now we are engaged in a great civil war, testing whether that nation or any nation so conceived and so dedicated can long endure. We are met on a great battlefield of that war. We have come to dedicate a portion of that field as a final resting-place for those who here gave their lives that that nation might live. It is altogether fitting and proper that we should do this.

But in a larger sense, we cannot dedicate, we cannot consecrate, we cannot hallow this ground. The brave men, living and dead who struggled here have consecrated it far above our poor power to add or detract. The world will little note nor long remember what we say here, but it can never forget what they did here. It is for us the living rather to be dedicated here to the unfinished work which they who fought here have thus far so nobly advanced. It is rather for us to be here dedicated to the great task remaining before us—that from these honored dead we take increased devotion to that cause for which they gave the last full measure of devotion—that we here highly resolve that these dead shall not have died in vain, that this nation under God shall have a new birth of freedom, and that government of the people, by the people, for the people shall not perish from the earth."

List and classify all the auxiliary verbs in the text above according to the three categories of auxiliaries discussed in the chapter, that is, 1) aspectual auxiliaries, 2) Do-support, 3) modal auxiliaries. If an auxiliary is mentioned more than once, list only the first occurrence.

No.	Aspectual Auxiliary	Do-Support	Modal Auxiliaries
1.			
2.			
3.			
4.			
5.			

EXERCISE 3—UNDERSTANDING GRAMMATICAL TERMINOLOGY

Make English sentences based on the grammatical information provided below:

1. Make a sentence with a future tense. Underline the morpheme of the future.

2. A sentence in which the tense-aspect combination is the past perfect progressive. Underline the past perfect progressive.

3. A sentence in which the tense of the modal verb in the past. Underline the modal verb.

4. Make a sentence with an ergative verb in the present perfect progressive. Underline the ergative verb and the present perfect progressive.

5. Make a sentence with a phrasal/periphrastic modal. Underline the phrasal modal.

6. Make a sentence in which a third person singular is the subject of a verb in the subjunctive mood. Underline the verb in the subjunctive mood.

7. Make a sentence in which a passive voice is used in combination with a future perfect progressive. Underline the passive voice and the future perfect progressive.

8. Make a sentence in the conditional mood. Make sure that the verb of the main clause is in the past tense. Pay attention to the tense-aspect agreement with the verb in the if-clause.

9. Make a sentence in the conditional mood. Make sure that the tense-aspect combination of the part of your sentence that begins with "**if**" is in the past perfect.

Chapter 8

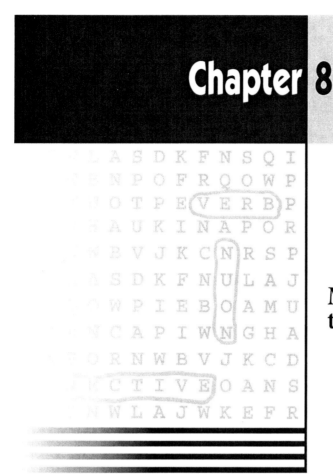

Main Verbs and the Verb Phrase

8.0 INTRODUCTION

Ancient Greek linguists and philosophers made a distinction between *logos* and *rhema*. These two concepts are reminiscent of the Sassurean distinction between *langue* and *parole,* or the Chomskyan opposition between *competence* and *performance.* However, the Greek *logos* was broader in meaning. In addition to designating word, speech, and wisdom, it also had a theological overtone.[1] Thus, Greek linguists used the term *rhema* exclusively for the spoken word. It is often translated into English as <verb>. The parallel that Latin grammarians found for this Greek word was the term <verbium>, that is, "verb." Both Greek and Latin grammarians considered the verb to be the most important part of speech. Contemporary linguists do not disagree with this three-thousand-year-old assessment. Fromkin et al. (2003:191) contend that the verb is the most important element in the sentence because "in all languages, the verb plays a central role in the meaning and structure of sentences. The verb determines the number of objects and limits the semantic properties of both its subject and its objects." With wit and a great sense of humor, Pinker (1994:113–4) highlights the centrality of verbs as follows:

> *Within a phrase, then, the verb is a little despot, dictating which of the slots made available by the super-rules are to be filled. These demands are stored in the verb's entry in the mental dictionary ... For a sentence to feel grammatical, the verb's*

---

[1] John 1:1–5 equates Jesus Christ and God with *logos.*

demands must be satisfied. . . . Because verbs have the power to dictate how a sentence conveys who did what to whom, one cannot sort out the roles in a sentence without looking up the verb.

The centrality of the verb is underscored by Aitchinson (1994:110) who quotes the French philosopher Victor Hugo as having said that "the word, it's the verb, and the verb it's God." Rodby and Winterowd (2005:44) concur with this assessment and give the following piece of advice to language professionals: "If you understand verbs, you will be ready to deal with sentences."

These quotes set the stage for what we will do in this chapter. They all emphasize the importance of verbs in sentence construction and interpretation. They all underscore the notion that a proper understanding of verbs can give teachers the needed confidence to explain many other aspects of grammar to their students. A good grasp of verbs can also provide knowledgeable feedback on students' writings. Thus, the goal in this chapter is to equip teachers with semantic, morphological, syntactic, and functional tools that will help them identify, classify, and explain the syntactic behavior of verbs in sentences.

8.1 Semantic Test for Verbs

Kaplan (1995:110) comments that the only things many people remember from English grammar lessons are the traditional definitions of nouns and verbs. A verb is defined traditionally as "a word that names an action or state." This definition of verbs is as problematic as that of nouns discussed in 6.2. The problem with this definition is that all classificatory systems based on semantics fail more often than not. Commenting on the endless possibilities of classifying and sub-classifying verbs, Lobeck (2000:110) writes: "In short, when it comes to classifying verbs on the basis of their meaning, there are numerous possibilities." The table following shows only a small fraction of meaning-based classifications of verbs that I have encountered in just a few grammar books (see Table 1).

A purely semantic definition is not very profitable to classroom teachers. For one, the list is endless. Secondly, there are too many overlapping categories. Teachers are best served if they are equipped with morphological and syntactic tools that can help them identify and classify verbs. For this reason, this chapter de-emphasizes the semantics of verbs and focuses more on their morphological patterns and their syntactic distributions.

8.2 Morphological Test for Main Verbs

As we did for nouns, we argue here that information obtained from inflectional morphology, derivational morphology, and word formation processes can allow teachers to successfully distinguish verbs from other parts of speech. Inflectional morphology, as will be seen shortly, distinguishes between finite and non-finite forms of verbs on the one hand, and verbs from the other parts of speech, on the other hand. It also distinguishes main verbs from auxiliary verbs. Using this information, we can set morphological features such as those in the tables below to distinguish between different types of verbs in the English lexicon.

8.2.1 Finite Test for Main Verbs

Traditional and contemporary grammarians make a distinction between **finite** and **non-finite** forms of verbs. Knowing what these two concepts entail can help identify verbs fairly easily. Cumes (1931:448) defines these two notions as follows: "Finite forms of verbs are those limited by **person, number,** and **mood.** Those not thus limited, verbal forms without person, number, and mood are non-finite forms." Most English verbs have

No.	Meaning-based Classification	Illustration
1.	Verbs of motion (Lobeck 2000:110)	Run
2.	Verbs of emotion (Lobeck 2000:110)	Love
3.	Verbs of perception (Lobeck 2000:110)	Hear
4.	Verbs of measurement (Lobeck 2000:260)	Weigh
5.	Verbs of containing (Celce-Murcia 1999:348)	Hold
6.	Verbs of fitting (Celce-Murcia 1999:348)	Suit
7.	Verbs of possession (Celce-Murcia 1999:348)	Own
8.	Verbs that involve vehicles (Celce-Murcia 1999:350)	Drive
9.	Verbs of cooking (Celce-Murcia 1999:350)	Bake
10.	Verbs of occurrence (Celce-Murcia 1999:352)	Happen
11.	Verbs of description (Celce-Murcia 1999:352)	Vanish
12.	Verbs of transfer (Celce-Murcia 1999:367)	Throw
13.	Verbs of permission (Celce-Murcia 1999:367)	Offer
14.	Verbs of making or creating (Celce-Murcia 1999:367)	Carve
15.	Verbs of entertaining	Read
16.	Verbs of telling (Celce-Murcia 1999:367)	Fax
17.	Verbs of teaching (Celce-Murcia 1999:367)	Teach
18.	Verbs of showing (Celce-Murcia 1999:367)	Show
19.	Verbs of cognition (Celce-Murcia 1999:367)	Think
20.	Verbs of information (Celce-Murcia 1999:367)	Tell
21.	Verbs of change of state (Celce-Murcia 1999:367)	Grow
22.	Verbs of existence (Disterheft 2003:145-6)	Remain
23.	Verbs of ingestion (Bickford 1999:79)	Eat
24.	Verbs of emission (Disterheft 2003:167)	Beep
25.	Touch verbs of existence (Disterheft 2003:163)	Pat
26.	Hit verbs (Disterheft 2003:163)	Bang
27.	Destroy verbs (Disterheft 2003:163)	Kill
28.	Admire verbs (Disterheft 2003:163)	Appreciate
29.	Amuse verbs (Disterheft 2003:163)	Entertain
30.	Cut verbs (Disterheft 2003:167)	Grind
31.	Break verbs (Disterheft 2003:167)	Smash
32.	Roll verbs (Disterheft 2003:167)	Bounce
33.	Pronominal verbs (Disterheft 2003:169)	Shave
34.	Psyche-verbs (Berk 1999:108)	Believe
35.	Punctual verbs (Berk 1999:110)	Blink
36.	Reciprocal verbs (Berk 1999:117)	Resemble[2]
37.	Sensory verbs (Berk 1999:117), Lobeck (2000:110)	Smell

Table 1 *Semantic Classification of Verbs*

[2] Other verbs in this category include <to collide, to shake hands, to argue, to fight, to kiss, to embrace, to hug, to make love, to reconcile>. These verbs have a reciprocal meaning if their subject is third person plural.

three persons in their conjugation, two numbers, and four moods. These characteristics are summarized in the tables below:

No.	Person	Number Singular	Number Plural
1.	1st person	I	We
2.	2nd person	You	You
3.	3rd person	He/She/ It	They

Table 2 *Person and Number*

No.	Mood
1.	Conditional
2.	Imperative
3.	Indicative
4.	Subjective

Table 3 *English Verb Moods*

Based on the information presented so far, a criterion for identifying finite verbs can be stated as follows:

Finite Verb Criterion

Any lexical item in a sentence that has the morphological marking for tense, mood, person, and number is a verb.

To see how this criterion applies, let us consider the examples below:

(1)   *Caleb **loves** math.*

(2)   *Andrew **played** with his sister.*

(3)   *The students will **receive** their diplomas in December.*

Sentence (1) is in the present tense. We know this because the inflectional suffix <-s> appears on the main verb <love>. Sentence (2) has the past tense suffix <-ed>. This tells us that the word <play> is a verb. Lastly, the presence of the future marker <will> signals that <receive> is a verb. Additionally, all three verbs are in the indicative mood. They are also in the third person. The verbs <love> and <play> are morphologically marked as singular. The verb <receive> is plural. In traditional grammar, the process of providing tense, mood, person, and number information about verbs is called **parsing.** This term is also used in computational linguistics. In second and foreign language books, <parsing> is also called **conjugation.** The inflectional morphology information useful for identifying finite verbs is summarized as a set of binary features in the following table:

No.	Test	Main Verb	Noun[3]	Adjective	Adverb	Pronoun	Conjunction	Preposition
1.	Tense	+	–	–	–	–	–	–
2.	Mood	+	–	–	–	–	–	–
3.	Person	+	–	–	–	+	–	–
4.	Number	+	+	–	–	+	–	–

Table 4 *Finite Verb Test*

Any lexical item that bears these features all at once is a finite/conjugated verb. The group of words "all at once" is very important here. As the table shows, nouns and pronouns have a [+Number] feature. However, the fact that they have this feature in isolation does not turn them into verbs. It is actually not surprising that nouns and pronouns have this feature because we saw in Chapter 6 that they transmit these features to auxiliary verbs or to main verbs through agreement in AUX.

8.2.2 Non-finite Test for Main Verbs

Main verbs that do not carry tense, mood, and number information are called non-finite verbs. Grammarians have identified three forms of main verbs to which they have given the label of non-finite verbs. These are:

1. the past participial form of verbs

2. the present participial form of verbs

3. the infinitive form of verbs

These forms are illustrated by the sentences below:

(4) *Jeff has **written** a computer program.*

(5) *A computer program is **written** by Jeff.*

(6) *Jeff is **writing** a computer program.*

(7) *Jeff wants **to write** a new computer program.*

We have already seen in Chapter 7 that the discontinuous morphemes (Have-EN), (Be-EN), and (Be-ING) are participial markers. In (4) and (5) the suffix <-EN> signals that the main verb <write> has taken a **past participial** form and is now <written>. In (6) the suffix <-ING> turns the main verb <write> into a **present participle** <writing>. We know from Chapter 7 that the rule of Affix Hopping moves the affixes <-EN> and <-ING> and attaches them only to verbs, and not to any other parts of speech. Consequently, the presence of these discontinuous morphemes on a word is a strong indication that that word is a verb.[4]

The free morpheme <to> which occurs in (7) can appear with verbs and nouns. If <to> precedes a word that has the properties of nouns as discussed in Chapter 6, then that word is a noun. However, if <to> precedes a word that is not a noun, then that word is an **infinitive** verb. The morpheme <to> is an infinitive marker for verbs. A distinction

---

[3] The part of speech category <article> is not listed separately here because it is considered part of the noun phrase (NP).

[4] This observation applies to all verbs in English except for modal verbs which do not take <-EN> and <-ING> suffixes. Also the verb <beware> does not accept participial suffixes.

is usually made between two kinds of infinitives in English. Some verbs take a <to-infinitive> marker but there is a small subset of verbs that, even though they are in the infinitive, do not take the marker <to>. An infinitive verb that does not have <to> is called a <bare infinitive>. This distinction can be illustrated by the two sentences below:

    (8)   *The rich heir wants **to buy** an airplane.*

    (9)   *The mother of the rich heir made him **buy** a bicycle.*

Both <to buy> and <buy> are in the infinitive, but the former is a <to-infinitive> and the latter a <bare infinitive>.

The preceding information allows us to propose the following test to identify non-finite verbs.

Non-finite Test for Verbs

Any lexical item in a sentence that has participial suffixes or is marked as an infinitive is most likely a verb.

This information can reliably help distinguish verbs from other parts of speech as indicated in the table below:

No.	Test	Main Verb	Noun	Adjective	Adverb	Pronoun	Conjunction	Preposition
1.	Past Participle	+	−	±[5]	−	−	−	−
2.	Present Participle	+	−	±	−	−	−	−
3.	Infinitive	+	−	−	−	−	−	−

Table 5 *Non-finite Test for Verbs*

We will see in 8.6 that the suffixes <-EN> and <-ING> appear on verbal forms that perform different functions in the sentence. The same is true for <to-infinitive> verbs.

8.3 *Derivational Morphology Tests for Verbs*

Derivational morphemes that help identify a lexical item as being a verb are not many in English. The most common derivational suffixes are <-ate>, <-ify>, <-ize> and <-en>. These suffixes change adjectives and nouns into verbs. The discontinuous morpheme <en- ... -en> also changes adjectives into verbs. Finally, the derivational prefix <be-> changes some adjectives and nouns into verbs.

---

[5] With regard to function, both past and present participles can function as adjectives. We will discuss this in Chapter 9.

No.	Suffixes	Adjective →	Verb	Noun →	Verb
1.	<-ate>	masculine →	emasculate	pontiff →	pontificate
2.	<-ize>	slender →	slenderize	union →	unionize
3.	<-ify>	null →	nullify	liquid →	liquefy
4.	<-en>	dark →	darken	fright →	frighten
5.	<en->	rich →	enrich	list →	enlist
6.	<en-.....-en>	light →	enlighten		
7.	<be->	little →	belittle	siege →	besiege

Table 6 *Non-finite Test for Verbs*

Apart from <-ify> and <-ize>, the other derivational affixes are either not very productive or they appear in lexical items that are not necessarily verbs. Therefore, a word of caution is in order. The suffix <-ate> appears in words such as <appropriate> and <mandate>. The former is both an adjective and a verb and the latter can be both a verb and a noun. In resolving cases where derivational morphology does not provide a clear-cut answer, one can rely on the finite and non-finite tests discussed earlier.

There is also a marginal phonological rule that changes voiceless sounds into voiced sounds. This phonological process changes a few adjectives into verbs. The most often cited examples are <safe>/<save> and <strife>/<strive>. Thus, the adjective <safe> is turned into a verb by changing <f> to <v>, as in <save>. Similarly, <f> becomes <v> when the noun <strife> becomes a verb, <strive>.

8.3.1 Word Formation Processes

New verbs are being constantly added to the English lexicon, but not necessarily through affixation. One of the most widely used word formation strategies for creating new verbs in English is conversion/backformation. This word formation process changes nouns to verbs without the need of additional suffixes. Thus, <an arm> becomes <to arm>, and <an eye> becomes <to eye>, <a mouth> becomes <to mouth>, <a house> becomes <to house>, <a party> becomes <to party>, <a boot> becomes <to boot>, etc. In such instances, only the finite and non-finite tests can help us distinguish between the nominal form and the verbal form of the same word, as in the examples below:

(10) *The police charged the couple because they **house** criminals.*

(11) *The police charged the couple because their **house** was full of criminals.*

The words <house> in both (10) and (11) are identical. It is hard to determine their part of speech just by looking at them. However, when they are parsed, we see that they belong to different parts of speech. The word <house> in (10) is a verb because it can be parsed as 3rd person plural in the present indicative mood. These features which are characteristic of verbs do not appear in (11). Instead, the presence of the determiner <their> makes us realize that <house> in (11) is not a verb, but rather a noun. Thus, the finite and non-finite tests and the various tests proposed in Chapter 6 can help distinguish between cases where verbs are created from existing nouns through conversion/back formation.

8.4 Syntactic-Semantic Interface

The firewalls that structural linguists erected between syntax and semantics began falling down with the advent of generative grammar. Early on, Chomsky (1965:90) introduced the notion of **subcategorization.** He divided subcategorization into two types: **strict subcategorization** and **selectional restriction.** The former consists of specifying all the syntactic elements that follow the verbs in the verb phrase. Originally subcategorization applied only to verbs but the notion has now been extended to nouns, adjectives, adverbs, prepositions, and adjectives. Since this chapter deals with verbs, we will concern ourselves mostly with their subcategorization. **Selectional restriction,** on the other hand, consists in specifying the semantic features that make a sentence acceptable or not acceptable. Chomsky (1965:153) and Radford (1981:139) argue that selectional restriction belongs in the lexicon, not in the syntactic component. A positive consequence, though controversial, is that in theory the semantic features are assigned early. Thus, they allow speakers to rule out sentences even before they are uttered.

The twin notions of subcategorization and selectional restriction are so important in contemporary syntax that Fromkin et al. (2003:133) argue that "the well-formedness of a phrase depends on at least two factors: whether the phrase conforms to the phrase structure requirements of the language, and whether the phrase conforms to the selectional requirements of the head." Teachers can benefit from knowing these two notions because they can help explain why some sentences made by their students "do not sound right" even though there might not be anything syntactically wrong with them.

8.4.1 Formalizing Subcategorization and Selectional Restriction

Chomsky (1965) proposes a formal notation for representing subcategorization information. Let us illustrate how this is done with the verb <to eat>:

$$\boxed{\text{Eat, V, [— (NP)]}}$$

The formalism is interpreted as follows: the lexical item <to eat> is first presented in its citation (dictionary) form. Then, it is followed immediately by its part of speech. Within the brackets[6] we find a place holder — for the verb and the possible complement(s) that occur with the verb. All the above information is contained in what is called a **subcategorization frame.** Chomsky (1965:93) states that subcategorizations are positively stated. By this he means that only the elements that must occur with the verb are to be specified. If one wishes to add selectional restriction to the subcategorization frame, one proceeds as follows:

$$\boxed{\begin{array}{llll} \text{Eat, V,} & \text{[NP} & \text{—} & \text{NP]} \\ & \text{[+ Animate]} & & \text{[- Liquid, +Edible]}^7 \end{array}}$$

In this case the subcategorization frame of the verb <to eat> also includes the following selectional restriction information. It states that the verb <to eat> requires that its subject be [+Animate] and that the direct object, i.e., the thing eaten, be [-Liquid, +Edible]. The inclusion of the selectional restriction in the subcategorization frame has the added

---

[6] Some linguists do not use brackets. In that case, <eat> is subcategorized as follows: Eat, V, [—(NP)].

[7] The formalism used here is slightly different from the one used in Radford (1986:129, 141) who uses semantic/ thematic rules instead of semantic features.

benefit of preventing the generation of semantically unacceptable sentences such as the ones below:

(12) ?*Charlie ate the orange juice.*

(13) ?*The sink ate the orange juice.*

(14) ?*Charlie ate the tree.*

Subcategorization and selectional restriction have complementary but different functions. Chomsky (1965:149)[8] notes that violating subcategorization constraints leads to grammatically ill-formed sentences whereas violating selectional restrictions results in sentences that are semantically unacceptable. Such sentences become acceptable only metaphorically as in (15):

(15) *The dead shall hear his voice.*

The verb <to hear> requires that its subject be alive because technically, dead people cannot hear. However, metaphorically this is possible (Chomsky 1965:149).

8.5 The Verb and Its Complements

In subcategorizing VPs, the concepts of **head** and **complement** become very useful. A head is defined as any lexical item that determines the syntactic category of the whole phrase. A complement is also defined as any word or group of words that follows the head and "completes" its meaning. There are five lexical categories that can head phrases, as shown in the table below:

No.	Lexical Heads	Phrasal Categories[9]
1.	N	NP
2.	V	VP
3.	Adj	AdjP
4.	Adv	AdvP
5.	P	PP

Table 7 *Lexical Heads*

Since the focus of this chapter is on verbs, we will focus only on the kind of complements that they take. In subcategorizing verbs, a distinction is often made between **phrasal complements** and **sentential complements**. The discussions in this section deal mainly with phrasal complements. We will study sentential complements in Chapter 13.

Both traditional and contemporary approaches to grammar classify verbs into four major groups according to their phrasal complements:

1.   intransitive verbs

2.   transitive verbs

3.   ditransitive verbs

4.   stative verbs

---

[8] The by-now famous sentence "*Colorless green ideas sleep furiously*" was used to illustrate this point (Chomsky 1965:149).

[9] The X-bar theory recognizes units that are larger than the phrase. However, X-bar theory is beyond the scope of this introductory material.

This classification is primarily based on the grammatical functions fulfilled by the noun phrases selected by the verb. These noun phrases are known either as the **arguments** of the verbs or as the **valences** of the verbs. Jurafsky and Martin (2000:343) observe that this traditional classification is woefully inadequate and that contemporary linguists have proposed between 50 and 100 new categories. However, for our purposes we will use the traditional categories and expand on them only when necessary.

Six important **grammatical functions** have been identified in English and many world languages. These functions are listed in the table below:

No.	Grammatical Functions of Noun Phrases
1.	Subject
2.	Subject Complement
3.	Direct Object
4.	Indirect Object
5.	Objective Complement
6.	Object of Preposition
7.	Adverbial Complement

Table 8 *Summary of Grammatical Functions of Noun Phrases*

These grammatical functions are also known as **grammatical relations, semantic roles,** or **thematic roles** in modern linguistic jargon. Their importance in sentence interpretation becomes obvious when we consider the two sentences below:

(16) *Tony loves Susie.*

(17) *Susie loves Tony.*

Sentences (16) and (17) have different meanings even though both have exactly the same words. The only thing that differs is the order in which the elements occur. Word order per se does not contribute to the semantic difference between the two sentences because we know that in some languages, namely Greek and Latin, word order does not lead to semantic differences in many instances. Grammarians argue that these two sentences are different because of differences in the grammatical function. In (16) <Tony> is **the subject** and <Susie> is the direct object. In (17) <Susie> is the subject and <Tony> is **the direct object.**

The focus in the remaining sections is on the subcategorization of verbs. In doing so, we do not deal with the subject of verbs because, according to Chomsky (1965:96), "verbs are not strictly subcategorized in terms of types of subject NPs or type of Auxiliary." For the subject, what matters the most is the selectional restrictions that the verb places on its NP subjects. Notions such as these are at the heart of traditional and contemporary approaches to grammar. Consequently, teachers should be familiar with them. They should be able to identify and label verbs and the grammatical functions that they assign. The remainder of this section will focus on the skills needed to carry out this task.

8.5.1 Intransitive Verbs

A verb is classified as **intransitive** if in its subcategorization frame, it does not allow a noun phrase. Verbs included in this group are <to laugh>, <to sleep>, <to smile>, <to rest>, <to arrive>, <to ring>, <to complain>, <to snore>, <to laugh>, <to cry>, <worry>.[10] The following sentences are ill-formed precisely because intransitive verbs do not accept an NP.

(18) *Mary slept her child.*

(19) * *The children laughed the old man.*

(20) * *The students complained the dean about their professor.*

Semantically, intransitive verbs do not need an NP in the VP for their meaning to be complete. The subcategorization frame of intransitive verbs is as follows:

> Verb, + Intransitive, [— Ø]

The null symbol "Ø" is used here to indicate that no NP can occur with intransitive verbs.

8.5.2 Transitive Verbs with Direct Object Complements

By definition, a **transitive verb** is a verb that takes an object. Grammarians make a distinction between transitive verbs that take a **direct object** (D.O.) and those that take an **indirect object** (I.O.). Let us consider direct objects first. Verbs that take a direct object are subcategorized as follows:

> Verb, + Transitive, [— NP]
> [+D.O]

Verbs in this category include <to eat>, <to drink>, <to need>, <to kiss>, <to pass>, <to study>, and <to solve> as in the sentences below:

(21) *Jill kissed her boyfriend.*

(22) * *Jill kissed.*

(23) *Rachel needs a ride.*

(24) * *Rachel needs.*

Sentences (22) and (24) are ill-formed because the verbs <kiss> and <need> require a direct object to make their meaning complete. Verbs such as <kiss> and <need> that necessarily require a direct object in their subcategorization frames are said to be **obligatory transitive** (LeTourneau 2001:144). It means that without a direct object, the sentence is ill-formed, as are (22) and (24). However, there are other transitive verbs that can set aside their direct objects in some sentences. Sentences (26) and (27) exemplify such cases:

(25) *Ryan ate an apple.*

(26) *Ryan ate.*

---

[10] In sentences such as <She cried herself to sleep> and <He worried himself sick>, the verbs <cry> and <worry> are not used intransitively.

(27) *Dale smoked a cigarette.*

(28) *Dale smoked.*

Transitive verbs that are used without a direct object are said to be used **absolutely.** According to Cumes (1931:437), when transitive verbs are used absolutely "we are not thinking of a particular person or things as receiving the action, but have in mind only the action itself pure and simple." The subcategorization frame of such verbs is as follows:

> Verb, + Transitive, [— (NP)]
> [+D.O]

Transitive verbs that fit this subcategorization frame are sometimes called **optional transitive** (LeTourneau (2001:144)).

8.5.3 Transitive Phrasal Verbs and their Complements

Some verbs are called phrasal verbs in English grammar because the verb is followed by a word that looks like a preposition. This preposition look-alike is called a particle. Verbs in this category include <to look **at**>, <to look **after**>, <to look **for**>, <to look **into**>, <to rely **on**>, <to contend **with**>, <to chat **with**>, etc. Transitive phrasal verbs must be subcategorized like regular transitive verbs, as in the example below:

> Verb, + Transitive, [— (NP)]
> [+D.O]

If the particle is missing, the sentence becomes ungrammatical as in (29):

(29) ** The police looked the missing boy but did not find him.*

The ungrammaticality of (29) comes from the fact that the particle <for> is missing. Since it contributes meaning to the verb <to look>, <for> cannot be omitted without affecting the grammaticality of the sentence. It will be argued in Chapter 11, sections 11.3.3 through 11.5.1, that words such as <at, after, for, with, on, into> etc., are not prepositions but rather particles.

8.5.4 Ditransitive Verbs with both Direct and Indirect Object Complements

Ditransitive verbs are verbs that can be subcategorized with two NPs. The prefix <di-> means <two>. Ditransitive verbs are also known as **dative verbs.** Verbs in this class include the following: <to give>, <to award>, <to hand>, <to buy>, <to feed>, <to lend>, <to loan>, <to offer>, <to promise>, <to bring>, <to send>, <to ship>, <to transfer>, <to throw>, <to kick>, <to pass>, etc. The subcategorization frame of these verbs is as follows:

> Verb, +Ditransitive, [— NP^1 to/for NP^2]
>   [+D.O]   [+I.O] or
> Verb, +Ditransitive, [— NP^2 NP^1]
>   [+I.O]   [+D.O]

The following sentences illustrate the syntactic behavior of these sentences:

(30) *Kim gave her transcript to the dean.*

(31) *Kim gave the dean her transcript.*

In (30) <her transcript> is the direct object and <the dean> is the indirect object. In (31) the order of the two NPs is reversed. However, the semantic/thematic roles are the same. NP^2 is still the direct object, and NP^1 is still the indirect object. Presumably, (30) is closer to the deep structure form and (31) is obtained as a result of the application of transformations. These sentences will be ungrammatical if one of the complements or both of them are missing.

Verbs such as <to bake>, <to make>, <to write>, <to tell>, etc. can be used as simple transitive verbs in phrases such <to bake a cake>, <to make dinner>, <to write a book>, <to tell a story>, etc. However, they can also be used ditransitively when a recipient of the action needs to be specified, as in the sentences below:

(32) *Mary baked her sister a cake.*

(33) *Mary baked a cake for her sister.*

(34) *Brenda wrote Jean a long letter.*

(35) *Brenda wrote a long letter to Jean.*

(36) *Lori made Joel a delicious fish dinner.*

(37) *Lori made a delicious fish dinner for Joel.*

This new information leads to a slight revision of the subcategorization rule proposed above. The new proposal takes into account transitive verbs that can be used ditransitively:

> Verb, + Transitive, [— NP^1 (to/for NP^2)]
>   [+D.O]   [+I.O] or
> Verb, + Transitive, [— NP^2 NP^1]
>   [+I.O]   [+D.O]

The parentheses are omitted in the second subcategorization because once the indirect object occurs first, it is expected that the direct object will follow or else the resulting sentence would be ill-formed as <*Karen made her parents>. Sentences such as (32) with ditransitive verbs are diagrammed as follows:

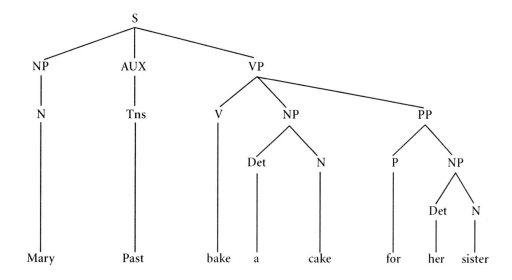

8.5.5 Linking Verbs and their Complements

Linking/stative verbs describe the physical, emotional, or positional state of the subject. Verbs belonging to this category are <to be>, <to become>, <to go>, <to run>, <to turn>, <to get>, <to appear>, <to seem>, <to remain>, <to stay>, <to feel>, <to taste>, <to smell>, <to look>, <to sound>. The subcategorization frame of linking verbs is as follows:

$$\text{Verb, +Stative,} \left\{ \begin{array}{l} [\text{— NP}] \\ [\text{— AdjP}] \\ [\text{— AdvP}] \\ [\text{— PP}] \end{array} \right\}$$

Sentences (38) through (41) illustrate the use of linking verbs:

(38) *My best friend became **a surgeon.***

(39) *Janet remained **optimistic.***

(40) *The doctor is **here.***

(41) *Brenda stayed **in the kitchen.***

The verbs in this group behave differently with regard to the complements with which they can be subcategorized, as seen in the table below:

No.	Linking Verbs	NP	AdjP	PP	AdvP
1.	be	+	+	+	+
2.	become	+	+	−	−
3.	seem	+	+	−	−
4.	sound	−	+	−	−
5.	feel	+	+	−	−
6.	remain	+	+	+	+
7.	stay	−	+	+	+
8.	taste	+	+	−	−
9.	smell	+	+	−	−
10.	appear	−	+	+	+
11.	turn	+	+	+	+
12.	get	+	+	+	+
13.	look	−	+	+	+
14.	grow	+	+	+	+
15.	keep	+	+	−	−

Table 9 *Complements of Linking Verbs*

Sentence (39), which is the most characteristic of constructions involving linking verbs, can be diagrammed as follows:

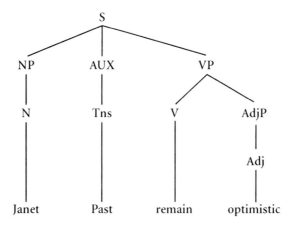

8.5.6 Transitive Verbs with Objective Complements

Some transitive verbs can have two direct objects, one right after the other, or the direct object may be followed by either an adjective phrase or a prepositional phrase. Such verbs are subcategorized as follows:

$$\text{Verb, +transitive, } [— \quad NP^1 \left\{ \begin{array}{l} NP^2 \\ AdjP \\ PP \end{array} \right\}]$$

This pattern can be illustrated by the sentences below:

(42) *Jeremy considers **Ben a friend.***

(43) *Some people find **linguistics fascinating.***

(44) *The audience found **the joke in poor taste.***

Some of the most common verbs in this category are <find>, <call>, <prove>, <make>, <declare>, <buy>, <appoint>, and <elect>. Sentences such as (42) with objective complements are diagrammed as follows:

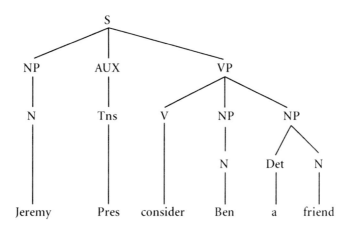

Notice the two NPs under the VP node. The main verbs in this group are as follows:

No.	Objective Complements	NP1	NP2
1.	find	+	-
2.	call	+	+
3.	prove	+	-
4.	make	+	+
5.	declare	+	+
6.	buy	+	+
7.	consider	+	+
8.	elect	+	+
9.	appoint	+	+

Table 10 *Verbs that take Objective Complements*

The verb <to find> for example cannot take a second objective complement that is an NP. If a complement must follow NP1, that complement must be an adjective. The main verbs that take adjectival complements appear in Table 11.

No.	Adjectival Complement	NP1	AdjP
1.	find	+	+
2.	call	+	+
3.	prove	+	+
4.	make	+	+
5.	declare	+	+
6.	buy	+	+
7.	consider	+	+

Table 11 *Verbs that take Adjectival Complements*

When such verbs are used in sentences, they can be diagrammed as follows:

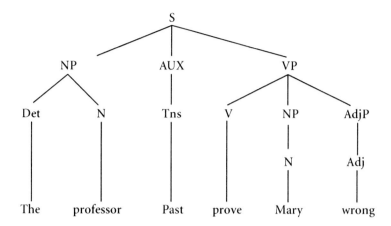

There is also a small sub-group of verbs whose objective complements are prepositional phrases, as shown here:

No.	Verb with PP Complements	NP	PP[11]
1.	put	+	+
2.	place	+	+
3.	pour	+	+
4.	take	+	+
5.	tell	+	+
6.	blame	+	+

Table 12 *Verbs with PP Complements*

More will be said about prepositions in Chapter 11. Suffice it to say here that in many instances, specific prepositions must be chosen from among the group of possible prepositions (Clark 2003:116-118). Thus, the verbs in the table here not only select their NP complements, they also select the kind of prepositions they can co-occur with. This can be illustrated by (45):

(45)   *Annie told **her mother about her boyfriend.***

The subcategorization frame of <tell> is as follows:

> Tell, Verb, [— NP   P   NP]
> <about>

---

[11] The discussion of particles will be delayed until Chapter 11.

Sentence (45) is diagrammed as follows:

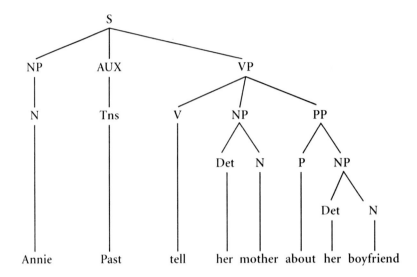

Constructions in which verbs select very specific types of prepositions appear to be problematic for English as a Second Language learners.

8.5.7 Verbs with Adverbial NP Complements

Some English verbs take NPs that function as **adverbial complements.** Lobeck (2000:260–1) explains that they are called "adverbial noun phrase complements" because "they express information about time/manner/place, or in other cases measurement such as height, weight, age, cost." Verbs of motion such as <drive>, <lurk>, <go>, and verbs of measurement such as <weigh>, <cost>, and <measure> take adverbial NP complements. These verbs have the following subcategorization frame:

Verb, [—   NP   ]
          [+adverb]

The NPs in the following sentences are not direct objects but adverbial complements because they answer the questions <where> and <how much> respectively:

(46) *John went* **home.**

(47) *This linguistics textbook costs* **an arm and a leg.**

In contrast to (46), notice that in (48) below, the word <home> is a direct object because it answers the question <what>.

(48) *John bought* **a home.**

The best way to determine if a noun phrase functions as a direct object or an adverbial complement is to perform the **passive test.**[12] If a sentence can be turned into a passive construction, then the NP is a direct object. If it cannot, then it functions as an adverbial complement, as seen in the two sentences below:

(49) **Home was gone by John.*

(50) *A home was bought by John.*

---

[12] Berk (1999:116–118) warns that some transitive verbs such as <want>, <enjoy>, <smell>, <have>, etc. are not readily passivized.

If the same test is applied to (47), the result will be ungrammatical. We conclude then that <an arm and a leg> is not a direct object complement, but rather an adverbial complement. The linguistic analysis of words such as <home> and <an arm and a leg> is always difficult because the formal characteristic of the word says one thing while the functional analysis says another thing. Normally, <home> and <an arm and a leg> are nouns. However, in these instances, they do not function as nouns, but rather as adverbs. It is in such cases where one must invoke the MAT Condition discussed in 1.14. For the analysis to be minimally accurate, one must rely both on formal and functional characteristics. There is also quite a bit of disagreement regarding the label used to name the syntactic category on tree diagrams. Some, following formal features, will label <home> as NP while others will label the node as AdvP because of functional properties. Either approach is correct but, following Chomsky (1965:68–9), my preference goes to labeling nodes based on formal characteristics. In the tree diagram below both labels are used to show that both are acceptable. The label that is "more acceptable" is in bold.

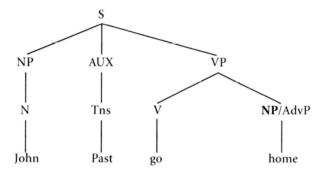

8.5.8 Verbs Listed in Multiple Categories

A word of caution is in order before concluding this section on the subcategorization of English verbs. There are verbs that can belong to more than one category. Let us illustrate this point with the verb <to feel> in the following sentences:

(51) Phil **feels** good about the future.

(52) Phil **feels** a pain in his knee.

(53) Phil doesn't **feel** well today.

In these three sentences, the verb <to feel> has three different complements. In (51) <feel> is used as a linking verb. Its complement is the adjective <good>. In (52) <feel> is a transitive verb because <a pain> is its direct object complement. Lastly, in (53) <feel> is an intransitive verb, not having any complement. Several English verbs can be used this way. It all depends on the function that they fulfill in the sentence and the syntactic category with which they are subcategorized.

8.6 Functional Tests for Verbs

English main verbs have four non-finite forms, namely, the infinitive, the gerund, the present participle, and the past participle. In simple sentences, they can function as subjects or adjectives, as will be discussed in the sections following.

8.6.1 Non-finite Verbs as Nominals

In the sentences below, <learning> and <to learn> fulfill the grammatical function of subject:

(54)   *Learning a foreign language helps you understand English grammar better.*

(55)   *To learn a foreign language helps you understand English grammar better.*

Both are also main verbs because they pass the non-finite test for verbs proposed in 8.2.2. However, in these two sentences they are the grammatical subjects of the verb <help>. This underscores once again the fact that a lexical item can be analyzed according to its function or its form. Traditional grammars give the label of **nominal** to words such as <learning> and <to learn> which fulfill the function of noun without being formally nouns.

The word <learning> in (54) is also known as a **gerund.** A gerund is a verbal form ending in <-ING> that functions as a subject or an object. To distinguish gerunds from present participial forms, an <it>-substitution test is often used. If a word or the phrase containing the <-ING> word can be replaced by <it> and if the sentence remains grammatical, then the word with the <-ING> ending is a gerund. However, if the substitution results in an ungrammatical sentence, then the form is a present participle, as seen in the examples below:

(56)   ***Learning*** *classical languages is good for you.*

(57)   ***It*** *is good for you.*

(58)   ***Smiling*** *from ear to ear, the bride kissed the groom.*

(59)   *****It,** *the bride kissed the groom.*

The word <smiling> is not a gerund because the phrase it occurs in cannot be substituted for by <it>. This test can be summarized by the table below:

No.	Test	Present Participle	Gerund
1.	It-substitution	–	+
2.	Determiner	–	+
3.	Possession	–	+

Table 13 *The Gerund Test*

Additionally, an <-ING> word that cannot be possessed or cannot be preceded by a determiner is most likely a participle. If it can be possessed or can be preceded by a determiner, then it is a gerund.

8.6.2 Non-finite Verbs as Adjectives

The present and past participial forms of verbs often function as adjectives. More will be said about adjectives in the next chapter. Here we will only say that when used this way, these participial forms modify the head noun they occur with, as seen in the sentences below:

(60) ***The smiling*** *bride kissed her groom.*

(61) *They escaped a bad plane crash with only **broken** legs.*

In both of these sentences, <smiling> and <broken> function as adjectives. They modify <bride> and <legs> respectively.

8.7 The Relevance of Subcategorization for ESL/EFL Teachers

Verbs are the "engine" of the sentence. Knowing which complement a verb takes or does not take is a very important step towards becoming a proficient speaker or writer. Many grammatical mistakes made by ESL/EFL students can, in many instances, be traced to a violation of one or more selectional criteria. ESL/EFL teachers will find it easier to explain students' ungrammatical sentences by familiarizing themselves with the subcategorization frames of verbs. It is important to keep in mind that verbs are positively subcategorized. Chomsky (1965:93) explains it as follows:

> *We then have a general rule of subcategorization to the effect that a Verb is positively specified with respect to the contextual feature associated with the context in which it occurs. [Italics in the original]*

According to Chomsky, verbs are subcategorized in relation to the complement(s) that they take. Once a verb is found to take a certain complement, this complement cannot be omitted[13] or replaced by another one. Doing so results in ill-formed sentences. The following sentences taken from the writings of an ESL student serve to illustrate the point:

(62) * *He further explains that it helps **to** children to go outside and enjoy the cold environments rather than relying **in** indoor games.*

(63) * *I agree **him** on that point.*

(64) * *She said **me** that one can get many benefits if his or her roommate is cooperative and helpful for my next question.*

Sentence (62) is ungrammatical because the transitive verb <help> is wrongly subcategorized as an intransitive verb. In the second part of the sentence, the preposition that is subcategorized with <rely> is <on>, not <in>. In (63) the intransitive verb <agree> has been forced to take a direct object pronoun. This violates its subcategorization frame. Consequently, the sentence becomes ill-formed. Lastly, there is a problem with the subcategorization frame of the verb <to say> in (64). This verb is inherently intransitive. Therefore, it cannot be used transitively as is the case in this sentence. Proficiency with the subcategorization frame of verbs provides a principled way of accounting for ungrammatical sentences. It can also help students improve their writing skills.

---

[13] Some transitive verbs such as <to eat> can appear with or without any complement. In the sentence <we ate a hamburger>, <hamburger> is the direct object. However, in the sentence <we ate>, there is no direct object. When this happens, grammarians say that the verb <to eat> is used absolutely.

8.8 Summary of Phrase Structure Rules

The subcategorization frames and the types of complements of verbs discussed in this chapter can be summarized by phrase structure rules as follows:

No.	Phrase Structure Rules	Description
1.	VP → V	Intransitive verb used alone
2.	VP → V PP	Intransitive verb with prepositional phrase
3.	VP → V NP	Transitive verb
4.	VP → V NP NP	Transitive verb with objective complement
5.	VP → V NP AdjP	Transitive verb with adjectival complement
6.	VP → V NP to/for NP	Ditransitive verb
7.	VP → V AdjP	Linking verb
8.	VP → V NP	Linking verb with a subject complement
9.	VP → V AdvP	Linking verb with an adverbial complement
10.	VP → V CP[14]	This occurs in subordinate clauses

Table 14 *Summary of Verb Subcategorization Frames*

8.9 Conclusion

The various tests proposed in this chapter can help distinguish verbs from the other parts of speech. Being able to do so is an important step in raising one's grammatical awareness. The subcategorization frames and the selectional restrictions of the four basic verb groups provide the necessary tools to classify the different arguments of the verb according to their grammatical function. This, too, is an important step in explaining sentence meaning. Furthermore, understanding selectional restrictions can help teachers explain in a principled way why some of the sentences produced by their students sound "funny." Clark (2003:121) alleges that native speakers intuitively choose the correct pattern for each verb. She states that "children who learn English as a native language use all the VP patterns correctly by the time they enter school." This assessment is probably true for grammatical competence in using BICS, i.e., conversational English. Our experience with the written composition of American college students does not lend support to Clark's claims when it comes to CALP (English used in academic circles). Mistakes related to the types of complements selected by verbs such as <loan> and <borrow>, <scratch> and <itch>, <lie> and <lay> show that the subcategorization frames of certain verbs are still troublesome, even for native speakers. However, Clark is right in encouraging ESL/EFL teachers to focus on the subcategorization and selectional restriction of verbs for English language learners. Interlingual errors in ESL and EFL speech can often be attributed to the fact that the speaker's first and second languages may subcategorize some verbs differently.

---

[14] This phrase structure rule will be examined in Chapter 13.

Key Terms to Know

These are the key terms that you should be able to use and define after reading this chapter:

1. argument: 8.5

2. bare infinitive: 8.2.2

3. complement: 8.4.1, 8.5, 8.5.2, 8.5.3, 8.5.4, 8.5.5, 8.5.6, 8.5.7, 8.5.8, 8.7, 8.8, 8.9

4. conjugation: 8.2.1

5. direct object: 8.4.1, 8.5, 8.5.2, 8.5.4, 8.5.6, 8.5.7, 8.5.8, 8.7

6. ditransitive verb: 8.5, 8.5.4, 8.8

7. finite verb: 8.2, 8.2.1

8. gerund: 8.5.8, 8.6

9. grammatical function/grammatical relation: 8.5, 8.6.1, 8.9

10. head: 8.4, 8.5, 8.6.2

11. indirect object: 8.5, 8.5.2, 8.5.4

12. infinitive: 8.2, 8.2.2, 8.6

13. intransitive verb: 8.5.1, 8.5.8, 8.7

14. linking/stative verb: 8.5, 8.5.5, 8.8

15. main verb: 8.2, 8.2.1, 8.2.2, 8.5.6, 8.6.1

16. non-finite verb: 8.2.2, 8.6.1, 8.6.2

17. objective complement: 8.5.6

18. parsing: 8.2.1

19. past participle: 8.2.2

20. phrasal complement: 8.5

21. present participle: 8.2.2, 8.6, 8.6.1

22. selectional restriction/criteria: 8.4, 8.4.1, 8.7, 8.9

23. subcategorization frame: 8.4.1, 8.5.1, 8.5.4, 8.5.5, 8.5.7, 8.7, 8.8, 8.9

24. subcategorization: 8.4, 8.4.1, 8.5.1, 8.5.4, 8.5.5, 8.5.7, 8.5.8, 8.7, 8.8, 8.9

25. subject: 8.0, 8.4.1, 8.5, 8.5.5, 8.6.1, 8.8

26. transitive verb: 8.5.2, 8.5.3, 8.5.5.8, 8.8.7

27. transitive (absolutely): 8.5.2

28. transitive (obligatory): 8.5.2

29. transitive (optional): 8.5.2

30. valence: 8.5

EXERCISE 1—SENTENCE DIAGRAMMING

Diagram the following sentences:

1. Laurie is outside in the garden.

2. Melissa bought Dan a computer.

3. Business owners give kickbacks to officials.

4. The banker declared the check void.

5. The farmer grows vegetables in her garden.

6. The farmer grows tired of locusts in her flowers.

7. Beth could have been an occupational therapist.

EXERCISE 2—MAIN VERB IDENTIFICATION

Classify the highlighted verbs according to the model below.

The Gettysburg Address
by Abraham Lincoln

"Fourscore and seven years ago our fathers **brought forth** (1) on this continent a new nation, conceived in liberty and dedicated to the proposition that all men are created equal. Now we are engaged in a great civil war, **testing** (2) whether that nation or any nation so conceived and so dedicated can long **endure** (3). We are met on a great battlefield of that war. We **have** (4) come to dedicate a portion of that field as a final resting-place for those who here gave their lives that that nation **might** (5) **live** (6). It is altogether fitting and proper that we should do this.

But in a larger sense, we **cannot** (7) dedicate, we cannot consecrate, we cannot **hallow** (8) this ground. The brave men, living and dead who **struggled** (9) here have consecrated it far above our poor power to **add** (10) or detract. The world **will** (11) little note nor long **remember** (12) what we **say** (13) here, but it can never forget what they did here. It is for us the living rather to be dedicated here to the unfinished work which they who fought here have thus far so nobly advanced. It is rather for us to be here **dedicated** (14) to the great task **remaining** (15) before us—that from these honored dead we **take** (16) increased devotion to that cause for which they **gave** (17) the last full measure of devotion—that we here highly **resolve** (18) that these dead shall not have **died** (19) in vain, that this nation under God **shall** (20) have a new birth of freedom, and that government of the people, by the people, for the people shall not perish from the earth."

No.	Verbs	Verb Type	Non-Finite Verbs	Finite Verbs
1.	brought forth	Intransitive: _____ Transitive: **X** Ditransitive: _____ Linking: _____	Bare Inf.: _____ To-Inf.: _____ Pres. Part: _____ Past Part: _____	Person: **3rd** Number: **Pl** Tense: **Past**
2.	testing	Intransitive: _____ Transitive: _____ Ditransitive: _____ Linking: _____	Bare Inf.: _____ To-Inf.: _____ Pres. Part: _____ Past Part: _____	Person:_____ Number: _____ Tense: _____
3.	endure	Intransitive: _____ Transitive: _____ Ditransitive: _____ Linking: _____	Bare Inf.: _____ To-Inf.: _____ Pres. Part: _____ Past Part: _____	Person:_____ Number: _____ Tense: _____
4.	have	Intransitive: _____ Transitive: _____ Ditransitive: _____ Linking: _____	Bare Inf.: _____ To-Inf.: _____ Pres. Part: _____ Past Part: _____	Person:_____ Number: _____ Tense: _____

No.	Verbs	Verb Type	Non-Finite Verbs	Finite Verbs
5.	might	Intransitive: ____ Transitive: ____ Ditransitive: ____ Linking: ____	Bare Inf.: ____ To-Inf.: ____ Pres. Part: ____ Past Part: ____	Person:_____ Number: _____ Tense: _____
6.	live	Intransitive: ____ Transitive: ____ Ditransitive: ____ Linking: ____	Bare Inf.: ____ To-Inf.: ____ Pres. Part: ____ Past Part: ____	Person:_____ Number: _____ Tense: _____
7.	cannot	Intransitive: ____ Transitive: ____ Ditransitive: ____ Linking: ____	Bare Inf.: ____ To-Inf.: ____ Pres. Part: ____ Past Part: ____	Person:_____ Number: _____ Tense: _____
8.	hallow	Intransitive: ____ Transitive: ____ Ditransitive: ____ Linking: ____	Bare Inf.: ____ To-Inf.: ____ Pres. Part: ____ Past Part: ____	Person:_____ Number: _____ Tense: _____
9.	struggle	Intransitive: ____ Transitive: ____ Ditransitive: ____ Linking: ____	Bare Inf.: ____ To-Inf.: ____ Pres. Part: ____ Past Part: ____	Person:_____ Number: _____ Tense: _____
10	to add	Intransitive: ____ Transitive: ____ Ditransitive: ____ Linking: ____	Bare Inf.: ____ To-Inf.: ____ Pres. Part: ____ Past Part: ____	Person:_____ Number: _____ Tense: _____
11.	will	Intransitive: ____ Transitive: ____ Ditransitive: ____ Linking: ____	Bare Inf.: ____ To-Inf.: ____ Pres. Part: ____ Past Part: ____	Person:_____ Number: _____ Tense: _____
12.	remember	Intransitive: ____ Transitive: ____ Ditransitive: ____ Linking: ____	Bare Inf.: ____ To-Inf.: ____ Pres. Part: ____ Past Part: ____	Person:_____ Number: _____ Tense: _____
13	say	Intransitive: ____ Transitive: ____ Ditransitive: ____ Linking: ____	Bare Inf.: ____ To-Inf.: ____ Pres. Part: ____ Past Part: ____	Person:_____ Number: _____ Tense: _____
14.	dedicated	Intransitive: ____ Transitive: ____ Ditransitive: ____ Linking: ____	Bare Inf.: ____ To-Inf.: ____ Pres. Part: ____ Past Part: ____	Person:_____ Number: _____ Tense: _____
15.	remaining	Intransitive: ____ Transitive: ____ Ditransitive: ____ Linking: ____	Bare Inf.: ____ To-Inf.: ____ Pres. Part: ____ Past Part: ____	Person:_____ Number: _____ Tense: _____
16.	take	Intransitive: ____ Transitive: ____ Ditransitive: ____ Linking: ____	Bare Inf.: ____ To-Inf.: ____ Pres. Part: ____ Past Part: ____	Person:_____ Number: _____ Tense: _____

No.	Verbs	Verb Type	Non-Finite Verbs	Finite Verbs
17.	gave	Intransitive: _____ Transitive: _____ Ditransitive: _____ Linking: _____	Bare Inf.: _____ To-Inf.: _____ Pres. Part: _____ Past Part: _____	Person:_____ Number: _____ Tense: _____
18.	resolve	Intransitive: _____ Transitive: _____ Ditransitive: _____ Linking: _____	Bare Inf.: _____ To-Inf.: _____ Pres. Part: _____ Past Part: _____	Person:_____ Number: _____ Tense: _____
19.	died	Intransitive: _____ Transitive: _____ Ditransitive: _____ Linking: _____	Bare Inf.: _____ To-Inf.: _____ Pres. Part: _____ Past Part: _____	Person:_____ Number: _____ Tense: _____
20.	shall	Intransitive: _____ Transitive: _____ Ditransitive: _____ Linking: _____	Bare Inf.: _____ To-Inf.: _____ Pres. Part: _____ Past Part: _____	Person:_____ Number: _____ Tense: _____

EXERCISE 3—UNDERSTANDING GRAMMATICAL TERMINOLOGY

1. Make a sentence with an intransitive verb. Underline the intransitive verb.

2. Make a sentence with a transitive verb. Underline the transitive verb.

3. Make a sentence with a ditransitive/dative verb. Underline the ditransitive/dative verb.

4. Make a sentence with a stative/linking verb. Underline the stative/linking verb.

5. Make a sentence with a direct object complement. Underline the direct object complement.

6. Make a sentence with an indirect object complement. Underline the indirect object complement.

7. Make a sentence in which there is a present participle verb. Underline the present participle verb.

8. Make a sentence in which there is an irregular past participle verb. Underline the irregular past participle verb.

9. Make a sentence which is subcategorized with an adverbial complement. Underline the adverbial complement.

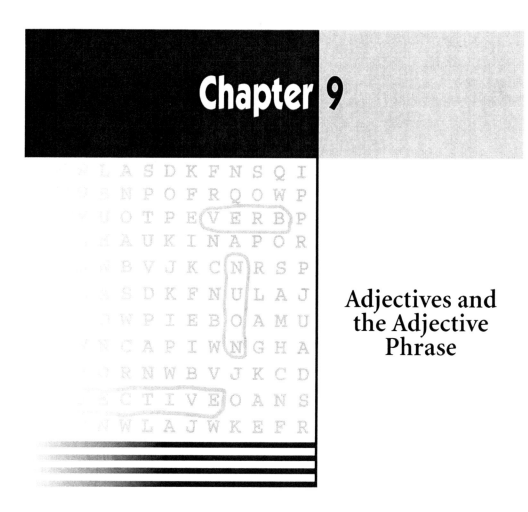

Chapter 9

Adjectives and the Adjective Phrase

9.0 INTRODUCTION

The Greek word for **"adjective"** is *"onoma epitheton."* Braun (1947:1) translates it as "that which is thrown near the noun." It can also be translated as "the one lying near the noun." This Greek phrase captures the essential function of adjectives, that is, describing, modifying, or qualifying nouns and pronouns. In other words, where there is an adjective, there is necessarily a noun or a pronoun. Or conversely, where there is no noun or pronoun, there is no adjective. This is an important syntactic constraint that teachers should know and communicate to their students. This chapter provides teachers with the necessary tools to identify, classify, and distinguish adjectives from other lexical categories.

9.1 Adjectives in World Languages

Cross-linguistic studies have revealed that the part of speech called <adjective> is found in all languages. Adjectives function the same everywhere but their form, their number, and their frequency vary greatly from language to language. Some languages have only a few dozen words that can be categorized as adjectives. Others, on the other hand, have thousands of adjectives in their lexicon. English is one of those languages where there is an overabundance of adjectives. We will see in this chapter that English has limitless possibilities of creating adjectives or turning other parts of speech into adjectives. Consequently, teachers and other language professionals who use English should familiarize themselves with the semantic, morphological, syntactic, and functional behavior of this important part of speech.

9.1.1 The Semantic Classification of Adjectives

In many grammar textbooks one often finds that adjectives are grouped according to their semantic categories. The number of these categories varies from author to author. However, irrespective of the theoretical approach used, there seems to be a consensus about the following semantic classifications:

No.	Semantic Classes	Illustrative Examples
1.	Nationality/origin	Ivorian, Australian, American
2.	Quality/opinion	good, bad, nice, charming
3.	Material	wooden, cotton
4.	Age	old, young, childish
5.	Size/shape	small, big, large, long
6.	Color	blue, yellow, orange, green

Table 1 *Semantic Classification of Adjectives*

We will see later in 9.5.8 that this semantic classification has an impact on what may be called the Adjectival Order Hierarchy.

9.1.2 Restrictive Meaning of Adjectives

Adjectives are like the spices that one adds to a sauce. Without adjectives, most sentences would have a general and non-specific meaning. With adjectives, however, all kinds of additional information are provided about nouns and pronouns. An interesting thing happens with the addition of adjectives to phrases or sentences. The more information the adjective provides about the noun or pronoun, the more limited the scope of that noun or pronoun. Without adjectives, the scope of the noun or pronoun is broad and general. With adjectives, the scope is more limited. Let us illustrate this with the following two sentences:

(1)   *A student came to see me in the office.*

(2)   *A **brilliant** student came to see me in the office.*

The first sentence is more general. It could be any student: mediocre, average, smart, lazy, hardworking, careless, etc. However, the use of the adjective <brilliant> in (2) restricts the pool of possible students who came to see me in the office. So, in this sense, all adjectives have a restrictive function. The more adjectives that are used to describe the same noun or pronoun, the more restrictive the scope of the noun or pronoun, as seen in (3) below:

(3)   *A **brilliant** and **good-looking** student came to see me in the office.*

The addition of <good-looking> restricts the scope of the noun <student> even further. Not any brilliant student came to see me, but a student who is both brilliant and good-looking. This restrictive meaning of adjectives can be represented by the following diagrams:

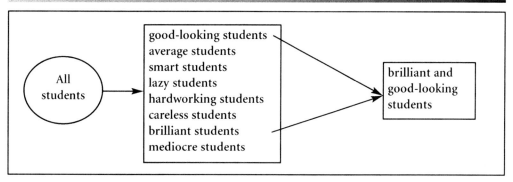

Table 2 *Illustration of the Restrictive Meaning of Adjectives*

9.1.3 Shades of Meaning of Adjectives

Many adjectives seem to encode two important semantic notions: **gradability** and **polarity.** Fromkin et al. (2003: 182) define gradable adjectives as follows: "The meaning of adjectives in gradable pairs is related to the object they modify. The words themselves do not provide an absolute scale. . . . with gradable pairs, the negative of one word is not synonymous with the other." Gradable adjectives can be placed on a continuum, as illustrated by the adjectives <miniscule> and <gargantuan>. Between the two, one may find other adjectives such as <small>, <medium>, <large>, <extra large>, <huge>, and <humongous>. We will see in 9.3 that gradation is often expressed morphologically in English. Polarity is similar to gradation, with the only exception that adjectives in this classification have a clear positive and negative contrast. There is no in-between gradation. Adjectives in this group include such pairs as <dead> vs. <alive> and <awake> vs. <asleep>. The distinction between gradable and polarity adjectives allows us to propose a semantic test for identifying adjectives:

Gradability/Polarity Test

> Any lexical item that lends itself to gradability/polarity **and** modifies a noun is most likely an adjective.

This rule of thumb works well for many types of commonly used adjectives. However, it fails to correctly identify other adjectives. Celce-Murcia and Larsen-Freeman (1999:392) note that it does not work for reference or nationality adjectives such as <former> and <American>.[1] In spite of these limitations, gradability and polarity are useful preliminary diagnostic tools that one can rely on to identify most adjectives. More refined tests will be provided as we proceed.

9.2 Derivational Morphology and English Adjectives

Barry (2002:105) makes the following observation with regard to the morphology of adjectives: "Adjectives are more easily identified by their function than by their form." This observation is pertinent because there are numerous adjectives that do not bear any morphological marking that one can use to identify them correctly. She cites the case of words such as <tall>, <short>, <certain>, <complicated>, <mere>, and <amazing>. This observation is generally valid. However, it is also true that English has a number of

---

[1] Except in ideologically loaded speech, we do not say that one U.S. citizen is more American than another.

derivational affixes that convert other parts of speech into adjectives. Adjectives created by such processes bear morphological characteristics that can be used to identify them easily. The next five sections will discuss these processes and indices.

9.2.1 Noun-to-Adjective Derivation

The derivational suffixes that change nouns to adjectives are by far the most numerous in English. The main ones are listed in the table below. The presence of any of these suffixes on a lexical item is a strong clue that the item in question is an adjective.

No.	Derivational Suffixes	Original Noun	Derived Adjectival Stem
1.	<-al>	economy	economical
2.	<-ate>	affection	affectionate
3.	<-ar>	consul	consular
4.	<-(e)ous>	danger	dangerous
5.	<-ary>	discipline	disciplinary
6.	<-ic>	alcohol	alcoholic
7.	<-ful>	fruit	fruitful
8.	<-ist>	legal	legalist
9.	<-less>	hope	hopeless
10.	<-ly>	friend	friendly
11.	<-ish>	boy	boyish
12.	<-(i)an>	America	American
13.	<-ine>	crystal	crystaline
14.	<-ive>	offense	offensive
15.	<-y>	salt	salty

Table 3 *Noun-to-Adjective Derivation*

9.2.2 Verb-to-Adjective Derivation

There are several suffixes that convert some verbs into adjectives. It is almost impossible to predict which verbs can be turned into adjectives and which cannot. Nevertheless, the presence of these suffixes on verbal stems is an indication that the word in question is probably an adjective.

No.	Derivational Suffixes	Original Verb	Derived Adjectival Stem
1.	<-al>	continue	continual
2.	<-ive>	create	creative
3.	<-ory>	migrate	migratory
4.	<-ent>	exist	existent
5.	<-ant>	resist	resistant
6.	<-ous>	prosper	prosperous
7.	<-able>/ <-ible>	read	readable
8.	<-y>	shake	shaky
9.	<-some>	win	winsome

Table 4 *Verb-to-Adjective Derivation*

9.2.3 Adjective-to-Adjective Derivation

English has a small set of suffixes that are added to adjectives to create other adjectives. The most common suffixes in adjective-to-adjective derivation are the following:

No.	Derivational Suffixes	Adjectives	Derived Adjectives
1.	<-ly>[2]	dead →	deadly
2.	<-ish>	red →	reddish
3.	<-some>	tired →	tiresome

Table 5 *Adjective-to-Adjective Derivation*

The suffixes <-ish> and <-some> are added to numbers in informal speech to convey an idea of approximation. This informal register is probably not appropriate for academic writing.

9.2.4 Adjectives Derived from Bound Roots

Some adjectives are attached to bound roots, that is, roots that cannot stand alone. It is not easy to reconstruct the original root by relying on contemporary evidence alone. In some cases, the root has been borrowed from another language. For instance, the adjective <eligible> comes from French root <élire> which means to <to elect>. Stageberg and Oaks (2000:172) list some of the most common bound roots to which derivational suffixes are added:

No.	Derivational Suffixes	Bound Root	Derived Adjectives
1.	<-ive>	<pens-> →	pensive
2.	<-ible>	<cred-> →	credible
3.	<-al>	<loc-> →	local
4.	<-id>	<splend-> →	splendid
5.	<-ile>	<frag-> →	fragile
6.	<-ain>	<cert-> →	certain
7.	<-ic>	<domest-> →	domestic
8.	<-ous>	<curi-> →	curious
9.	<-fic>	<terri-> →	terrific

Table 6 *Adjectives Created from Bound Roots*

9.2.5 Adjective-to-Adjective Derivation through Prefixation

All the derivational affixes that we have seen so far are suffixes. However, English has half a dozen derivational prefixes that convert existing adjectives into other adjectives. These prefixes often express gradability and polarity, as seen in the table below:

---

[2] Some adjectives take the suffix <-ly>. We will see in Chapter 10 that the suffix <-ly> turns some adjectives into adverbs. However, the words <friendly>, <bubbly>, <lively>, and <deadly> are adjectives.

No.	Derivational Prefixes	Adjective	Derived Adjectives
1.	<un->	happy →	unhappy
2.	<in->[3]	tolerant →	intolerant
3.	<a-, ab->	normal →	abnormal
4.	<non->	native →	nonnative

Table 7 *Derivational Prefixes*

When all these derivational suffixes and prefixes are put together, we see that English has a sizable number of adjective-making affixes. This underscores the importance of adjectives in English.

9.3 *Inflectional Morphology*

One important morphological characteristic of adjectives is their ability to encode gradation through inflectional morphology.[4] Grammarians recognize three degrees of gradation with adjectives: **the positive, the comparative,** and **the superlative.** The positive is the base form of the adjective. The comparative is subdivided into three levels: **the comparison of inferiority, the comparison of equality,** and **the comparison of superiority.**

9.3.1 The Morphemes of the Comparative

Discontinuous morphemes are frequently found in connection with comparative adjectives. The comparison of inferiority is characterized by the discontinuous morpheme <less ... than>. The adjective is sandwiched between the free morphemes <less> and <than> as shown in the sentence below:

(4)   *Corinne is **less** energetic **than** usual.*

If comparative and superlative adjectives are taken as discontinuous morphemes, then the best way to diagram a sentence such as (4) is as follows:

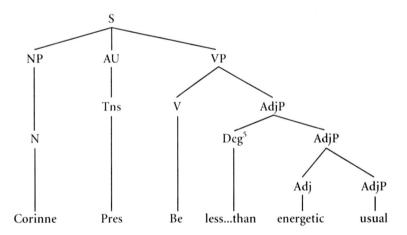

---

[3] Following Kaplan (1995:100) I contend that the prefixes <im-> (impossible), <il-> (illogical), and <ir-> (irresponsible) are allomorphs of the same basic morpheme <in->.

[4] Adverbs also use the same inflectional morphemes to express gradation. However, we will not deal with adverbs in this chapter.

[5] Deg. stands for "degree." More will be said about degree words in 9.5.1.

According to this view, to obtain sentence (4), the first adjective is moved and inserted between the elements that constitute the discontinuous morpheme. Thus, in this case, the adjective <energetic> is moved and inserted between <less> and <than>. The same is true for the comparison of equality which is formed by using the discontinuous morpheme <as ... as> as illustrated by sentence (5):

(5) *For some students, linguistics is* **as** *challenging* **as** *mathematics.*

There are two ways of forming the comparison of superiority. The first is through the affixation of the inflectional morpheme <-er> to the adjective. Generally, if the adjective is **monosyllabic** or **disyllabic,** the suffix <-er> is used. If the two elements being compared are explicitly mentioned, then the free morpheme <than> immediately follows the adjective that has been inflected with the suffix <-er>, as in the sentence below:

(6) *The Mississippi River is longer* **than** *the Arkansas River.*

The second way of forming comparisons of superiority in English consists in using the discontinuous morpheme <more ... than>. If the entities being compared are more than two syllables long, then <more ... than> becomes necessary:

(7) *The Mississippi River is* **more** *navigable* **than** *the Arkansas River.*

9.3.2 The Morphemes of the Superlative

The superlative expresses the highest degree of gradation. Semantically, it is used when at least three items are being compared and one of the three stands out as having more or less of the attributes that has been singled out for comparison. Morphologically, the superlative is identifiable by the suffix <-est> and by optional elements such as <the> and <of> that may occur with it. The suffix <-est> is used with adjectives that are less than three syllables long, as illustrated by sentence (8):

(8) *Gates is* **the tallest** *girl in her fifth grade class.*

If the adjective has three or more syllables, then the free morpheme <most> is used to express the superlative, as seen in (9):

(9) *Her* **most humiliating** *experience was being on academic probation her first year of college.*

9.3.3 Regular, Irregular, and Suppletive Comparative Adjectives

The comparative forms of regular, irregular, and suppletive adjectives are presented in Tables 8 and 9.

No.	Uninflected Form	Comparison of Inferiority	Comparison of Equality	Comparison of Superiority	Superlative
1.	One- or two-syllable Adjectives	less ... than	as ..... as	-er ... than	(the) ... -est
2.	Three-syllable Adjectives	less ... than	as ..... as	more ... than	(the) most

Table 8 *Regular Gradation*

As one might expect, there are exceptions to the syllable-conditioned rule discussed previously. Not all one-syllable or two-syllable adjectives can take the inflectional suffixes <-er> and <-est>. The following sentences are ill-formed even though the adjectives meet the syllable criterion:

(10) *This twenty dollar bill is **faker** than this one.

(11) *My son thinks that BMX racing is **funner**[6] than playing tennis.

Curme (1931:500) lists the following adjectives as common exceptions to the two-syllable rule: <tender, bitter, sober, able, eager, famous, comic, docile, fertile, active, passive, content>. Moreover, a number of high frequency adjectives have irregular or suppletive comparative forms, as shown here:

No.	Uninflected Form	Comparison of Inferiority	Comparison of Equality	Comparison of Superiority	Superlative
1.	good, well	–	as good as	better	(the) best (of)
2.	bad, ill, evil	worse	as bad as	–	(the) worst (of)
3.	far	–	as far as	farther/further	(the) farthest/furthest (of)
4.	old	–	as old as	older/elder	(the) oldest/eldest (of)
5.	up	–	–	upper	uppermost/upmost
6.	much	–	as much as	more than	(the)[7] most
7.	many	–	as many as	more than	(the) most
8.	few	fewer than	as few as	–	(the) fewest
9.	little	less than	as little as	–	(the) least

Table 9 *Irregular Gradation*

The morphology clues discussed in the previous sections help identify adjectives. These clues can be translated into a test which I formulate as follows:

Morphological Gradability Test

Any lexical item that lends itself to three levels of gradability, i.e., positive, comparative, and superlative, **and** modifies a noun is an adjective.

The phrase "and modifies a noun" is very important in this formulation because without it there is no way to distinguish adjectives formally from some adverbs.

9.3.4 Pedagogical Implications

The inflectional morphology of adjectives is not usually problematic for native and proficient speakers. However, Calderonello et al. (2003:151–2, 284–6) report that even native

---

[6] My nine-year-old daughter and her friends of the same age use <funner> and <funnest> all the time.

[7] Superlative adjectives that have the structure "the most + adjective + of" are called "absolute superlatives."

speakers are confused sometimes. They are not sure when to use the syllable-based rule to inflect comparative adjectives. As a result, the following ill-formed structures appear in native students' compositions: <*more prettier>, <*more great>, or <*magnificentest>.[8]

9.4 Terminological Differences between Traditional and Descriptive Grammars

There is a terminological consensus about the morphology and the semantics of adjectives. However, when it comes to the syntax of adjectives, traditional grammarians and descriptive grammarians disagree strongly. The former give the label of "adjective" generously to many lexical items whereas the latter do so very sparingly. There is a good explanation for this state of affairs. Contemporary linguists try as much as possible not to take semantic realities into account when describing syntactic behavior. Traditional grammarians, on the other hand, often mix semantic and syntactic behaviors indiscriminately. Unfortunately for students, many textbook writers do not make this difference sufficiently clear. Consequently, students finish grammar classes without understanding what the different labels entail. The following sections discuss the main terminological differences. In each case where important disagreements exist, brief comments are made to explain the rationale behind the choice of different terms to label the same syntactic reality.

9.4.1 Demonstrative Adjectives vs. Determiners

According to Cumes (1931:508), **demonstrative adjectives** "point out persons or things either by gesture, or by the situation, or by an accompanying description." English has two types of demonstrative adjectives, as shown in the table below:

No.	Demonstrative Adjectives	Singular	Plural
1.	Proximity	this + NP	these + NP
2.	Distance	that + NP	those + NP

Table 10 *Table of Demonstrative Adjectives*

These lexical items are known in traditional grammar as adjectives because they modify nouns by indicating their proximity or distance in relation to the speaker. However, in descriptive linguistics, they are referred to as **determiners** because they have the same syntactic distribution as the determiners <a> and <the>.

9.4.2 Possessive Adjectives vs. Determiners

English has some function words whose sole purpose is to indicate a relationship of possession between the possessor and the thing possessed. Traditional grammar labels these words <possessive adjectives> if they are used in conjunction with a noun, as seen in the table following:

---

[8] There is a change in progress. As a result, there is confusion with some forms. For instance, though <commonest> is well-formed, one hardly encounters <commoner>. Instead <more common> is used for more frequently. Similarly <sadder> is well-formed but less used than <more sad>. However, <saddest> is more frequently heard than <most sad>.

No.	Possessive Adjectives	Singular	Plural
1.	First person	my + NP	our + NP
2.	Second person	your + NP	your + NP
3.	Third person	his/her/its + NP	their + NP

Table 11 *Table of Possessive Adjectives*

Many students confuse possessive adjectives with possessive pronouns. However, the two are morphologically and syntactically different. Possessive pronouns have their own specific endings. Moreover, they are never followed by NPs. For a word to qualify as a possessive adjective in English, it must necessarily be followed by an NP as in the following structure:

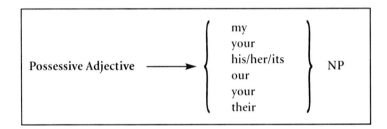

If the NP is missing, then the preceding closed class words are not adjectives because by definition one cannot have an adjective without a noun. Descriptive grammarians prefer the term <determiner> because "possessive adjectives" have the same distribution as other determiners. So, in sentences such as <this is his book> and <the book is his>, the <his> in the phrase <his book> is a possessive adjective whereas the <his> in the second sentence is a possessive pronoun. We will deal with possessive pronouns in Chapter 13.

9.4.3 Interrogative Adjectives vs. Determiners

For traditional grammarians, any lexical item that helps to ask a question about the head noun is an <**interrogative adjective**>. English has only two such adjectives:

No.	Interrogative Adjectives
1.	which + NP
2.	what + NP

Table 12 *Table of Interrogative Adjectives*

Descriptive linguists, however, use the label <determiner> for the same reasons discussed in the two previous sections.

9.4.4 Indefinite Adjectives vs. Quantifiers

Indefinite adjectives are words that express an idea of quantity. However, the exact amount involved is not known. When such quantity words precede or follow a noun, traditional grammarians label them <**indefinite adjectives**>. The terminology used by descriptive linguists varies. Some lump indefinite adjectives together with determiners. However, others use the label <quantifier> to refer to such words as discussed in 6.5 and 6.5.1.

No.	Indefinite Adjectives
1.	any
2.	some
3.	both
4.	neither
5.	enough
6.	each
7.	every
8.	few
9.	a lot of
10.	plenty of

Table 13 *Table of Indefinite Adjectives*

9.4.5 Cardinal and Ordinal Adjectives vs. Numerals

So long as cardinal numbers, ordinal numbers, multipliers, fractions, and percentages modify nouns, traditional grammarians call them <adjectives>. Some descriptive linguists, on the other hand, use the term <Numeral>, abbreviated as (Num), to refer to all these number words. However, as noted in 6.5, there is no terminological consensus among linguists. Thus, in the sentence below, <two> is known as an adjective in traditional grammar books but in contemporary linguistics, it is referred to as a numeral or as a quantifier, <Q>. I use the term <numeral> when exact quantities are known, and <quantifier> when the exact amount is not known.

(12) **Two** *students are on academic probation.*

9.4.6 Adjectives vs. Premodifiers

From the perspective of traditional grammar, the NP in (13) would be diagrammed as follows:

(13) **All our first three presidents** *graduated from Harvard.*

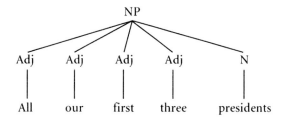

However, labeling all the terms "adjectives" is excessive and obscures important grammatical insights. Instead, descriptive linguists would diagram the same NP as follows:

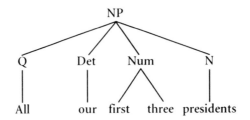

This way of labeling the constituents of the NP is more revealing than the previous one because it uses relevant names to specify the constituents of the NP. Even more revealing of the internal structure of this NP is the way X-bar theory diagrams such phrases. As alluded to in 6.5, this theory of syntax shows better the internal organization of words within phrases. Thus, <all our first three presidents> can be diagrammed as follows:

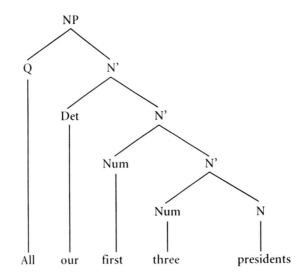

The intricate details of X-bar theory are irrelevant here. Suffice it to say that <N'> "n bar" is not necessarily a lexical category but could be an intermediate category that is halfway between the phrasal category and the lexical category. This intermediate category anchors grammatical information in the process of building phrases and sentences. The diagram above reveals clearly the hierarchy of modification of <presidents>. The quantifier <all> modifies all the words in lower branches, and so on and so forth. This insight is not obvious in the first two diagrams. However, as noted in 6.5, diagrams such as this, though very informative about the internal structure of phrases, are not our primary concern in this book. The main focus is the correct identification and labeling of words in phrases and sentences.

Contemporary linguistics still struggles to find a term that is general enough and revealing enough to capture the essence of what traditional grammarians lump together as "adjective." Some have recently proposed the "super-term" <premodifier>. Even though this seems like a good compromise, it has not been widely adopted. Pre-service teachers who are preparing for the praxis exam would be well advised to familiarize themselves with both sets of terminologies since it is not always clear what labels the test writers will use in the exam. Usually they tend to err on the side of caution by sticking to traditional grammar terms.

9.5 *The Distributional Patterns of Adjectives in English*

The syntax of English adjectives offers three distributional patterns: adjectives can occur **before** the head noun, **after** the head noun, or **inside** the VP after a small set of verbs. A number of other lexical items also occur in these same environments. In order to determine which ones can qualify as adjectives, linguists have developed a battery of tests. Let us now turn our attention to the syntactic tests.

9.5.1 The Syntactic Test for Adjectives

One reliable way of finding out whether a lexical item is an adjective or not is to submit it to the degree test. This test is reliable because it works irrespective of the position in which adjectives occur. The degree test can be formulated as follows:

Degree Test

Any lexical item that can be preceded or followed by a degree word and modifies a noun is an adjective.

Some have nicknamed this the <Very Test> because <very> is usually used for it. However, the words in Table 15 below can also be used. But <very> works best. The use of the Degree Test can be summarized as follows:

No.	Test	Main Verb	Noun[9]	Adjective	Adverb	Pronoun	Conjunction	Preposition
1.	Degree Word	–	–	+	+	–	–	–
2.	Noun	–	–	+	–	–	–	–
3.	Pro	–	–	+	–	–	–	–

Table 14 *Degree Test*

The degree test works for both adjectives and adverbs. A priori, it cannot help distinguish between adjectives and adverbs. However, in reality it can. Since adverbs never modify nouns, and since only adjectives can do so, if a degree word is used in conjunction with a noun, then the lexical item in question is an adjective. In sentences (14) and (15) following, we can say that <lucrative> is an adjective, not an adverb because of the word <job> which is a noun. Consequently, the Degree Test is reliable because it helps identify words that are adjectives.

Degree words belong to a closed class of words which not only express some idea of comparison, but also convey the idea of "**degree.**" Some authors refer to degree words as "**intensifiers**" or "**modifiers.**" The degree words that occur frequently with adjectives are the following:

---

[9] The part of speech category of <article> is not listed separately here because it is considered part of the noun phrase (NP).

No.	Degree Words
1.	very
2.	really
3.	so
4.	too
5.	quite
6.	somewhat
7.	much
8.	more
9.	most
10.	only
11.	fully
12.	completely
13.	at all
14.	sort of
15.	kind of
16.	rather
17.	somewhat
18.	extremely
19.	barely
20.	entirely
21.	scarcely
22.	simply
23.	enough
24.	a little (bit)
25.	especially

Table 15 *List of Main Degree Words*

The use of degree words in sentences can be illustrated as follows:

(14)   *Deanna landed a lucrative job.*

(15)   *Deanna landed a **very** lucrative job.*

(16)   *Deanna landed an **extremely** lucrative job.*

Sentences (15) and (16) are different from (14) because they both contain degree words that modify the adjective <lucrative>. The occurrence of degree words in sentences such as the ones above has led linguists to reformulate the phrase structure rule for NPs. Lobeck (2000:163) proposes the following rule:

$$\boxed{\begin{array}{l} \text{NP} \rightarrow \quad \text{(Det) (AdjP) N} \\ \text{AdjP} \rightarrow \text{DegP Adj} \end{array}}$$

The number of degree words that can modify an adjective is in theory unlimited.[10] But language users do not usually string together more than two or three degree words in the same sentence, as shown in (17):

(17)   *Deanna landed an **extremely very** lucrative job.*

This sentence can be diagrammed as follows:

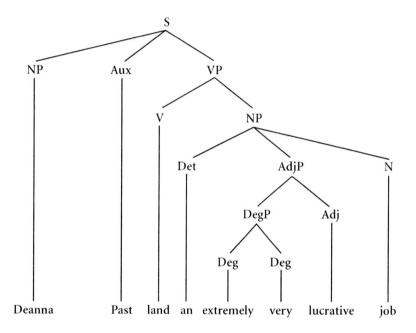

This tree diagram shows that (17) has two degree words. In informal speech, speakers use more degree words than in written texts. In conversational speech, it is not uncommon to hear speakers use degree words that are not categorized as such by linguists. The highlighted words in the sentences below are degree words:[11]

(18)   *Bethany was **dog** tired when she stumbled home last night.*

(19)   *Mary colored her hair **beet** red.*

(20)   *I'm hungry **like a bear.***

9.5.2 The Distribution of Adjectives in the NP

Let us now turn our attention to the position of adjectives in the NP. Grammarians have names for adjectives depending on whether they precede the head noun or follow it. If an adjective precedes the head noun, it is called an **attributive adjective** or **prenominal adjective.** If an adjective follows the head noun, it is known as a **postnominal adjective.**

---

[10] The phrase structure rule is written this way to show that there may be more than one degree word such as "very very very tired."

[11] Lobeck (2000:168) considers <sky> in the phrase <sky blue> to be a degree word. Words such as <navy> and <forest> in the phrases <navy blue> and <forest green> can also be considered degree words.

The preferred position for English adjectives is before the head noun. For this reason, the usual phrase structure rule of NPs is as follows:

$$NP \rightarrow (Det)\ (DegP)\ (AdjP^n)\quad Noun$$
$$DegP \rightarrow Deg^n$$

The superscript "n" indicates that theoretically, the number of degree words that can modify an adjective is unlimited. But in actuality, no more than two or three degree words are used in a sentence, as is the case of (17). Similarly, the number of adjectives that can modify a noun is unlimited but for pragmatic and physiological reasons, speakers limit the number of adjectives that can modify the same noun.

The word <former> in sentence (21) illustrates this position.

(21) *My wife and I met a **former** U.S. president.*

The word <former> belongs to a small set of English adjectives that cannot occur in any other position except before the head noun.

9.5.3 Postnominal Adjectives in the Noun Phrase

Just as <former>, there are a few adjectives that occur only after the head noun, as shown in Table 16 below:

No.	Postnominal Adjectives
1.	ago
2.	later
3.	alive
4.	afloat
5.	afraid
6.	alone
7.	awake
8.	asleep

Table 16 *Postnominal Adjectives*

This pattern can be illustrated by the sentence below:

(22) *I visited the Grand Canyon a decade **ago**.*

The verbs listed in Table 11 in section 8.5.6 tend to take post-nominal adjectival complements.

9.5.4 "Ambidextrous" Adjectives

The vast majority of adjectives in English can either precede or follow the head noun. The adjective <new> can occur before the head noun as in <a **new** house>. It can also follow the head noun as in <something **new**>. In some limited syntactic environments, especially if indefinite nouns such as <something>, <nothing>, or <anything> are used, adjectives prefer to occur after the head noun, as shown in sentences (23) and (24):

> (23) *Give me something **new** to think about.*

> (24) ** Give me **new** something to think about.*

Evidence such as this has compelled linguists to expand the phrase structure rule of NPs as follows:

$$\text{NP} \rightarrow \text{(Det) (Deg) (\textbf{Adj})}\quad \text{Noun}\quad \text{(\textbf{Adj})}$$

9.5.5 Distributional Test for Adjectives in the NP

The ability that adjectives have to occur immediately either before or after the head noun is a strong syntactic clue that can help identify them. For this reason, the following test can be proposed:

Distributional Test

Any open class lexical item that occurs immediately before the noun or immediately after the noun is likely to be an adjective.

The distributional test is summarized as follows:

Test	Main Verb	Noun[12]	Adjective	Adverb	Pro- noun	Con- junction	Pre- position
Occurs before head noun	−	−	+	+	−	−	−
Occurs after head noun	−	−	+	+	−	−	−
Modifies NPs	−	−	+	−	−	−	−
Modifies Pronouns	−	−	+	−	−	−	−

Table 17 *Distributional Test for Adjectives*

Kaplan (1995:119) observes that this distributional pattern is "a useful indication that the word in question is likely to be an adjective, and privilege of occurrence in both positions is even stronger evidence that the word is an adjective."

9.5.6 The Syntax of Adjectives in the VP

Adjectives that occur in a VP that is headed by a linking/stative/copular verb are also given the label of **predicative adjectives.** Adjectives that occur before or after the noun are normally called **attributive adjectives.** However, in English the label of "attributive adjective" is mostly given to adjectives that occur before the noun. Because of this terminological confusion, more and more linguists prefer the terms <**prenominal adjective**>

---

[12] The part of speech category of <article> is not listed separately here because it is considered part of the noun phrase (NP).

and <**postnominal adjective**>. Refer to the discussion in 8.5.5 and Table 8 of Chapter 8 to see the list of the most common linking verbs in English. The following subcategorization frame was given for these verbs:

$$
\text{Verb, +Linking,} \quad
\begin{Bmatrix}
[\text{— NP}] \\
[\text{— AdjP}] \\
[\text{— AdvP}] \\
[\text{— PP}]
\end{Bmatrix}
$$

This subcategorization frame shows that nouns, adjectives, adverbs, and prepositions can occur with these linking verbs. To find out conclusively if a lexical item that occurs with a linking verb is an adjective or not, Lobeck (2000:164) proposes the <Degree Test> discussed in 9.5.1. If the use of a degree word in conjunction with another word results in an ill-formed sentence, then we conclude that the word in question is not an adjective. However, if the result is a well-formed sentence, and the word modifies a noun, then we conclude that the word in question is an adjective. Let us illustrate how this test works with the words in the sentences below:

(25)   *Pam stayed calm in spite of her injury.*

(26)   *Pam stayed home because of her injury.*

(27)   *Pam stayed **very** calm in spite of her injury.*

(28)   **Pam stayed **very** home because of her injury.*

The word <calm> in (25) is an adjective because (27) does not fail the Degree Test. By the same token, we conclude that the word <home> in (26) is not an adjective because (28) fails the Degree Test. Bickford (1999:186) observes that a word such as <calm> in (25) and (27) is an adjectival complement because it expresses an abstract quality of the subject. This is probably the reason why in traditional grammar the adjective <calm> is known as a **subject complement.** It completes the subject <Pam>.

9.5.7 Subcategorization of Adjectives

When some adjectives are used, they require that a complement be added. Kolln and Funk (2006:271) argue that such adjectives are complements rather than modifiers because "they complete the idea expressed by the adjective, in much the same way that direct objects are complements of verbs." Following the pattern of verbs, LeTourneau (2001:226) labels such adjectives <**transitive adjectives**>. Here is a small sample of adjectives and their preferred complement types:

No.	Subcategorization Patterns of Adjectives
1.	afraid to/that
2.	fearful of/that
3.	aware that/of
4.	conscious of/that
5.	certain to/that
6.	fond of
7.	skeptical of/about
8.	cognizant of
9.	(un)prepared for/to
10.	anxious about/for
11.	eager to
12.	impatient to/with
13.	tired of
14.	interested in
15.	surprised by/that
16.	nervous about/over
17.	loyal/disloyal to
18.	ready for
19.	careful with/to
20.	concerned about/over
21.	angry at/with
22.	bored of/with
23.	good at/in/with
24.	different from
25.	tantamount to
26.	subject to
27.	bad at/in/with
28.	mad at/about

Table 18 *Adjectives and their Complements*

Let us illustrate how adjectives select their complements by examining the subcategorization frame of the word <resentful>:

$$\text{Resentful, Adj.} \quad \left(\quad - \left\{ \begin{array}{c} \varnothing \\ \text{PP} \\ \text{CP}^{13} \end{array} \right\} \quad \right)$$

The subcategorization frame above shows us that this adjective can take at least three types of complements, as illustrated by the following sentences:

(29) *Sarah was resentful.*

(30) *Sarah was resentful of Hagar.*

(31) *Sarah was resentful that Hagar was pregnant.*

Berk (1999:184) remarks, rather accurately, that "predicate adjectives are often followed by prepositional phrases that are clearly working with the adjective in a single grammatical structure. . . . The relationship of the prepositional phrase to the preceding adjective is semantically rather like the relationship of a direct object to the preceding verb."

9.5.8 Adjectival Word Order

In theory, because of the principle of linguistic recursion, languages can queue up an unlimited number of adjectives to modify nouns and pronouns. No matter how many adjectives one may wish to use, they must conform to a rigid order determined by the semantic category in which they fall (Calderonello et al. 2003:266–7 and Celce-Murcia and Larsen-Freeman 1999:394). The studies that these authors cite indicate that there is an **Adjectival Order Hierarchy** in English and other languages. The hierarchy constraint for English appears to be the following:

**Opinion > Condition > Size > Shape > Age >
Color > Material/Origin/Nationality + Head noun**

This hierarchy can be interpreted as follows: if adjectives having these semantic properties are to appear in a sentence, the order in which they will occur is specified by the hierarchy above. Calderonello et al. (2003:266) illustrate the hierarchy with the following sentence:

(32) *The beautiful but decrepit big round old brown Italian marble coffee table was sold at an auction.*

It is unlikely that a student will produce such a sentence. However, whether a student will produce a sentence such as (32) or not is beside the point. The point of this argument is that it is still good for teachers to know this hierarchy so as to explain to students why a sentence "sounds funny." Knowing that adjectives in a sequence conform to a **hierarchy constraint** can help teachers avoid impressionistic and subjective explanations.

---

[13] CP stands for Complementizer Phrase. These phrases will be discussed in Chapter 13.

9.5.9 Adjectives and Syntactic Ambiguity

Attributive adjectives are prone to structural/syntactic ambiguity, especially when a single adjective precedes two nouns in the same NP, as shown in (33) below:

(33) *High winds and waves pummeled the ship.*

This sentence is structurally ambiguous because it could be interpreted and diagrammed in at least two different ways. In one case, both <the winds> and <the waves> are high. This interpretation is represented by the first tree diagram:

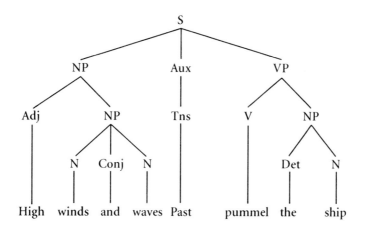

The second interpretation is that only the winds are high but we know nothing about the strength of the waves. The tree diagram below captures the second interpretation of the same sentence:

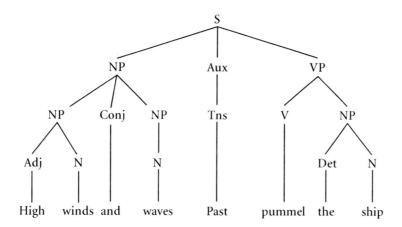

Notice, however, that there is no syntactic ambiguity when two or more adjectives modify a single NP as in the sentence below:

(34) *Rare and colorful monkeys live in Madagascar.*

In this sentence, both the adjectives <rare> and <colorful> modify <monkeys>. So, the tree diagram is as follows:

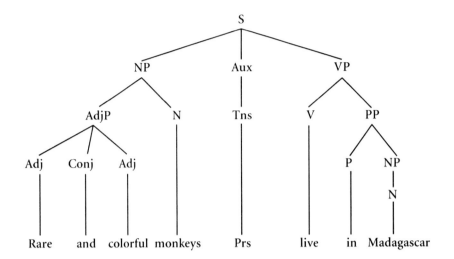

9.6 *Functional Analysis of Adjectives*

Many words that are not morphologically and syntactically categorized as adjectives behave as such because they modify nouns or pronouns. Traditional grammarians have coined the term <**adjectival**> to name these words. On the other hand, some "true" adjectives lose their "adjectiveness" and function as nouns. The sections below discuss these two cases.

9.6.1 Adjectives Used as Nouns

In traditional grammar, any lexical item that is not formally a noun but functions as one is called a **nominal** or a **substantive**. Adjectives fit this category because they are regularly used as collective nouns. Adjectives such as <poor>, <rich>, <uneducated>, <dead> are used as nouns to refer to a whole class of individuals, as in the sentence below:

(35) *The rich exploit the poor and the poor exploit the rich.*

Normally, <rich> and <poor> are adjectives. However, in this sentence, they are used as nouns. This new classification is based on the presence of the determiner <the>. Recall from 6.5 that any lexical item that is preceded by a determiner is a noun except in comparative constructions such as <*the* more I study syntax, *the* more I pay attention to how people speak>, or in superlative constructions such as <you are *the* best>. Thus, here <rich> and <poor> have become nouns.

9.6.2 Adjectives Used as Adverbs

Some English verbs have "split personalities." Sometimes they function as linking verbs and other times they do not. The verb <feel> is notorious for having this dual personality. When used as a linking verb, it requires an adjectival complement. However, if it is used as a transitive verb, it takes a direct object complement. Both usages are illustrated by (36) and (37) below:

(36) *Audrey feels **some pain** in her legs.*

(37) *Beth is not feeling **sad** today.*

In (36) <feel> is a transitive verb. In (37), on the other hand, it is a linking verb. We know this because <sad> is an adjectival complement whereas <some pain> is a direct object complement. Constructions such as these in which the same verb can have an adjectival complement and an object complement are misleading because people apply this dual function to other verbs which do not fit the pattern. Consequently, it is not uncommon to hear people say <drive careful> or <drive safe>. In such sentences, the verb <drive> is made into a linking verb even though it is not. Only linking verbs can take adjectival complements. Transitive verbs cannot. Therefore, the appropriateness of <drive safe> and <drive careful> in written compositions is questionable. The same confusion is responsible for the road signs in Saint Cloud, Minnesota, which read <Drive friendly>. In this case, the <-ly> ending misled the sign writer to believe that <friendly> is an adverb. However, it is an adjective. And since <drive> is not a linking verb, the sentence on the sign is ill-formed.

9.6.3 Nouns Used as Adjectives

Just as adjectives can be used as nouns or adverbs, nouns also frequently function as adjectives. The rule of thumb is the following: when two or more nouns appear in a row, the ones that appear before the head function as adjectives:

(38)   *The **English** language is full of surprises.*

(39)   *Kikuyo speaks **English** very well.*

In (38) <English> is an adjective that modifies <language>. However in (39), it is a noun. The first example underscores the fact that nouns can function as adjectives in English.

9.6.4 Infinitives Used as Adjectivals

To-infinitive verbs also can function as adjectivals, as seen in the sentence below:

(40)   *The college football team **to beat** is USC.*

In this sentence, the infinitive <to beat> functions as an adjective because it modifies the noun phrase <the college football team>. Notice also that in this sentence both <college> and <football> are adjectivals that modify the noun <team>.

9.6.5 Participles Used as Adjectivals

We saw in 8.6.2 that main verbs have present and past participial forms. Both of these forms can set aside their "verbness" and behave like adjectives in some sentences:

(41)   *Dan bought a used BMW.*

(42)   *Debi has a glowing smile.*

In (41) <used> is the past participial form of the verb <use>. However, in this sentence, it behaves like an adjective because it modifies <BMW>. Similarly, in (42) the present participle <glowing> functions as an adjective because it modifies the noun <smile>.

Verbs used as past participial adjectives sometimes have pronunciations that are different from their past tense forms. The word <blessed> is a case in point. If used in the past tense, it is pronounced [blɛst]. However, when used as a participial adjective, the correct pronunciation is [blɛsəd]. Other examples of participial forms in which the final <-ed> is pronounced [əd] or [ɪd] include <learned>, <crooked>, <jagged>, <wicked>,

<rugged>, <naked>, <legged>. Morphologically, participial adjectives of one or two syllables cannot take the comparative suffix <-er> nor the superlative suffix <-est>. They only take the free morphemes <more> or <most> as seen in the sentences below:

(43) *People seem tireder on Mondays than on Wednesdays.*

(44) *People seem more tired on Mondays than on Wednesdays.*

(45) *People seem most tired on Mondays.*

9.6.6 Dangling Adjectivals

If participles can be adjectives as noted in the preceding section, it means that they can also modify nouns. Recall that where there is an adjective or an adjectival form, there must necessarily be a noun or a pronoun. However, in some sentences, the noun that the participial adjective is supposed to modify is missing. When this happens, grammarians say that the participle is dangling, hence the term **<dangling participle>**. Dangling participles are common in oral speech but frowned upon in writing. It is not at all uncommon to hear the following sentence in weather forecasting:

(46) *Becoming increasingly cloudy, the temperature will rise to 60 in the afternoon with thunderstorms expected in the evening.*

In this sentence, <becoming> is a dangling participle because the noun that it is supposed to modify is missing. The word <temperature> in the second clause is not modified by <becoming>. We know this because the adjective <cloudy> cannot be subcategorized with the noun <temperature>. The reason why <becoming> is a dangling participle becomes more obvious when we spell out the deep structure form of (46). It is something like (47):

(47) *The weather Pres Be + ING become increasingly cloudy. The temperature Fut rise to 60 in the afternoon Pro Be + EN expect thunderstorms in the evening.*

Between the deep structure and the surface structure, a number of transformations take[14] place. First, the subject of the verb <become> in the first clause, i.e., <weather>, is deleted. The auxiliary <Be> that makes the progressive aspect possible is also deleted after Affix Hopping has taken place. As a result, in the surface structure sentence, the clause has neither subject nor auxiliary.

Infinitives can also dangle. Klammer et al (2004:392) illustrate the case of dangling infinitives with the following sentence:

(48) *Unable to start my car, my dog and I never arrived at the vet's office.*

In this instance, the deletion of the subject is not the reason for the dangling infinitive. There is a dangling infinitive because of the selectional criteria involved in <start my car>. The direct object complement <a car> makes it necessary for the verb <to start> to require a [+human] subject. However, in this sentence, the dog and the speaker seem to be the underlying subject of <to start my car>. Since dogs cannot drive, the sentence appears to be pragmatically ill-formed.

---

[14] We will overlook transformations that are irrelevant in this analysis.

9.6.7 Dangling Adjectivals in Written Compositions

Dangling participles and infinitives receive a lot of attention in composition textbooks. In spite of concerted efforts made by teachers to get rid of this phenomenon, it seems invincible. According to Calderonello et al. (2003:288) dangling adjectivals are found mostly in the writing of inexperienced writers because "[they] can lose track of the relationship between an adjective modifier and the noun it describes, particularly, when the modifier is a lengthy phrase or clause."

Dangling adjectivals can be accounted for in generative grammar as the violation of a syntactic constraint involving an illicit deletion of NP subjects in the adjectival clause. Klammer et al. (2004:392) state this constraint as follows:

> *The subject of a nonfinite verb can be deleted only if it is the same as the subject of the verb in the main clause.*[15]

Teachers can help their students avoid this error in their writing by having them identify the deleted NP subject in the adjectival clause. After that, students should also be taught how to pair off the deleted subject in the adjectival clause with the overt subject in the surface structure to see if their semantic and syntactic features match.

9.6.8 Prepositional Phrases Used as Adjectivals

Prepositions will be discussed fully in Chapter 11. For now, suffice it to say that prepositional phrases too can modify nouns and pronouns by giving information about location, duration, time, or frequency. Since they perform these functions, traditional grammarians take prepositional phrases to be adjectival, as shown in the two sentences below:

(49) *The couple **in the next apartment** is noisy.*

(50) *The student **with sunglasses** is my assistant.*

In these two sentences, the prepositional phrases <in the next apartment> and <with sunglasses> provide additional information about the nouns <the couple> and <the student>. Consequently, these PPs function as adjectives.

Prepositional phrases found in NP of NP constructions also function as adjectives. Thus, in phrases such as <a man of honor>, <the war of independence>, and <the fountain of youth>, the prepositional phrase is an adjectival. Phrases such as <a fountain of youth> are commonly diagrammed as follows:

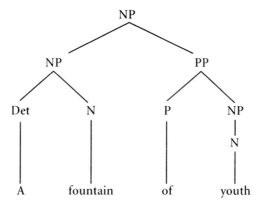

The PP functions as an adjective because it modifies the NP.

---

[15] The grammatical notion of <clause> will be discussed in Chapter 13. However, it is introduced early to make note of this important constraint.

9.7 Phrase Structure Rule Summary

Adjectives are found in two separate phrasal categories: in noun phrases and in verb phrases. Adjectives that occur in the noun phrase are labeled attributive adjectives. In more recent years, the labels pre-nominal and post-nominal adjectives have been coined to distinguish between two types of attributive adjectives. Adjectives that occur in the verb phrase are called predicative adjectives. Attributive adjectives and predicative adjectives are represented by the phrase structure rules below:

No.	Phrase Structure Rules	Description
1.	NP → (Det) Adj N	Pre-nominal attributive adjective
2.	NP → (Det) Deg Adj N	Pre-nominal attributive adjective with a degree word
3.	NP → (Det) N Adj	Post-nominal attributive adjective
4.	NP → (Det) N Deg Adj	Post-nominal attributive adjective with a degree word
5.	VP → V AdjP	Predicative adjective
6.	VP → V Deg AdjP	Predicative adjective with a degree word
7.	VP → V NP AdjP	Adjectival complement
8.	VP → V NP Deg AdjP	Adjectival complement with a degree word
9.	VP → {be/seem} Adj CP[16]	Some adjectives call for subordinate clauses

Table 19 *Summary of Adjective PSR*

9.8 Conclusion

The part of speech called <adjective> has semantic, morphological, and syntactic characteristics that make it relatively easy to identify in English. However, in some instances, accurate identification may be hampered for a number of reasons. Some adjectives lack morphological markings. Moreover, terminological squabbles between traditional grammarians and descriptive linguists sometimes make what counts as an adjective unclear. In spite of these difficulties, this chapter has given teachers the tools they need to identify adjectives. Additionally, this chapter has provided information about the distributional patterns of adjectives in English, their subcategorization frames, their word order hierarchy, and the rationale behind the various types of <adjectivals>. Moreover, the generative grammar account of dangling participles and infinitives offers a principled explanation that is relevant to the teaching of writing.

---

[16] This phrase structure rule will be examined in 13.6.

Key Terms to Know

These are the key terms that you should be able to use and define after reading this chapter:

1. adjective: 9.0, 9.1, 9.1.1, 9.1.2, 9.1.3, 9.2, 9.2.1, 9.2.2, 9.2.3, 9.2.4, 9.2.5, 9.3, 9.3.1, 9.3.2, 9.3.3, 9.3.4, 9.4, 9.4.1, 9.4.2, 9.4.3, 9.4.5, 9.5, 9.5.1, 9.5.2, 9.5.3, 9.5.5, 9.5.6, 9.5.7, 9.5.8, 9.6, 9.6.1, 9.6.2, 9.6.3, 9.6.5, 9.6.6, 9.6.7, 9.6.8, 9.7, 9.8.

2. adjectival order hierarchy: 9.1.1, 9.5.8, 9.8

3. adjectival: 9.1.1, 9.5.3, 9.5.6, 9.5.8, 9.6, 9.6.2, 9.6.4

4. attributive adjective: 9.5.1, 9.5.2, 9.5.6, 9.5.9, 9.7

5. comparative adjective: 9.3, 9.3.1, 9.3.3, 9.3.4

6. comparison of equality: 9.3, 9.3.1, 9.3.3

7. comparison of inferiority: 9.3, 9.3.1, 9.3.3

8. comparison of superiority: 9.3, 9.3.1, 9.3.3

9. dangling adjectival: 9.6.6, 9.6.7

10. dangling infinitive: 9.6.6

11. dangling participle: 9.6.6, 9.6.7, 9.8

12. degree word/intensifier/modifier: 9.5.1, 9.5.2, 9.5, 9.7

13. demonstrative adjective: 9.4.1

14. disyllabic: 9.3.1

15. gradability/gradable: 9.1.3, 9.2.5

16. indefinite adjective: 9.4.4

17. interrogative adjective: 9.4.3

18. linking verb: 9.6.5, 9.6.2

19. monosyllabic: 9.3.1

20. nominal: 9.6.1

21. ordinal adjective: 9.4.5

22. polarity: 9.1.3, 9.2.5

23. positive: 9.3

24. possessive adjective: 9.4.2

25. postnominal adjective: 9.5.2, 9.5.3, 9.5.6

26. predicative adjective: 9.5.6, 9.7

27. prenominal adjective: 9.5.2, 9.5.6

28. subject complement: 9.5.6

29. substantive: 9.6.1

30. superlative adjective: 9.3.1

31. syllable: 9.3, 9.3.1, 9.3.2, 9.3.4, 9.6.5

32. syntactic ambiguity: 9.5.9

EXERCISE 1—TREE DIAGRAMMING

Diagram the following sentences that contain adjectives. Be careful: some of the sentences may be ambiguous.

1. Some very smart minority actors and actresses play dumb in popular sitcoms.

2. We all live in a busy world.

3. Dolphins are smarter than dogs.

4.   New international students find the American culture intriguing.

5.   This linguist wrote a bestseller chemistry book.

6.   Frustrated employees could have become disgruntled employees.

EXERCISE 2—ADJECTIVAL COMPLEMENTS

Write the subcategorization frame of the following adjectives.

1. absent

2. ready

3. alive

4. eager

5. oblivious

6. uncommon

7. peculiar

8. hungry

EXERCISE 3—ADJECTIVE IDENTIFICATION

Find 10 adjectives in the text below. Use semantic, morphological, and syntactic evidence to support your finding. Base your classification on both descriptive linguistics and traditional grammar terminology. Indicate any degree word that occurs with the adjective. If a word occurs more than once, provide an analysis only of the first occurrence.

The Gettysburg Address

by Abraham Lincoln

"Fourscore and seven years ago our fathers brought forth on this continent a new nation, conceived in liberty and dedicated to the proposition that all men are created equal. Now we are engaged in a great civil war, testing whether that nation or any nation so conceived and so dedicated can long endure. We are met on a great battlefield of that war. We have come to dedicate a portion of that field as a final resting-place for those who here gave their lives that that nation might live. It is altogether fitting and proper that we should do this.

But in a larger sense, we cannot dedicate, we cannot consecrate, we cannot hallow this ground. The brave men, living and dead who struggled here have consecrated it far above our poor power to add or detract. The world will little note nor long remember what we say here, but it can never forget what they did here. It is for us the living rather to be dedicated here to the unfinished work which they who fought here have thus far so nobly advanced. It is rather for us to be here dedicated to the great task remaining before us—that from these honored dead we take increased devotion to that cause for which they gave the last full measure of devotion—that we here highly resolve that these dead shall not have died in vain, that this nation under God shall have a new birth of freedom, and that government of the people, by the people, for the people shall not perish from the earth."

No.	Adjective Classification and Analysis
1.	
2.	
3.	
4.	
5.	
6.	
7.	
8.	
9.	
10.	

EXERCISE 4—DANGLING PARTICIPLES

Here are some sentences that contain dangling participles. Identify the dangling participle and fix the sentence.

1.   My friend Larry found my missing shoe driving to work last week. (Calderonello 2003:288)

2.   On the way to Houghton we ran into a car going 90 miles per hour.

3.   Lying on the beach, the sun felt hot. (Calderonello 2003:288)

4.   Stored in the refrigerator, we can keep oranges for six weeks. (Klammer et al. 2004:390).

5.   Looking beyond the fact that the slave trade was beyond profitable for Europeans, once the 19th century rolled around, many began to rethink their methods. (From a student's chapter summary in my Introduction to African Studies course)

6.   To keep farm machinery in good repair, a regular maintenance schedule is necessary. (Kolln and Funk 2006:126)

EXERCISE 5—UNDERSTANDING GRAMMATICAL TERMINOLOGY

1. Make a sentence with an attributive adjective. Underline the attributive adjective.

2. Make a sentence with an interrogative adjective. Underline the interrogative adjective.

3. Make a sentence with a predicative adjective. Underline the predicative adjective.

4. Make a sentence with a linking verb. Underline the linking verb.

5. Make a sentence in which there is a subject complement. Underline the subject complement.

6. Make a sentence with an infinitive functioning as an adjectival. Underline the adjectival infinitive.

7. Make a sentence with a comparative adjective. Underline the comparative adjective.

8. Make a sentence with a prepositional phrase that functions as an adjective. Underline the prepositional phrase.

9. Make a sentence in which the adjective is in the comparative of superiority. Underline the adjective in the comparative of superiority.

10. Make a sentence in which the present participle functions as an adjective. Underline the present participle.

11. Make a sentence in which the past participle functions as an adjective. Underline the past participle.

12. Make a sentence in which the adjective is in the comparative of inferiority. Underline the adjective in the comparative of inferiority.

13. Make a sentence in which the adjective is in the superlative. Underline the superlative adjective.

14. Make a sentence in which the adjective is used as a substantive. Underline the substantive.

15. Make a sentence in which a degree word is used to modify an adjective. Underline the degree word.

16. Make a sentence in which the adjective is in the comparative of equality. Underline the adjective in the comparative of equality.

17. Make a sentence with a possessive adjective. Underline the possessive adjective.

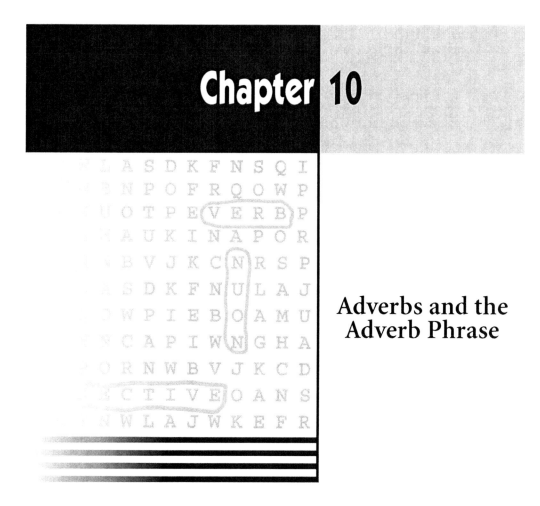

Chapter 10

Adverbs and the Adverb Phrase

10.0 INTRODUCTION

According to both Greek and Latin grammarians, the main function of adverbs is to modify verbs. This is reflected in how these two languages chose to name this part of speech. The Greeks labeled it *<epirhemata>* which is a compound word consisting of the preposition *<epi>* and the root *<rhema>*. The preposition *<epi>* means, among other things, "near," "after," or "by." The root *<rhema>* is translated by *<verb>*, as noted in 8.0. The compound word thus formed can be loosely translated as "that which in thrown or lies near the verb." Latin grammarians often relied on Greek in naming the parts of speech found in their own language. They, therefore, calqued the Greek term directly into their own language and labeled it *<adverbium>*. This Latin word is also a compound consisting of the prefix *<ad>* which means "near" or "toward" and the root *<verbium>* which stands for "verb." According to experts, the English word <adverb> comes straight from this Latin compound through Middle French.

10.1 Definitional Woes

It is clear from the etymological analysis that has just been sketched that ancient grammarians connected adverbs closely with verbs. They were also aware that adverbs did more than modify verbs. For this reason, traditional grammar books often define the adverb as "a word that modifies a verb, an adjective, or another adverb." This covers the three main functions of adverbs. However, contemporary linguists are not happy with this definition. For reasons that will become obvious in the remainder of this chapter, they see this definition as problematic. Bickford (1998:99), for example, frames the issue this way:

> *The term adverbial, however, leaves much to be desired. For one thing, the most common types of obliques[1] are PPs and NPs, neither of which are adverbs. But worse, the traditional class of adverbs is an ill-defined conglomeration of very different types of words, many of which cannot be used as obliques. The core of this group, what we call true adverbs, consists of words that can be modified in English by degree words; in this way they are adjectives. The true adverbs thus include words like* possibly, quickly, well, *and* far, *and we reserve the word 'adverb' for a class of words that contain similar meanings. Many other words traditionally called adverbs are clearly* not *in the same syntactic category as true adverbs. Degree words, for example, are traditionally considered adverbs, but they cannot be interchanged freely with true adverbs.*

Kaplan (1995:120, 159) also bemoans the traditional conception of adverbs, arguing that it is unsatisfactory for the following reasons:

This definition has two problems: (1) it does not include certain kinds of words which are usually called adverbs, and (2) there are big differences between verb-modifying adverbs on the one hand, and basically adjective and adverb-modifying adverbs, on the other. The differences are so striking that 'adverb,' as a name of a grammatical category, does not have much meaning.

Later, on page 159, he states that "in traditional grammar, the class of 'adverbs' is often used as a kind of trash-heap to put hard-to-classify words in." Jurafsky and Martin (2000:291) also observe that "[the lexical category] adverb, is rather a hodge-podge, both semantically and formally." Quotes such as these are found throughout the linguistic literature. They also set the stage for what will follow in this chapter, namely, that adverbs remain to this day an ill-defined part of speech.

10.1.1 A Point of Clarification

An important caveat is in order before we proceed further. Many grammar books give the labels <**adverb**> and <**adverbial**> generously to a vast array of words or constructions. However, these same words are given other labels under different circumstances. To minimize cross-classifications which often confuse students, I have resolved to use the term <adverb> to refer only to lexical items that are truly adverbs. The term <adverbial> will be used later in 10.8 to refer to words or phrases that are not adverbs but function as such in a given sentence. I, in addition, exclude from consideration a group of words that some grammarians have called "conjunctive adverbs." In my opinion, these so-called adverbs are actually conjunctions. Therefore, they will be dealt with in Chapter 12, rather than here.

10.2 Semantic Characteristics of Adverbs

Adverbs have been categorized and sub-categorized semantically in multiple ways. However, irrespective of the classification scheme that is used, the following five major types always resurface:

1. degree adverbs

2. manner adverbs

---

[1] The term "oblique" is the exact of opposite of the term "complement." Any word or group of words that is not subcategorized with a verb, an adverb, or a preposition, but occurs with it in a sentence is called "an oblique."

3. place adverbs

4. time adverbs

5. modality/sentential adverbs

The presentation in this section will focus on these adverbial categories. Semantic clues/tests will be given to help teachers and their students identify and classify adverbs according to these five broad categories.

10.2.1 Degree Words Used as Adverbs

The concept of degree words was introduced in 9.5.1. It was claimed then that the presence of these closed class words provided reliable clues for identifying adjectives. The same words perform double duty because traditional grammar classifies them as adverbs when they modify an adverb, an adjective, or a verb. Therefore, from the perspective of traditional grammar, the word <absolutely> in (1) is an adverb because it modifies the adjective <brilliant>:

(1)   Peter is **absolutely** brilliant.

(2)   Peter is **absolutely** a fool.

However, this traditional definition runs into a problem when one considers the same word in (2). Can it be said in this case that <absolutely> is an adverb? If it is an adverb, what does it modify? It should be recalled that according to traditional grammar, an adverb modifies only verbs, other adverbs, or adjectives. In (2) <absolutely> does not modify any verb, adjective, or adverb; and yet the sentence is grammatical. Difficulties such as this have led contemporary linguists not to consider <absolutely> in (2) as an adverb. Instead, they use the label <degree word> (<**intensifier**>, or <**modifier**> are also used).

The point of all this is that the part of speech called "adverb" is too broad. It consists of different subsets, including <degree words>. The most common degree words that were traditionally classified as "adverbs" are the following:

No.	Degree Words[2]
1.	totally
2.	really
3.	awfully
4.	scarcely
5.	especially
6.	barely
7.	entirely
8.	extremely
9.	completely
10.	absolutely
11.	incredibly
12.	terribly
13.	amazingly

Table 1 *List of Common Degree Words*

[2] Other degree words are listed in 9.5.1.

Here traditional grammar and descriptive linguistics clash in their labeling of words. For the former, all the words in Table 1 are "manner adverbs," whereas the latter considers them to be "degree words," "intensifiers," or "modifiers."

10.2.2 Manner Adverbs

Manner adverbs are words that primarily modify verbs. When adverbs are used in this fashion, they can be paraphrased as "in an X manner," where "X" stands for an adjective, as illustrated by the sentence below:

(3)   *The faculty responded **sarcastically** to the dean's proposal.*

The word <sarcastically> can be paraphrased as <in a sarcastic manner>. Kaplan (1995:122–5) has drawn attention to the fact that not all adverbs that end in <-ly> are manner adverbs as is commonly asserted. He gives the example of the word <scientifically> in (4) to show that, even though the word has the suffix <-ly>, it is not a manner adverb because it fails the "in an X manner" test as shown below:

(4)   *That is **scientifically** impossible.*

(5)   * *That is impossible in a **scientific manner.***

Lobeck (2000:180) also cautions against relying solely on the suffix <-ly> to classify an adverb as a "manner adverb." She argues that words such as <terribly>, <amazingly>, <incredibly>, and <absolutely> are not manner adverbs even though they end in <-ly>. She classifies them as degree words.

It appears from the preceding paragraph that the presence of the suffix <-ly> is not a guarantee that the word in question is a manner adverb.[3] For this reason, a <How-Test> has been proposed that can help distinguish manner adverbs that end in <-ly> from other words that are morphologically similar but are not manner adverbs. Generally, the <How-Test> helps identify all manner adverbs, whether they end in <-ly> or not. It can be formulated as follows:

The How-Test

Any lexical item that can be substituted for by <how> without causing the derived sentence to be ungrammatical is most likely a manner adverb.

Let us apply it to the two sentences below to see if it can adequately discriminate between <sarcastically> and <scientifically>:

(6)   *The faculty responded **sarcastically** to the dean's proposal.*

(7)   *That is **scientifically** impossible.*

When the <How-Test> is applied, it yields the following results:

(8)   *The faculty responded **how** to the dean's proposal?*

(9)   * *That is **how** impossible?*

The fact that (9) is ill-formed shows that <scientifically> is not a manner adverb. However, since <sarcastically> can be replaced by <how> without resulting in an ill-formed sentence, we conclude it is a manner adverb.

---

[3] We will see in 10.8.3 that some words that end in <-ly> are adjectives.

10.2.3 Place Adverbs

The next group of adverbs under consideration is <**place adverbs**>. This is a cover term for a wide range of adverbs that include "locative adverbs" and "adverbs of direction." To test whether a word is a place adverb or not, we can apply the following <Where-Test>:

The Where-Test

> Any lexical item that can be substituted for by <where> without causing the derived sentence to be ungrammatical is most likely a place adverb.

When applied to the word <downtown> in the sentences below, it yields the following results:

(10) *The mayor rebuilt downtown.*

(11) ** The mayor rebuilt where?*

(12) *The mayor works downtown.*

(13) *The mayor works where?*

We conclude based on these results that <downtown> in (10) is not a place adverb because it fails the test. However, <downtown> in (12) is a place adverb because it can be replaced by <where> without leading to an ungrammatical sentence. Using this test, one can classify the words in Table 2 as place adverbs:

No.	Common Place Adverbs
1.	here
2.	there
3.	over there
4.	over here
5.	anywhere
6.	somewhere
7.	nowhere
8.	everywhere
9.	inside
10.	upstairs
11.	downstairs
12.	downtown
13.	uptown
14.	behind
15.	ahead
16.	around
17.	overhead
18.	underneath
19.	aboard
20.	overboard

Table 2 *Place Adverbs*[4]

[4] We will see in 11.8.3 that when some of the words listed here are followed by NPs, they are classified as prepositions.

10.2.4 Time Adverbs

Time adverbs answer the question <when>. The test to help distinguish time adverbs from all other adverbs can be formulated as follows:

The When-Test

> *Any lexical item that can be substituted for by <when> without causing the derived sentence to be ungrammatical is most likely a time adverb.*

Time adverbs fall into different subcategories among which one finds "adverbs of duration," "frequency adverbs," and "adverbs of sequence." However, for the sake of simplicity, I have lumped all these various semantic classes together as "time adverbs." The time adverbs that have high frequency of occurrence are listed in Table 3 on the following page.

The <When-Test> can be applied to <tomorrow> in the list to see if it is really a time adverb:

(14) *Classes will be cancelled **tomorrow.***

(15) *Classes will be cancelled **when?***

As mentioned previously, time adverbs fall into many different semantic subcategories. Consequently, they do not all respond to the "When-Test." The example below would lead one to think that the word <yet> is not a time adverb because when it is replaced by "when," the sentence becomes ill-formed:

(16) *The train has not departed **yet.***

(17) ** The train has not departed **when?***

The ungrammaticality of (17) does not mean that the test is unreliable. All it shows is that different test words have to be found for different types of time adverbs. In the case of (16), if we use the test phrase "for how long," the derived sentence becomes grammatical. This must be kept in mind when administering the <When-Test>. One must be willing to use as many test words as necessary for the identification and classification of time adverbs. Some examples of test words include *"how long," "since when," "how often."*

10.2.5 Modality Adverbs

Modality adverbs can be defined simply as adverbs that express speakers' attitudes towards their utterances. The attitude can be measured by degrees of certainty, obligation/necessity, or probability. Modality adverbs are also sometimes referred to as <**sentential adverbs**>. The following list contains some of the most widely used modality adverbs (see Table 4 on page 266):

No.	Common Time Adverbs
1.	today
2.	tomorrow
3.	yesterday
4.	now
5.	noon
6.	midnight
7.	this/last/next week
8.	this/last/next month
9.	this/last/next year
10.	later
11.	seldom
12.	usually
13.	daily
14.	seasonally
15.	twice
16.	often
17.	rarely
18.	during
19.	for
20.	since
21.	awhile
22.	recently
23.	lately
24.	indefinitely
25.	for ever
26.	until
27.	continually
28.	still
29.	before
30.	next
31.	after
32.	then
33.	first
34.	finally
35.	already
36.	yet
37.	again

Table 3 *Temporal Adverbs*

No.	Common Modality Adverbs
1.	fortunately/unfortunately
2.	luckily
3.	obviously
4.	generally
5.	supposedly
6.	allegedly
7.	assuredly
8.	probably
9.	perhaps
10.	certainly
11.	surely
12.	typically
13.	clearly
14.	evidently
15.	hopefully
16.	regrettably
17.	seemingly
18.	undoubtedly
19.	possibly
20.	truly
21.	honestly
22.	surprisingly
23.	understandably
24.	frankly

Table 4 *Modality Adverbs*

There is not a single semantic test that one can rely on to identify a word as a modality adverb. Instead, one must combine the semantic and the syntactic environments in which a word occurs. Modality adverbs have a unique distributional pattern that somehow distinguishes them from many other adverbs and from other parts of speech. The test for these adverbs can be called the <Mobility Test>. It is formulated as follows:

The Mobility Test

Any lexical item that can freely move to sentence-initial position **and** express at the same time degrees of certainty, obligation, necessity, or probability without causing the sentence to be ungrammatical, is most likely a modality adverb.

It seems as though this test falls more in the domain of syntax than semantics. However, this is only partially true. Many adverbs and some other parts of speech can move around in the sentence without qualifying as modality adverbs. In addition to distributional mobility, a word that qualifies as a modality adverb must also express degrees of certainty, obligation, or probability. To illustrate this, let us consider the sentences below:

(18) **Admittedly,** *many students are afraid of grammar.*

(19) *?Many students are afraid of grammar* **admittedly.**

(20) *The striking workers passed by* **noisily.**

(21) **Noisily,** *the striking workers passed by.*

In (21) <noisily> moves to sentence-initial position. This satisfies the distributional requirement. However, since the word <noisily> does not meet the semantic requirements, it cannot be classified as a modality adverb. We conclude therefore, that the semantic test is crucial in distinguishing modality adverbs from all other adverbs.

10.2.6 Summary of Semantic Tests

The preceding analysis shows that semantics gives some important clues for identifying and classifying adverbs. Semantic clues help distinguish one class of adverbs from another. Additionally, these clues help distinguish adverbs from other parts of speech. Table 5 summarizes these findings.

No.	Test[5]	Main Verb	Noun	Adjective	Adverb	Pro-noun	Con-junction	Pre-position[6]
1.	How	−	−	−	+	−	−	±
2.	Where	−	−	−	+	−	−	±
3.	When	−	−	−	+	−	−	±

Table 5 *Summary of Semantic Tests*

10.3 *The Morphology of Adverbs*

In this section we will examine the morphological processes that English uses to create new adverbs. There are two main processes: compounding and derivation. We will also study the inflectional characteristics of adverbs but we will not dwell on them because they are strikingly similar to those of adjectives. Lastly, we will examine a group of adverbs that grammarians have labeled **"flat adverbs."** The main conclusion that we will draw from the analysis of adverbial morphology is that, unlike the parts of speech that we have seen so far, morphology does not provide us with strong clues to distinguish adverbs from other parts of speech.

10.3.1 Compounding

A large number of English adverbs are formed by combining two minor parts of speech to form a single word. The meaning of such compounds is not **compositional,** that is,

---

[5] The word <why> is missing from the list of tests because the <why-test> usually calls for a subordinate clause that is introduced by the subordinating conjunction "because." Issues related to "why" and to subordinating conjunctions will be addressed in Chapter 13.

[6] We will see in 11.8.3 that prepositions and adverbs are semantically similar. The symbol "±" is used because in some cases prepositional phrases answer the questions "why," "how," "where," and "when."

the total meaning of the derived word cannot be calculated on the basis of the meaning of the individual words that make up the compound. Here are some of the most frequent adverbial compounds:

No.	Word Formation Processes	Derived Adverbs
1.	how + ever	however
2.	never + the + less	nevertheless
3.	more + over	moreover
4.	none+the+less	nonetheless
5.	some + what	somewhat
6.	some + how	somehow
7.	like + wise	likewise
8.	ever+ more	evermore
9.	hence + forth	henceforth
10.	not+with+standing	notwithstanding
11.	further + more	furthermore
12.	some + where	somewhere
13.	in+side	inside
14.	with + in	within
15.	through + out	throughout
16.	there + after	thereafter
17.	other + wise	otherwise
18.	mean + while	meanwhile
19.	there + abouts	thereabouts

Table 6 *Compound Adverbs*

These adverbs form a closed class because new adverbs of this type are not readily created by English speakers.

10.3.2 Derivational Morphology

By far the most productive process whereby adverbs are formed in English, and a number of European languages (including French and Spanish), is through the affixation of the suffix <-ly> to an adjectival stem. This process is so productive and so regular that there is virtually no limit to the number of adverbs that English can generate. This is another vexing characteristic of adverbs. One subset of adverbs forms a closed class while another subset is an open class. Here are some examples of adverbs derived from adjectival stems:

No.	Adjectives	Derived Adverbs
1.	beautiful	beautifully
2.	honest	honestly
3.	warm	warmly
4.	enthusiastic	enthusiastically
5.	bright	brightly
6.	obvious	obviously
7.	certain	certainly
8.	sure	surely
9.	assured	assuredly
10.	surprising	surprisingly
11.	foolish	foolishly
12.	handsome	handsomely

Table 7 *Regular <-ly> Adverbial Derivation*

10.3.3 The Suffix <-ly> in other Parts of Speech

The presence of the suffix <-ly> in a word is a very reliable clue that it is most likely an adverb. However, it is not one hundred percent reliable because, as shown in Table 8 below, some adjectives can also take the suffix <-ly>:

No.	Test	Main Verb	Noun[7]	Adjective	Adverb	Pronoun	Conjunction	Preposition
1.	<-ly>	−	−	±	+	−	−	−

Table 8 *The Suffix <-ly> and other Parts of Speech*

The adjective column has the feature "±" because there are a dozen or so adjectives that end in <-ly> , as listed in Table 9:

No.	Adjectives/Nouns	Adjectives
1.	friend	friendly
2.	bubble	bubbly
3.	love	lovely
4.	dead	deadly
5.	live	lively
6.	heaven	heavenly
7.	home	homely
8.	world	worldly
9.	beast	beastly
10.	leisure	leisurely
11.	coward	cowardly
12.	earth	earthly

Table 9 *Adjectives Ending in <-ly>*

[7] The part of speech category of <article> is not listed separately here because it is considered part of the noun phrase (NP).

10.3.4 Other Derivational Morphemes

English has three other minor derivational suffixes whose presence suggests that the word in which they appear may be an adverb. These three adverbial suffixes are of unequal productivity. The suffix <-wise> can be added to almost any noun to derive an adverb. However, this is not the case for <-wards> which appears only on locative adverbs or prepositions. Adverbs having this suffix denote motion toward a place. This suffix is in **free variation** with <-ward>. For example, both <toward> and <towards> are acceptable. Free variation means that the choice of one form or another does not lead to differences in meaning. Finally, the suffix <-ways> is added to a few nouns to derive adverbs. However, this process is not for the moment very productive. It occurs only in a handful of words. Table 10 below illustrates this derivational process:

No.	<-wise>	<-ward>	<-ways>
1.	lengthwise	downward(s)	sideways
2.	clockwise	backward(s)	crossways
3.	timewise	afterward(s)	
4.	otherwise	inward(s)	
5.	schoolwise	outward(s)	
6.	moneywise	toward(s)	
7.	cashwise	upward(s)	
8.	weatherwise	forward(s)	
9.	budgetwise		

Table 10 *Additional Derivations*

The preceding observations can be turned into a derivational test for identifying and classifying adverbs. It can be formulated as follows:

Derivational Morphology Test for Adverbs

The presence of the suffixes <-ly>, <-wise>, <-ways>, and <-ward> is strong but not conclusive evidence for identifying and classifying a word as an adverb.

10.4 *Inflectional Morphology*

English adverbs and adjectives have a great deal of inflectional characteristics in common. The comparative morpheme <-er> works for both of them. The superlative morpheme <-est> is common to both. Both adverbs and adjectives follow the same syllable rules discussed in 9.3.1 through 9.3.3. Table 11 on the following page summarizes the similarities in the inflectional morphology of both parts of speech:

No.	Test	Main Verb	Noun	Adjective	Adverb	Pro-noun	Con-junction	Pre-position
1.	Regular <-er> comparative	–	–	+	+	–	–	–
2.	Regular<-est> supperlative	–	–	+	+	–	–	–
3.	Irregular comparative	–	–	+	+	–	–	–
4.	Suppletive comparative	–	–	+	+	–	–	–
5.	Irregular supperlative	–	–	+	+	–	–	–
6.	Suppletive superlative	–	–	+	+	–	–	–

Table 11 *Inflectional Similarities between Adverbs and Adjectives*

The discussions in 9.3.1 regarding the deep structure form of comparative, equative, and superlative forms of adjectives also apply to adverbs. Discontinuous morphemes such as <more ... than>, <less ... than>, <the ... -est>, <-er ... than>, <the best>, <the worst>, etc. are taken to be degree words. Thus, a sentence such as *<Jeremy runs the fastest>* can be diagrammed as follows:

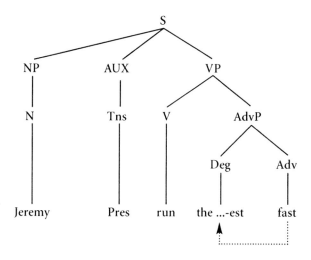

Here, as in 9.3.1, the adverb <fast> is moved and inserted between the elements of the discontinuous morphemes <the ...-est> during the derivation, as shown by the dotted arrow.

10.4.1 Adverbial Suffixes that End in <S>

A small number of English adverbs take a suffix <-s> which is neither the plural morpheme nor the third person singular <-s>. This adverbial suffix appears on the following words:

No.	Adverbs with Plural Endings
1.	unawares
2.	nowadays
3.	besides
4.	backwards
5.	thereabouts
6.	towards
7.	downwards
8.	afterwards
9.	inwards
10.	outwards
11.	upwards
12.	sideways
13.	crossways

Table 12 *Adverbial Plural Suffixes*

Pinker (1999:35) labels this suffix "the affective <s>" when it occurs in nouns. However, to the best of my knowledge, no attempt has been made to name it when it appears in adverbs. A closer examination shows that almost all the words involved denote some kind of direction. A similar suffix occurs in biblical Hebrew where a suffix called "directional <hé> [he^1]" is added to place names to indicate movement toward a geographical location.

10.4.2 Flat Adverbs

Many English adverbs do not bear any morphological markings whatsoever that can help us identify and classify them as adverbs. However, these words are adverbs. Grammarians have given the uninspiring name of <**flat adverbs**> to these words. Lobeck (2000:178) remarks that flat adverbs are very easy to mistake for adjectives because they both have the same comparative and superlative inflectional morphemes. Therefore, one must rely on other elements in the sentence to make the proper diagnosis. Let us illustrate this point with (22) and (23):

(22) *Jeremy is **faster** than Tallie.*

(23) *Jeremy runs **faster** than Tallie.*

The word <faster> in (22) is an adjective because it modifies both "Jeremy" and "Tallie." We arrive at this classification because <Be> is a linking verb. However, <faster> in (23) is an adverb because it modifies how both "Jeremy" and "Tallie" run. There is nothing that formally distinguishes <faster> in the two sentences. Only their syntactic functions help classify them differently. Some of the most common flat adverbs are the following:

No.	Adverbs with no Suffix
1.	fast
2.	hard
3.	later/late
4.	sharp
5.	often
6.	seldom
7.	never
8.	soon
9.	now
10.	early
11.	long
12.	high
13.	low
14.	near
15.	deep
16.	here
17.	there
18.	then
19.	far
20.	straight
21.	quick

Table 13 *Common Flat Adverbs*

In concluding this section, it must once again be noted that morphology alone cannot help distinguish adverbs from other parts of speech. To make a decision whether a lexical item is an adverb or not, one must take syntactic clues into account.

10.5 *The Syntax of Adverbs*

One of the most important characteristics of English adverbs is their mobility. They can occur in five different positions in the sentence with or without significant semantic differences in the idea being conveyed. The ability of adverbs to occur in different positions raises important theoretical questions. Teachers do not usually care about theoretical speculations. They are task oriented professionals who want practical solutions that they can readily apply. However, I must digress here and go on a little theoretical expedition. Given the difficulties that we have alluded to in the previous paragraphs, it is necessary to use a little bit of theory to help us understand the behavior of adverbs. Some of the theoretical issues that we will investigate are the following: 1) what position do adverbs occupy in the deep structure? 2) What kinds of transformations take place in deriving surface structure sentences that contain adverbs from their deep structure counterparts?

3) What is the status of \<Not\>? But before delving into these issues, let us first examine what constitutes an adverbial phrase.

10.5.1 The Adverbial Phrase

An adverbial phrase is defined as a word or group of words that is formally an adverb. How many such adverbs can occur in a single sentence? In theory, speakers can string together as many adverbs as they have stamina to produce. With this in mind, linguists have proposed the following phrase structure rules to account for adverbial phrases:

$$VP \rightarrow V \ AdvP^n$$
$$AdvP \rightarrow (Deg)^n \ Adv^n$$

The superscript "ⁿ" means that the rule allows as many adverbs as possible to be generated. Even though this is theoretically possible, no more than two or three adverbs are used to modify the same verb, adverb, or adjective. Sentence (24) below illustrates how adverbs can be piled up one after the other in the same verb phrase:

(24) *Students will **probably always** complain **very very loudly** about grammar.*

In this sentence, there are five adverbs \<probably\>, \<always\>, \<very\>, \<very\>, and \<loudly\>.

10.5.2 The Distribution of Adverbs

Adverbs as a lexical category can occur in five different positions in English sentences, as stated in 10.5. This does not in any way imply that all adverbs can occur in all five different positions. Baker (1989:284), who is well known for his research on adverbial positions, illustrates the distributional pattern of adverbs with the sentences in Table 14 below and Table 15 on the following page:

No.	Syntactic Positions of Adverbs
1.	**Position One:** sentence initial *Already,* George has been making plans.
2.	**Position Two:** before the first auxiliary George *already* has been making plans.
3.	**Position Three:** after the first auxiliary George has *already* been making plans.
4.	**Position Four:** before the main verb George has been *already* making plans.[8]
5.	**Position Five:** sentence final George has been making plans *already.*

Table 14 *Distribution Patterns of Adverbs*

[8] Baker (1989:284) has a star by this sentence, meaning that he considers it ill-formed. However, this sentence is judged grammatical by many other speakers of English.

After an extensive series of experiments to determine where various adverbs are acceptable, Baker (1989:283) summarizes his findings about the behavior of individual adverbs in the chart below:

No.	Adverb	S-Initial	Before Finite Verb	After Finite Verb	Before Action Verb	End of VP
1.	now	+	+	+	-	+
2.	then	+	+	+	-	+
3.	already	+	+	+	-	+
4.	still	+	+	+	-	+
5.	yet	-	-	-	-	+
6.	Any more	-	-	-	-	+
7.	often	+	+	+	-	+
8.	sometimes	+	+	+	-	+
9.	always	-	+	+	-	+
10.	never	+	+	+	-	+
11.	modality	+	+	+	-	-
12.	also	-	-	+	-	+
13.	too	-	-	-	-	+
14.	even	+	+	+	-	+?
15.	only	+	-	+	-	-

Table 15 *Distribution Pattern of High Frequency Adverbs*

Findings such as these have led linguists to propose the following phrase structure rule:

$$S \rightarrow (AdvP)\ NP\ (AdvP)\ Aux^1\ (AdvP)\ Aux^2\ (AdvP)\ VP\ (AdvP)$$

The number of adverbial positions available in a sentence depends a great deal on the number of auxiliary verbs that occur in the same sentence. If a sentence has two auxiliary verbs, as indicated in Table 14 on previous page, some adverbs can appear in five positions. If a sentence has only one auxiliary verb, the number of available positions is reduced to four. Let us illustrate this with (25). The adverb <already> can be inserted in four positions, as illustrated by (26) through (29):

(25) *George has made plans.*

(26) *George **already** has made plans.*

(27) *George has made plans **already.***

(28) *George has **already** made plans.*

(29) ***Already,** George has made plans.*

The number of adverbs that can occur in a sentence is reduced to three if a sentence consists of one main verb only:

(30)   *George made plans.*

(31)   *George **already** made plans.*

(32)   *George made plans **already.***

(33)   ?***Already,** George made plans.*

It is worth noting, as does Curme (1931:13) that "adverbs can freely stand in almost any position except between a verb and its direct object, where it is much less common than elsewhere." In all the examples discussed here, if the adverb <already> stands between the verb <made> and its direct object <plans>, the sentence becomes ill-formed, as is the case below:

(34)   **George made **already** plans.*

10.5.3 The Default Adverbial Position

The distributional pattern of adverbs raises theoretical questions about the position of adverbs in the deep structure. Do adverbs occur in all these five different positions in the deep structure? Are the surface structure positions the by-product of transformation rules? Let us consider the various alternatives and their theoretical implications.

Most traditional grammar books subscribe to the view that the most natural position of adverbs in English sentences is after the main verb. This distribution can be illustrated by the following phrase structure rule:

$$S \rightarrow NP \quad Aux \quad VP \quad \textbf{AdvP}$$

However, some theoretical linguists dispute this widely held view. Baker (1989:292) makes the following observation:

> *The only verbs that allow these adverbs to follow them are the modals, the finite forms of BE, and the finite forms of perfect HAVE. Thus, all finite verbs allow these adverbs to precede them, but only a few allow the same adverbs to follow them. This observation might lead us to suspect that the position before the finite verb, which is available to all verbs, is more basic than the position after the verb, which is available only to a few.*

Culicover (1997:341) and Baker (1978:399) adopt the same view. Those who hold this view propose the following phrase structure rule to account for the distribution of adverbs in the deep structure:

$$S \rightarrow NP \quad Aux \quad \textbf{AdvP} \quad VP$$

For the sake of simplicity, I propose, rather reluctantly, that the default position of adverbs is after the main verb. This is the position that we will take in this book from now forward. Some linguists who refuse to take sides in this debate propose the following phrase structure rule:

$$S \rightarrow NP \quad Aux \quad (AdvP) \quad VP \quad (AdvP)^9$$

It should be noted, however, that the subcategorization frame of the verb takes precedence. For transitive verbs, the noun phrase occurs with the main verb. And if there is an adverb in the sentence, it comes after the NP. This is illustrated by sentence (35) in 10.5.4 below. The adverb "*already*" occurs after the NP "*plans*" in the deep structure because the verb "*make*" is a transitive verb.

If one takes the position that adverbs occur after the main verb, then one must go one step further and posit that for transitive verbs, the adverb occurs after the NP in the deep structure. This requirement is strongest for verbs such as <to buy> which are strictly subcategorized as taking a direct object. This requirement is less stringent for optionally transitive verbs such as <to eat>. The difference between the two types of transitive verbs is that the verb <to buy> cannot be used without an NP whereas the verb <to eat> can. However, for the sake of simplicity, one can avoid having to distinguish between the two types of transitive verbs by always placing adverbs directly after the direct object if there is one, as shown in the phrase structure rule below:

$$VP \rightarrow V \quad (NP) \quad \mathbf{AdvP}$$

10.5.4 Adverbial Movement Rules

Irrespective of the view that one holds with regard to the position of adverbs, there is a consensus that a movement rule applies to move adverbs from their default position to elsewhere in the sentence. According to this view, the four sentences below derive from the same underlying form, namely,

(35)   George Pres Have—EN Be-ING make plans *already.*

By moving <already> around, we have four different sentences with slightly different emphasis:

(36)   *George **already** has been making plan.*

(37)   *George has **already** been making plans.*

(38)   *George has been **already** making plans.*

(39)   ***Already,** George has been making plans.*

In all these four sentences the adverb <already> is moved from its default position from after the NP to a different location in the sentence depending on the degree of emphasis that the speaker wants the sentence to convey. Adverbial movement rules, therefore, appear to be stylistically motivated.

10.6 To Transform or Not to Transform?

Most linguists, except for Kaplan (1995:159–160), consider <NOT> to be an adverb. This is one of the arguments that some linguists use to support their claim that the preverbal position is the default position for adverbs in the deep structure. Since its inception, generative grammar has used negative constructions as evidence that transformational rules

---

[9] Fromkin, Victoria et al. (2000:200).

apply to deep structures to derive surface structures. However, even before the advent of *The Minimalist Program* (refer to section 3.6), some linguists had questioned the rationale for deriving negative sentences from underlying affirmative sentences. This debate has implications for adverbs, especially the status of the verbal negator <NOT>.

10.6.1 Negative Construction and the Status of <NOT>

In early generative grammar, all negative sentences were derived from their affirmative equivalent in the deep structure, as discussed in 3.6.2.3. Thus, sentence (40)

> (40) *Many students don't take linguistics,*

is believed to have been derived from its deep structure equivalent which is *<many student plural Pres take linguistics>*. The derivational steps that were used to arrive at the surface structure are as follows:

Deep structure:	many student plural Pres take linguistics
1. Negative Insertion:	many student plural Pres **NOT** take linguistics
2. DO-Support addition:	many student plural Pres **DO NOT** take linguistics
3. NOT-Contraction:	many student plural Pres **DON'T** take linguistics
4. Affix Hopping:	many student plural ___ **DON'T** Pres take linguistics
5. Spell-Out Rules:	many students **DON'T** take linguistics

Syntactic Surface Structure: <Many students don't take linguistics>.

Underlying this process is the assumption that the negator <NOT> has a fixed position, namely that it always occurs before the main verb. The insertion of the negator <NOT> sets off the derivational process.

10.6.2 A Non-Generative Account of Negation

A great deal has happened since the early days generative grammar.[10] Today, a number of linguists take the position that negative sentences are not derived from an underlying affirmative sentence. Instead, they argue that a single phrase structure rule can be formulated to generate all English sentences in which verbs are negated. This rule is as follows:

$$S \rightarrow NP \quad AUX \quad NEG \quad VP$$

The phrase structure rule generates two types of negative constructions. If an auxiliary verb or a modal verb occurs in the sentence, either can be negated directly as seen in (41):

> (41) *You **shouldn't** sell this book at the end of the semester.*

> (42) *Many students don't take linguistics.*

However, if no auxiliary or modal verb is present, <DO> is inserted to negate the main verb. The second rule generates negative sentences in which the main verb is negated. This rule can generate (42) directly without deriving it from a positive deep structure counterpart. The proponents of this approach would diagram (42) as follows:

---

[10] The transformational bases for questions and negations have been contested, see Jurafsky and Martin (2000:408, 417).

Many students do NOT take linguistics.

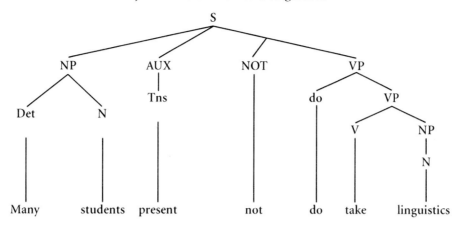

There are a number of implicit assumptions that need to be made explicit. First, in the X-Bar theory which downplays transformations, auxiliary verbs and modals occur under the main VP, not in AUX. Secondly, <NOT> **must** occur immediately to the left of the **main** verb. The third assumption is that AUX contains only inflectional information (Tense, Aspect) but no real lexical item. The surface structure sentence *<many students do not take linguistics>* is obtained by moving <DO> out of the first VP and placing it in AUX. This process is called **verb raising.** The same process accounts for (43) and (44) below:

(43) *The officer should not have killed the rapist.*

(44) *The officer should have not killed the rapist.*

(45) ** The officer should have killed not the rapist.*

In the case of (43) only <should> moves into AUX. In (44) both <should> and <have> are raised into AUX. Sentence (45) is ill-formed because <Not> must always occur to the left of the main verb, namely <killed>.[11] This can be illustrated by the following tree diagram and the arrows that point to where movements have taken place.

The officer should not have killed the rapist.

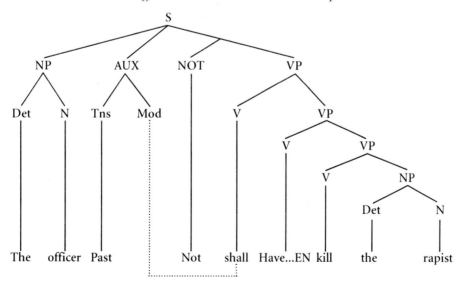

[11] The proponents of the non-transformational account dismiss apparent counterexamples such as, "Ask **NOT** what your country can do for you, but what you can do for your country," found in JFK's memorable speech. They claim that it is an instance of stylistic transformation that is of little interest in theoretical linguistics!

To derive < *The officer should not have killed the rapist* >, <should> is moved from its position from under VP and placed under AUX. If one wanted to derive < *The officer should have not killed the rapist* >, one would do the same by moving <Have ...EN> from under the second VP and placing it under AUX and before <should>.

10.6.3 The Occam Razor Principle in Use

In dealing with negation, teachers have now two approaches that they can draw from. They can follow the transformational route or they can take the non-transformational route. Moreover, they can rationalize their choice by appealing to the Occam Razor discussed in 4.1. *The Minimalist Program* by eliminating the transformational component, seems to suggest that the non-transformational approach is simpler. However, the transformational approach is valuable as a pedagogical tool because it highlights how transformations work to derive surface structure sentences from their underlying deep structure counterparts. I personally favor the transformational approach because, as we will see in 10.9, it offers teachers great insights about the role that adverbs can play in composition.

10.7 *Adverbs and Syntactic Ambiguity*

Just as we noted in 9.5.9 for adjectives, adverbs also are prone to syntactic ambiguities. This is particularly true when the same degree word is made to modify two or more adverbs, as in the following sentence:

(46) *Teenagers talk **rather** fast and loud.*

This sentence is syntactically ambiguous because it can be interpreted in at least two different ways. In one case, <rather> modifies both <fast> and <loud>, as represented by the diagram below:

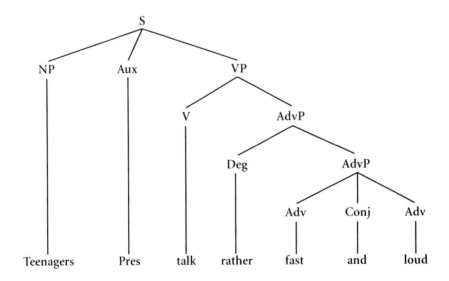

The other possible meaning is that <rather> modifies only <fast> but not <loud>. This interpretation is reflected in the following diagram:

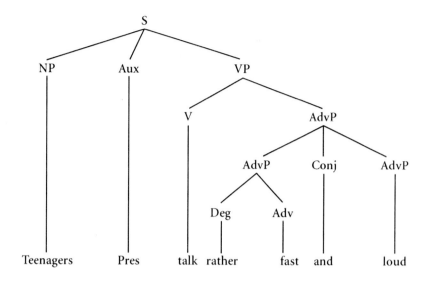

10.8 The Function of Adverbs

Adverbs are hard to classify and identify because semantic, morphological, and syntactic tests do not give definitive answers. Consequently, more often than not, one must rely on functional analysis in deciding whether or not a word is an adverb. This difficulty is compounded by the fact that other parts of speech that are not formally adverbs can function as adverbs in some sentences. Let us now see how functional clues can help us in the identification and classification of adverbs.

10.8.1 Noun Phrases Used as Adverbs

The words <yesterday> and <home> in (47) and (49) are nouns. However, the same words function as adverbs in (48) and (50):

(47) *I'll always remember* **yesterday** *as long as I live.*

(48) *They arrived* **yesterday** *from Cairo.*

(49) *Our* **home** *is your* **home.**

(50) *They went* **home** *discouraged.*

The part of speech of <yesterday> in (47) is a noun because it is the direct object complement of the verb <remember>. It also answers the question "what." However, in (48) <yesterday> is an adverb because it answers the question <when>. Similarly, <home> in (49) is a noun because it is preceded by the determiners <our> and <your>. In (50), on the other hand, it is an adverb because it answers the question <where>. This example shows clearly that one must take contextual clues into account in deciding whether or not a lexical item is an adverb.

10.8.2 Prepositional Phrases Used as Adverbs

Many adverbs have prepositional equivalents. For instance <hurriedly> and <in a hurry> have the same meaning. Additionally, some grammarians give the label of adverb to prepositional phrases that answer the question <where>, <when>, <why>, and <how>. This is the reason why Disterheft (2003:229) considers "up a tree" to be an adverb in the sentence below:

(51) *Did Shadow chase Noami up a tree?*

In mainstream generative grammar, even though prepositional phrases may function semantically as adverbs, they are represented in tree diagrams as prepositional phrases, not as adverbs. The reasoning behind this position is that functional information is not represented in tree diagrams (see section 4.2.7). Since the theoretical underpinning of this book is classical generative transformational grammar, we reserve the label "Adverbial Phrase" only for lexical items that are formally adverbs.

10.8.3 Adjectives Used vs. Adverbs

Some words that end in <-ly> can be classified either as adverbs or adjectives, depending on how they are used in a sentence. The words that belong to this category often denote time, frequency, or chronology. Table 16 contains some of these words:

No.	Nouns	Derived Adjectives/adverbs
1.	day	daily
2.	hour	hourly
3.	week	weekly
4.	month	monthly
5.	annual	annually
6.	year	yearly
7.	season	seasonally

Table 16 *Adjectives or Adverbs Derived from Nouns*

These words are derived from nominal roots instead of being derived from adjectival roots, as is the case for most manner adverbs. In deciding whether or not these words are adverbs, one has to rely on the lexical elements being modified. Let us illustrate this with the two sentences, (52) and (53):

(52) *Sarah works out **daily** at the gym.*

(53) *A **daily** dose of humor is good medicine.*

In (52) <daily> is an adverb because it modifies the phrasal verb <work out>. However, in (53) <daily> is an adjective because it modifies the noun <dose>. These examples show once again that the presence of the suffix <-ly> does not guarantee that the word in question is an adverb. In some cases, contextual clues must be taken into account before one can make a decision about the status of a word that ends in <-ly>.

10.8.4 Clauses Used as Adverbs

The label of "adverb" is also applied to clauses that answer the questions <why> or <for what purpose/reason>. So, in (54) below, the group of words < *because she was fed up with the faculty*> is referred to in traditional grammar books as an adverbial clause.

(54) *The chancellor resigned **because she was fed up with the faculty.***

Here too, I follow mainstream generative grammar in not considering such a clause as an adverb. We mention this only in passing. Clausal constructions will be dealt with later in Chapters 12 and 13. Adverbs such as <because> which introduce clauses are called "conjunctive adverbs," as will be discussed in 12.5.4 and 12.9.1.

10.8.5 Adverbial Complements

It was noted in 8.5.7 that some English verbs select adverbial complements. These complements appear in the form of NPs and are used mostly with verbs denoting quantity, cost, and measurement. Thus, in (55), (56) and (57), the NP functions as an adverbial complement:

> (55) *My friends spent **half a million dollars** on their home.*

> (56) *Their house cost **an arm and a leg**.*

> (57) *This baby weighs **a ton!***

In these constructions, the various NPs function semantically as adverbs because they answer the question <how much>. Again, according to Chomsky (1965:68–9) as reported in 4.2.7, functional information is not to be indicated on tree diagrams. Consequently, in diagramming any of the sentences above, the highlighted phrases will appear as NPs, not AdvPs.

10.9 *Unleashing Adverbial Power in Writing*

Adverbs play an important role in communication. They play an even bigger role in writing. Simply by moving an adverb from its default position to another location in the sentence, writers can turn an ordinary sentence into an extraordinary one. Speech writers and novelists have known the power of adverbial movement for a long time, and they often use it to communicate their message very effectively. To illustrate this point, let us compare the two sentences below. In (58) the adverbs occur in their unmarked positions. In (59), on the other hand, they have been moved to sentence initial position:

> (58) *We hope **fondly**—we pray **fervently**—that this mighty scourge of war may pass away **speedily**.*

> (59) ***Fondly** do we hope—**fervently** do we pray—that this mighty scourge of war may **speedily** pass away.*[12]

The stylistic effect of the two sentences is clearly noticeable. Teachers can unleash their students' creative powers by helping them understand how and where to move adverbs from one position to another for maximum impact. The issues of movement involved in these stylistic transformations are discussed below.

10.9.1 Adverbial Fronting

Adverbial fronting, also known as **"adverbial preposing,"** consists of moving an adverb from its default position and placing it at the very beginning of the sentence. According to Curmes (1931:130–1), adverbial fronting is used for emphasis. Sentence (60) <***Already,** George has been making plans*>, is an example of adverbial fronting. Modality adverbs and some temporal adverbs are often fronted for stylistic reasons.

---

[12] Taken from Abraham Lincoln's *Second Inaugural Address.*

In oral speech, the fronted adverb is heavily stressed. There is also a slight pause between the pre-posed adverb and the rest of the sentence. In writing, the same information is conveyed by the placement of a comma between the fronted adverb and the rest of the sentence, as in (60).

(60) *Already, George has been making plans.*

10.9.2 Adverbial Fronting and Inversions

Moving adverbs can set in motion other syntactic constructions. For instance, when place adverbs such as <here>, <there>, <up>, <down> are moved to the front of the sentence in an elevated style, an Auxiliary-Subject Inversion transformation is expected, as seen in (61) below:

(61) *Here comes the dean again with his unreasonable expectations from the faculty.*

In addition to place adverbs, the use of the adverbs in Table 17 often calls for both adverbial fronting and Auxiliary-Subject Inversion. Unlike the inversion discussed in the paragraph above which connotes surprise or annoyance, the use of the adverbs in Table 17 signals an elevated style most suitable in formal registers.

No.	Fronting Adverbs
1.	never
2.	seldom
3.	rarely
4.	scarcely
5.	hardly
6.	here
7.	now
8.	there
9.	nor
10.	not once

Table 17 *Inversion Adverbs*

In his memorable *"I Have a Dream"* speech, Rev. Dr. Martin Luther King, Jr. uses adverbial inversion very effectively in the last stanza of his speech.

(62) *"Now is the time to rise from the dark and desolate valley of segregation to the sunlit path of racial justice. Now is the time to open the doors of opportunity to all of God's children. Now is the time to lift our nation from the quicksands of racial injustice to the solid rock of brotherhood."*

The derivational process involved in adverbial inversion is similar to that of negation and Yes/No question formation. If no auxiliary verb is found in the deep structure sentence, <Do –insertion> is necessary for the sentence to be grammatical. Otherwise, the sentence becomes ill-formed as shown in (63):

(63) *?Fondly we hope—fervently we pray—that this mighty scourge of war may speedily pass away.*

10.10 Summary of Adverbial Positions

The position taken in this chapter is that in an SVO pattern, the adverb occurs immediately after the main verb, as was noted in several places in 10.5.3. Consequently, if an adverb is found in any other position in the sentence, it means that the adverb has been moved from its original post-verbal position. The various adverbial movement transformations can be described as noted in Table 18 below:

No.	Syntactic Positions of Adverbs	Description
1.	**AdvP** SVO	Adverbial Fronting
2.	S **AdvP** Aux 1 Aux 2 VO	The adverb moves between the subject and first auxiliary verb.
3.	S Aux 1 **AdvP** Aux 2 VO	The adverb moves between the first and the second auxiliary verbs.
4.	S Aux 1 Aux 2 **AdvP** VO	The adverb moves right before the main verb.
5.	S Aux 1 Aux 2 VO **AdvP**	The adverb moves to a sentence final right after the object.

Table 18 *Adverbial Positions and Transformation*

10.11 Conclusion

Adverbs are notoriously difficult to identify and classify for a number of reasons. They are semantically and functionally similar to prepositions. Morphologically, adjectives and adverbs share the same inflectional morphemes. The derivational morpheme <-ly> that is characteristic of adverbs is sometimes found on adjectives as well. Syntactically, both adverbs and adjectives take degree words. The only true clue that one can use to distinguish between adverbs and adjectives is mobility. Even then, adverbs are not the only parts of speech that can move from their default position to another part of the sentence. All this gives credence to contemporary linguists' suspicion of adverbs as forming a coherent part of speech. These objections are valid, but they should not paralyze teachers to the point of giving up on adverbs. When their syntactic and functional behaviors are properly understood, adverbs can enhance the quality of students' writing.

Key Terms to Know

These are the key terms that you should be able to use and define after reading this chapter:

1. adverb: 10.0, 10.1, 10.1.1, 10.2, 10.2.2, 10.2.3, 10.2.4, 10.2.5, 10.2.6, 10.3.1, 10.3.2, 10.3.3, 10.4, 10.4.1, 10.4.2, 10.5, 10.5.1, 10.5.3, 10.5.4, 10.6.3, 10.7, 10.8, 10.8.1, 10.8.2, 10.8.3, 10.8.4, 10.9, 10.9.1, 10.9.2, 10.10, 10.11

2. adverbial fronting/preposing: 10.9.1, 10.9.2

3. adverbial phrase: 10.5.1, 10.8.2

4. auxiliary-subject inversion: 10.9.2

5. degree word/intensifier/modifier: 10.1, 10.2.1, 10.2.2, 10.4, 10.7, 10.11

6. flat adverb: 10.3, 10.4.2

7. free variation: 10.3.4

8. manner adverb: 10.2, 10.2.1, 10.2.2

9. mobility adverb: 10.2.5, 10.5

10. modality/sentence adverb: 10.2.5

11. Occam Razor Principle: 10.6.3

12. place adverb: 10.2, 10.2.3, 10.9.2

13. stylistic transformation: 10.5.4, 10.9, 10.9.1, 10.9.2

14. time adverb: 10.2, 10.2.4

15. verb raising: 10.6.2

EXERCISE 1—SENTENCE DIAGRAMMING

Diagram the following sentences. Be careful, some of the sentences may be ambiguous. Assume in all these diagrams that the adverb occurs in a post-verbal environment.

1.   The wise speak softly but convincingly.

2.   The county built the new stadium downtown.

3.   It is altogether fitting and proper.

4.   The world will long remember the fallen heroes in this place.

EXERCISE 2—DEEP STRUCTURES

Determine the most likely deep structure forms of the following sentences. Comment on where the adverb used to be and where it is in the surface structure sentence. Focus mostly on adverbs and ignore any other detail that is not pertinent to your analysis. Keep in mind that the deep structure of English sentences has an SVO pattern.

1.   Now we are engaged in a great civil war.

     Deep structure:

2.   They have thus far nobly advanced our cause.

     Deep structure:

3.   She has probably committed a felony.

     Deep structure:

EXERCISE 3—MORE ON TRANSFORMATIONS

Examine the sentence below and answer the following questions:

Students will probably always complain loudly about grammar.

1. The deep structure of <*Students will probably always complain loudly about grammar*> has been provided. Proceed with all the transformations that must take place to derive the surface structure.

    Deep structure: Student Pl Fut. complain probably always loudly about grammar

    Surface structure: *Students will probably always complain loudly about grammar*

2. Draw a tree diagram of this sentence so as to reflect its deep structure form.

EXERCISE 4 ADVERB IDENTIFICATION

Fill the table below with five adverbs from the text. Use semantic, morphological, and syntactic evidence to support your classification. Group your adverbs according to the following categories:

1. manner adverb

2. modality/sentential adverb

3. time adverb

4. place adverb

5. degree word

Note: Keep in mind that some categories listed here may not appear in the text. If an adverb occurs many times, list it only once.

The Gettysburg Address

by Abraham Lincoln

"Fourscore and seven years ago our fathers brought forth on this continent a new nation, conceived in liberty and dedicated to the proposition that all men are created equal. Now we are engaged in a great civil war, testing whether that nation or any nation so conceived and so dedicated can long endure. We are met on a great battle-field of that war. We have come to dedicate a portion of that field as a final resting-place for those who here gave their lives that that nation might live. It is altogether fitting and proper that we should do this.

But in a larger sense, we cannot dedicate, we cannot consecrate, we cannot hallow this ground. The brave men, living and dead who struggled here have consecrated it far above our poor power to add or detract. The world will little note nor long remember what we say here, but it can never forget what they did here. It is for us the living rather to be dedicated here to the unfinished work which they who fought here have thus far so nobly advanced. It is rather for us to be here dedicated to the great task remaining before us—that from these honored dead we take increased devotion to that cause for which they gave the last full measure of devotion—that we here highly resolve that these dead shall not have died in vain, that this nation under God shall have a new birth of freedom, and that government of the people, by the people, for the people shall not perish from the earth."

No.	Place Adverbs	Manner Adverbs	Modality Adverbs	Time Adverbs	Degree Words
1.					
2.					
3.					
4.					
5.					

EXERCISE 5—UNDERSTANDING GRAMMATICAL TERMINOLOGY

1. Make a sentence with a place adverb. Underline the place adverb.

2. Make a sentence with a manner adverb. Underline the manner adverb.

3. Make a sentence with a degree word. Underline the degree word.

4. Make a sentence with a modality adverb that functions as a sentential adverb. Underline the modality/sentential adverb.

5. Make a sentence with a time adverb. Underline the time adverb.

```
I N W B V J K C D R S P O
S K W L A S D K F N S Q I
W B W B N P O F R Q O W P
N R M U O T P E V E R B P
W E G H A U K I N A P O R
I V N W B V J K C N R S P
D D L A S D K F N U L A J
F A Q O W P I E B O A M U
P E W N C A P I W N G H A
N A P O R N W B V J K C D
A D J E C T I V E O A N S
D K F N W L A J W K E F R
```

MINOR PARTS OF SPEECH

Chapter 11

Prepositions, Particles, and the Prepositional Phrase

11.0 INTRODUCTION

Prepositions can be defined simply as closed class words that indicate a relation between two words, the last of which must be a noun. This definition spells out right away the relationship of dependency that exists between prepositions and nouns. The former, like a parasite, depends on the latter for its survival. Nouns can exist without prepositions, but prepositions cannot exist without nouns. To put it slightly differently, where there is a preposition, there must also be a noun. A preposition without a noun is unheard of in grammar. In English syntax and in the syntax of many languages, prepositions occur before a noun. However, there are hundreds of languages in which "prepositions" occur after the noun. In such languages, "prepositions" are called **postpositions**.

Etymologically, the word "preposition" is a compound consisting of the prefix "pre-" and the stem "position." The name of this part of speech was calqued from the Greek <*prothesis*> into Latin. The Greek prefix <pro-> means "before," and the stem <thesis> means "position." The Latin word that "begat" the English term "preposition" is also made up of the prefix "prae" (before) and the stem "position."

11.1.1 Frequency of Prepositions

Estimates of the number of English prepositions range from sixty to seventy. This is an impressive number because prepositions are closed class items. Prepositions occur with high frequency in both written and spoken English. The table below lists thirty of the most frequent prepositions.

No.	Prepositions and their Frequency Count[1]
1.	of (540,085)
2.	in (331,235)
3.	for (142,421)
4.	to (125,691)
5.	with (124,965)
6.	on (109,129)
7.	at (100,169)
8.	by (77,794)
9.	from (74,843)
10.	about (38,428)
11.	than (20,210)
12.	over (18,071)
13.	through (14,964)
14.	after (13,670)
15.	between (13,275)
16.	under (9,525)
17.	per (6,515)
18.	among (5,090)
19.	within (5,030)
20.	towards (4,700)
21.	above (3,056)
22.	near (2,026)
23.	off (1,695)
24.	past (1,575)
25.	worth (1,563)
26.	toward (1,390)
27.	till (686)
28.	amongst (525)
29.	via (351)
30.	amid (222)

Table 1 *List of High Frequency Prepositions*

Prepositions are also frequent because they appear in a wide variety of syntactic contexts, as illustrated by the examples below:

(1)   *The house **on** the hill collapsed.* (after a noun)

(2)   *She ran **up** the hill.* (after a verb)

[1] Jurafsky, Daniel and James H. Martin. (2000:292). The Frequency counts are from COBUILD 16 million word corpus.

(3)   *Mary is fond **of** chocolate.* (after an adjective)

(4)   *We saw her **at** the airport.* (after a pronoun)

(5)   *They drove quickly **into** the street.* (after an adverb)

(6)   *They go in and **out** of the penitentiary as a normal way of life.* (after a conjunction)

11.1.2 Frustration with Prepositional Meaning

Prepositions are everywhere. Consequently, one would think that they are easy to classify semantically. But in fact, accurate semantic classification of prepositions in English has eluded linguists for centuries. Assessing prepositional meaning and classifying prepositions semantically is frustrating because they are generally **polysemous. Polysemy** is a semantic characteristic of words that have multiple meanings. To illustrate the polysemous nature of prepositions, let us consider the word <with> in the examples below:

(7)   *The alumni association presented the dean **with** the Distinguished Scholar Award.*

(8)   *Jeremy went camping **with** Ben.*

(9)   *Tallie cut Olivia's hair **with** scissors.*

(10) *She still lives **with** her parents.*

(11) *You need to soak in the bath tonight because you are covered **with** dirt.*

The preposition <with> has a different meaning in each one of these sentences. Linguists have also had difficulty pinning down the exact meaning of <of> because in examples such as the following, it has several different meanings:

(12) *The declaration **of** independence*

(13) *A woman **of** great integrity*

(14) *Saul **of** Tarsus*

(15) *A piece **of** my mind*

(16) *The triangle **of** death*

(17) *A litany **of** complaints*

(18) *The Son **of** David*

In each one of these phrases, the preposition <of> has a different meaning. We encounter the same semantic classification difficulties with the prepositions <in>, <from>, and <out>. As a result, most linguists have given up on a semantic classification as a way of identifying prepositions. Instead, they resort to thematic role analysis.

11.1.3 Prepositions and Thematic Roles

The concept of thematic roles was introduced and discussed in 6.2.5. Suffice it to say here that verbs and prepositions are the two main parts of speech that assign thematic roles to nouns. Consequently, the thematic role that a noun receives gives us a very important clue as far as the meaning of the preposition is concerned. Table 2 is a modified version of Table 2 in 6.2.5. In these examples, we can deduce the meaning of the preposition by examining the thematic role of the noun.

No.	Thematic Roles	Definitions	Examples
1.	Agent	The volitional causer of an event	The car was damaged *by the demonstrators.*
2.	Accompaniment/ Commitative	The involved in an event participant	Tallie is playing *with Chloe.*
3.	Force	The non-volitional causer of an event	The house was destroyed *by the tornado.*
4.	Instrument	An instrument used in an event	Joni paints with *her teeth.*
5.	Beneficiary	The beneficiary of an event	Parents work hard *for their children.*
6.	Source	The origin of an object or a person	Men are *from Mars* and women are *from Venus.*
7.	Goal	The destination of an object or a person	Our friends are flying *to Ghana.*
8.	Location	The place where an object or a person is found	Melissa and Brit used to live *in Kazakhstan.*
9.	Path	The path followed by a person or an object	Jeff went to Casablanca *through Paris.*

Table 2 *Prepositions and Thematic Roles*

Thematic role analysis provides us with a reliable semantic test for identifying prepositions and for distinguishing them from other parts of speech. This test can be stated as follows:

Thematic Role Test

Any closed class word that assigns a thematic role to the NP that follows it, is a preposition.

The only potential drawback is that the analyst must know the names of the different thematic roles in order to identify and classify prepositions. However, it is not a herculean task to ask language professionals to memorize these thematic role labels. Their colleagues in the medical profession, in chemistry, in physics, and in the sciences have to commit to memory far more technical vocabulary items than the few mentioned here.

11.2 Morphology of Prepositions

Prepositions, like other minor parts of speech, are not rich in morphology. There is practically nothing worth saying concerning the morphology of prepositions, except to note that occasionally the prepositions <in> and <out> are used as nouns, as shown in the sentence below and in 11.8.1:

(19) *Politicians want to investigate the **ins** and **outs** of scandals when it is to their advantage.*

Apart from this unusual case, prepositions do not take inflectional affixes. The two areas where the morphology of prepositions is worth investigating are case assignment and word formation. Let us begin with the former.

11.2.1 Prepositions and Case

Prepositions and verbs assign **case** to nouns and pronouns. A case is an inflectional suffix that is added to nouns or pronouns to indicate their grammatical function. English used to have a case system but it has now lost its case endings except for personal and relative pronouns, as seen in Table 3 below:

List of Cases	Definition	Personal Pronouns	Relative Pronouns	Illustrations
Nominative/ Subjective	The doer of the action or the subject of the verb	I, you, he, she, it, we, you, they	who	*She* met the man *who* saved her life.
Genitive/ Possession	Primarily indicates a relationship of possession	mine, yours, his, hers, its, ours, yours, theirs	whose	She met the man *whose* heroic act saved *her* life.
Dative	Indicates indirect object	to/with me, you, him, her, it, us, you, them	to/ with whom	She met the man *to whom* she is indebted.
Accusative/ Objective	Indicates the direct object	me, you, him, her, it, us, you, them	whom	She met the man *whom* she admires for saving *her* life.

Table 3 *Pronouns, Prepositions, and Case*

The dative and genitive cases that prepositions assign to relative pronouns are illustrated by the examples below:

(20)   *The professor **to whom** you were talking is a Nobel laureate.* (Dative case)

(21)   *The professor **whose** textbook we are using in this class is a Noble laureate.* (Genitive case)

Since the advent of the Government-Binding theory (1981), it is now assumed that all NPs in English are marked with case, whether case is reflected in words orthographically, phonetically, or not at all.[2] From this we conclude that prepositions assign cases to all NPs or pronouns that follow them. Therefore, evidence of case marking by a closed class word is proof that that word is a preposition. Consequently, case marking is a reliable morphological clue for identifying prepositions. The <Case Marking Test> can be formulated as follows:

Case Test

Any closed class word that assigns case to an NP or a pronoun is a preposition.

The close connection between English prepositions and case was stated long ago by Curme (1931:562) who argued that the loss of various case endings led to the creation of prepositions.

---

[2] Case that is not phonetically realized is called "abstract" case.

11.2.2 Prepositions and Word Formation Processes

Prepositions often combine with verbs and nouns to create new words. Examples of prepositions that frequently combine with verb stems are listed in Table 4. Some that interact with nouns to create compound prepositions are found in Table 5.

No.	Prepositions	Verbs	Compound Verbs
1.	for +	bear →	forbear
2.	down +	play →	downplay
3.	out +	do →	outdo
4.	under +	estimate →	underestimate
5.	over +	estimate →	overestimate

Table 4 *Prepositions and Compound Verbs*

No.	Prepositions	Nouns	Compound Nouns
1.	in +	mate →	inmate
2.	out +	doors →	outdoors
3.	in +	side →	inside
4.	out +	side →	outside
5.	under +	garment →	undergarment
6.	over +	seas →	overseas
7.	off +	shore →	offshore
8.	by +	product →	byproduct
9.	above +	board →	aboveboard
10.	after +	thought →	afterthought
11.	on +	line →	online
12.	in +	fighting →	infighting
13.	down +	turn →	downturn

Table 5 *Prepositions and Compound Nouns*

Occasionally two prepositions combine to create a single preposition. The words <throughout>, <within>, and <without> illustrate this process. Compounding two prepositions to create single prepositions such as these is not a very productive word formation process in English, that is, no such new prepositions are being added to the language.

11.2.3 Prepositions and Word Formation Processes

In addition to the compounds listed in Tables 4 and 5, frequently two or three parts of speech are strung together with a preposition to form a complex preposition called a **"phrasal preposition."** Two-word phrasal prepositions are listed in Table 6 while three-word and four-word prepositions are found in Table 7.

No.	Compound Prepositions
1.	according to[3]
2.	across from
3.	alongside of
4.	apart from
5.	up to
6.	away from
7.	ahead of
8.	along with
9.	as for
10.	aside from
11.	because of
12.	but for
13.	contrary to
14.	except for
15.	instead of
16.	next to
17.	out of
18.	prior to
19.	up to
20.	thanks to
21.	together with
22.	down from
23.	up against

Table 6 *Two-word Prepositions*

Two-word prepositions generally consist of an adverb and a preposition, as in <aside from>, or of two prepositions, as in <up to>. The difference between this compounding process and the compounding process that resulted in the creation of <within>, <throughout>, and <without> is orthographical. For reasons that are unclear, these three compounds are represented orthographically as one word while the others in Table 6 are written as two separate words. Similarly, English has created complex prepositions that consist of three or four words. Generally in these prepositions, a noun is sandwiched between two prepositions, as shown in Table 7 on page 304:

---

[3] Most of the words in Tables 6 and 7 are taken from Curme's (1931:502-566) extensive list of English prepositions.

No.	Complex Prepositions
1.	on account of
2.	at the cost of
3.	at the hands of
4.	at the risk of
5.	at the peril of
6.	at the point of
7.	in accordance with
8.	in addition to
9.	in advance of
10.	in agreement with
11.	in care of
12.	in conformity with
13.	in contrast with
14.	in the event of
15.	in the matter of
16.	in the middle of
17.	in the midst of
18.	in the name of
19.	in the presence of
20.	in return for
21.	in relation to
22.	in spite of
23.	in support of
24.	in back of
25.	on behalf of
26.	by means of
27.	by order of
28.	by reason of
29.	by virtue of
30.	by way of
31.	in case of
32.	in charge of
33.	in connection with
34.	in front of
35.	in lieu of
36.	for the sake of
37.	for fear of
38.	for lack of
39.	for the benefit of
40.	for the purpose of
41.	from lack of
42.	on top of
43.	in/on the face of
44.	next door to
45.	under cover of
46.	with reference to
47.	with the exception of

Table 7 *Three-Word Prepositions*

In tree diagrams, two-word or three-word prepositions behave just like one-word prepositions, that is, they are dominated by a single preposition node, as seen in the tree diagram below of (22). The phrasal preposition <next door to> is under P.

(22)   *My aunt lives **next door to** a millionaire.*

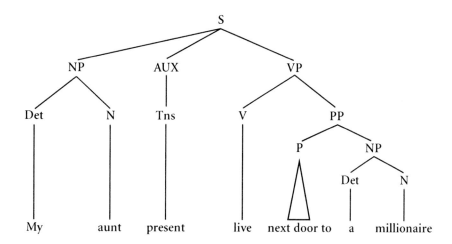

So long as <next door to> is perceived as a complex preposition, there is no reason to parse it out into its constituent parts in the tree diagram. Thus, it would be laborious and fruitless to think of <next door to> as consisting of an adjective <next>, of a noun <door> and of a preposition <to>. It has been argued that complex phrases such as those in Table 7 are entered in the mental lexicon as non-compositional chunks.

11.3 Syntactic Characteristics of PP

The syntax of prepositions will be studied from three different angles. First, we will consider distributional issues. Secondly, the similarities and differences between prepositions and particles (see 11.3.3) will be examined. Finally, we will study the subcategorization frames in which prepositions occur.

11.3.1 The Distribution Pattern of Prepositions

By far the most important distributional characteristics of prepositions is that they must occur with a noun phrase. In English and other languages that have prepositions, a noun must necessarily follow the preposition, as evidenced by (23) and (24) below:

(23)   *Mary ran **into** the house.*

(24)   **Mary ran the house **into**.*

The preposition <into> must precede the noun phrase <the house>. This requirement is met by (23). Sentence (24) is judged ungrammatical because the preposition fails to precede the noun. As noted in the introduction, there are many languages in which (24) would be grammatical because these languages take postpositions instead of prepositions. If English were a postposition language, (24) would be well-formed. That a noun or pronoun should always follow a preposition is a necessary and sufficient criterion for identifying prepositions. This constraint can be stated as a diagnostic test:

Distributional Test

Any closed class lexical item that precedes a noun phrase or pronoun and receives case or thematic role assignment from it is a preposition.

In a way, the distributional test as formulated above is a super-test. It includes the two other tests formulated in 11.1.3 and 11.2.1. The same information can be presented as a set of distinctive features:

Test	Noun	Verb	Adjective	Adverb	Preposition	Conjunction	Pronoun	Article
Closed Class item Followed by a Noun or Pronoun with case or Thematic Role	–	–	–	–	+	–	–	–

Table 8 *Distributional test*

This test is so reliable that we will use it later in 11.8.3 to distinguish between prepositional phrases and adverbial phrases. This constraint has also allowed linguists to propose a very precise phrase structure rule for prepositional phrases (PPs).

11.3.2 Phrase Structure Rules and Recursion

The phrase structure for PPs is formulated simply as follows:

$$PP \rightarrow P\ NP$$

Notice that because of the constraint stated above, a phrase structure rule of the following type has not been attested in English:

$$*PP \rightarrow P\ (NP)$$

One of the most important syntactic characteristics of prepositional phrases is **recursion**. Noun phrases can generate prepositional phrases and prepositional phrases can, in turn, "beget" noun phrases up to infinity:

$$NP \rightarrow N\ PP$$
$$PP \rightarrow P\ NP$$

Prepositional phrases can also be modified by degree words such as "straight" and "right." This new piece of information leads to the expansion of the phrase structure rule for PPs as follows:

$$PP \rightarrow (Deg)\ P\ NP$$

Prepositional Phrases which conform to the phrase structure rule above can be illustrated by (25):

(25) *The student walked **straight** up to the professor.*

Sentence (25) can be diagrammed as follows:

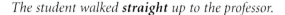

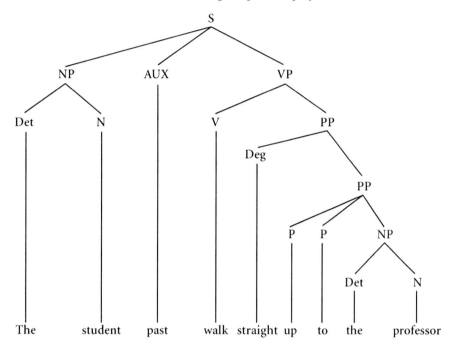

The lower PP deserves a parenthetical comment. The sentence <*The student walked **straight** to the professor* > is well-formed. This means that <up> does not form a unit with <straight>. The sentence <* *The student walked **straight** up the professor* > is ill-formed. This means that <to> is the indispensable preposition in this sentence because omitting it results in an ill-formed sentence. What then is the role of <up> in (25) and how should it be represented in a tree diagram? Does <up> form a compound with <to>? The fact that <up> can be omitted without the sentence being ill-formed tells us that <up> and <to> do not constitute a compound preposition. In the tree diagram, <up> has been given the ad hoc label of "preposition" without necessarily deserving it. This parenthetical comment forewarns us that, as will be discussed below, not everything that looks like a preposition is actually a preposition. There are preposition "wannabes" in English. These are words that look like prepositions but act differently from "real" prepositions.

11.3.3 Prepositions vs. Particles

By far the most important issue in dealing with the syntax of prepositional phrases is the distinction between **prepositions** and preposition look-alikes that linguists call <particles>. Martin (2000:292) defines the particle as "a word that resembles a preposition or an adverb, and that often combines with a verb to form a larger unit called a phrasal verb." Prepositions and particles are like identical twins. They are phonetically and orthographically indistinguishable. They are true **homophones** because they are pronounced the same; and they are true **homographs** because they are spelled the same. There are only two ways to tell prepositions and particles apart from each other. The first is by applying a semantic test, and the second is through a series of syntactic tests. Let us focus on the semantic test here. The syntactic tests will be considered in sections 11.3.5 and following.

11.3.4 Semantic Distinctions between Prepositions and Particles

As noted in 11.1.3, the meaning of prepositions can be deduced from the thematic roles that they assign to the nouns and pronouns. In (26) <in> and <trunk> have different meanings. The preposition <in> assigns a locative meaning to <trunk>:

> (26)   *The criminal locked up the victim **in the trunk.***

In semantic analysis, it is said that the meaning of the prepositional phrase <in the trunk> is **compositional,** that is, each word in the phrase keeps its own meaning. Notice that this is not the case when particles are used. When a particle is used with a verb, together they form an **idiomatic phrase.** Kolln and Funk (2006:37) define an **idiom** as a "combination of words whose meaning cannot be predicted from the meaning of its parts." Idioms are set expressions that act as single semantic units. To distinguish between prepositions and particles, linguists often rely on semantics. Here is a useful test that yields very good results.

Semantic Test for Particles

A preposition look-alike whose meaning is not compositional in the phrase in which it occurs is not a preposition, but a particle.

Let us now use this criterion to reanalyze (26).

> (26)   *The criminal **locked up** the victim in the trunk.*

The word <up> is normally a preposition. However in (26) it does not have a semantic meaning of its own. Instead, it teams up with <locked> to convey a single idea, that of "imprisonment." English uses a large number of phrasal verbs in which the "preposition" is actually a particle. Table 9 gives a sample of thirty high frequency phrasal verbs.

Proficient speakers have no trouble distinguishing particles from prepositions. However, beginning and intermediate ESL/EFL students need a great deal of exposure to such constructions before mastering them.

No.	Verb with a Particle
1.	give away
2.	put out
3.	call off
4.	look up
5.	pass out
6.	find out
7.	turn off
8.	turn on
9.	call up
10.	look over
11.	drink down
12.	gobble up
13.	fire up
14.	write up
15.	write down
16.	sound off
17.	throw up
18.	carry out
19.	rub out
20.	blend in
21.	roll over
22.	put off
23.	give up
24.	take away
25.	put on
26.	throw away
27.	cut down
28.	mix up
29.	chew out
30.	tune out

Table 9 *Phrasal Verbs*

11.3.5 Syntactic Characteristics of Prepositions and Particles

The semantic distinction made previously between prepositions and particles can be bolstered by three important syntactic tests. Let's now review these tests to see how they are applied.

11.3.5.1 The Particle Shift Test

The test commonly used to distinguish between particles and prepositions is the <Particle Shift Test>. It is a transformation that consists of shifting the particle to the right of the NP. If the resulting sentence is well-formed, it is concluded that the preposition look-alike is a particle, not a true preposition. If, on the other hand, the resulting sentence is ill-formed, it is concluded that the word is a preposition, not a particle. The particle shift test can be illustrated by examining the two sentences below:

(27)   *Jamie ran **up** the hill.*

(28)   *Jamie ran **up** the bill.*

When the particle shift test is applied to both sentences, it yields the following results:

(29)   ******Jamie ran the hill **up**.*

(30)   *Jamie ran the bill **up**.*

Sentence (29) is ill-formed but (30) is well-formed. We conclude, based on the Particle Shift Test, that <up> in (27) is not a particle but a preposition. We also conclude that <up> in (28) is a particle. The distinction between preposition and particle is made clear in tree diagrams. Sentences (27) and (28) are represented in tree diagrams as follows:

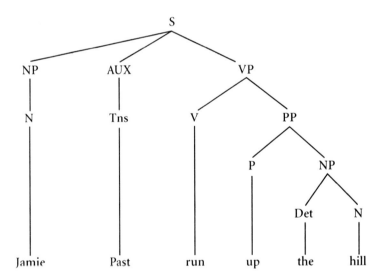

Notice that in (27) <up> occurs under PP. However, this is not the case for <up> in sentence (28).

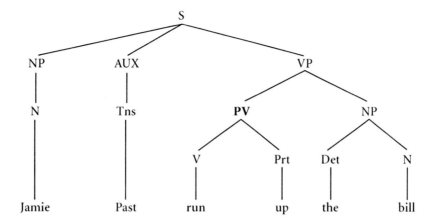

In (28) <up> occurs under <**PV**> which stands for "**phrasal verb.**" So, in diagramming prepositional phrases, the VP node dominates the P. In diagramming particles, on the other hand, the particle is part of the phrasal verb.

Linguists disagree on precisely the best way to diagram particles. While some represent particles as in the diagram above, others place the particle directly under the VP. According to this view, there is no PV node as such. The benefit of this way of representing particles becomes obvious when Particle Shift Transformation is involved. Instead of moving the particle from under PV, it is moved directly from under VP to the right side of NP as seen in the diagram of (30):

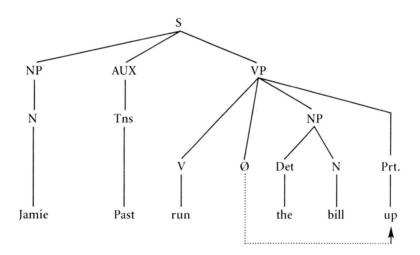

The symbol "Ø" indicates the original position of the particle before shifting took place. Theoretically, there is not a major difference between the two different ways in which particles are represented in tree diagrams. The approach which consists in placing the particle in the PV node indicates clearly that it is a phrasal verb. Therefore, this approach is syntactically informative. However, the approach which consists in placing the particle directly under the VP is also good because it makes it easier to represent particle shift directly in tree diagrams. Students should know that these two approaches are available to them.

11.3.5.2 Constraint on Particle Shift

Particle shift is an optional transformation, meaning that speakers may choose to move or not move the particle to the right of the NP. However, when a direct object NP is replaced by a direct object pronoun, particle shifts becomes an obligatory transformation, as seen in the sentences below:

(31)   *Jamie ran **up** the bill.*

(32)   *Jamie ran **it up.***

(33)   **Jamie ran **up it.***

Sentence (33) is ill-formed because the obligatory particle shift rule failed to apply. The particle shift rule can be represented by the tree diagram below:

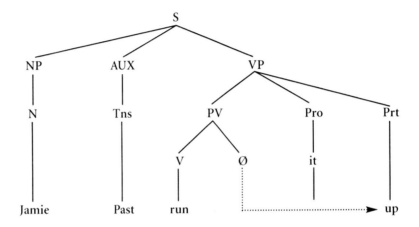

11.4 Movable vs. Immovable Particles

The preceding sections can lead to the erroneous conclusion that all particles can undergo particle shift. However, this is not the case. For this reason, Kaplan (1995:158–9) and other linguists make a distinction between **movable** and **immovable particles.**[4] A movable particle is a particle that can shift to the right of NP. Immovable particles, on the other hand, cannot be shifted in a similar fashion. Kaplan illustrates the distinction between the two types of particles with these examples:

(34)   *I came across a promising review.*

(35)   *?I came a promising review across.*

The existence of immovable particles makes it hard to rely solely on syntax to distinguish between prepositions and particles. Consequently, a semantic test should be used to tell immovable particles apart from prepositions. Kaplan explains the usefulness of semantics as follows: "an immovable particle forms a semantic unit with the verb immediately preceding it, whereas prepositions are semantically independent of preceding verbs." With this explanation, we should be able to explain which <into> in the following sentences is a particle and which is a preposition:

(36)   *My best friend in college turned into a recluse.*

(37)   **My friend turned into a corner very abruptly.*

---

[4] The terms "separable phrasal verbs" and "inseparable phrasal verbs" are also used by Jacobs (1995:248–250) in the same way.

Based on semantic clue, we conclude that <into> in (36) is a particle whereas <into> in (37) is a preposition. The next sections will give us more amunition to distinguish between prepositions and particles.

11.4.1 The PP-Preposing Test

Another test that is useful in distinguishing between particles and prepositions is the <PP-preposing Test>. This transformation consists of moving any preposition look-alike to a sentence initial position. If the resulting sentence is grammatical, then it is concluded that the word that moved is a preposition. However, if the result is an ill-formed sentence, we say that it is a particle. This test is illustrated by the examples below:

(38) *Jamie ran **up** the hill.*

(39) *Jamie ran **up** the bill.*

The transformation yields the following sentences:

(40) ***Up** the hill Jamie ran.*

(41) ****Up** the bill Jamie ran.*

The fact that (41) is ungrammatical shows that <up> is a particle. Conversely, the grammaticality of (40) indicates that <up> is a preposition.

11.5 The Adverbial Insertion Test

The purpose of the insertion test is to see if the verb and the particle form an indivisible semantic unit. The thought behind this test is that if an adverb can be inserted between the verb and the preposition look-alike, and if the resulting sentence is ill-formed, then it means that the preposition look-alike is actually a particle. However, if the resulting sentence is acceptable, then it means that the preposition look-alike is a true preposition. The rationale is that, since verb-particle combinations are idioms, no external element should be able to separate them. Let us apply this test to the same two sentences from above and see if this test confirms the preceding results:

(42) *Jamie ran **quickly** up the hill.*

(43) **Jamie ran **quickly** up the bill.*

This test confirms the two previous tests, namely that in (42), <up> is a preposition whereas in (43) it is a particle. If an adverb is inserted between a verb and what looks like a preposition, and if the resulting sentence is ill-formed as in sentence (43), then we conclude that the preposition look-alike is a particle, not a real preposition. In other words, prepositions allow adverbial insertion but particles do not tolerate it.

11.5.1 The Passivization Test

The first three tests can reliably allow us to distinguish between prepositions and particles. However, they fail to help us distinguish between movable and immovable particles. The movable particle can undergo particle shift but the immovable one cannot, as seen in the examples below:

(44) *The University's legal team is looking **into** this matter.*

(45) *The president relies **on** the University's legal team.*

Grammarians have labeled the verb and its immovable particle <u>intransitive phrasal verb</u>, while the verb and its mobile particle are called a <u>transitive phrasal verb</u>. Recall from 8.5.1 and 8.5.2 that transitive verbs are subcategorized with a direct object but intransitive verbs cannot be followed by a direct object. Again, it must be emphasized here that the passivization test is meant only to distinguish moveable and immoveable particles. If the NP that follows a phrasal verb can be passivized, it means that the phrasal verb is transitive. However, if it cannot, we conclude that the phrasal verb is intransitive. Let us see how this test applies to (46) and (47) to help us distinguish between transitive and intransitive phrasal verbs:

(46)   *This matter is being looked into by the university's legal team.*

(47)   *The university's legal team is relied on by the president.*

The fact that (47) is ungrammatical shows that <on> in the phrasal verb <rely on> is not a mobile particle. Thus, we conclude that <to rely on> is an intransitive phrasal verb. On the other hand, the grammaticality of (46) is an indication that <into> is a movable particle. However, both <on> and <into> are particles. The main difference between the two types of phrasal verbs is that <rely on> is an intransitive phrasal verb whereas <look into> is a transitive phrasal verb.

The previous tests can be summarized as follows:

No.	Tests	Preposition	Particle
1.	PP-Preposing	+	−
2.	Adverbial Insertion	+	−

Table 10A *Summary of Distributional Tests*

No.	Tests	Intransitive PV	Transitive PV
1.	Particle Shift	−	±[5]
2.	Passivization	−	+

Table 10B *Summary of Distributional Tests*

These tests reliably distinguish between prepositions and particles. If linguists wish to make further distinctions between types of particles, they resort to the passivization test to separate transitive phrasal verbs from intransitive ones. Now, let's summarize the various tests with a flow chart that can, hopefully, make it easy to distinguish between prepositions and particles:

---

[5] One characteristic of some transitive phrasal verbs is that they are separable; that is, the particle may move away from its verb to position behind the direct object by a transformation called Particle Movement (PM)," Disterheft (2003:178). The symbol "±" is used here because not all particles can undergo particle shift.

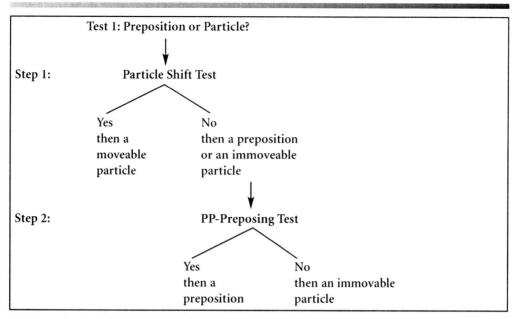

Table 10C *Flow Chart 1 Particle Shift vs. Preposition*

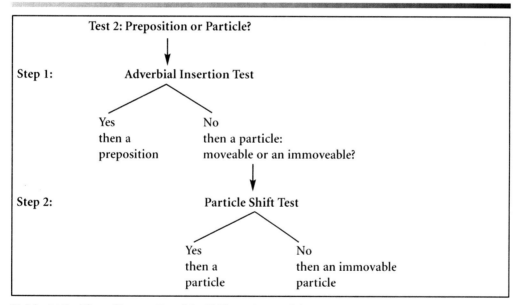

Table 10D *Flow Chart 2 Particle Shift vs. Preposition*

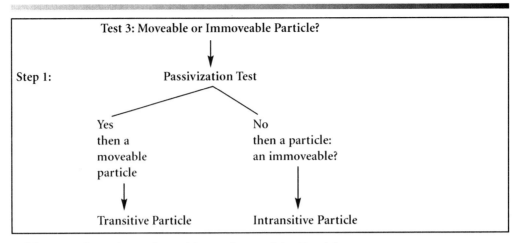

Table 10E *Flow Chart 3 Transitive vs. Intransitive Particles*

11.6 Prepositions and Subcategorization

This section is devoted to the subcategorization frame of parts of speech that must be followed by a PP. The parts of speech that we have in mind are verbs and adjectives.

11.6.1 Verbs that Require Prepositions

Many English verbs must be followed by a PP, otherwise the sentence is ill-formed. There are even verbs that cannot exist by themselves without a preposition. Take the verb <rely> for example. Its subcategorization frame must necessarily include the preposition <on> and only the preposition <on>. No other preposition can occur with <rely>, as illustrated by the sentences below:

(48) *The president **relies on** the University's legal team.*

(49) **The president **relies over** the University's legal team.*

(50) **The president **relies by** the University's legal team.*

(51) **The president **relies in** the University's legal team.*

(52) **The president **relies from** the University's legal team.*

(53) **The president **relies with** the University's legal team.*

Linguists have hypothesized, based on similar evidence, that in the mental lexicon the words <to rely> and <on> appear as a single lexical entry. Furthermore, they hypothesize that in the process of acquiring English verbs, learners acquire subconsciously which preposition is subcategorized with which verb. Native speakers and proficient speakers would know, for instance, that the verb <abide> is usually subcategorized with the prepositions <by> or <with>. Table 11 lists some verbs and the prepositions with which they are often subcategorized:

No.	Subcategorization with Prepositions
1.	to conform <to>
2.	to hint <at>
3.	to commit <to>
4.	to interfere <with>
5.	to intercede <for>
6.	to plead <for>
7.	to suffer <from>
8.	to consist <of>
9.	to part <with>
10.	to depart <from>
11.	to detract <from>
12.	to substitute <for>
13.	to compete <with>, <against>
14.	to provide <with>, <for>
15.	to long <for>
16.	to differ <from>, <with>
17.	to abstain <from>
18.	to refrain <from>
19.	to object <to>
20.	to approve <of>

Table 11 *Verbs and their Subcategorizing Prepositions*

11.6.2 Complex Phrasal Verbs

Some phrasal verbs also appear to be subcategorized with specific prepositions, as found in Celce-Murcia and Larsen-Freeman (1999:427):

No.	Complex Phrasal Verbs
1.	put up <with>
2.	look in <on>
3.	look down <on>
4.	get away <with>
5.	get down <on>
6.	get back <to>
7.	get along <with>
8.	check up <on>
9.	check out <of>
10.	go in <for>
11.	come up <with>
12.	give in <to>
13.	cut down <on>
14.	catch up <with>
15.	stand up <for>
16.	keep up <with>
17.	end up <with>
18.	pick up <on>
19.	close in <on>
20.	make away <with>
21.	make up <for>
22.	drop in <on>
23.	run up <against>
24.	break up <with>
25.	stand up <for>
26.	keep up <with>
27.	go through <with>
28.	drop in <on>

Table 12 *Phrasal Verbs with Prepositions*

Very little research has been done on complex phrasal verbs. For this reason, it has been assumed without much analysis that the words in Table 12 that appear between the brackets are prepositions. However, this assumption may be false, as shown by the following sentences:

(54) *George cannot put up with Melissa anymore.*

(55) **George cannot put up Melissa **with** anymore.*

(56) ***With Melissa** George cannot put up anymore.*

(57) ?***Up with Melissa** George cannot put anymore.*

The ungrammaticality of (55) may be accounted for by the fact that <with> is an immovable particle. The ungrammaticality of (56) on the other hand shows that <with> is not a preposition. If it were, PP preposition could take place. If it is born out that the words in angle brackets are immovable particles, then the VP of (54) can be diagrammed as follows:

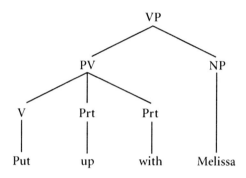

The fact that Particle Shift Movement is not possible shows that such particles are immovable. There are other instances such as <*the politician gave up under pressure*> where <*under pressure*> is clearly a prepositional phrase. In such cases, the VP can be diagrammed as follows:

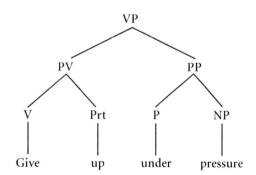

11.6.3 Particles in the Noun Phrase

In English, the preposition precedes the noun. However, there a few constructions in which a preposition look-alike occurs after the noun. These preposition look-alikes are not real prepositions. They are particles. We know that they are not prepositions because such words can take the plural suffixes. However, we know that prepositions never take the plural suffixes. Orthographically, a hyphen usually (but not always) separates the noun and the particle. The following list of words illustrates <noun + particle> constructions in English:

No.	Complex Phrasal Verbs
1.	a seat-in
2.	a dine-in
3.	kindergarten round up
4.	a push over
5.	a stare down
6.	a blow up
7.	a blow out
8.	a check up
9.	a check out
10.	a check-in
11.	a cook out
12.	a smoke out
13.	a shut-in
14.	a catch up

Table 13 *Particles in the NP*

It is perfectly legitimate to refer to such nouns as **phrasal nouns** (PN) even though, to my knowledge, such a label has not been used before. Phrasal nouns can be generated by the following phrase structure rule:

$$PN \rightarrow (Det)\ N\ Prt$$

The tree diagram of phrasal nouns can be as follows:

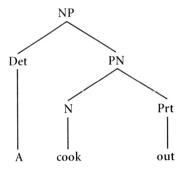

11.6.4 Adjectives that Require Prepositions

A number of adjectives in English have prepositions in their subcategorization frames. Adjectives can normally occur by themselves. However, if they occur in a distribution such as the one below, some require that a preposition occur between them and the following NP:

> Linking/Stative Verb + Adjective + P + NP

Table 14 gives us a sample of such adjectives:

No.	Subcategorization with Adjectives
1.	to be proud <of>
2.	to be fond <of>
3.	to be angry <at>, <with>
4.	to be good/bad <at>, <in>
5.	to be afraid <of>, <for>
6.	to be satisfied <with>
7.	to be different <from>
8.	to be suspicious <of>
9.	to be absent <from>
10.	to be present <at>, <with>
11.	to be interested <in>

Table 14 *Subcategorization with Adjectives*

If the preposition is omitted, the sentence becomes ill-formed, as seen in (59):

> (58) *Sue is mad **at** Scot over their divorce.*

> (59) **Sue is mad—Scot over their divorce.*

11.7 *Pedagogical Implications*

Three main pedagogical implications stand out from the preceding analysis. The first two have to do with L1 composition and the last with the teaching of prepositions to ESL/EFL learners.

11.7.1 Subcategorization and Composition

It is a linguistic truism that native speakers know the subcategorization frames of their native tongue. For this reason Clark (2003:121) argues that native speakers "intuitively choose the correct patterns and produce natural and grammatical utterances." This is generally true for spoken language, but it is not necessarily so for academic English. Some subcategorizations that are acceptable in spoken English are not acceptable in written compositions. Take the phrase <to be different>, for example. In informal conversations speakers subcategorize it with <than>. But in academia, it takes the preposition <from>.

It is therefore not accurate to assume that the subcategorization frames of spoken English will always coincide with those of written English.

11.7.2 Phrasal Verbs and their Latinate Equivalents

Phrasal verbs occur both in writing and in speech. However, they are more prevalent in spoken English. Many phrasal verbs have Latinate counterparts. The presence of these Latinate words can be explained by the massive amount of **prestige borrowing** that took place over three centuries of French colonial rule in England. English noblemen borrowed thousands of French words out of snobbism, even though the same concepts had equivalents in their native tongue. Consequently, English vocabulary doubled in some semantic fields. Native English words were used in informal conversations while Latinate words were used in elevated speech. In contemporary written English both forms are equally acceptable. However, teachers should make sure that their students do not use phrasal verbs exclusively at the expense of Latinate forms. Familiarity with Latinate forms is important because they occur in literary texts and in the verbal portions of a number of standardized tests such as the GRE and the SAT. Encouraging students to include Latinate forms in their composition increases their vocabulary power and elevates their style. Berk (1999:128–9) provides a short list of English phrasal verbs and their Latinate equivalents.

No.	Phrasal Verbs	Latinate Equivalents
1.	conform to	meet
2.	put out	extinguish
3.	call on	visit
4.	throw up	vomit
5.	give back	return
6.	put down	denigrate
7.	take off	remove/leave
8.	hint at	suggest
9.	give in	yield
10.	give up	relinquish
11.	break in on	interrupt
12.	look down on	disdain
13.	look up to	admire
14.	put up with	tolerate

Table 15 *Latinate Equivalents of Phrasal Verbs*

Extensive lists such as this one can be found in thesauruses.

11.7.3 Preposition Stranding and Written Compositions

Preposition stranding is a syntactic transformation that consists of moving the NP out of the PP node so that the preposition stands alone at the end of the clause or sentence. Sentence (61) is an illustration of preposition stranding:

(60) *The professor **from whom** you took linguistics is a Nobel laureate.*

(61) *The professor **who** you took linguistics **from** is a Nobel laureate.*

Prejudice against preposition stranding is very strong. Students get chastised for ending their sentences or clauses with a preposition. It is not clear how this prohibition originated. Stageberg and Oaks (2000:331–2) conjecture that the prohibition "may have arisen from the name of that part of speech itself: pre-position. As some prescriptivists probably reasoned, if a preposition by its name should precede the noun it is associated with, then it should never follow it—and certainly not at the end of the sentence." The classic case of preposition stranding is that of Winston Churchill who was chastised for ending his sentence with the preposition <with>. In a response to this rebuke, he allegedly produced (62).

(62) *This is the sort of nonsense up with which I shall not put.*

The consensus among linguists today is that preposition stranding is perfectly acceptable. Oaks and Stageberg argue that trying to avoid it at all costs may result in unnatural sentences. They give the following piece of advice "labored attempts to avoid a preposition at the end of a clause or sentence are unnecessary. . . . in some constructions, the preposition must come at the end of the clause or sentence. . . . A number of grammatical constructions in fact call for postponement of the preposition," (p. 332). They also note how hard it is to avoid placing <of> at the end of sentences such as "one that most people have heard of." They go on to show that resorting to "of which," "to whom," "from whom," or "with whom," would sound unnatural in some instances. Kaplan (1995:158) states that not stranding the preposition can lead to charges of "too high a level of formality."

Furthermore, preposition stranding is often syntactically necessary if particle shift movement is used. We noted in 11.4 that if the direct object is a pronoun, the particle must obligatorily move to the end of the sentence or clause, otherwise the sentence is ill-formed. Prescriptivists overlook this aspect in forbidding preposition stranding. Academic journals and serious publications have relaxed the prohibition against preposition stranding. Composition teachers need not rebuke their students for ending their sentences with a preposition.

11.7.4 The Acquisition of Prepositions by ESL/EFL Learners

The importance of teaching the subcategorization of verbs and adjectives to ESL and EFL learners cannot be emphasized enough. Celce-Murcia and Larsen-Freeman (1999:401) state the problems that English language learners have with English prepositions as follows:

Prepositions are notoriously difficult to learn. Long after ESL/EFL students have achieved a high level of proficiency in English, they still struggle with prepositions. Why do such little words as, in, on, and at cause so many problems? . . . [prepositions] not having correspondence from one language to the next become even more problematic when the meaning of prepositions is extended beyond expressing spatial relations to establishing relationships of a more abstract nature.

It is easy to overlook preposition errors when they occur infrequently. However, if a composition has a fair number of such errors, the overall quality of the work is diminished.

Subcategorization mistakes should not be taken lightly because, as Fromkin et al. (2003:133) observe, "the well-formedness of a phrase depends on at least two factors: whether the phrase conforms to the phrase structure requirements of the language, and whether the phrase conforms to the selectional requirements of the head."

Negative syntactic transfer is partly to blame for subcategorization errors. Students tend to transfer the subcategorization frames of their native language into English. When this happens, the resulting sentence is likely to be ill-formed. There are three types of subcategorization errors. Students may use a preposition where none is required in English, or they may omit a preposition where one is needed in English, or they may use the wrong preposition altogether, as is the case in the example below:

(63) *Undesirable side effects related **with** the presence of quinine. . . .*

This sentence is found in a phamaceutical leaflet warning about the sides effects of a malaria drug. It was translated from French into English by a professional French-speaking translator. The translator transfered the subcategorization frame of the equivalent of the verb <to relate> into English. The French equivalent of the verb <relate> is subcategorized with the preposition <avec> translated in English by <with>. Thus, the translation in (63) is a clear case of negative transfer.

11.7.5 Prepositions and Syntactic Ambiguities

Finally, to conclude this section on the syntax of prepositions, it is worth pointing out that prepositions, especially the prepositions <in> and <by>, contributes frequently to sentences that are syntactically ambiguous. Sentence (64), for instance, has two separate meanings.

(64) *Dale saw a bird **in** the garage.*

This sentence is syntactically ambiguous because it has two different deep structures as revealed by the two tree diagrams below:

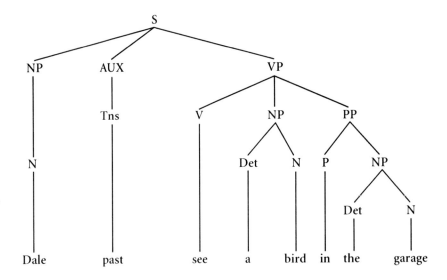

The first diagram can be interpreted to mean that Dale saw the bird while standing in the garage. The bird could have been in the flowers or on a tree outside the garage. But the bird is not in the garage. The next tree diagram conveys a different meaning, namely that the bird was in the garage.

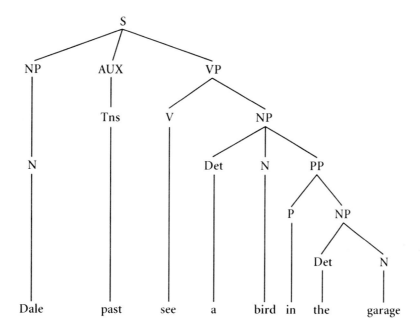

The different meanings assigned to sentence (64) depend on the node that dominates the prepositional phrase. In the first case, PP is dominated directly by VP while in the second interpretation it is dominated by the NP under VP.

11.8 The Functions of Prepositions

Prepositions, like the other parts of speech, can assume functions that are different from the part of speech under which they are normally classified. They can function as nouns, adjectives, and adverbs. Let us consider some sentences in which prepositions can fulfill these diverse roles.

11.8.1 Prepositions Used as Nouns

It is not common for prepositions to function as nouns. The words <in> and <out> function as nouns in the following sentence:

(65)   *The senators want to get to the **ins** and **outs** on this matter.*

In this sentence <in> and <out> meet two formal requirements that qualify them as nouns. First, the presence of the determiner <the> suggests that the two are nouns. Secondly, the inflectional morphology test of plurality shows that they are nouns because they have the suffix <s>. Thus, these two prepositions function as nouns in (65).

11.8.2 Prepositions Used as Adjectives

Some prepositions are used as adjectives because they can modify nouns. In the sentences below, the prepositions <in>, <off>, <over>, and <after> function as adjectives:

(66)   *Code-switching is often used for **in**-group communication.*

(67)   *The faculty senate made an **over** the board statement.*

(68) *An **off** hand comment about minorities put an end to her political ambition.*

(69) *In the summer, the beach comes alive in the **after** dinner hours.*

Numerous prepositions, including <across>, <out>, and <between> are used regularly as adjectives.

11.8.3 Prepositions vs. Adverbs

Prepositions function semantically as adverbs, as shown by Table 16. Five important semantic features are shared by both parts of speech:

No.	Semantic characteristics	Prepositions	Adverbs
1.	Direction	The boy ran *into the house.*	The boy ran *home.*
2.	Location	He fell flat *on his back.*	She teaches *here.*
3.	Manner	The plane took off *in a hurry.*	The plane took off *hurriedly.*
4.	Time	She got up *in the morning.*	She got up *early.*
5.	Frequency	She visits Grandma *in the evenings.*	She *always* visits Grandma before traveling overseas.

Table 16 *The Semantics of Prepositions and Adverbs*

As far back as 1934, Robertson, (p. 554) stated that "between adverbs and prepositions no distinct line can be drawn." Some grammarians of a generation or so ago even speculated that prepositions were originally adverbs of place. This similarity between the two parts of speech has led some linguists to give the label of "Adverb" to prepositional phrases in their tree diagrams. However, a distinction must be made between the two on formal grounds. The test for distinguishing between the two is the presence or absence of an NP. Prepositions absolutely need an NP for their syntactic "survival." Therefore, if a preposition occurs in a sentence and is not followed by an NP, that preposition is not functioning as a preposition, but rather as an adverb. The only caveat is cases of prepositional stranding at the end of clauses, as discussed in 11.7.3. The table below captures the essence of this test:

No.	Test	[+ NP]	[-NP]
1.	Preposition	+	−
2.	Adverb	−	+

Table 17 *Distinctive Feature Test*

The same information can be stated in prose as follows:

Preposition vs. Adverb Test

Any word that looks like a preposition but is not followed by an NP is an adverb.[6]

Let us apply this test to the two words <inside> in the sentences below to see which one is a preposition and which one is an adverb:

(70)   *The police went **inside** the house.*

(71)   *The police went **inside**.*

In (70) <inside> is a preposition because it is followed by an NP. However, in (71) it is an adverb because no NP follows. Both (70) and (71) answer the question <where>.

11.8.4 Are Prepositions Necessary?

Curne (1931:562) alleges that English dropped its case system and opted for prepositions in order to achieve a fuller expression of thoughts. Cross-linguistic evidence shows that this claim is patently false. Prepositions are actually cumbersome and are not necessary at all to communicate thoughts fully. For this reason, hundreds of world languages only have a very small set of prepositions. The prepositions found in such languages are limited to spatial prepositions. Language acquisition also indicates that prepositions are not needed for thoughts to be communicated. Psycholinguists have noted that prepositions, especially those that function as **deixis,** are one of the last parts of speech to be acquired in language development. Deixis are often defined as words or expressions whose meaning can be determined by relying solely on the context of the utterance (Fromkin et al 2003:218, 395). Furthermore, evidence from pidgin languages shows that prepositions are often omitted without significant impairment in the communication process.

11.9 Conclusion

Prepositions are an important part of speech in English for teachers to know and teach to their students for a number of reasons. First, prepositions contribute to the meaning of phrases and sentences. Knowing the thematic roles that they assign can help in sentence interpretation. Being knowledgeable about prepositions can help untangle many of the syntactic ambiguities that they cause. This insight can result in a deeper and richer interpretation of texts. Familiarity with the morphological case that prepositions assign to nouns and pronouns can help students avoid basic grammar mistakes. When the distinction between true prepositions and particles is presented, students can benefit by knowing why in some instances a "preposition" can move while in others it cannot. Students will also be less intimidated by the outdated prohibition against preposition stranding. Finally, the syntactic requirement that prepositions be followed by nouns can help teachers explain better the persistent confusion between prepositions and adverbs.

---

[6] We should add except for "particles" because if they occur with a pronoun, they must be in sentence-final position.

Key Terms to Know

These are the key terms that you should be able to use and define after reading this chapter:

1. case: 11.2, 11.2.1, 11.3.1, 11.6.3, 11.9
2. deixis: 11.8.4
3. homograph: 11.3.3
4. homophone: 11.3.3
5. idiom: 11.3.4, 11.3.5.5
6. idiomatic phrase: 11.3.4
7. immovable particle: 11.5.1
8. intransitive phrasal verb: 11.5.1
9. Latinate form: 11.7.2
10. movable particle: 11.4
11. particle: 11.3, 11.3.3, 11.3.4, 11.3.5, 11.3.5.1, 11.3.5.2, 11.4.1, 11.5, 11.5.1, 11.6.2, 11.6.3, 11.7.3, 11.9
12. particle shift: 11.3.5.1
13. phrasal noun: 11.6.3
14. phrasal verb: 11.3.5.1
15. polysemy: 11.1.2
16. postposition: 11.0, 11.3, 11.3.1
17. pp-preposing: 11.4.1
18. preposition stranding: 11.7.3, 11.9
19. preposition: 11.0, 11.1.1, 11.1.2, 11.1.3, 11.2, 11.2.1, 11.2.2, 11.2.3, 11.3.1, 11.3.2, 11.3.3, 11.3.4, 11.3.5, 11.6, 11.6.1, 11.6.2, 11.6.3, 11.6.4, 11.7, 11.7.4, 11.7.5, 11.8, 11.8.1, 11.8.2, 11.8.3, 11.8.4, 11.9
20. prepositional phrase: 11.3.1, 11.3.2, 11.4, 11.4.1, 11.6.2, 11.7.5, 11.8.3
21. prestige borrowing: 11.7.2
22. recursion: 11.3.2
23. thematic roles: 11.1.3, 11.3.4, 11.9
24. transitive phrasal verb: 11.5.1

EXERCISE 1—SENTENCE DIAGRAMMING

1. The dog came in from the storm.

2. Jacob pinned down his opponent.

3.   Annie broke up with her boyfriend.

4.   The acrobatic catch fired up the crowd.

5.   The cat goes in and out of the door.

EXERCISE 2—MOVABLE AND IMMOVABLE PARTICLES

English has two types of particles: movable particles that undergo particle shift and immovable particles that cannot be shifted. When immovable particles and the phrases in which they occur are pre-posed, the grammaticality of the sentence is questionable. This shows that immovable particles are not prepositions, as in the example below.

> Example: My best friend turned **into** a recluse.
> *My best friend turned a recluse **into.**
> ?**Into** a recluse my best friend turned.

Examine the following sentences and determine whether the highlighted words are prepositions or particles. If they are particles, say whether they are movable or immovable particles. Support your finding with the **PP-Preposing Test** and the **Particle Shift Test**. The PP-Preposing discriminate between prepositions and particles but cannot discriminate between movable particles and immovable particles. To distinguish between these two types of particles, you will need the Particle Shift Test.

1. The therapist brought **up** uncomfortable issues.

2. We will need to go **over** the syntax lecture.

3. The disgruntled boxer turned **in** his medal.

4. My friend has turned **into** a recluse.

5. Drugs mess **up** your brain.

6. The politician gave **in** under pressure.

7. This business gives **back** millions of dollars to the community.

8. My parents brought me up to stand **up** for the truth.

9. This girl stood John **up** several times.

EXERCISE 3—PREPOSITION AND PARTICLE IDENTIFICATION

List **10** prepositions and/or particles that you find in the text below.

The Gettysburg Address

by Abraham Lincoln

"Fourscore and seven years ago our fathers brought forth on this continent a new nation, conceived in liberty and dedicated to the proposition that all men are created equal. Now we are engaged in a great civil war, testing whether that nation or any nation so conceived and so dedicated can long endure. We are met on a great battle-field of that war. We have come to dedicate a portion of that field as a final resting-place for those who here gave their lives that that nation might live. It is altogether fitting and proper that we should do this.

But in a larger sense, we cannot dedicate, we cannot consecrate, we cannot hallow this ground. The brave men, living and dead who struggled here have consecrated it far above our poor power to add or detract. The world will little note nor long remember what we say here, but it can never forget what they did here. It is for us the living rather to be dedicated here to the unfinished work which they who fought here have thus far so nobly advanced. It is rather for us to be here dedicated to the great task remaining before us—that from these honored dead we take increased devotion to that cause for which they gave the last full measure of devotion—that we here highly resolve that these dead shall not have died in vain, that this nation under God shall have a new birth of freedom, and that government of the people, by the people, for the people shall not perish from the earth."

No.	Prepositions/Particle
1.	
2.	
3.	
4.	
5.	
6.	
7.	
8.	
9.	
10.	

EXERCISE 4—UNDERSTANDING GRAMMATICAL TERMINOLOGY

1. Make a sentence with a locative preposition. Underline the locative preposition.

2. Make a sentence with a preposition that expresses instrument. Underline the instrumental preposition.

3. Make a sentence with a preposition of possession. Underline the possessive preposition.

4. Make a sentence with a movable particle. Underline the movable particle.

5. Make a sentence in which <up> is an immovable particle. Underline the immovable particle.

6. Make a sentence in which <up> is a movable particle. Underline the movable particle.

7. Make a sentence with a preposition that expresses path. Underline the preposition that expresses path.

8. Make a sentence with a complex phrasal verb structure consisting of two particles. Underline both particles.

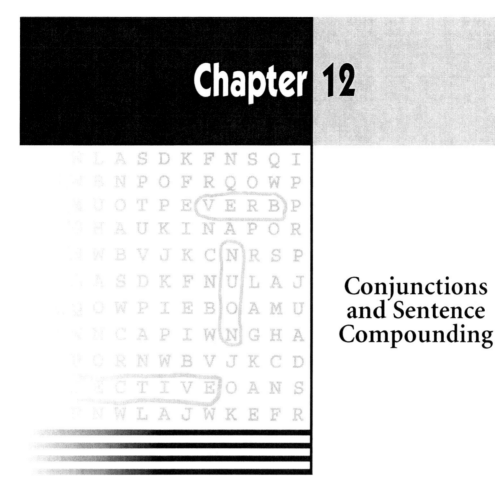

Chapter 12

Conjunctions and Sentence Compounding

12.0 INTRODUCTION

Conjunctions are closed class words whose sole purpose in language is to join words, phrases, and clauses together. In a sense, conjunctions are to grammar what the ligaments and the tendons are to the body. They join two parts of the body together. Similarly, conjunctions connect elements of discourse together. According to Robertson (1934:1177), the word <**conjunction**> can be traced back to the Greek word <*sundesmoi*> which is comprised of the prefix <*sun->* (with) and the root <*desmoi*> ("bond," "fetters," or "chains").[1] Ancient Greek grammarians compared conjunctions to glue that bonds linguistic elements together. Roman grammarians translated <*sundesmoi*> literally as <*conjungo*> into Latin.

12.1 Frequency and Distribution

Conjunctions, like prepositions, are extremely frequent parts of speech. Jurafsky and Martin (2000:294) give us the occurrences of the thirty most frequent English conjunctions. The frequencies are from the databank COBUILD based on a 16 million word corpus:

---

[1] The word <desmoi> is in the plural. Its singular is "desmos." In the Greek New Testament it is translated metaphorically as "prison."

Rank	Conjunctions	Frequency
1.	and	514,946
2.	that	134,773
3.	but	96,889
4.	or	76,563
5.	as	54,917
6.	if	53,917
7.	when	37,975
8.	because	23,626
9.	so	12,933
10.	before	10,720
11.	though	10,329
12.	than	9,511
13.	while	8,144
14.	after	7,042
15.	for	5,935
16.	although	5,424
17.	until	5,072
18.	yet	5,040
19.	since	4,843
20.	nor	3,078
21.	unless	2,205
22.	now	1,209
23.	neither	1,209
24.	whenever	1,120
25.	whereas	913
26.	except	867
27.	till	864
28.	provided	594
29.	lest	131
30.	albeit	104

Table 1 *Conjunction Frequency*

The word <and> is the most frequent and the most studied of all conjunctions. Entomologists take the fruit fly to be the prototype for insects; similarly linguists consider <and> to be the prototypical conjunction. For this reason, <and> will figure prominently in the examples used in this chapter.

12.2 Semantic Classification of Conjunctions

Conjunctions are function words; as such they are extremely hard to define. Categorizing them semantically has been a vexing problem for linguists for a long time. No matter the classification scheme used, conjunctions are simply hard to put in clear and neat semantic categories. For this reason, linguists have resigned themselves to using functional categories such as the following:

No.	Classes of Conjunctions
1.	Additive Conjunctions
2.	Adversative Conjunctions
3.	Cause and Effect Conjunctions
4.	Temporal Conjunctions

Table 2 *Broad Semantic Classes of Conjunctions*

The semantic problem with classifying conjunctions is compounded by the fact that some conjunctions are polysemous; that is, the same conjunction can assume different functions depending on its use in the sentence, as shown by Table 3 and the examples below:

No.	Words	Adverb	Preposition	Conjunction	Determiner
1.	so	+	−	+	−
2.	for	−	+	+	−
3.	that	+	−	+	+
4.	after	+	+	+	−
5.	before	+	+	+	−
6.	from	+	+	+	−
7.	but	+	−	+	−

Table 3 *Polysemy and Conjunctions*

(1) *Remy is **so** tired, he is falling asleep in front of the TV.*

(2) *Remy is tired, **so** he is falling asleep in front of the TV.*

In sentence (1) <so> is an adverb, or more accurately, a degree word. However, in (2) it is a conjunction. Haliday and Hasan (1981) tried to find a better semantic classification for conjunctions. However, in spite of their best efforts, their new semantic categories failed to supplant the traditional terminology used by Greco-Roman grammarians. For this reason, many linguists continue to rely on the traditional grammar terminology in classifying conjunctions. The traditional labels seem to work best because they balance syntactic considerations with semantic ones. Additionally, they offer terminological continuity and stability. Table 4 lists these age-old labels on which the remainder of this chapter is based.

No.	Classes of Conjunctions
1.	Coordinating Conjunction
2.	Correlative Conjunction
3.	Conjunctive Adverb
4.	Subordinating Conjunction[2]

Table 4 *Traditional Classification*

12.3 Morphological Characteristics

Conjunctions do not have much to offer by way of morphology because they have neither inflection nor derivation. Morphology is only relevant in so far as word formation processes are concerned. In this regard, there are four major types of conjunctions, as illustrated by Table 5:

No.	Classes of Conjunctions
1.	Simple Conjunctions
2.	Compound Conjunctions
3.	Complex Conjunctions
4.	Correlative/Discontinuous Conjunctions

Table 5 *Traditional Classification of Conjunctions*

Simple conjunctions are conjunctions without prefix or affix. Table 6 shows that the fifteen most common conjunctions in English (as per Table 1) are simple conjunctions:

No.	Simple Conjunctions
1.	and
2.	that
3.	but
4.	or
5.	as
6.	if
7.	when
8.	because
9.	so
10.	before
11.	though
12.	than
13.	while
14.	after
15.	for

Table 6 *Simple Conjunctions*

---

[2] Subordinating conjunctions will be dealt with in Chapter 13.

Compound conjunctions are formed by combining two or more words, as in Table 7 below:

No.	Compound Conjunctions
1.	Notwithstanding[3]
2.	whereupon
3.	inasmuch as
4.	forasmuch as
5.	insomuch as
6.	moreover
7.	furthermore
8.	however
9.	despite

Table 7 *Compound Conjunctions*

Complex conjunctions are usually, but not always, written as a single orthographic word. Linguists rely on spelling to distinguish between compound conjunctions and complex ones. The latter is made up of two or three words written as separate orthographic words. Table 8 lists the most common complex conjunctions:

No.	Complex Conjunctions
1.	in order to
2.	in order that
3.	so that
4.	on condition that
5.	provided that
6.	even if
7.	even though
8.	in spite of
9.	that is to say
10.	that is
11.	for instance
12.	let us say
13.	as soon as
14.	for example

Table 8 *Complex Conjunctions*

---

[3] The conjunctions <notwithstanding, whereupon, inasmuch as, forasmuch as, insomuch as> are classified as compound conjunctions because they are spelled as single orthographic words. However, as far as word formation processes are concerned, they could be classified as complex conjunctions.

Finally, correlative conjunctions are different from all the other conjunctions because they are discontinuous morphemes. Lexical or phrasal elements can be inserted between the two members of correlative conjunctions, as seen in (3) below:

(3)   *The professor is **both** understanding **and** tough.*

The discontinuous conjunction is <both ... and>. It will be argued later in 12.5.2 that a conjunction movement rule moves <both> to the left of the adjective <understanding>. Table 9 lists the six main correlative conjunctions found in English.

No.	Classes of Conjunctions
1.	either .... or
2.	neither ... nor
3.	both .... and
4.	not .... but
5.	not only ... but also
6.	whether ... or

Table 9 *Correlative Conjunctions*

12.4 *The Syntax of Coordinating Conjunctions*

English has seven coordinating conjunctions which are collectively known under the mnemonic label of FANBOYS. This acronym stands <for, and, nor, but, or, yet, so.> These conjunctions are further sub-classified according to their meaning, as seen in the table below:

No.	Conjunction	Meaning	Illustration
1.	and	additive/sequential	She came home **and** went to sleep.
2.	but	adversative[4]	She came home **but** did not go to sleep.
3.	or	positive disjunction	They will study **or** party all night.
4.	nor	negative disjunction	They will not study **nor** party all night.
5.	so	clausal	Many people left the island **so** they could escape from political violence.
6.	for	explicative	His accusers recanted their testimony **for** they could not find any fault in him.
7.	yet	adversative/ temporal/ concession	He is bright, **yet** he is down to earth.

Table 10 *Coordinating Conjunctions*

The syntax of coordinating conjunctions is worth investigating because it offers insights into contemporary linguistic concepts such as **recursion, combinatoriality,** and **constraints.** Understanding these concepts is crucial to understanding the issues involved in sentence compounding.

---

[4] The conjunction <but> can also be used as a degree word with the meaning of "almost" as in "the election is all but over," or as in "she is but a poor child."

12.4.1 The Arithmetic of Coordinating Conjunctions

Coordinating conjunctions illustrate perfectly two important linguistic principles: **recursion** and **combinatoriality**. Pinker (1999:8–9) playfully and insightfully defines the former as follows:

> *Now grammar rules are recursive: the rule creates an entity that contains an example of itself. In this case, a sentence contains a Verb Phrase which in turn can contain a sentence. An entity that contains an example of itself can just as easily contain an example of itself that contains an example of itself that contains an example of itself, and so on . . . A recursive grammar can generate sentences of any length, and thus can generate an infinite number of sentences. So a human being possessing a recursive grammar can express or understand an infinite number of distinct thoughts, limited in practice only by stamina and mortality.*

The principle of combinatoriality, on the other hand, expands the sentence-making possibilities of human languages tremendously by allowing various syntactic elements to combine among themselves. Pinker (1999:6–7) underscores the astounding combinatorial power of natural languages as follows:

> *The rules [of grammar] are combinatorial. They don't just have a single slot, like fill-in-the blank exam questions; every position in the sentence offers a choice of words from a lengthy menu. Say everyday English has four determiners (a, any, one, and the), and ten thousand nouns. Then the rule for a noun phrase allows four choices for the determiner, followed by ten thousand choices for the head noun, yielding $4 \times 10,000 = 40,000$ ways to utter a noun phrase. The rule for a sentence allows these forty thousand subjects to be followed by any four thousand verbs, providing $40,000 \times 4,000 = 160,000,000$ ways to utter the first three words of a sentence. Then there are four choices for the determiner of the object (640 million four-word beginnings) followed by ten thousand choices for the head noun of the object, or $640,000,000 \times 10,000 = 6,400,000,000,000$ (6.4 trillion) five-word sentences. Suppose it takes 5 seconds to produce one of these sentences. To crank them out, from* The abandonment abased the abbey *and* The abandonment abased the abbot, *through* The abandonment abased the zoologist, *all the way to* The zoologist zoned the zoo, *would take a million years.*

These two properties give a great deal of flexibility and power to humans in their sentence-making abilities. According to Dell (1980:3), English can create roughly a hundred billion billion possible sentences of twenty words. He also alleges that it would take one hundred billion centuries to say them all one after another!

12.4.2 Symmetry Constraints in Coordinating Conjunctions

The principles of recursion and combinatoriality rely on coordination and subordination to accomplish this linguistic feat. However, sentence compounding is subject to a **syntactic symmetry constraint.** This means that the conjoined structures must belong to the same syntactic category, as illustrated by the following sentences:

(4) *He was denied tenure, **yet** he still teaches as an adjunct faculty.*

(5) *He was denied tenure, **for** he did not publish enough.*

(6) *He was denied tenure, **so** he left the university.*

(7) **She studied chemistry yet physics.*

(8)　*She studied chemistry for physics.

(9)　*She studied chemistry so physics.

The conjunctions <for>, <so>, and <yet> can only conjoin clauses. Sentences (7), (8), and (9) use the same conjunctions; and yet they are ill-formed. We deduce from these ill-formed examples that <yet>, <for>, and <so> cannot conjoin phrases. The syntactic symmetry constraint that they must satisfy is that whenever they are used, they must conjoin clauses. So, (7), (8), and (9) are ungrammatical because they fail the clausal symmetry constraint. The remaining coordinating conjunctions, that is, <and>, <but> <or>, and <nor> can conjoin both phrases and sentences, as seen in (10) through (16):

(10)　*Mary bought a house **and** a car **and** a plasma TV **and** a couch.*

(11)　*Mary will buy a house **or** a car **or** a plasma TV **or** a couch.*

(12)　*Mary will not buy a house **nor** a car **nor** a plasma TV **nor** a couch.*

(13)　*Mary bought a house **but** not a car.*

(14)　*Remy played ball in the park **and** Colton swam in the pool.*

(15)　*Ken talks softly **but** he is not a pushover.*

(16)　*Public officials must take their oath of office seriously **or** they will be fired.*

In addition to the syntactic symmetry constraint, individual conjunctions may impose more constraints. Take the conjunction <but>; it cannot conjoin more than two elements in any given sentence, as seen by the ungrammaticality of (17) below:

(17)　*Mary bought a house **but** not a car **but** not plasma TV **but** not a couch.*

To sum up, English has two types of coordinating conjunctions. The conjunctions <yet, so, for> conjoin only clauses, while the conjunctions <and, but, nor, or> can conjoin both clauses and phrases. Both groups of conjunctions are subject to the same syntactic symmetry constraint.

12.4.3　Constraints and Parts of Speech Identification

The syntactic symmetry constraint has proven to be a very important tool in identifying the parts of speech of conjoined words. If two or more words are connected, and if the part of speech of one is known and the part of speech of the other words is not known, by virtue of the fact that only syntactically similar elements can be conjoined, we can infer that the unknown word belongs to the same part of speech as the known word. Let us illustrate this point with the following sentence:

(18)　***Fourscore** and **seven** years ago our fathers brought forth on this continent a new nation . . .*

Let us assume that one knows that <seven> is a numeral adjective but one does not have any idea what part of speech <fourscore> is. The symmetry constraint can help deduce accurately that <fourscore> is also a numeral adjective by virtue of the fact that only syntactically similar elements can be conjoined.

12.4.4　Pragmatic Constraints vs. Symmetry Constraints

The syntactic symmetry constraint alluded to in the preceding section is a necessary but not a sufficient condition for a sentence to be grammatically acceptable. It may be overridden by pragmatic constraints. This means that the conjoined elements can satisfy the symmetry constraint, and yet the sentence can be ill-formed, as shown by the following examples taken from Oirsouw (1978:8):

(19) *I could not decipher the rest of the message **and** I could not decipher the rest of the message.*

(20) *I wrote my grandmother a letter today, **and** six men can fit in the back seat of a Ford.*

In these two sentences <and> conjoins clauses as it is supposed to do. However, the sentences are ill-formed. Sentence (19) is ill-formed because there is a pragmatic constraint against conjoining two identical clauses. As for (20), it seems to be unacceptable because the ideas expressed in the two clauses arc disjointed. In both of these examples, the sentences are unacceptable even though the syntactic symmetry constraint has not been violated.

The syntactic symmetry constraint is very useful. However, it is so strong that it makes wrong predictions. For instance, if we adhere to it closely, (21) would be rejected as ungrammatical because, on the surface, the syntactic symmetry constraint is violated:

(21) *Kim baked turkey, **and** Beth duck.*

The conjunction <and> conjoins a clause <Kim baked turkey> and a phrase <Beth duck.> However, this sentence is still perfectly grammatical. Sentences (19), (20), and (21) show that the symmetry constraint can be overridden under certain circumstances. We will explain why (21) is grammatical in 12.7.2 even though it apparently violates the syntactic symmetry constraint.

12.5 Generating and Diagramming Conjoined Phrases

The syntactic symmetry constraint discussed previously allows us to propose the following phrase structure rules for generating conjoined phrases in English:

No.	Conjoined Constituents			
1.	NP	$\rightarrow$	NP	Conj	NP^{n}[5]
2.	VP	$\rightarrow$	VP	Conj	VP^{n}
3.	AdjP	$\rightarrow$	AdjP	Conj	$AdjP^{n}$
4.	AdvP	$\rightarrow$	AdvP	Conj	$AdvP^{n}$
5.	PP	$\rightarrow$	PP	Conj	PP^{n}
6.	S	$\rightarrow$	S	Conj	S^{n}[6]

The superscript "n" in these formulas stands for "infinite number." By displaying syntactic categories, tree diagrams help us see whether the syntactic symmetry constraint is fulfilled or violated. The tree diagram of (22) shows that the conjoined elements are similar, in that they are both NPs.

---

[5] The principle of combinatoriality allows an unlimited number of phrasal and clausal conjunctions, except in the case of the conjunction <but>.

[6] We will see later that this formulation is also problematic.

(22) *Mary bought a house **and** a car.*

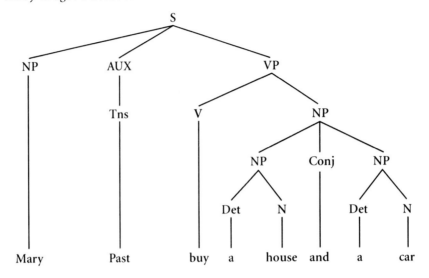

The tree diagram of (23) shows clearly that the syntactic symmetry constraint is met. Here two VPs are conjoined.

(23) *Tallie ate **and** went to bed.*

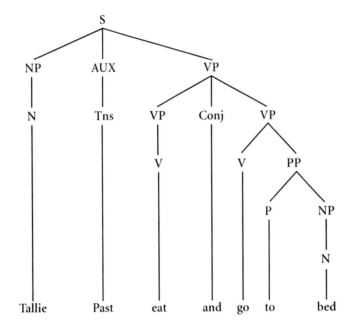

12.5.1 Diagramming Compound Sentences

Clauses can also be joined together into what is referred to in 1.12.1 as **compound sentences.** A compound sentence is defined as a sentence that is generated by the following phrase structure rule:

$$S \rightarrow S \text{ Conj. } S$$

Sentence (24) below is an example of a compound sentence because the higher S dominates two lower Ss which are, in turn, bound together by the conjunction <but>. Sentences of this type are diagrammed as follows:

(24) *Susie bought a book **but** she lost it.*

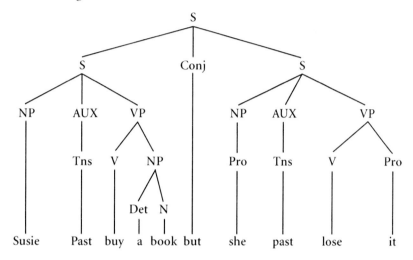

12.5.2 The Syntax of Correlative Conjunctions in Phrases

It was noted in 12.3 that English has only six correlative conjunctions. All these conjunctions are discontinuous morphemes. On the surface structure, syntactic elements are sandwiched between the two members of discontinuous morphemes. However, in the deep structure, the discontinuous morphemes appear next to each other, as shown in the tree diagram of (25). The points that were made in 9.3.1 and 10.4 about comparative and superlative adjectives are valid here also.

(25) *Syntax is **both** exciting **and** challenging.*

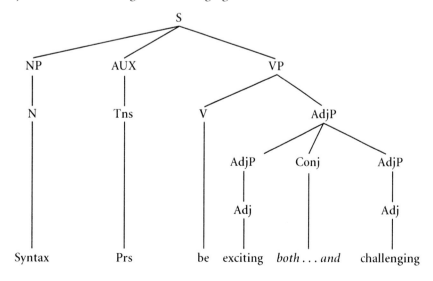

During the derivation process, a correlative conjunction movement rule is responsible for moving <both> and placing it before the adjective <exciting>.

12.5.3 The Syntax of Correlative Conjunctions

Correlative conjunctions connect phrases as well as clauses. In (24) the conjunction <both... and> conjoins the adjective phrases <exciting> and <challenging>. In (26) on the other hand, the discontinuous morpheme <either...or> joins two independent clauses, as shown in the tree diagram below:

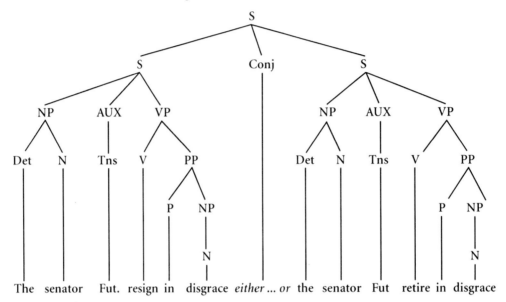

Here too, the correlative conjunction movement rule moves <either> from its original position in the deep structure and places it before the verb <resign>. As a result of this movement, and deletion of identical elements, the surface structure form of (26) is:

(26)   *The senator will **either** resign **or** retire in disgrace.*

12.5.4 The Syntax of Conjunctive Adverbs

The last group of conjunctions to be examined is conjunctive adverbs. They are by far the largest group of conjunctions in English. A dozen of them occur rather frequently in speech, while some such as <notwithstanding> occur primarily in written texts. Conjunctive adverbs encode various relationships between clauses. They are called "adverbs" because they express the same kind of information normally associated with adverbs, as illustrated by Table 11 below:

No.	Semantic Classification
1.	Result/logical deduction/cause and effect
2.	Concession
3.	Explanation/apposition
4.	Addition
5.	Time
6.	Contrast
7.	Conclusive
8.	Reinforcement

Table 11 *Conjunctive Adverbs*

Syntactically, conjunctive adverbs are easy to identify because, like "normal" adverbs, they are moveable. The mobility of conjunctive adverbs can be illustrated by the examples below:

(27) *The professor is old;* **however,** *he lectures with enthusiasm.*

(28) *The professor is old; he,* **however,** *lectures with enthusiasm.*

(29) **However** *old the professor is, he lectures with enthusiasm.*

Unlike other conjunctions, most conjunctive adverbs join only independent clauses. Some of them, including <now,> serve as discourse connectives without necessarily conjoining clauses (Kaplan 1995:31). The word <now> as used in sentence (30) does not connect clauses:

(30) **Now,** *what are you going to do about it?*

12.5.5 Diagramming Compound Sentences with Conjunctive Adverbs

Diagramming compound sentences with conjunctive adverbs is similar to diagramming any other compound sentences. Thus, (27) repeated here as (31) can be diagrammed as follows:

(31) *The professor is old;* **however,** *he lectures with enthusiasm.*

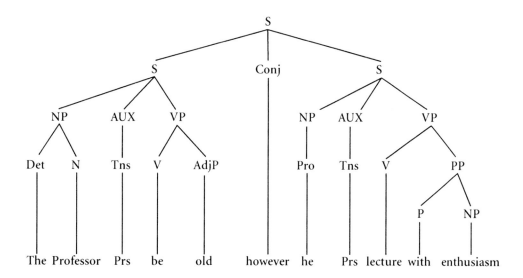

Even though conjunctive adverbs may appear in other positions in the sentence, we contend that in the deep structure they occur between the two clauses, as represented by the diagram above.

12.6 Coordination in Generative Transformational Grammar

So far our study of coordination has been fairly traditional. We have ignored some of the most hotly debated issues which have led to an overhaul of some of the basic tenets of generative transformational grammar. Even though the focus of this book is on the practical side of grammar, we cannot overlook matters of theoretical importance altogether. Now is the appropriate time to review some theoretical aspects of coordination that are of pedagogical interest.

12.6.1 A Transformational Account of Coordination

Early on in generative transformational grammar, it was believed that compound sentences and phrases were generated by transformational rules. According to this view, transformations apply to conjoined sentences in the deep structure to derive the surface structure. The key transformation in this derivational process is **deletion.** However, to prevent deletion from being applied haphazardly, the constraints of **identity** and **recoverability** were imposed (Oirsouw 1987:31, 38). By the former, it is meant that if two elements of a sentence are identical, one can be deleted. As for the recoverability condition, Oirsouw (1987:38) describes it as follows:

> *Hankamer (1973) proposes a number of strong restrictions on coordinate deletions which he intends to be part of a larger restriction on the recoverability of deletions and movement, which he construes as 'the ability of a hearer to recover the underlying representation of a sentence which may have undergone various processes of ellipsis or rearrangement in the course of its derivation.' The motivation for such constraint on recoverability will be clear: in a model of grammar where semantic interpretation is done on deep structure alone, the hearer must be able to find the deep structure on the basis of the surface structure that he is confronted with—in other words, he will have to undo the derivation, which, in the case of deletions, involves recovering the material that has been lost in the surface structure as a result of such rules as ellipsis and deletion. Recoverability of deletion is therefore not a constraint that ensures correct syntactic patterning of sentences, but one which helps to ensure an unequivocal relation between surface structure and interpretation of a sentence.*

Let us apply Hankamer's concepts of identity and recoverability to (32) to see if it works:

(32)   *The senator will either resign or retire in disgrace.*

Deep structure:	The senator Fut resign in disgrace either... or the senator Fut retire in disgrace.
Indexing/Matching Condition:	The senator[1] Fut[2] resign in disgrace[3] either... or the senator[1] Fut[2] retire in disgrace.[3]
Deletion Rule:	The senator[1] Fut[2] resign Ø either... or Ø Ø retire in disgrace.[3]
"Either...or"-Dislocation:[7]	The senator[1] Fut[2] either resign Ø either —... or Ø Ø retire in disgrace[3]
Spell-Out Rules:	The senator[1] will either resign Ø or Ø Ø retire in disgrace.[3]
Surface Structure:	The senator will either resign or retire in disgrace.[8]

The rationale for applying Indexing/Matching Condition is that is helps us identify the elements of the sentence that are identical in the underlying clauses. In the deep structure of (32), <the senator>, <Fut>, and <in disgrace>, and are identical. Consequently, they are deleted in the second clause. As a result of the application of the deletion rule and other rules, we arrive at the surface structure sentence, <*The senator will resign or*

---

[7] The dislocation rule is a movement rule that applies to discontinuous morphemes to move one element of the complex morpheme to another part of the sentence.

[8] A slightly different transformation rule is envisaged if the surface structure is "The senator will resign in disgrace or retire." But we need not concern ourselves with that now.

retire in disgrace>. So far so good. However, the examples to be discussed below show that a transformational account of coordination raises serious doubts about the validity of this approach in explaining all compound sentences.

12.6.2 Problems with Conjoined Structures

A sentence such as (33) below brings to light the weakness of generative transformational grammar in dealing with certain types of compound sentences:

(33) *Tony **and** Suzy bought a house.*

A transformation account of this sentence would propose the following as the deep structure:

Deep structure: Tony Past buy a house and Suzy Past buy a house.

Such a deep structure form raises a number of important questions: how many houses were bought? Do Toni and Suzy own the same house? Does Tony own his house and Suzy her house? A commonsense interpretation of this sentence would tell us that Tony and Suzy own the same house. However, an interpretation that relies solely on generative transformational grammar would lead to the conclusion represented by the following tree diagram:

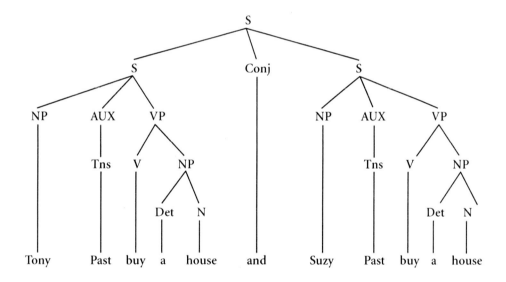

To prevent an interpretation such as this, some linguists have rejected the transformational account of compound sentences. Instead, they have proposed that conjoined sentences can be generated exclusively by phrase structure rules. To achieve this result, the semantic feature [± joint] has been made part of the apparatus of phrase structure rules. Thus (33) can be generated by the phrase structure rule below:

$$
\begin{aligned}
S &\rightarrow \text{NP} \quad \text{AUX} \quad \text{VP} \\
\text{NP} &\rightarrow \text{NP} \ \text{Conj} \ \text{NP}^n
\end{aligned}
$$

The NP → NP Conj NP^n formula is to be interpreted as [+joint]. Armed with this new device, compound sentences can be generated without the need of transformations. By inserting the feature [+joint] directly in the deep structure of compound sentences, the deep structure of sentence (33) can be interpreted as follows:

Deep structure: Toni and Suzy [+joint] Past buy a house.

The diagram below represents this new interpretation of sentence (33):

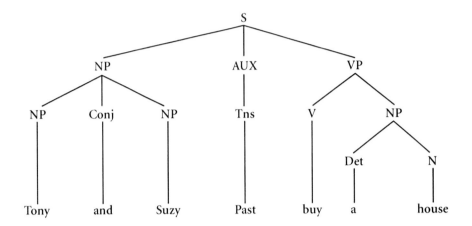

It has been argued by Oirsouw (1987:26) that in addition to the feature [± joint], the feature [± respectively] is also needed. Without such a feature, (34) may be interpreted wrongly:

(34)   *The bride **and** the groom kissed.*

The addition of the feature [± respectively] makes it possible to interpret the action of kissing as being reciprocal.

12.6.3 Sentence Compounding Made Simple

The introduction of these two semantic features has made it is easy to generate large numbers of sentences directly through phrase structure rules instead of through transformations. Without such a provision, Celce-Murica and Larsen-Freeman (1999:467–70) note that generating (35) would be unwieldy.

(35)   *Kim, Beth, **and** Melissa ate at the new restaurant.*

A transformation-based approach to coordination would posit that this sentence is derived from four separate sentences in the deep structure:

Deep structure: Kim Past eat at the new restaurant and Beth Past eat at the new restaurant and Melissa Past eat at the new restaurant.

To derive (35) many deletion rules would have to apply. It is doubtful that when a person hears a sentence such as (35), he/she processes it along the lines suggested by the deep structure above.

12.6.4 A Non-Transformational Account of VPs

The same non-transformational approach to conjoined sentences advocated above can help generate sentences in which two or more verb phrases are conjoined, as in (36) below:

(36)   *Tim ran for the senate **but** lost.*

Here, two verbs are conjoined. Both verbs have the same subject, namely <Tim>. Thus, the deep structure of (36) is as follows:

Deep structure: Tim Past run for the senate and Past lose the senate.

Here as in the case of (33), a number of deletion rules have to be posited to derive the surface structure sentence <Tim ran for the senate and lost.> For the same reason as invoked earlier, most linguists prefer to generate sentences in which two or more verb phrases are conjoined through phrase structure rules rather than through transformations. The following rule can be proposed to account for cases where verb phrases are conjoined:

$$
\begin{array}{l}
S \;\to\; NP \quad AUX \quad VP \\
VP \to \; VP \; Conj \; VP^n
\end{array}
$$

Sentence (36) can be represented by the following tree diagram:

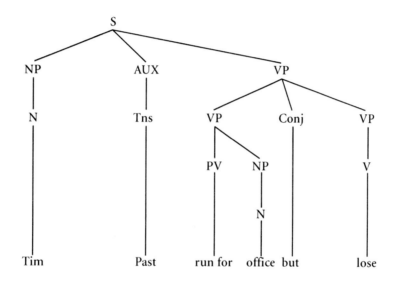

A non-transformational account of coordination works well for all the phrasal categories. It can generate each of the following sentences:

(37)   *Grammar is fascinating **but** challenging.*

(38)   *Mary speaks softly **but** assertively.*

(39)   *The cat jumps on **and** off the sofa.*

Following the same line of reasoning as previously, we see that (37), (38) and (39) are generated respectively by the phrase structure rules below:

$$
\begin{array}{lll}
AdjP & \to & AdjP \quad Conj \quad AdjP^n \\
AdvP & \to & AdvP \quad Conj \quad AdvP^n \\
PP & \to & PP \quad Conj \quad PP^n
\end{array}
$$

Transformations, therefore, appear to be irrelevant in the derivation of compound phrases and sentences. However, this is only an appearance. As will be seen in the next sections, without transformations, it is impossible to account for some sentences in English and other languages.

12.7 The Usefulness of Transformations

One may conclude rather erroneously based on the previous analysis that transformations are not needed in dealing with compound sentences. However, it is impossible to account for **ellipsis** and **gapping** in English and many other languages without appealing to transformations.

12.7.1 Coordination, Transformation, and Ellipsis

The study of coordination cross-linguistically has shown that the syntactic symmetry constraint discussed in 12.4.2 is widespread. This constraint stipulates that conjoined elements must belong to the same syntactic category. If this is true, then how can we explain the fact that (40) is well-formed?

(40)   *Betsy wrote a textbook **and** Bruce, too.*

Obviously, the symmetry constraint is violated because <Betsy wrote a textbook> is a sentence but <Bruce, too> is a noun phrase. The phrase structure rule that generated (40) could be rewritten as follows:

$$S \rightarrow S \quad Conj \quad NP$$

However, this rule violates the syntactic symmetry constraint because the conjoined elements do not belong to the same syntactic category. How can we account for this apparent violation of the symmetry constraint that does not result in ungrammaticality? The only way to save the Syntactic Symmetry Constraint is to claim that it applies only to deep structures, not necessarily to surface structures. Thus, the deep structure of (40) is as follows:

Deep structure: Betsy Past write a textbook and Bruce Past write a textbook.

If this is the case, then the surface structure of <*Betsy wrote a textbook **and** Bruce too* > is obtained as a result of the application of various transformations, as outlined in the derivation below:

Deep structure:	Betsy Past write a textbook and Bruce Past write a textbook.
Indexing/Matching:	Betsy Past[1] write[2] a textbook[3] and Bruce Past[1] write[2] a textbook.[3]
Deletion:	Betsy Past write a textbook and Bruce Ø Ø Ø Ø
Too-Addition:	Betsy Past write a textbook and Bruce Ø Ø Ø Ø too
Affix Hopping:	Betsy write Past a textbook and Bruce Ø Ø Ø Ø too
Spell-Out Rules:	Betsy wrote a textbook and Bruce too.
Surface structure:	Betsy wrote a textbook and Bruce, too.

Words such as "too" and "also" can be inserted in the derivation because it was noted in 4.5.2.1 that words that do not carry lexical meaning can be inserted during the derivational process. Linguists give the label of <**ellipsis**> to syntactic constructions such as (40) in which a clause is conjoined with a phrase without resulting in an ungrammatical sentence. In (40) all the elements of the second clause except for the subject are identical with those of the first clause.

Ellipsis is used in daily conversations as well as in compositions. It comes in various forms, as illustrated by the dialogue below:

(41) - *"May I borrow your textbook?"*

(42) - *Yes, you may.*

Sentence (42) is an elliptical construction because the portion of (41), namely <borrow my textbook>, that is identical with (42) is deleted. The examples of (40) and (42) lead us to propose the following definition for ellipsis: An ellipsis is a syntactic transformation that deletes elements of the second clause if they are identical with those of the previous clause. Ellipses are used effectively by all languages in order to avoid unnecessary repetitions of known information. The respondent could have said "yes, you may borrow my textbook." However, what is the point of this if the portion <borrow my textbook> can be deleted without affecting the meaning of the sentence?

12.7.2 Coordination, Transformations, and Gapping

Gapping is a syntactic construction that is very similar to ellipsis. Like ellipsis, it involves the deletion of the verb of the second clause. Also, like ellipsis, gapping can be accounted for only if we take a transformational approach to sentence compounding. Phrase structure rules cannot generate gapped sentences without violating the Symmetry Constraint. In spite of these similarities, gapping is different from ellipsis in one important respect. The NP object in the second clause must necessarily be different from the NP object in the first clause for a construction to qualify as gapping. Let us illustrate this with the sentences below:

(43) *Kim baked turkey,* **and** *Beth duck.*

(44) * *Kim baked turkey,* **and** *Beth turkey.*

Sentence (44) is ill-formed because the direct object is the same in both clauses. The following test has been proposed to help distinguish ellipsis and gapping:

No.	Distinguishing Features	Ellipsis	Gapping
1.	Emphatic Pro-form	+	−
2.	Identical NP Object	+	−
3.	Deleted NP Object in second clause	+	−
4.	Identical Verb	+	+

Table 12 *Ellipsis vs. Gapping*

Let us see how these tests can be used to discriminate between gapping and ellipsis.

(45) * *Kim baked turkey,* **and** *Beth duck too.*

Sentence (45) is ungrammatical because gapping requires that the objects in the conjoined clauses be different. Sentence (45) is also ungrammatical from the point of ellipsis because ellipsis requires that the second identical NP be deleted. Sentence (45) is ill-formed because gapping constructions cannot take the pro-form <too> or <also>. Consequently, any sentence that has <too> or <also> is an ellipsis. On the other hand,

<Kim baked turkey, and Beth duck> is an example of gapping because the direct objects are different, and no emphatic pro-form such as *<too>* can be used with the undeleted NP object in the second clause.

12.8 Syntactic Ambiguity and Conjoined Phrases

Let us now turn our attention to the semantic interpretation of conjoined phrases. The coordinating conjunctions *<and>*, *<or>*, and *<but>* frequently contribute to making sentences structurally ambiguous. This syntactic ambiguity occurs most often when adjective phrases, adverb phrases, and prepositional phrases are conjoined. The syntactic ambiguity caused by these constructions is illustrated by the sentences and the tree diagrams discussed in this section.

12.8.1 Syntactic Ambiguity in Conjoined Adjective Phrases

In sentence (46) *<Annie is very sensitive and generous>* below, the adjectives *<sensitive>* and *<generous>* are preceded by the degree word *<very>*. This sentence is ambiguous because *<very>* can either modify only *<sensitive>* but not *<generous>*, or *<very>* can modify both *<sensitive>* and *<generous>*. This causes the sentence to be interpreted in at least two different ways, as illustrated by the following tree diagrams:

(46)   *Annie is very sensitive **and** generous.*

The first diagram represents cases where Annie is both very sensitive and very generous:

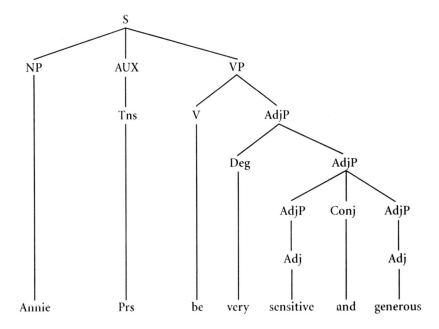

Here, the degree word <very> is sister to the adjective phrase node which dominates two lower adjective phrases. If, on the other hand, Annie is "very sensitive" but only somewhat "generous," the sentence can be diagrammed as follows:

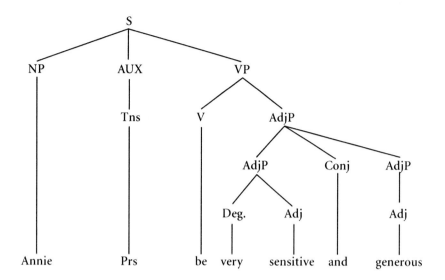

12.8.2 Syntactic Ambiguity in Conjoined Adverbial Phrases

Coordinated structures involving adverbial phrases are also often syntactically ambiguous when the degree word precedes the conjoined elements, as in the sentence and tree diagrams below:

(47) *Mary talks very softly **but** assertively.*

Just as in the case discussed in the section above, the degree word <very> can modify both <softly> and <assertively>, or it can modify only <softly> but not <assertively>. The first interpretation is as follows:

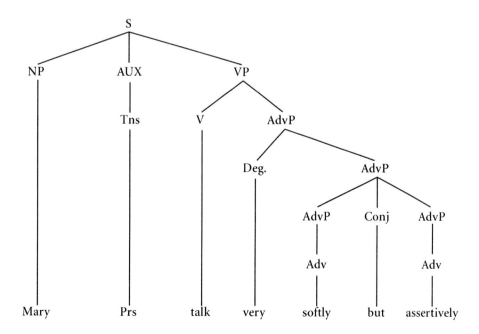

If, on the other hand, <very> modifies only <softly> but not <assertively, the sentence would have the following tree diagram representation:

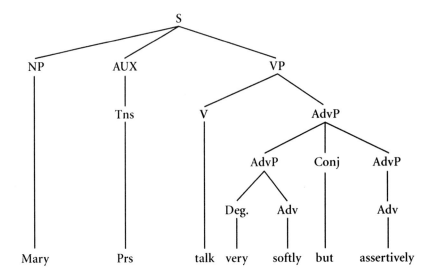

12.8.3 Syntactic Ambiguity in Conjoined Prepositional Phrases

Prepositional phrases that are modified by degree words can also be ambiguous as shown by (48):

(48) *The cow stepped right over the fence **and** onto the highway.*

The first diagram can be paraphrased as meaning that the cow stepped right over the fence and right onto the highway:

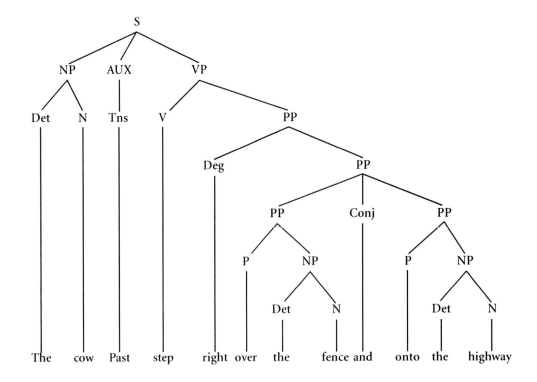

This interpretation is plausible because the degree word <right> dominates the lower prepositional phrases. The second possible interpretation suggests that the cow stepped right over the fence, but not right onto the highway. This interpretation is represented by the tree diagram below:

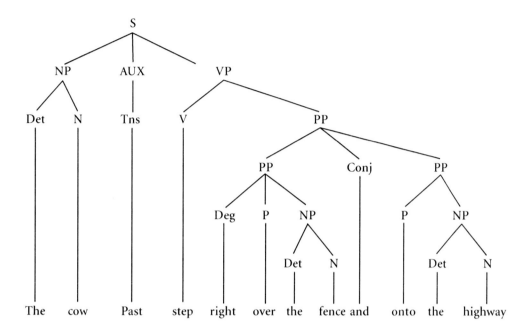

Once again, we see that syntactic ambiguities of this type can be clearly represented by tree diagrams.

12.9 *Pedagogical Implications*

The importance of conjunctions in oral and written communication cannot be emphasized enough. Halliday and Hasan (1985:10–1) contend that without cohesive devices such as conjunctions, communication would be an incoherent heap of words that listeners and readers would have difficulty processing. They claim that thanks to conjunctions, we have "the semantic resources for linking a sentence with what has gone before." Conjunctions facilitate processing the load of information, and making it manageable and understandable. In oral communication, the speaker uses many conversational devices, including modulations in the tone of voice, to indicate cohesion between utterances. The array of cohesive elements available for written communication is far more limited. However, in spite of these limitations, written communication has developed mechanisms to connect ideas.

12.9.1 Conjunctions and Composition

As far as composition is concerned, it has been found that students do not have problems using conjunctions to connect phrases. However, researchers have found deficiencies in students' ability to use clausal conjunctions. Wardhaugh (2002:333–8) cites the insightful yet controversial findings of Bernstein, a British sociologist of education, showing that students with "restricted linguistic code" were more likely to fail in school than those with "an elaborated code." One of the main differences between the two types of codes is that students with a restricted code have a deficiency in the use of conjunctive adverbs and subordinating conjunctions, or they use the same ones over and over again.

However, the students with an elaborate code use a variety of clausal conjunctions. Wardhaugh describes this situation as follows:

> *Elaborate code uses accurate grammatical order and syntax to regulate what is said; uses complex sentences that employ a* range of devices for conjunction and subordination; *employs prepositions to show relationships of both temporal and logical natures. . . . In contrast, restricted code employs short, grammatically simple, and often unfinished sentences of poor syntactic form, uses a few conjunctions simply and repetitively; employs little* subordination; *tends toward a dislocated presentation of information. [Italics added.]*

Since conjunctions contribute not only to the cohesion of the text but also to its overall meaning, composition teachers should highlight the semantic and grammatical functions of conjunctions. A simplified version of the table that Halliday and Hasan (1985:242–3) propose is very useful for this purpose. The leftmost column lists the four most important semantic classes of conjunctions. Each "supercategory" is subdivided into smaller categories. The second and third columns indicate the syntactic functions of conjunctions. The fourth column further sub-classifies conjunctions semantically (see Table 13 on page 361).

Yule (2006:126) highlights the importance of conjunctions in composition by making the following statement: "Analysis of these cohesive ties within a text gives us some insight into how writers structure what they want to say and *they may be crucial factors in our judgments on whether something is well written or not*" (emphasis added). Teachers should make every effort to instruct their students in the use of cohesive devices in their compositions. For this reason, they should not only teach the dos and don'ts, they should also teach the meanings of conjunctions, and their proper usages at the clausal level.

12.9.2 Conjunctions and Punctuation

Punctuation marks are devices of written communication that are meant to imitate aspects of spoken language. Two punctuation devices that are often associated with conjunctions are the **comma** and the **semicolon.** Opinions differ as to which of the two should be used in compound clauses. Burch (2003:120) explains the use of the semicolon as follows: "Conjunctive adverbs will accomplish two goals: first, they will ask the reader to slow down (they are usually set off with commas); second, they will demonstrate the relationship between the clauses." On pages 118 and 119 she argues that using the semicolon to join two independent clauses is more formal than using just the comma. The analysis in this chapter leads me to propose three simple heuristic principles for the use of commas and semicolons:

1. Conjoined phrases are not set off by commas, except when a list is involved.

2. Conjoined independent clauses are often separated by commas.

3. Conjunctive adverbs can be separated by semicolons.

These principles explain the syntactic motivations behind the use of commas and semicolons.

12.9.3 Coordinating Conjunctions in Sentence Initial Position

The prohibition against beginning a sentence with the coordinating conjunctions <and> and <but> is still so strong that Kolln and Funk (2006:294) find themselves on the defensive for going against it. They appeal to authoritative writers to justify going against it: "We should also mention that well-respected writers use both *and* and *but* as sentence

No.	Semantic Category	Phrasal Conjunction	Clausal Conjunction
Addition			
1.	Simple	and	and, furthermore, in addition, besides,
2.	Expository/Explanatory		that is, I mean, in other words, for instance, thus
3.	Comparison: similar		likewise, similarly, in the same way
4.	Comparison: dissimilar		on the other hand, by contrast, in contrast
5.	Disjunction/Alternative	or	or, or...else, either...or, neither...nor
6.	De-emphasis/afterthought		incidentally, by the way
7.	Reinforcement		further, in particular, indeed, in fact, above all
Adversative			
1.	Simple	but	yet, however, nevertheless, despite
2.	Contrastive		in fact, actually, as a matter of fact, at the same time
3.	Correction	but	instead, rather, on the contrary
Cause and Effect			
1.	Simple		for, because
2.	Reason		for this reason, on account of this, it follows, on this basis, under the circumstances
3.	Result		as a result, consequently
4.	Purpose		for this purpose, with this in mind, to this end
Temporal			
1.	Simple	and	as soon as, meanwhile, in the meantime, up to now, up to this point
2.	Sequential	and	then, next, after that, first, second, from now on, henceforward, afterwards, earlier, subsequently, previously, before that
3.	Simultaneous	and	just then, at the same time
4.	Conclusive		in the end, finally, in conclusion, thus, at last
5.	Summary		to sum up, in short, briefly, to return to the point
6.	Durative		meanwhile

Table 13 *Semantic Classification of Conjunctive Adverbs*

openers in spite of what you may have read or been told to the contrary." The translators of the King James Version of the Bible were among the first authoritative writers to have violated the prohibition against the use of <and> and <but> in sentence initial position. These respected translators followed closely the Hebraic tradition of opening paragraphs or starting sentences with <and> or <but.> Given the prestige and the influence of this version on literary English, writers since the Renaissance have felt safe in opening their sentences with either one of these two conjunctions.

12.9.4 Idiosyncratic Properties of Conjoined Prepositional Phrases

Conjoined prepositional phrases in English display an asymmetrical behavior that may not be found in other languages. For this reason, teachers of English as a Second/Foreign Language must make sure to explain the idiosyncrasies of conjoined prepositional phrases in English. The following sentences exemplify this syntactic behavior:

(49)   *The cat jumps on **and** off the sofa.*

(50)   ?*The cat jumps on the sofa **and** off the sofa.*

(51)   * *The cat jumps on the sofa **and** off.*

We notice in these sentences that two different prepositions are conjoined. Sentence (49) is well-formed while (50) is unnatural. Sentence (51) is outright ungrammatical. This seems to suggest that in English, when conjoined prepositions share the same noun phrase, the first NP is the one that undergoes deletion. Now let us examine the case when the conjoined prepositional phrases have different noun phrases, as is the case in (52), (53) and (54):

(52)   *Janet flew to Arizona **and** to Florida.*

(53)   ?*Janet flew to Arizona **and** Florida.*

(54)   * *Janet flew Ø Arizona **and** to Florida.*

In spoken English (53) is acceptable, but some purists question its use in composition. Sentence (54) is ungrammatical both in spoken and written English. There seems to exist a rule that prevents the deletion of the preposition in the first clause if the noun phrases of the compound prepositional phrases are different. Since this constraint may not exist in other languages, English as a Second/Foreign Language teachers should be aware of it in order to explain it to their students.

12.10 Conclusion

Conjunctions exist and function the same in all languages, that is, they allow speakers to string together lexical, phrasal and sentential elements in speech or writing. English conjunctions fall into four categories, depending on their semantic, morphological, and syntactic characteristics. The advent of Generative Transformation Grammar has brought a great deal of excitement and many challenges to the study of conjunctions. New theoretical issues have surfaced that traditional grammarians did not anticipate. Conjunctions, especially coordinating conjunctions, have been used by theorists within this framework to prove the usefulness of "phrases" in syntactic analyses. Insights gained by the study of the Symmetry Constraint have advanced our contemporary understanding of the processes involved in conjoining sentences. We now know that neither phrase structure rules nor transformations are sufficient in themselves to explain compound sentences. However, when both are taken together, they can account for a wide variety of conjoined sentences.

Last but not least, the study of conjunctions is important to language teachers because it enables them to help their students meet the demands of CALP (Cognitive Academic Language Proficiency) at school. Though still in its infancy and somewhat controversial, preliminary studies seem to indicate that a correlation exists between assessment of written communication and proficiency in the use of conjunctions, especially those conjunctions that connect clauses. Compositions that display proficiency in the use of conjunctions are evaluated more positively than those that do not.

Key Terms to Know

These are the key terms that you should be able to use and define after reading this chapter:

1. combinatoriality: 12.4, 12.4.1, 12.4.2

2. complex conjunction: 12.3

3. compound conjunction: 12.3

4. conjunction: 12.0, 12.1, 12.3, 12.4, 12.4.1, 12.4.2, 12.4.4, 12.5.1, 12.5.2, 12.5.3, 12.5.4, 12.8, 12.9, 12.9.1, 12.9.2, 12.9.3, 12.10

5. conjunctive adverb: 12.2, 12.5.4, 12.5.5, 12.9.1, 12.9.3

6. coordinating conjunction: 12.2, 12.4, 12.4.1, 12.4.2, 12.8, 12.9.3, 12.10

7. correlative conjunction: 12.2, 12.3, 12.5.2, 12.5.3

8. deletion: 12.5.3, 12.6.1, 12.6.3, 12.6.4, 12.7.2, 12.9.4

9. dislocation: 12.6.1

10. ellipsis: 12.6.1, 12.7, 12.7.1, 12.7.2

11. gapping: 12.7, 12.7.2

12. identity: 12.6.1

13. polysemy: 12.1

14. recursion: 12.4, 12.4.1, 12.4.2

15. simple conjunction: 12.3

16. syntactic ambiguity: 12.8, 12.8.1, 12.8.2, 12.8.3

17. syntactic symmetry constraint: 12.4.2, 12.4.3, 12.4.4, 12.5, 12.7.1

EXERCISE 1—GAPPING AND ELLIPSIS

Part A: Assume that the deep structure of "*Ryan majored in physics, and Mary in linguistics*," is as indicated in the deep structure below. Show all the derivational steps needed to generate the surface structure.

Deep structure: Ryan Past major in physics and Mary Past major in linguistics

Surface structure: *Ryan majored in physics, and Mary in linguistics*

Part B: Assume that the deep structure of "*Ryan majored in physics, and so did Mary*," is as indicated in the deep structure below. Show all the derivational steps needed to generate the surface structure.

Deep structure: Ryan Past major in physics and Mary Past major in physics

Surface structure: *Ryan majored in physics, and so did Mary.*

Now answer the following questions:

1. What is the name given to syntactic constructions such as *"Ryan majored in physics, and Mary in linguistics"*?

2. What is the name given to syntactic constructions such as *"Ryan majored in physic, and so did Mary"*?

3. The two sentences are very similar; yet there are differences between them. What are the syntactic differences between the two sentences?

EXERCISE 2—SENTENCE DIAGRAMMING

Diagram the sentences below.

1. The student arrived exactly on time and at the right place.

2. The rioters should step up their demands or give up the fight.

3. Beth baked and served turkey for Easter.

4. Bruce is sick today, therefore he is skipping class.

5. Tuition is expensive but parents want a good education for their children.

6. People are either for him or against him.

EXERCISE 3—CONJUNCTION IDENTIFICATION

List all the conjunctions found in the text below. Classify them according to the following categories: 1) coordinating conjunction, correlative conjunction, and conjunctive adverbs. [**Note:** Keep in mind that there may be more or less conjunctions to fill the table below. Some of the categories may not be represented in the text.]

The Gettysburg Address

by Abraham Lincoln

"Fourscore and seven years ago our fathers brought forth on this continent a new nation, conceived in liberty and dedicated to the proposition that all men are created equal. Now we are engaged in a great civil war, testing whether that nation or any nation so conceived and so dedicated can long endure. We are met on a great battlefield of that war. We have come to dedicate a portion of that field as a final resting-place for those who here gave their lives that that nation might live. It is altogether fitting and proper that we should do this.

But in a larger sense, we cannot dedicate, we cannot consecrate, we cannot hallow this ground. The brave men, living and dead who struggled here have consecrated it far above our poor power to add or detract. The world will little note nor long remember what we say here, but it can never forget what they did here. It is for us the living rather to be dedicated here to the unfinished work which they who fought here have thus far so nobly advanced. It is rather for us to be here dedicated to the great task remaining before us—that from these honored dead we take increased devotion to that cause for which they gave the last full measure of devotion—that we here highly resolve that these dead shall not have died in vain, that this nation under God shall have a new birth of freedom, and that government of the people, by the people, for the people shall not perish from the earth."

	Coordinating Conjunction	Correlative Conjunction	Conjunctive Adverbs
1.			
2.			
3.			
4.			
5.			

EXERCISE 4—UNDERSTANDING GRAMMATICAL TERMINOLOGY

1.   Make a sentence with a disjunctive conjunction which conjoins two phrases. Underline the disjunctive conjunction.

2.   Make a sentence with a conjunctive adverb. Underline the conjunctive adverb.

3.   Make a sentence with an additive coordinating conjunction. Underline the coordinated conjunction.

4.   Make a sentence with a correlative conjunction. Underline the correlative conjunction.

5.   Make a sentence with an adversative coordinating conjunction. Underline the coordinating conjunction.

Chapter 13

Subordinating Conjunctions and Subordinate Clauses

13.0 INTRODUCTION

The distinction that is made in English grammar between **independent/main clauses** and **dependent/subordinate clauses** is inherited from Greek grammarians. They labeled the former <*parataktika axiomata*> and the latter <*upotaktika axiomata*>, (Robinson 1934:911–24). The Greek prefixes <*para*> and <*upo*> can be translated contextually as <*major*> and <*minor*>, respectively. Some grammar books still use the Greek borrowing <*paratactic*> and <*hypotactic*> constructions to refer to main and subordinate clauses. The main distinction between these two types of clauses lies in the fact that the latter is usually, but not always, introduced by a subordinating conjunction. English conjunctions fall into two major categories. The previous chapter was devoted to the conjunctions that conjoin independent clauses. The present chapter focuses on subordinating conjunctions that connect subordinate clauses to main clauses.

13.1 Frequency and Distribution

Subordinating conjunctions are used only where a dependency relationship exists between two or more clauses. In all cases, the clauses rely on each other to convey the full thought expressed by the sentence. English has a wide variety of conjunctions that express various types of dependency relationships. In Table 1 on page 374, Jurafsky and Martin (2000:294) give us the frequency count of the most common subordinating conjunctions:

No.	Conjunctions	Frequency
1.	that	134,773
2.	as	54,917
3.	if	53,917
4.	when	37,975
5.	because	23,626
6.	so	12,933
7.	before	10,720
8.	though	10,329
9.	while	8,144
10.	after	7,042
11.	for	5,935
12.	although	5,424
13.	until	5,072
14.	yet	5,040
15.	since	4,843
16.	unless	2,205
17.	now	1,209
18.	neither	1,209
19.	whenever	1,120
20.	whereas	913
21.	except	867
22.	till	864
23.	provided	594
24.	lest	131
25.	albeit	104
26.	providing	96
27.	whereupon	85
28.	notwithstanding	3
29.	as long as	no data
30.	as if	no data
31.	in so far as	no data
32.	for as much as	no data
33.	as though	no data
34.	however	no data
35.	now that	no data
36.	only	no data

Table 1 *Frequency Count of Subordinating Conjunctions*

13.2 Semantic Classification of Conjunctions

When subordinating conjunctions conjoin clauses, they encode various types of semantic relationships between the clauses. The most common meanings expressed by these conjunctions are listed in Table 2 below:

No.	Meaning	Illustration
1.	Time	when, whenever, after, as, before, once, since, till, until, now that, while, as long as, as soon as
2.	Concession	though, although, if, while, despite, in spite of
3.	Contingency	if, once
4.	Condition	if, in case, as long as, unless, provided that, whether, except
5.	Reason/Cause	because, since, as long
6.	Result	so that
7.	Comparison	as, just as, as if, as though
8.	Contrast	while, whereas

Table 2 *Semantic Classification of Subordinating Conjunctions*

We saw in 12.2 that the semantic classification of conjunctions paved the way to their syntactic labeling. The same is true also for subordinating conjunctions. Linguists and grammarians rely on the interface between semantics and syntax to label the different types of subordinate clauses. Kaplan (1995:254) finds the following to be the main types of subordinate clauses in English:

No.	Meaning
1.	Adverbial subordinate clause of time
2.	Adverbial subordinate clause of cause/reason
3.	Adverbial subordinate clause of condition
4.	Adverbial subordinate clause of concession
5.	Adverbial subordinate clause of result

Table 3 *Classification of Subordinate Clauses*

Kaplan undoubtedly uses the label "adverbial" to show that all subordinate clauses perform an adverbial function, namely that they modify the main clause. However, in everyday usage, most linguists omit the label "adverbial" when referring to subordinate clauses.

13.3 Morphological Characteristics

An analysis based on the word formation processes allows us to classify subordinating conjunctions into three groups, as shown in Table 4:

No.	Classification of Subordinating Conjunctions
1.	Simple Subordinating Conjunctions
2.	Compound Subordinating Conjunctions
3.	Complex Subordinating Conjunctions

Table 4 *Traditional Classification of Subordination Conjunctions*

Simple subordinating conjunctions are monomorphemic words, that is, they have neither prefixes nor suffixes. The most common simple subordinating conjunctions are the following:

No.	Simple Subordinators
1.	that
2.	when
3.	after
4.	as
5.	before
6.	once
7.	when
8.	why
9.	how
10.	where
11.	since
12.	till
13.	while
14.	though
15.	if
16.	for
17.	lest
18.	except
19.	whether

Table 5 *Simple Subordinating Conjunctions*

Compound subordinating conjunctions, on the other hand, are made up of two or more separate words written as single orthographic words, as those listed in Table 6:

No.	Compound Subordinators
1.	notwithstanding[1]
2.	whenever
3.	unless
4.	although

Table 6 *Compound Subordinating Conjunctions*

Complex subordinating conjunctions are made up of two or more separate words and are written as separate orthographic words, as in Table 7 below:

No.	Complex Subordinators
1.	in order to
2.	in order that
3.	as though
4.	on condition that
5.	provided that
6.	even if
7.	even though
8.	so that
9.	as if
10.	for the purpose of
11.	as soon as
12.	as long as

Table 7 *Complex Subordinating Conjunctions*

Opinions differ on the exact classification of groups of words such as <the fact that, the idea that, the claim that>. Some consider them to be complex subordinating conjunctions, but others do not. Fromkin et al. (2003:200–1) separate <the fact that> into an NP <the fact> and the complementizer <that>. However, Celce-Murcia and Larsen-Freeman (1999:667) consider such groups of words to be complex subordinating conjunctions.

---

[1] The conjunctions <notwithstanding, whereupon, inasmuch as, forasmuch as, insomuch as> are classified as compound conjunctions because they are spelled as single orthographic words. However, as far as word formation processes are concerned, they could be classified as complex conjunctions.

13.4 Defining Subordinate Clauses

A few definitions are in order before we proceed any further. First and foremost, we must define the concept of "clause." It was defined earlier in 1.12 as "a group of words that has a subject (expressed or unexpressed) and a tensed (conjugated) or untensed (not conjugated) verb." Though the presence of a subject is required, it need not be present on the surface structure. Similarly, a clause must have a verb, but this verb must be a main verb. It cannot be an auxiliary verb. Let us illustrate these two requirements with the two sentences:

(1) *Rhoda wants to travel to Africa.*

(2) *I hope that she can.*

According to the definition given above, (1) is a complex sentence consisting of two clauses: <Rhoda wants> and <to travel to Africa>. The first clause, <Rhoda wants>, meets the criteria set forth in the definition of the clause, because <Rhoda> is the subject and <wants> is the main verb. The second group of words, <to travel to Africa>, is also a clause. However, the main verb <to travel> does not have a surface structure subject. Generative linguists claim that the subject of <to travel> is also <Rhoda> even though it does not appear on the surface structure. Thus, it has been proposed that the deep structure of (1) can be represented as follows:

*Deep structure: Rhoda Pres. want **Rhoda**[2] to travel to Africa.*

Now, let us examine (2) to see if it meets the two criteria set forth above to identify clauses. The portion <I hope> is certainly a clause because the group of words <I hope> has a subject, <I>, and a main verb, <hope>. However, does the second portion of the sentence, <that she can>, qualify as a clause? The pronoun <she> is subject; however, there is no main verb. We know that <can> is an auxiliary verb. Auxiliary verbs are there to help main verbs carry aspectual and tense information. But in this sentence there is no main verb. In spite of the absence of a main verb, sentence (2), especially the portion <that she can>, is a legitimate clause. Linguists arrive at this conclusion not by looking at the surface structure, but by relying on the deep structure. Generative transformational grammarians claim that a main verb existed in the deep structure of (2) but that it was deleted by an ellipsis transformation of the type discussed in 12.7.1. Thus, a simplified deep structure of (2) can be presented as follows:

Deep structure: I Pres. hope that she Pres can travel to Africa.

The preceding analysis leads us to redefine the clause as follows:

A clause is a group of words that consist of a subject and a main verb in the deep structure.

The notion of "main verb" is important for another reason. It helps calculate the number of clauses in a sentence. In general, the number of main verbs in a sentence is proportionate to the number of clauses. We know that the sentence <Rhoda wants to travel to Africa> has two clauses because it has two main verbs, <want> and <travel>. Now consider the following sentence:

(3) *The professor could have been lying under oath.*

This sentence has four verbs: <could>, <have> <been> and <lying>. However, <lying> is the only main verb amongst all these four verbs. All the other verbs are auxiliaries. For this reason, we conclude that (3) has only one clause.

---

[2] The second <Rhoda> does not actually appear in the deep structure. It is kept here for the sake of argument. The correct deep structure of this sentence will be discussed in 13.5.2.1. In the meantime we will continue using Rhoda in the subordinate clause until noted otherwise.

13.4.1 Types of Clauses

Grammarians and linguists give different syntactic labels to the types of clauses found in subordinate constructions. One of the clauses is named **main clause** and the other is called **subordinate clause.** The two are also respectively known as **independent** and **dependent clauses.** In many traditional grammar books, the main or independent clause has been defined as a clause that "can stand on its own," while the subordinate clause is said to be unable to stand on its own. This definition is "the mother of all confusion." For this reason, we do not use it in this book. Instead, we will use Loebeck's (2000:225) simple but accurate definition which describes a main/independent clause as "a clause that is not dominated by a phrase that is dependent." Let us contrast this with her definition of the subordinate/dependent clause: "a subordinate or dependent clause is a clause dominated by a phrase that is dependent." Let us go back to (1) reproduced here as (4) to illustrate Loebeck's definitions:

(4)   *Rhoda wants to travel to Africa.*

According to Loebeck's definition, the main difference between the main clause and the subordinate clause is domination or lack of domination by a phrase. The main/independent clause is not dominated, whereas the subordinate clause is dominated by a phrase. Let us illustrate this by a tree diagram:

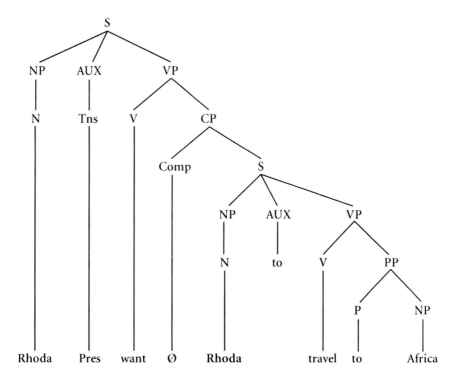

This tree diagram contains more information than we have seen so far. Ignore for now the unfamiliar details. We will return to them later. For now, let us focus on how Loebeck's definition can be used to illustrate main and subordinate clauses in this sentence. When we examine the tree diagram above, we see that the group of words <Rhoda wants> is not dominated by a phrase. However, the group of words <Rhoda to travel to Africa> is dominated by the VP <want>. We conclude then that <Rhoda wants> is the main clause while <to travel to Africa> is the subordinate clause. This way of defining main and subordinate clauses is far superior to the one which makes standing alone or not standing alone the main criterion. In reality, neither the clause <Rhoda wants> nor <to travel to Africa> can stand by itself.

13.4.2 Formal Characteristics of Subordinate Clauses

The phrase structure rule that we have relied on to generate all the sentences that we have encountered so far in the book is the following:

$$S \rightarrow NP \quad AUX \quad VP$$

This phrase structure rule must now be expanded to cover subordinate clauses. As we do so, we must keep in mind the definition of the subordinate clause, namely a clause dominated by a phrase. Though subordinate clauses can be dominated by NPs, AdjPs, and VPs, in this section and the next, we will concern ourselves only with subordinate clauses that are dominated by VPs. The standard formulation of the phrase structure rule for subordinate clauses dominated by verb phrases is the following:

$$VP \rightarrow V \quad CP$$
$$CP \rightarrow Comp \ S$$

According to this formula, a verb phrase can be rewritten as a verb and a **complementizer phrase** (CP). This is a new syntactic category that was introduced a couple of decades ago by generative grammarians. It consists of a word or a group of words that introduces a subordinate clause.[3] The complementizer phrase is in turn rewritten as Comp and S. The abbreviation "Comp" stands for "complementizer." Comp is the modern linguistic equivalent of the traditional term for "subordinate conjunctions." The phrase structure rule for Comp can be formulated as follows:

$$Comp \rightarrow \left\{ \begin{array}{l} \text{that} \\ \text{for} \\ \text{whether} \\ \text{if} \\ \text{when} \\ \text{Possession}[4] \\ \varnothing \end{array} \right\}$$

Celece-Murcia et al. (1999:667) argue that Comp can be made up of one word or of complex subordinating conjunctions such as <because of the fact that>, <due to the fact that>, <on account of the fact that>, and <in spite of the fact that>. The presence of null, that is, "Ø," in Comp means that English allows for subordinate clauses that are not introduced by a subordinating conjunction. This means that a clause can still qualify as a

[3] It has been proposed by some linguists that all clauses, including main clauses, are also introduced by "Comp." However, such an assumption, though correct, will not be pursued in this book.

[4] The possessive element here is in most cases a gerund, as in the sentence <Mary's *singing* in the shower at 4:00 A.M. annoys me> or <Her *singing* in the shower at 4:00 A.M. annoys me.>

subordinate clause even if it does not have an overt subordinating conjunction, as is the case of (5) below:

(5)   *I hope Ø Rhoda can travel to Africa.*

(6)   *I hope that Rhoda can travel to Africa.*

Sentence (5) does not have an overt complementizer but (6) has the complementizer <that>. Radford (1986:172, 174) observes that in contemporary linguistics, all sentences, (not only subordinate clauses) are dominated by CP. This means that Comp may or may not have an overt complementizer.

13.4.3 Recursion in the Subordinate Clause

The principle of recursion is at play here again. It makes it possible to generate subordinate clauses up to infinity. CP can be rewritten as Comp and S. This S can also be rewritten as NP AUX VP, and the VP can, in turn, be rewritten again as V CP. Sentence (7) illustrates the recursive aspect of the phrase structure rules that generate subordinate clauses:

(7)   *I know that you know that she knows that they know that I love linguistics.*

This sentence contains four subordinate clauses. But in theory, it can contain as many subordinate clauses as one may wish to produce.

13.4.4 Expanded AUX

We have expanded the original phrase structure rule for generating subordinate clauses. To accommodate this expansion, some linguists have also proposed that AUX be expanded to contain additional elements such as the infinitive marker <To>, the present participial suffix <-ING>, and the past participial suffix <-EN>. Following Celce-Murcia and Larsen-Freeman (1999:645) and LeTourneau (2001: 359, 371, 381), AUX is expanded as follows:

$$
\text{AUX} \rightarrow
\left\{
\begin{array}{l}
\text{Tense} \\
\text{To} \\
\text{-ING} \\
\text{-EN} \\
\text{- Ø} \\
\text{- Imp}
\end{array}
\right\}
\text{(Perf) (Prog) (Pass) [+ MV]}
$$

Detailed explanation will follow in subsequent sections. For now, suffice it to make only a few cursory observations about <To>, <-ING>, and <-EN>. When <To> follows a verb, it is not a preposition. It is an infinitive marker. This <To> is placed in AUX. Thus in (8) the first <To> is part of AUX. Similarly, the <-ING> and the <-EN> of (9) and (10) are considered part of AUX:

(8)   *Rhoda promised Larry to go to Africa.*

(9)   *Bethany enjoyed studying linguistics.*

(10)   *The police wanted the suspect arrested.*

We will see later that <studying linguistics> and <arrested> are both subordinate clauses. These clauses are dominated by the verbs <enjoyed> and <wanted>. Since <studying linguistics> and <arrested> are clauses, then the participial suffixes <-ING> and <-EN> are under AUX. We will return to these examples in 13.5.2, 13.5.4.3, and 13.5.4.5, and tree diagrams will be drawn to illustrate the positions of <To>, <-ING> and <-EN> in these diagrams.

13.5 The Syntactic Classification of Subordinate Clauses

There are two main schemes for classifying subordinate clauses. One approach relies on semantics and functional information while the other focuses primarily on the syntactic properties of the verb. It is not uncommon in syntactic analysis to take the verb as the key variable. Fromkin et al. (2003:191) justify this position as follows: "In all languages, the verb plays a central role in the meaning and structure of sentences." Indeed, in the study of subordination in English, a verb-centered classification seems to be very sensible.

A number of verbs in English and in other languages are subcategorized with complementizer phrases (CP). These verbs can be said to fit into the following subcategorization frame:

> V, [— CP] where CP is rewritten as
> CP → Comp S

This formula means that when such verbs are used, they must be followed by a subordinate clause. Linguists have found that subordinate clauses in English fall into two broad categories: **tensed** vs. **untensed clauses,** respectively known as **finite** and **non-finite clauses.** Some linguists prefer the labels "finite" and "non-finite" subordinate clauses but overall these terms are used interchangeably. Tensed/finite clauses are clauses in which the verb carries tense information. In other words, the verb is fully conjugated. In untensed/non-finite subordinate clauses on the other hand, the verb does not carry any tense information. These clauses are subdivided into four subcategories, as shown in the diagram below:

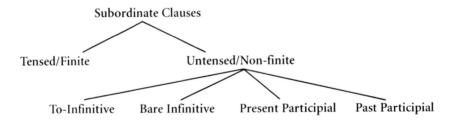

Additionally, we will see in 13.6 that some adjectives are also subcategorized as requiring subordinate clauses. For now, let us focus on the syntactic characteristics of each of these different types of subordinate clauses in English.

13.5.1 The Syntactic Characteristics of Tensed/Finite Subordinate Clauses

The main morphological characteristic of tensed/finite subordinate clauses is that the verb in the subordinate clause is morphologically marked for tense. It is either in the past tense, the present tense, or the future tense, as shown by the sentences below:

(11) *Some scientists believe that the globe **is** warmer.*

(12) *Some scientists fear that the globe **will** be warmer.*

(13) *Some scientists allege that the globe **was** warmer a century ago.*

The subordinate clauses of these three sentences carry tense information. The verb <be> in (11) is in the present tense, in (12) it is in the future tense, and in (13) it is in the past tense. The tree diagram of (11) reveals clearly that the verb in the subordinate clause is marked for tense, as indicated by the labels "Tns" and "Pres." under the AUX dominated by CP.

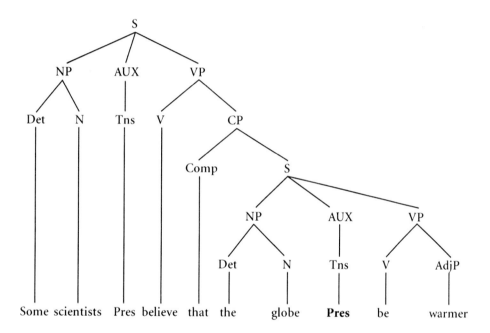

A very large number of English verbs that are subcategorized with CP take tensed subordinate clauses. The list includes verbs such as those in Table 8 on the following page:

No.	Syntactic Classification of Clauses
1.	to hope (that)
2.	to know (that)
3.	to remember (that)
4.	to propose (that)
5.	to believe (that)
6.	to think (that)
7.	to claim (that)
8.	to allege (that)
9.	to report (that)
10.	to assume (that)
11.	to imagine (that)
12.	to say (that)
13.	to understand (that)
14.	to see (that)
15.	to prefer (that)
16.	to observe (that)
17.	to decide (that)
18.	to explain (that)
19.	to observe (that)
20.	to wonder (if, whether)

Table 8 *Verbs Subcategorized with Tense*

The presence of the subordinating conjunction usually requires that the verb of the subordinate clause be marked morphologically for tense. However, this is not an absolute requirement since deleting the subordinating conjunction <that> is possible. In (15), the conjunction <that> is omitted but the verb of the subordinate clause still has tense:

(14)   *We hope that it doesn't rain on the parade tomorrow.*

(15)   *We hope it doesn't rain on the parade tomorrow.*

It is important to note that in a number of languages, including French and Spanish, the complementizer is not optional. The subordinate clause must be introduced by a complementizer, or else the sentence is ill-formed. English speakers sometimes delete the subordinating conjunction <que> when speaking Spanish or French. This usually results in a negative transfer because in these two languages <que> is obligatory to introduce the subordinate clause if its verb is inflected for tense.

13.5.2 The Syntactic Characteristics of To-Infinitive Subordinate Clauses

The label <To-Infinitive> subordinate clause is self-explanatory. When some verbs are used in the main clause, they require that the verb in the subordinate clause be preceded by the infinitive marker <To>. It was noted earlier in 13.4.4 that this infinitive marker appears in the AUX dominated by the CP, as seen in the following diagram of (16):

(16)   Rhoda promised Larry to go to Africa.

(17)   Rhoda hopes to go to Africa.

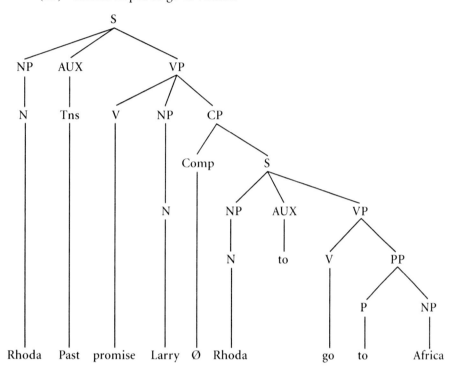

There are two important observations to be made about To-Infinitive subordinate clauses. First and foremost, in all such constructions, the Comp is empty. Secondly, determining the nature of the <To-Infinitive> clause is a major issue. Let us consider this question briefly.

13.5.2.1 Identifying the Subject of <To-Infinitive> Subordinate Clauses

Determining the subject of To-infinitive subordinate clauses has been a topic of fruitful theoretical discussions. Generative linguists claim that there are two main types of To-Infinitive subordinate clauses. In some, the subject of the To-infinitive verb is identical to the verb of the main clause, whereas in others it is not. Take the sentence <Rhoda wants to go to Africa.> All competent speakers of English understand <Rhoda> to be the subject of the verb <to go>. Now, contrast the same sentence with the following:

(18)   *Rhoda persuaded Larry to go to Africa.*

In this case, all proficient speakers take <Larry> to be the subject of the verb <to go>. Sentence (17) can be diagrammed as follows:

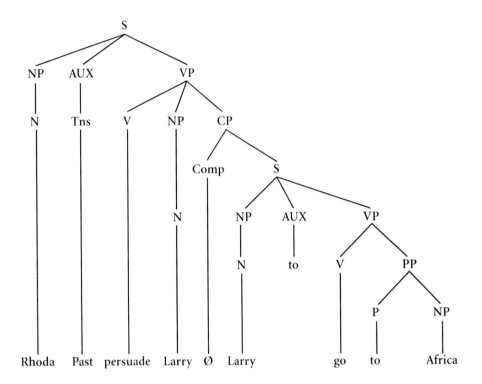

This tree diagram shows clearly that <Larry> is the subject of the verb <to go>. Previous attempts to account for such sentences were not very successful because they lacked all the theoretical insights necessary. However, since the advent of Government-Binding (GB) theory, such sentences are relatively easy to account for. A new syntactic category named "PRO" has been proposed to deal with <To-infinitive> subordinate clauses. This PRO stands for the subject of any verb that is not conjugated. Linguists distinguish between PRO and the "Pro" which is the abbreviation for "pronoun." More will be said about this in the next chapter. Radford (1989:380) explains the usefulness of this new category as follows:

> *Generalizing, we see that a PRO which is the subject of an infinitive complement after a verb like* want *or* promise *is controlled by the main sentence subject, whereas a PRO which is the subject of an infinitive complement embedded under a verb like* persuade *is controlled by the object of the verb* persuade. *This has led many linguists to propose a distinction between two types of verbs: those that take* subject control *(want, promise, etc.—i.e., verbs whose subject controls the PRO subject of the following infinitive); and those that take* nonsubject control *(persuade, etc. - i.e. verbs where the PRO subject of a following infinitive is governed by some complement of the higher verb which is not its subject, e.g., its object.*

Native and proficient speakers of English know intuitively which of the verbs in Table 9 require that the subject of the subordinate clause be identical with the subject of the main clause and which do not, as is the case of (16) and (17) previously:

No.	Syntactic Classification
1.	to promise to
2.	to persuade to
3.	to convince to
4.	to want to
5.	to hope to
6.	to need to
7.	to attempt to
8.	to try to
9.	to claim to
10.	to dare to
11.	to plead to
12.	to ask to
13.	to appeal to
14.	to vow to
15.	to choose to
16.	to proceed to
17.	to refuse to
18.	to tend to
19.	to expect to
20.	to fail to
21.	to intend to
22.	to remember to
23.	to hope to
24.	to manage to

Table 9 *Verbs Subcategorized with To-Infinitive*

When these verbs are used, PRO occupies an NP position in the subordinate clause.

13.5.2.2 Diagramming Sentences with PRO

The tree diagrams proposed for (16) and (18) are wrong from the perspective of Government-Binding theory because they do not include PRO. Let us re-draw (18) correctly now. With this new insight, the sentence <Rhoda persuaded Larry to go to Africa> can now be correctly diagrammed as follows:

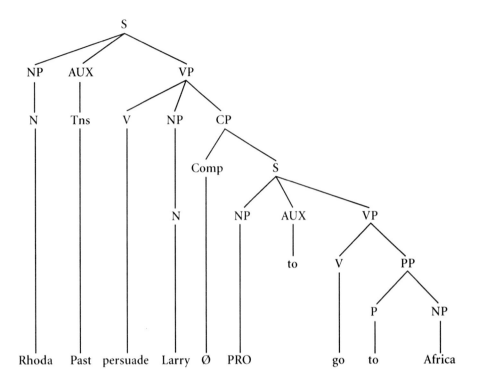

The main difference between this tree diagram and the preceding one is that in the former <Larry> appears under the NP subject of the subordinate clause whereas here, PRO occupies this position. This way of diagramming <To-infinitive> subordinate clause and all subordinate clauses with non-finite verbs is more accurate because it conforms to the PRO-Condition in Government-Binding. Radford (1986:331) states this condition as follows:

PRO-Condition

Any sentence containing PRO in a position where it is governed (or cased-marked) is ill-formed.

In other words, for PRO to occur in English, the verb in the subordinate clause must not have any tense information associated with it. It must either be in an infinitival or a participial form.

13.5.3 The Syntactic Characteristics of Bare Infinitive Subordinate Clauses

The use of verbs such as those listed in Table 10 requires that the verb of the subordinate clause be in the bare infinitive. When such verbs appear in the main clause, the verb in the subordinate clause takes an infinitival form without <To>. The number of English verbs that require that the verb of the subordinate clause be in the bare infinitive mood is small. The most common ones are here:

No.	Syntactic Classification
1.	to watch
2.	to hear
3.	to feel
4.	to let
5.	to make
6.	to see
7.	to demand
8.	to insist
9.	to require
10.	to suggest

Table 10 *Verbs Subcategorized with Bare Infinitive*

Sentence (19) illustrates the use of bare infinitive subordinate clauses:

(19) *The board made the professor resign.*

In contemporary linguistics, <resign>is a bare infinitive subordinate clause. It is dominated by a CP. Sentence (19) can be diagrammed as follows:

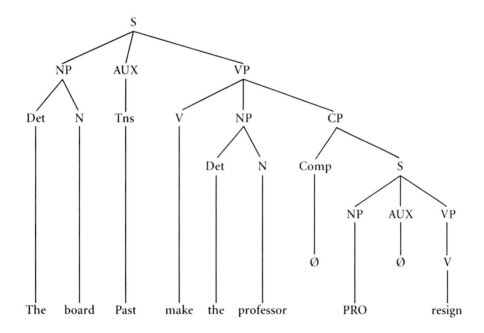

The tree diagram of bare infinitive subordinate clauses deserves a few comments. First, notice that Comp is empty in all such constructions. Secondly, for the first time since we have been diagramming sentences, the AUX of the subordinate clause is also empty, as shown by the symbol "Ø". In reality, it is occupied by the bare infinitive marker. However, since this infinitive marker is morphologically unrealized, there is no reason to indicate it under AUX.

13.5.4 The Syntactic Characteristics of Participial Subordinate Clauses

English has two types of participial subordinate clauses: **present participial clauses** and **past participial clauses**. As in the previous cases, certain verbs in the lexicon condition the use of a participial verbal form in the subordinate clause. Thus, the subcategorization frame of such verbs can be represented as follows:

V, [—CP],   where CP is rewritten as

CP, [Comp S],   where S is rewritten as

S → PRO AUX VP   where AUX is rewritten as

$$\text{AUX} \rightarrow \begin{Bmatrix} \text{-ING} \\ \text{-EN} \end{Bmatrix} \quad [+\text{MV}]$$

A rule of Affix Hopping similar to the one that we have seen in previous chapters applies to move the participial suffixes <-ING> and <-EN> to the main verb. The form <-EN> is the invariable deep structure form for the past participle. The present participle <-ING> has no irregular form.

13.5.4.1 Present Participial Subordinate Clauses

There are three semantic categories of verbs that introduce present participial subordinate clauses: verbs of liking, verbs expressing inherent time frame information, and a third group of verbs that defy any semantic classification. These three types are represented by Tables 11, 12, and 13 below:

No.	Syntactic Classification
1.	to love
2.	to like
3.	to enjoy
4.	to resent
5.	to appreciate
6.	to dislike
7.	to hate
8.	to loath
9.	to prefer

Table 11 *Verbs of Liking*

No.	Syntactic Classification
1.	to begin
2.	to start
3.	to finish
4.	to stop
5.	to continue
6.	to quit
7.	to resume

Table 12 *Verbs Denoting Time Frame*

No.	Syntactic Classification
1.	to regret
2.	to mind/do not mind
3.	can/cannot imagine
4.	to recall
5.	to remember
6.	to admit
7.	to deny
8.	to see[5]
9.	to hear
10.	to find
11.	to watch

Table 13 *Miscellaneous Verbs*

When most of these verbs or verbal constructions occur in the main clause, the verb of the subordinate clause takes the <-ING> suffix, as in the examples below:

(20) *Josh enjoys studying linguistics.*

(21) **Josh enjoys to study linguistics.*

(22) **Josh enjoys study linguistics.*

The ungrammaticality of (21) and (22) shows that the present participle is obligatory if the verb of the main clause is <enjoy>. Now, let us contrast these sentences with the following:

(23) *Josh loves studying linguistics.*

(24) *Josh likes studying linguistics.*

(25) *Josh loves to study linguistics.*

(26) *Josh likes to study linguistics.*

---

[5] The last four verbs are classified as verbs of perception.

(27) *Josh loves study linguistics.

(28) *Josh likes study linguistics.

Sentences (23), (24), (25), and (26) tell us that not all verbs of liking behave like <enjoy>. Some can take either a <To-Infinitive> subordinate clause or a present participial subordinate clause. Presumably, proficient speakers' mental lexicon is positively subcategorized as to indicate which of these verbs accept both types of subordinate clauses and which accept only the present participial subordinate clause. It is important to note that none of the verbs in Tables 11, 12 and 13 can accept a bare infinitive subordinate clause. The ungrammaticality of (27) and (28) illustrate this point.

It is also worth pointing out that verbs of perception such as <to see, to hear, to find> require that the verbs of the subordinate clause take the present participial suffix, as in the sentences below:

(29) The police found him lying in a pool of blood.

(30) *The police found him to lie in a pool of blood.

(31) *The police found him lie in a pool of blood.

Additionally, the presence of the complementizer <without> calls for the verb in the subordinate clause to take the present participial suffix <-ING>, as in the sentences below:

(32) The police accused her without finding any strong evidence.

(33) *The police accused her without to find any strong evidence.

(34) *The police accused her without find any strong evidence.

13.5.4.2 Diagramming Sentences with Present Participial Subordinate Clauses

The tree diagram of sentences such as those in the previous paragraph is straightforward. Let us use (20) to illustrate how such sentences are diagrammed:

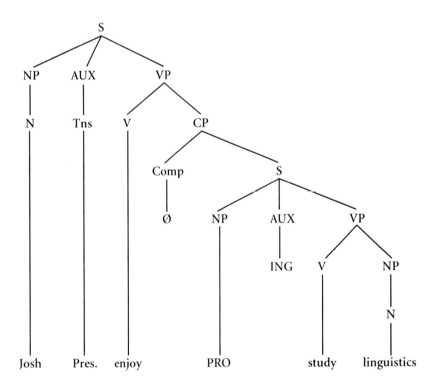

In deriving this sentence from the deep structure, the rule of Affix Hopping applies late to move <-ING> under AUX to the verb <study>. If (32) were to be diagrammed, <without> would occur under Comp.

13.5.4.3 Past Participial Subordinate Clauses

English has a small number of verbs that are subcategorized as taking a verb in past participle in the subordinate clause. Most of these verbs appear in Table 14 below:

No.	Syntactic Classification
1.	to want
2.	to see
3.	to hear
4.	to declare
5.	to consider
6.	to find
7.	to watch

Table 14 *Verbs Subcategorized with Past Participles*

When any one of these verbs occurs in the main clause, the verb of the subordinate clause can be in the past participle, as illustrated by the sentences below:

(35) *The whole nation wanted Nixon impeached.*

(36) *The orphan saw his mother raped.*

(37) *They found the precious jar broken into pieces.*

In these sentences, <impeached>, <raped>, and <broken into pieces> are subordinate clauses. One school of thought within Generative Transformational Grammar is that such sentences are reduced passive constructions in which the agent or the subject of the subordinate clause has been deleted.[6] This older view claims that all passive constructions have an active counterpart in the deep structure. However, as noted by Celce-Murcia and Larsen-Freeman (1999:675) such a position becomes indefensible since a verb such as <rumor> occurs mostly in the passive but does not have an active counterpart.

If, on the other hand, passive constructions are generated directly by phrase structure rules, as most linguists now believe, then sentences such as these are derived from underlying deep structure of the following type:

Deep structure: The whole nation Past want Nixon Be-EN impeach.

Thus, the surface structure, <the whole nation wanted Nixon impeached> is obtained by applying Affix Hopping, and then deleting <Be>. A third alternative exists which does not consider sentences such as (35), (36), and (37) to be derived from any passive construction at all. According to this view, a sentence such as (35) is produced to meet

---

[6] Some also refer to these sentences as "reduced subordinate clauses." Each one these three sentences can be derived respectively as follows: "The whole nation wanted Nixon to be impeached," "The orphan saw his mother being raped," and "They found that the precious jar had been broken into pieces."

the subcategorization frame of <want> and therefore has the following deep structure form:

Deep structure: The whole nation Past want Nixon EN impeach.

All these three analyses produce the same result. Here, the Occam Razor Principle discussed in 4.1.5 can be invoked to support the third alternative analysis. This analysis is simpler because it does not call for deletion. Only the Affix Hopping transformation is necessary.

13.5.4.4 Diagramming Past Participial Subordinate Clauses

Assuming that the simpler analysis is the best, the following tree diagram can be proposed to account for sentence (35) and similar sentences:

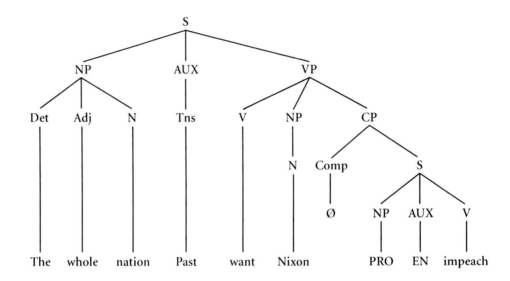

This concludes the discussion on verb-centered classification of subordinate clauses. This approach is simpler because it reduces the plethora of subordinate constructions in English to only four, namely, To-infinitive, bare infinitive, present participial, and past participial constructions.

13.6 Adjectives and Subordination

The syntactic similarities between verbs and adjectives have long been recognized (Chomsky 1965:92–3). Just like verbs, a good number of English adjectives are subcategorized as taking subordinate clauses when used as predicative adjectives. For instance, the adjective complex <*be eager to, be easy to, be hard to, be appropriate that, be uncommon that, be interesting that, be oblivious to the fact that, be happy to, be happy that, be sad that, be ready to, be peculiar that*> can all be subcategorized as follows:

Adjective, [— CP]

Here are a few sentences to illustrate this subcategorization frame:

(38) *Tallie is eager to please her father.*

(39) *This problem is easy to solve.*

(40) *It is appropriate to deal with this matter now.*

(41) *John is oblivious to the fact that Mary hates anchovies.*

(42) *It is fun watching/to watch children role play.*

(43) *Drew is happy that the meeting went well.*

The examples above show that some adjectives take tensed subordinate clauses while others take non-finite subordinate clauses. Some predicative adjective used with <be> such as <be appropriate that>, <be uncommon that>, <be necessary to>, <be important to/that> are subcategorized both with tensed and untensed subordinate clauses, as in the sentences below:

(44) *It is appropriate that I should give back to the community.*

(45) *It is appropriate to give back to the community.*

However, there others such as <to be eager to>, <to be easy to> that are subcategorized only with To-Infinitive subordinate clauses:

(46) *Sarah is eager to please her brother.*

(47) **Sarah is eager that she please her brother.*

Sentences such as (46) are diagrammed as follows:

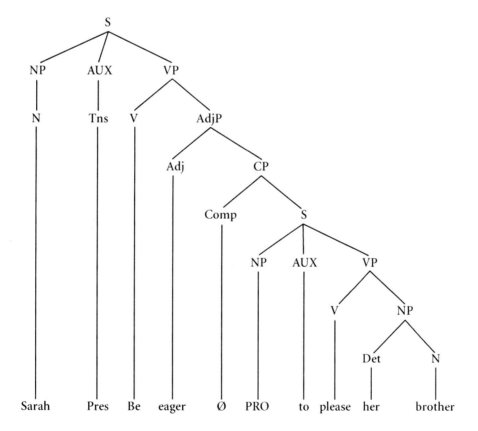

A small set of adjectives such as <to be interested in> is subcategorized with present participial subordinate clauses.

> (48) *Sarah is interested in pleasing her brother.*

> (49) **Sarah is interested to please her brother.*

> (50) **Sarah is interested that she please her brother.*

13.7 Transformations and Subordinate Clauses

Sentence relatedness has always been used to prove the existence and necessity of transformations. Fromkin et al (2003:152) explain that when two sentences differ in structure with small differences in grammatical morphemes but no difference in meaning, these sentences are to be related to each other. The conventional wisdom has been that one of the sentences is the basic sentence, that is, the one closer to the deep structure, and the other is the derived sentence. Moving from the basic or deep structure sentence to the derived sentence is done through transformations. We have examined many such transformations already. In this section we will focus on three transformations that apply in subordinate clauses: **topicalization, extraposition**[7], and **conditional clause fronting.**

The common denominator between these transformations is that they involve movement rules. Topicalization moves an NP from the subordinate clause leftward into the main clause. There are many types of topicalizations but we restrict our analysis only to those that move NPs from the subordinate clause into the main clause. As far as topicalization in the subordinate clause is concerned, experts distinguish between two main types: subject-raising and object-raising. These two will be discussed shortly. As for extraposition, it takes an NP from the main clause and moves it rightward into the subordinate clause. The last transformation to be considered is conditional clause fronting. It moves the whole subordinate clause, not just part of it, into sentence initial position.

13.7.1 Subject-Raising Topicalization

In **Subject-Raising** transformations, the deep structure subject of the verb in the subordinate clause is moved up to be the surface structure subject of the verb in the main clause. Let us illustrate the Subject-Raising transformation with (51) below:

> (51) *Larry seems to like Africa.*

A simplified deep structure form of this sentence is as follows:

> *Deep Structure: [NP e Prs. seem [CP Larry to like Africa]]*

Radford (1996:334–5, 377, 383) suggest that the NP in the sentence be treated as a nonlexical NP, or **empty NPs.** The symbol "*e*"[8] is used to represent empty NPs. This symbol is in complementary distribution with PRO. NP *e* occurs before tensed verbs while PRO occurs with non-finite verbs (infinitives and participles). The tree diagram of (51) can be represented as follows:

---

[7] A fourth transformation called "Cliticization" will be examined in 14.7.4 and 15.4.9.

[8] Some textbooks use the symbol "*e*" (empty) instead of "Ø" (null).

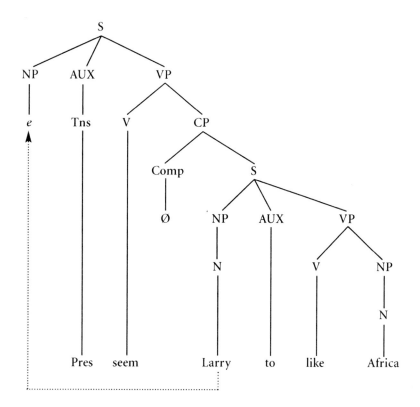

This type of topicalization is called "Subject-Raising" because the NP subject <Larry> of the subordinate clause is raised from the lower part of the sentence as shown by the dotted arrows in the tree diagram to the empty NP higher up in the tree diagram. The number of English verbs that call for Subject-Raising is very limited. The two that are most often mentioned are <seem> and <appear>.

13.7.2 Object-Raising Topicalization

The same movement rule that applies to move a subject of the subordinate clause to the beginning of the main clause can also apply to move a direct object from the subordinate clause to the same position in the main clause, as seen in the example below:

>   (52)   *This problem is hard to solve.*

The verb <solve> is a transitive verb that is strictly subcategorized with a direct object. When the direct object is omitted, the resulting sentence becomes ill-formed as in (53).

>   (53)   **Mary solved.*

The deep structure of (52) is said to be as follows:

>   *Deep structure: NP e Pres be hard CP PRO to solve this problem*

Its tree diagram can be represented as follows:

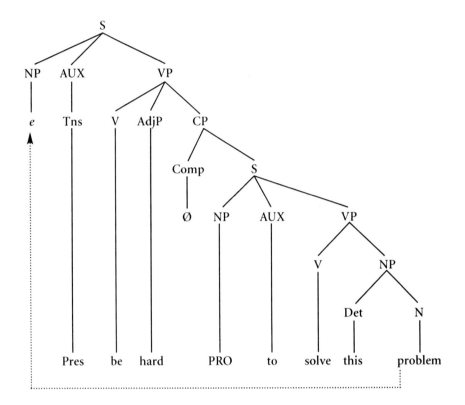

The dotted arrows in the tree diagram show the process whereby sentence (52) is generated. The direct object <this problem> has been raised leftward to the NP subject position. This is the reason why this topicalization has received the label of Object-Raising.

13.7.3 Extraposition Transformations

As noted earlier, extraposition is a mirror image of topicalization. It moves elements from the main clause rightward into the subordinate clause, whereas topicalization moves sentential elements leftward. Here are some examples of sentences in which the extraposition transformation has been applied:

(54) *It is hard to solve this problem.*

(55) *It is a shame that the reporter lied.*

(56) *It is forbidden to cheat on an exam.*

These three sentences seem to be related to the ones below:

(57) *To solve this problem is hard.*

(58) *That the reporter lied is a shame.*

(59) *To cheat on an exam is forbidden.*

Linguists postulate that (57) through (59) are the base sentences from which (54) through (56) are generated. These sentences are said to have undergone an extraposition transformation[9]. Extraposition consists of moving the NP subject (or parts of it) from the main clause rightward towards the end of the sentence, as seen in the example below"

> *Deep structure: That the reporter Past lie Pres Be a shame.*

> *Extraposition Movement:— is a shame that the reporter lied.*

Notice that <that the reporter lied> has moved from its subject position rightward. Since the subject <that the reporter lied> was moved out of the main clause, the verb <is> is left without a grammatical subject. This is a major violation of the NP-Subject Movement Constraint which is formulated as follows:

NP-Subject Movement Constraint

A tensed clause subject cannot undergo NP Movement (Radford 1986:341).

This constraint is violated because the subject of the verb <is> has been moved. In so doing, it has left <is a shame> subjectless. English has a very stringent requirement, namely that all finite verbs must have a grammatical subject. To prevent the output sentence from being ungrammatical, the "dummy" subject <It> is inserted. The addition of <It> is in keeping with the addition constraint stated in 4.5.2.1, namely that only no meaning-bearing elements can be introduced in the derivation. The addition of <It> satisfies the requirement that all tensed verbs must have an overt subject. The full derivational process that helps generate sentences such as (55) is detailed as follows:

Deep structure:	That the reporter Past lie Pres be a shame
Extraposition Movement:	—Pres be a shame that the reporter Past lie
"IT"- addition:	it Pres be a shame that the reporter Past lie
Affix Hopping:	it be Pres a shame that the reporter lie Past
Spell-Out rules:	it is a shame that the reporter lied
Surface structure:	It is a shame that the reporter lied.

Extraposition transformations of this type are said to apply cyclically. This means that they must follow a prescribed order such as this one or else the sentence would be ill-formed.

---

[9] There are very complex extraposition rules. Radford (1986:227) gives the following examples: "A critical review of *his latest book* has just appeared" and "A book *which deals with Constraints* has just appeared." As a result of the application of the extraposition rule, we have the following sentences: "A critical review has just appeared *of his latest book*" or "A book has just appeared *which deals with Constraints*." The elements that have undergone extraposition are in italics.

Sentences such as (58) that have heavy subjects still conform to the SVO pattern. They are diagrammed like other SVO pattern sentences, as seen below:

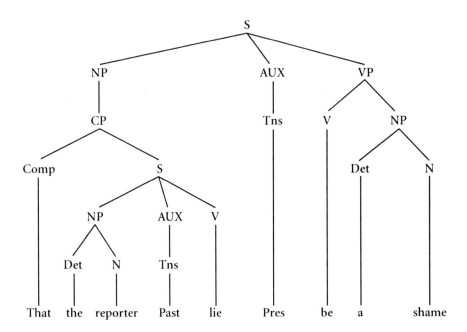

13.7.4 Extraposition and Information Structure

Linguists speculate as to why speakers resort to extraposition. Bickford (1998:325) proposes that "native speakers feel that clauses are usually too big to fit comfortably just before the verb and prefer them at the end of the clause." Clark (2003:260) concurs with this opinion because she, too, writes that "extraposition shortens the subject of the sentence by moving a CP or PP out of the subject position to the end of the sentence." Kaplan (1995:259) goes one step further and offers the following opinion:

> *All else being equal, longer constituents tend to be placed at the end of a sentence (e.g., in an extraposed structure). . . . Possibly part of the answer to the question of why sentential subjects are so uncommon in discourse is simply that the tendency to place longer elements toward the end of a sentence outweighs the tendency to place elements representing old information early. It is unclear why this should be so. More research is needed on this, and on the question of what motivates choices of a sentential structure, when it does occur, over one with the embedded sentence moved to the end.*

This linguistic behavior is puzzling because in extemporaneous communication, speakers usually tend to remain close to the deep structure pattern of the sentence. Non-obligatory transformations are used for reasons often associated with style and register. However, in this case, an extraposition transformation is preferred to the form of the sentence closer to the deep structure. We concur with Kaplan that this syntactic behavior is a mystery that needs to be investigated further.

13.7.5 Conditional Clause Fronting

The last transformation to be examined involves <If> subordinate clauses. These clauses are normally labeled "conditional clauses." However, given the preponderance of "If" in such constructions, more and more linguists are referring to them as "If subordinate clauses." Celce-Murcia and Larsen-Freeman (1999:557) note that 80% of all conditional subordinate clauses begin with <If>. Table 15 lists other subordinating conjunctions that introduce such clauses:

No.	Syntactic Classification
1.	if
2.	unless
3.	only if
4.	even if
5.	whether ... or not
6.	provided that
7.	given that
8.	assuming that
9.	as if
10.	so long as

Table 15 *Conjunctions of Condition*

Sentences (60) and (61) can be used to illustrate conditional clauses:

> (60)   *Rhoda will go to Africa if she makes money.*

> (61)   *If Rhoda makes money, she will go to Africa.*

Sentence (60) is said to be the basic sentence, whereas (61) is the derived sentence. Thus, sentence (60) can be diagrammed as follows:

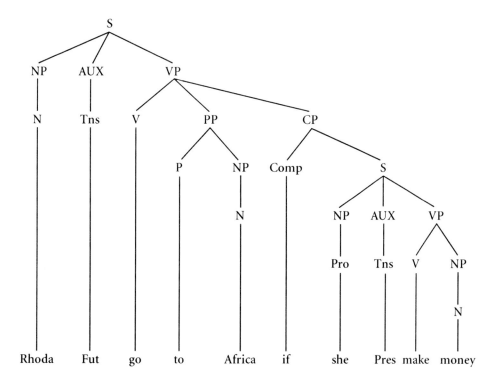

To derive sentence (61) from sentence (60) a number of transformations take place, chief among which is the Conditional Clause Fronting rule. The whole derivational process and all the necessary adjustments that are made to derive the surface structure from the underlying form can be illustrated as follows:

Deep structure:	Rhoda Fut go to Africa if Rhoda Pres make money
Matching/Indexing rule:	Rhoda[1] Fut go to Africa if Rhoda[1] Pres make money
Cond. Clause Fronting:	if Rhoda Pres make money Rhoda Fut go to Africa—
Pronominalization:	if Rhoda Pres make money she Fut go to Africa—
Affix Hopping:	if Rhoda make Pres money she Fut[10] go to Africa—
Spell-Out Rules:	if Rhoda makes money she will go to Africa—
Surface Structure:	If Rhoda makes money, she will go to Africa.

If-Conditional clauses have a complex morphosyntactic agreement system, as illustrated by the examples below:

(62)   Rhoda would go to Africa if she made money.

(63)   Rhoda would have gone to Africa if she had made money.

The morphosyntactic agreement pattern can be summarized by the table below:

No.	Verb in the Main Clause	Verb in the Subordinate Clause
1.	Present tense	will + bare infinitive
2.	Past tense	would + bare infinitive
3.	Past perfect	would + present perfect

Table 16 *Morphosyntax of Conditional Clauses*

Celce-Murcia and Larsen-Freeman (1999:557) report the result of an extensive study conducted by Hwang which shows that conditional clauses involving the perfect aspect is not favored in speaking or in writing. Out of 266 spoken utterances, only 10, that is, 3.8% involved the perfect aspect. Similarly, out of 948 written tokens, the sentences in which the perfect aspect appeared both in the main clause and the subordinate clause account only for 31 occurrences, that is, 3.3%.

---

[10] It is important to note that Affix Hopping does not apply with the future tense because English does not have an inflectional future affix. The future tense marker in English is the free morpheme <will>.

Sentence (60) discussed previously can be diagrammed as follows:

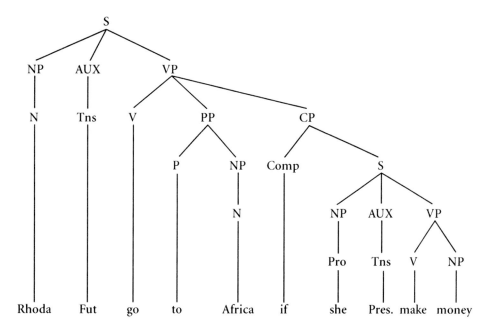

The fact that <if she makes money> is dominated by a VP shows clearly that this portion of the sentence is the subordinate clause.

13.7.6 Transformations and Composition

Chomsky (1965:125–7, 133) made it abundantly clear that there was a distinction between grammatical transformations and stylistic transformations. Furthermore, he added that

> In general, the rules of stylistic reordering are very different from the grammatical transformations, which are much more deeply embedded in the grammatical system. It might, in fact, be argued that the former are not so much rules of grammar as rules of performance. In any event, though this is surely an interesting phenomenon, it is one that has no apparent bearing, for the moment, on the theory of grammatical structure.

Generative Transformational Grammar, as noted previously, has not been interested for the most part in the application of its findings to the classroom. However, these insights provided by generative linguistics are extremely useful to teachers and to their students. The transformations discussed in this chapter can help enhance students' writing ability. Knowledge of Subject-Raising and Object-Raising can help reduce the repetitive use of "It" that is often characteristic of immature style. Teachers can help their students vary their usage of conditional clauses by teaching them explicitly the morphosyntactic agreement pattern when both the main clause and the subordinate clause have verbs in the perfect aspect. Not knowing this rule often leads to avoidance. However, avoidance of this construction in some instances leads to awkward sentence constructions. More will be said about this topic in Chapter 15.

13.8 Conclusion

Two main types of clauses exist in all languages: main/independent clauses and subordinate/dependent clauses. The generative grammar approach which defines subordinate clauses as clauses dominated by a phrase is far superior to the traditional definition of subordinate clause which alleges that subordinate clauses cannot "stand alone." Furthermore, the verb-centered approach used in this chapter has made it possible to reduce the types of subordinate clauses found in English to only four. It has also been shown that three major types of transformations that are important in writing operate in subordinate clauses. Understanding how these transformations apply and the steps involved in deriving surface structure sentences from deep structure forms can be an invaluable asset to teachers as they prepare their students for language use in academic settings.

Key Terms to Know

These are the key terms that you should be able to use and define after reading this chapter:

1. bare infinitive subordinate clause: 13.5.3

2. complementizer phrase (CP): 13.4.2, 13.5, 13.8

3. complementizers: 13.3, 13.4.2, 13.5, 13.5.1, 13.5.4.1

4. conditional clause: 13.7, 13.7.5, 13.7.6

5. cyclical application of rules: 13.7.3

6. dependent clause: 13.0, 13.2, 13.4, 13.4.1, 13.4.2, 13.4.3, 13.5, 13.5.2, 13.5.2.2, 13.5.3, 13.5.4, 13.5.4.1, 13.5.4.3, 13.5.4.4, 13.5.4.5, 13.6, 13.7, 13.7.1, 13.7.2, 13.7.3, 13.7.5, 13.7.6, 13.8

7. extraposition: 13.7, 13.7.3, 13.7.4

8. finite verb: 13.5, 13.7.1, 13.7.3

9. fronting transformation: 13.7, 13.7.5

10. independent: 13.0, 13.2, 13.4.1, 13.5.2, 13.5.2.1, 13.5.3, 13.5.4.1, 13.5.4.4, 13.7, 13.7.1, 13.7.2, 13.7.3, 13.7.5, 13.7.6, 13.8

11. main clause: 13.0, 13.2, 13.4.1, 13.5.2, 13.5.2.1, 13.5.3, 13.5.4.1, 13.5.4.4, 13.7, 13.7.1, 13.7.2, 13.7.3, 13.7.5, 13.7.6, 13.8

12. non-finite verb: 13.5, 13.5.2.2, 13.7.1

13. Occam Razor Principle: 13.5.4.4

14. object-raising transformation: 13.7, 13.7.2, 13.7.6

15. past participial subordinate clause: 13.5.4.3, 13.5.4.3

16. present participial subordinate clause: 13.5.4.1

17. PRO: 13.5.2.1

18. Pro: 13.5.2.1

19. stylistic transformation: 13.7.6

20. subject-raising transformation: 13.7, 13.7.1, 13.7.6

21. subordinate clause: 13.0, 13.2, 13.4, 13.4.1, 13.4.2, 13.4.3, 13.5, 13.5.2, 13.5.2.2, 13.5.3, 13.5.4, 13.5.4.1, 13.5.4.2, 13.5.4.3, 13.5.4.4, 13.6, 13.7, 13.7.1, 13.7.2, 13.7.3, 13.7.5, 13.7.6, 13.8

22. subordinating conjunction: 13.0, 13.1, 13.2, 13.3, 13.4.2, 13.5.1, 13.7.5

23. tensed clause: 13.5, 13.7.1, 13.7.3

24. To-infinitive subordinate clause: 13.5.2, 13.5.2.1, 13.6

25. topicalization:13.7, 13.7.1, 13.7.2, 13.7.3

26. untensed clause: 13.5, 13.5.2.2, 13.7.1

27. verb-centered classification: 13.5

EXERCISE 1

Underline the subordinate clauses in the following sentences. Include the subordinating conjunction (complementizer) inside of the subordinate clause.

1. The university expects to reduce its deficit.

2. The board of ethics wants the lawyer disbarred.

3. The convict tried to assassinate the politician.

4. We all wondered when the beloved professor would retire.

5. The administration persuaded the disgruntled professor to drop his lawsuit.

6. Everybody wants to be a winner.

7. The police made her sign an illegal affidavit.

8. Elected officials love playing politics with national security matters.

9. The distressed mother promised the parole board that her daughter would stop drinking and driving.

10. The nurse persuaded the patient to take his medecine.

11. That professors would inflate grades for their students is unbelievable.

12. If everything else fails, we have each other to depend on.

EXERCISE 2—SENTENCE RELATEDNESS AND TRANSFORMATIONS

From the following deep structure sentence forms, provide all the transformations that apply to derive the pairs of related sentences. What is the name of this transformational operation?

Deep structure: NP *e* Pres seem the students PRO to be ready for Christmas break

Surface structure: The students seem to be ready for Christmas break.

Deep structure: NP *e* Pres seem the students to be ready for Christmas break

Surface structure: It seems that the students are ready for Christmas break.

Deep structure: That grammar Pres Be-EN dread by students Pres surprise me

Surface structure: It surprises me that grammar is dreaded by students.

EXERCISE 3—TREE DIAGRAMMING

Provide a tree diagram of the following sentences.

1.   The board of ethics wants the lawyer disbarred.

2.   The convict tried to assassinate the politician.

3. The police made her sign an illegal affidavit.

4. This disease is easy to treat with penicillin.

EXERCISE 4—SUBORDINATE CLAUSES

Give the appropriate clause labels to the italicized clauses in the sentences below. [**Note:** Not all of the labels may apply. Some labels may be used more than once.]

Tensed subordinate clause

Bare infinitive subordinate clause

To-infinitive subordinate clause

Present Participial subordinate clause

Past Participial subordinate clause

1.   Jim promised *to marry Rebecca at the end of the semester.*

2.   They watched the candidate *giving a speech.*

3.   I made my son *clean his room this morning.*

4.   We saw Larry *drinking and driving.*

5.   The protesters heard the senator *jeered by the mob.*

6.   The kids saw the cat *catch a bird.*

7.   The climber felt her strength *give out.*

8.   The player came home *injured and bleeding.*

9.   Tallie thinks *that Dora the Explorer is a good show.*

EXERCISE 5—SUBORDINATING CONJUNCTION IDENTIFICATION

Identify the subordinating conjunctions found in the text below. [**Note:** Keep in mind that there may be more or there may be less subordinating conjunctions to fill the table below.]

The Gettysburg Address

by Abraham Lincoln

"Fourscore and seven years ago our fathers brought forth on this continent a new nation, conceived in liberty and dedicated to the proposition that all men are created equal. Now we are engaged in a great civil war, testing whether that nation or any nation so conceived and so dedicated can long endure. We are met on a great battlefield of that war. We have come to dedicate a portion of that field as a final resting-place for those who here gave their lives that that nation might live. It is altogether fitting and proper that we should do this.

But in a larger sense, we cannot dedicate, we cannot consecrate, we cannot hallow this ground. The brave men, living and dead who struggled here have consecrated it far above our poor power to add or detract. The world will little note nor long remember what we say here, but it can never forget what they did here. It is for us the living rather to be dedicated here to the unfinished work which they who fought here have thus far so nobly advanced. It is rather for us to be here dedicated to the great task remaining before us—that from these honored dead we take increased devotion to that cause for which they gave the last full measure of devotion—that we here highly resolve that these dead shall not have died in vain, that this nation under God shall have a new birth of freedom, and that government of the people, by the people, for the people shall not perish from the earth."

	Subordinating Conjunctions
1.	
2.	
3.	
4.	
5.	
6.	
7.	
8.	
9.	
10.	

EXERCISE 6—UNDERSTANDING GRAMMATICAL TERMINOLOGY

1. Make a sentence with a past participle subordinate clause. Underline the past participle subordinate clause.

2. Make a sentence with a subordinate clause introduced by a subordinating conjunction of result. Underline the subordinate.

3. Make a sentence with a To-infinitive subordinate clause. Underline the To-infinitive subordinate clause.

4. Make a sentence with a subordinate clause introduced by a subordinating conjunction of reason. Underline the subordinate.

5. Make a sentence with a Bare-infinitive subordinate clause. Underline the Bare subordinate clause.

6. Make a sentence with a tensed subordinate clause introduced by a subordinating conjunction of concession. Underline the subordinate.

7. Make a sentence with a subordinate clause introduced by a subordinating conjunction of time. Underline the subordinate.

8. Make a sentence with a subordinate clause introduced by a subordinating conjunction of purpose. Underline the subordinate.

9. Make a sentence with a subordinate clause introduced by a subordinating conjunction of condition.

10. Make a sentence with a present participial subordinate clause. Underline the subordinate clause.

Chapter 14

Pronouns and Pronominalization

14.0 INTRODUCTION

Pronouns are closed class words that are truly universal. None of the 6,000 or so languages spoken in the world today has been found to be lacking in pronouns. Though the number of pronouns may vary from language to language, pronouns in all languages have the same function, i.e., they are substitutes for nouns. The etymology of the English word for this part of speech says it all. The word "pronoun" is a direct translation of the Latin words <pro>, which means "for," and the root <nomen>, which is equivalent to "noun" or "name" in English. Brooks and Winbery (1988:80) define a pronoun as "a word which stands for or in the place of or instead of a noun. Pronouns are used to prevent the monotony which would result from unnecessary repetition of nouns. Inasmuch as pronouns take the place of nouns, they are used much the same way as nouns are used."

This chapter summarizes the essential information that ESL/EFL and language arts teachers need to know to understand pronouns and pronominalization in English. The semantic, morphological, and syntactic properties of various types of pronouns and pronominal constructions are investigated. The interface between functional and syntactic analysis will receive the lion's share of attention because most problems related to the use of pronouns straddle semantics, morphology, and syntax.

14.1 Classificatory Nightmare

Both traditional grammarians and contemporary linguists classify pronouns semantically and functionally into nine major groups, as listed in Table 1:

No.	Semantic Classification
1.	Personal Pronouns
2.	Possessive Pronouns
3.	Demonstrative Pronouns
4.	Interrogative Pronouns
5.	Indefinite Pronouns
6.	Reflexive Pronouns
7.	Reciprocal Pronouns
8.	Emphatic Pronouns
9.	Relative Pronouns

Table 1 *Semantic Classification of Pronouns*

In studying pronouns, it is not possible, nor is it desirable, to separate meaning from function, or function from form. They have been separated here for pedagogical purposes and also for the sake of continuity with the previous chapters.

14.1.2 Summary Definitions and Semantic Classifications

The definitions proposed here follow the order of the pronouns listed in Table 1. **Personal pronouns** are pronouns that are used to refer to the person who is speaking, the person who is being spoken to, or the person being spoken about. As for **possessive pronouns,** they establish a relationship of ownership between two entities. **Demonstrative pronouns** are pronouns that one uses to point to people, objects, or things. **Interrogative pronouns** as the name says are used to ask questions. **Indefinite pronouns** refer to people, objects, or things whose nature or identity is not clear, or is not intended to be clear. **Reflexive pronouns** are closely linked with personal pronouns. They show that the speaker or the addressee, or the entity being referred to does something to himself/herself/itself, or for his/her/its own benefit. The use of **reciprocal pronouns** entails that two agents are involved in the action or state described by the verb. The result of the action or of the state is beneficial to the two parties involved. A subclass of reciprocal pronouns is called "**distributive pronouns.**" The use of these pronouns signals that there are more than two participants who share in the benefits or consequences of the action or state expressed by the verb. **Emphatic pronouns** are also closely related to personal pronouns. When such pronouns are used, an extra emphasis is placed on the speaker, the addressee, or the person/thing being talked about. **Relative pronouns** are so named because the pronoun that is used has a "relative" in another clause, usually in the main clause. These brief definitions set the stage for a more extensive morphological and syntactic analysis in the upcoming sections where numerous examples are provided to illustrate the uses of these pronouns.

14.1.3 Additional Classifications

Further semantic divisions are made in studying world languages. Some of these distinctions do not apply in English, but a few do. In studying other languages, linguists distinguish between **inclusive** and **exclusive** pronouns. Inclusive pronouns are used when the speaker includes himself/herself among the group of people being referred to. Exclusive pronouns, on the other hand, exclude the speaker. Dobrin and Good (2009:621) note that this pronominal feature was first brought to the awareness of the worldwide linguistic community by missionaries. The pronoun most susceptible for such a usage is <we>, as in the examples below:

(1) *We are vacationing in Wyoming this summer.*

(2) *How are we doing today? (doctor to a patient)*

In sentence (1) <we> is an inclusive pronoun because the speaker includes himself/herself among the group of people going to Wyoming. However in (2) when the doctor uses <we>, he/she excludes himself/herself. This is a case of an exclusive <we> in English.

Another semantic distinction that is often made is the one between proximity and distance. In English, the use of the pronoun <this> or <these> suggests geographical proximity relative to the speaker, whereas the use of <that> and <those> implies a distance relative to the speaker. The idea of proximity and distance is taken a step further in some Amerindian languages. McWorther (2003:180) notes that some languages have a special class of pronouns called "**evidentials**" which are used to indicate whether the speaker is an eyewitness to the events that he/she is reporting, or whether he/she is reporting it as hearsay.

Furthermore, Spanish, French, Japanese, Indonesian, Vietnamese, and many other world languages distinguish between **honorific** and **non-honorific pronouns**. An honorific pronoun is used to signal a difference of social status between speakers. Participants in a discourse use the sociolinguistically correct pronouns when addressing each other.

14.2 The Morphology of Pronouns

The concept of **agreement** is a key notion in the study of pronouns. Pronouns are said to agree in **number, person, case,** and **gender** with the nouns that they replace, as noted already in 7.2.1. This means that if a pronoun is used as a substitute for a noun, both must agree in the four essential features just mentioned. These four features do not have equal importance in world languages. For instance, agreement in gender, though found in nearly all Western European languages, is absent in West African languages. Languages in which the pronoun agrees with the noun in gender do not all behave the same way. In some, such as Hebrew, a gender distinction is made between the masculine <you> and the feminine <you>. English does not make such a distinction. Distinctions such as these that are lacking in English are generally overlooked in this discussion. However, some may be mentioned in passing if they help to highlight aspects of pronominal acquisition. The main focus of this chapter is on English pronouns.

14.2.1 Agreement in Case

Case is generally defined as a suffix found on nouns. These case suffixes indicate the grammatical function performed by that noun in the sentence. The term **declension** is used sometimes with the same intended meaning. We begin our analysis of the pronominal morphology with case because, according to contemporary linguistics, case is a universal feature found in all NPs of all languages. However, languages fall into two distinct groups with regard to case. Some have a case system that is phonetically and/or orthographically realized, whereas others have only **abstract cases** (Radford 1986:312). The number of morphological cases that languages assign to NPs varies greatly from one language to the next. English has four main cases, which are described as follows:

No.	Case	Functional Equivalent	Examples
1.	Nominative	Subject of the verb	I, you, he/she, it, we, you, they, who
2.	Dative	Object of a preposition	me, you, him/her, it, us, you, them, whom
3.	Genitive	Possession	mine, yours, his, hers, its, ours, yours, theirs, whose
4.	Accusative	Direct Object	me, you, him, her, it, us, you, them, who/whom

Table 2 *The Case System*

Old English used to have case suffixes on all nouns. However, gradually morphological case ceased to be indicated on nouns. The only part of speech in which case has survived until now is on pronouns. The examples below serve to illustrate how case is used in the pronominal system of English. The examples show how the 1st person singular pronoun changes its form depending on its grammatical case/function in the sentence:

(3)   *I love Kim.*   → Nominative case

(4)   *Kim jogs with **me**.*   → Dative case

(5)   *This book is **mine**.*   → Genitive case

(6)   *Kim gave **me** flowers.*   → Accusative case

14.2.2 Agreement in Number and Persons

Brooks and Winbery (1988:130) define **person** as "that quality of [a pronoun or] a verb which indicates the relation of the subject to the action. If the subject is represented as speaking, the verb is in the first person. If the subject is being spoken to, the verb is in the second person. If the subject is being spoken about, the verb is in the third person." They also define **number** as "the quality of a verb or pronoun which indicates whether the subject is one person or one thing (singular number) or more than one (plural number)." Traditional and contemporary grammarians divide the pronouns found in English into six persons and two numbers, as seen below:

No.	Person	Example
	Singular	
1.	First person	I, me, me, mine
2.	Second person	you, you, you, yours
3.	Third person	he, she, it, to/for/with him, her, it, his, hers
	Plural	
1.	First person	we, us, us, ours
2.	Second person	you, you, you, yours
3.	Third person	they, them, them, theirs

Table 3 *Personal Pronoun System*

A number and person agreement system known as **resolution rules** has been found to be universal. Foley and Van Valin (1985:288) propose the following hierarchy for the agreement pattern found when two or more pronouns are conjoined or when pronouns are conjoined with lexical NPs:

speaker > addressee > 3rd person

The hierarchy is interpreted as follows: when the speaker <I>, is conjoined with the addressee <you>, agreement is made with <we>. Whenever the speaker <I> is coordinated with any pronoun or any NP, the first person plural <we> agreement applies. Whenever the addressee is involved, agreement is done with the second person plural <you>. Lastly, when a 3rd person is involved, agreement is done with the 3rd person plural <they>. In all these examples and in the table below, the nominative case is assumed. The information presented here is summarized in Table 4 as follows:

No.	Pronoun	Resolution Rule
1.	Speaker + addressee	→ <we>
2.	Speaker + 3rd person	→ <we>
3.	Addressee + Speaker	→ <we>
4.	Addressee + Addressee	→ <you>
5.	Addressee + 3rd person	→ <you>
6.	3rd person + Addressee	→ <you>
7.	3rd person + Speaker	→ <we>
8.	3rd person + 3rd person	→ <they>

Table 4 *Pronoun Resolution Rules*

The examples below illustrate how the person and number agreement system works in English:

(7) ?*You and I, **we** are going fishing tomorrow.*

(8) ?*You and you, **you** are going fishing tomorrow.*

(9) ?*You and he, **you** are going fishing tomorrow.*

(10) ?*He and she, **they** are going fishing tomorrow.*

These sentences are not deemed acceptable in written English. However, they are heard quite frequently in emphatic statements in spoken English. Cross-linguistic studies have shown variations in this agreement pattern. For instance, in Classical Greek, agreement in conjoined NPs is generally controlled by the NP closest to the verb. In other instances, it is the lexical NP that is more salient that controls the agreement. Koffi (1994: 434–41) has shown that misunderstanding this agreement pattern has led to the mistranslation of some Greek New Testament passages into English. ESL/EFL teachers can expect negative transfer in the person and number agreement system from their students, especially where agreement is not controlled by the same hierarchy patterns.

14.2.3 Agreement in Gender

Pronominal gender in English is confined only to the 3rd person singular where a three-way distinction is made between the masculine, the feminine, and neuter. This division is mostly based on biological gender, not on grammatical gender. The pronouns <he>, <him>, and <himself> replace masculine nouns, while <she>, <her> and <herself> are used for feminine nouns. The pronouns <it>, <its> and <itself> are used for lexical NPs that have the semantic feature [-animate], or for [+animate] beings whose sex is unknown or unimportant. Gender distinction is very limited in English; but it carries a very crucial information load. Table 5 summarizes the gender and pronouns in English.

No.	Person and Number	Masculine	Feminine	Neuter
	Singular			
1.	First person singular	unmarked	unmarked	unmarked
2.	Second person singular	unmarked	unmarked	unmarked
3.	Third person singular	He, him, him, his, himself	She, her, her, hers, herself	It, itself, its
	Plural			
1.	First person plural	unmarked	unmarked	unmarked
2.	Second person plural	unmarked	unmarked	unmarked
3.	Third person plural	unmarked	unmarked	unmarked

Table 5 *Gender in the Pronoun System*

Not using the gender of pronouns correctly can result in miscommunication and even embarrassment. Irrespective of dialectal differences, no native speaker of English is likely to produce sentences such as (11) and (12) below:

(11) **Mary is sick today. **He** has cancelled **his** office hours.*

(12) **Keith is fighting the flu, so **she** needs to rest in bed.*

Mismatch between the gender system of ESL/EFL students' L1 and English is the subject of concern for many teachers. Errors related to gender are more prevalent at the beginning and intermediate levels, but they decrease with exposure and practice. However, Celce-Murcia and Larsen-Freeman (1999:312) contend that their residual effects persist even at more advanced levels.

14.3 Functional Analysis of the Pronominal System

The nine pronouns listed in Table 1 get their names from their functions in the sentence, not from their formal characteristics. Consequently, understanding the function of pronouns is a key to understanding most of their syntactic behavior as well. The following sections will attempt to explain the rationale behind the traditional labels and their relevance to the syntax of pronouns.

14.3.1 Personal Pronouns

Personal pronouns fall into two main groups, "**subject**" and "**object**" pronouns. This classification owes a lot to the syntactic functions that the pronoun performs in the sentence. Subject pronouns in English have the nominative case. They function grammatically as the subject of the verb. Object pronouns, on the other hand, are either the direct object of the verb or the object of a preposition. Objective pronouns are inflected for the accusative or dative case. These three classes of pronouns are listed in Table 6 below:

No.	Person and Number	Subject	Direct Object	Indirect Object/ Object of a Preposition
	Singular			
1.	1st person singular	I	me	me
2.	2nd person singular	you	you	you
3.	3rd person singular	he, she, it	him /her /it	him, her, it
	Plural			
1.	1st person plural	we	us	us
2.	2nd person plural	you	you	you
3.	3rd person plural	they	them	them

Table 6 *Subject and Object Pronouns*

The examples below illustrate the use of the 3rd person plural pronoun in these three cases:

(13) ***They*** *came to the party.* (Nominative/subjective case)

(14) *Mary saw **them** at the party.* (Accusative/objective case)

(15) *Mary gave flowers **to them** at the party.* (Dative case)

We see that in these sentences, the 3rd person plural pronoun assumes two morphologically different forms depending on its grammatical function. In the nominative/ subjective case, the form is <they>, but it changes to <them> when it functions as a direct object or an indirect object (accusative and dative cases, respectively).

14.3.2 Possessive Pronouns

Possessive pronouns indicate possession. In English such pronouns are inflected for the genitive case. There is usually a great deal of confusion between possessive pronouns and what traditional grammar calls possessive adjectives. The difference between the two can be illustrated by the sentences below:

(16) *This is **my** book.* (Possessive adjective)

(17) *This book is **mine**.* (Possessive pronoun)

In (16) the word "my" is a possessive adjective because it modifies <book>. In (17) on the other hand, <mine> is a possessive pronoun. The difference between the two is one of syntactic environment. Since adjectives must modify nouns, whenever a possessive adjective is used, it must occur with a noun. Pronouns, on the other hand, replace nouns. Consequently, they cannot be followed by a noun. It is for this reason that (18) below is ill-formed:

(18) *This book is **mine** book.*

Table 7 lists both possessive pronouns and possessive adjectives side by side.

No.	Person and Number	Possessive Pronouns	Possessive Adjectives
1.	1st person singular	mine	my + NP
2.	2nd person singular	yours	your + NP
3.	3rd person singular	his, hers, its	his, her, its + NP
4.	1st person plural	ours	our + NP
5.	2nd person plural	yours	your + NP
6.	3rd person plural	theirs	their + NP

Table 7 *Possessive Pronouns*

In addition to the syntactic or distributional differences, there is also an inflectional morphology difference between the two. Possessive pronouns have the suffix <-s> that appears on all the pronominal forms except the first person singular. Most ESL/EFL students have more troubles with the possessive pronouns <his> and <her> than any other pronouns. The reason for this is often a fundamental difference between how grammatical gender and possession interact. In English the biological gender of the possessor controls the use of <his> or <her>. In other words, if the possessor is male, the pronoun <his> is used. If the possessor is female, the pronoun <hers> is used. In Spanish and French, on the other hand, the gender of the possessor does not control agreement with the possessive pronoun. Instead, it is the grammatical gender of the thing possessed that determines the kind of possessive pronoun used.

14.3.3 Demonstrative Pronouns

On the basis of Greek etymology, Robertson (1934:289) speculates that demonstrative pronouns may have been originally deictic words because they point to the position of an object in relation to the speaker.[1] Fromkin et al. (2003:218) note that deixis are words that require contextual information for their meaning to be complete. English has two main demonstrative pronouns, this/these and that/those, which agree in number with the noun that they replace. These pronouns also encode an idea of distance or proximity. Therefore, they agree with the speaker in the feature [± distance], as shown in the table below:

No.	Number	[-distance](close)	[+distance] (far)
1.	Singular	this	That
2.	Plural	these	Those

Table 8 *Demonstrative Pronouns*

[1] Demonstrative pronouns are called *"deitikai antonomai"* in Greek. This phrase can be translated literally as "pointing pronouns."

When the object referred to is close to the speaker, he/she uses the pronouns <this> and <these> to show proximity. The further the distance between the speaker and the object, the more likely he/she is to use the pronouns <that> and <those>. Here too, as was the case in 14.3.2, a distinction must be made between demonstrative pronouns and demonstrative adjectives. If the demonstrative word is followed by an NP, it is a demonstrative adjective. However, if it lacks an NP, it is a demonstrative pronoun, as illustrated by the sentences below:

(19) *I hate **this.*** (Demonstrative pronoun)

(20) *I hate **that.*** (Demonstrative pronoun)

(21) *I hate **this** attitude.* (Demonstrative adjective)

(22) *I hate **that** attitude.* (Demonstrative adjective)

14.3.4 Interrogative Pronouns

Interrogative pronouns are pronouns used to ask questions. They agree with their antecedents in the semantic features listed in Table 9.

No.	Semantic Features	Interrogative Pronouns
1.	[+human]	who, whom
2.	[±human]	whose
3.	[±human]	which
4.	[+locative]	where
5.	[+ reason]	why
6.	[+degree]	how
7.	[+time]	when

Table 9 *Interrogative Pronouns*

(23) ***Who** assassinated Lincoln?*

(24) ***Where** was he assassinated?*

(25) ***How** was he assassinated?*

The interrogative words in these three sentences are actually pronouns even though they do not replace any noun. They are called "free pronouns," about which more will be said in 14.7.1. Some refer to these same words as "interrogative adverbs." We will see in 14.5 that these same pronouns function as relative pronouns in other sentences. Interrogative pronouns must be distinguished from interrogative adjectives. The former appear without any noun, but the latter occur with nouns.

14.3.5 Reflexive Pronouns and Emphatic Pronouns

Reflexive and **emphatic pronouns** are similar morphologically and semantically. They emphasize the role of the personal pronoun in the sentence. Reflexive pronouns specify that the pronoun acts on itself or for its own benefit. Morphologically, they are formed by adding the suffixes <self> or <-selves> to the pronominal form, as shown in Table 10:

No.	Persons and Number	Pronouns
	Singular	
1.	1st person singular	myself
2.	2nd person singular	yourself
3.	3rd person singular	himself/herself oneself/itself
	Plural	
1.	1st person plural	ourselves
2.	2nd person plural	yourselves
3.	3rd person plural	themselves

Table 10 *Reflexive Pronouns*

Two different patterns can be observed in the formation of these pronouns. The pronouns <myself>, <yourself>, <ourselves>, and <yourselves> are formed on the basis of the possessive adjectives, whereas <himself>, <herself> and <themselves> are formed on the basis of the accusative form of personal pronouns. This explains why some native-speakers tend to use the form <hisself> instead of <himself> in casual register. Celce-Murcia and Larsen-Freeman (1999:299) also observe that errors involving these pronouns are common among ESL/EFL students.

14.3.6 Reciprocal and Distributive Pronouns

English has one true **reciprocal pronoun,** <each other>, and one **distributive pronoun,** <one another>. However, this distinction is not often made and both are lumped together as "reciprocal" pronouns. The distinction between the two is more numerical than syntactic. Normally, the pronoun <each other> is used only when two entities are involved, and <one another> is used when more than two entities participate in the action or event described by the verb, as in the sentences below:

(26) *Steve and Kim love **each other.***

(27) **Steve and Kim love **one another.***

(28) *All the students in the grammar class help **one another.***

(29) *?All the students in the class help **each other.***

The distinction between reciprocal and distributional pronouns was once clear but is disappearing in contemporary usage. For example, Robinson (1934:292) notes that Modern Greek does not make this distinction anymore even though Classical Greek used to make it.

14.3.7 Indefinite Pronouns

Indefinite pronouns are so called because they do not refer to anybody or anything in particular. The morphology of indefinite pronouns is worth describing briefly. These pronouns are formed by compounding indeterminate quantity terms such as <some>, <any>, <no> and <every> with the words <body>, <one>, <thing>, as shown in the table below:

No.		some	any	no	every
1.	+ body	somebody	anybody	nobody	everybody
2.	+ one	someone	anyone	no one	everyone
3.	+ thing	something	anything	nothing	everything

Table 11 *Indefinite Pronouns*

All these compounds are written as single orthographic words except for <no one> because writing it as <noone> would result in reading difficulties. Sentence (30) illustrates the use of indefinite pronouns:

(30)   *Somebody at Indiana University loves me.*

The combination of the indefinite pronoun <somebody> with the first person pronoun <me> in (30) is meant to make the alumni of Indiana University feel connected to their alma mater. Time will tell if this slogan plastered on mugs and other memorabilia is an effective campaign.

14.4 *The Syntax of Anaphoric Pronouns*

Pronominalization is a syntactic operation which consists of replacing a lexical NP with a pronoun. The noun that is replaced by the pronoun is called the **antecedent.** Pronominalization has been the subject of intense linguistic research since the 1980s. A whole theory of syntax called Government-Binding has been devoted to investigating how syntax interacts with semantics when nouns are pronominalized. Government-Binding has provided linguists with useful tools in their quest for more knowledge about the behavior of pronouns and pronominalization. It has uncovered and formalized a set of constraints under which pronominalization takes place in natural languages. These conditions are known collectively as **anaphora.** The prefix <ana-> is a Greek prefix which means "before." Therefore, an anaphoric pronoun is a pronoun that refers to an NP that precedes it. A distinction is sometimes made between anaphora and **cataphora.** The latter is derived from the Greek prefix <cata> which means "ahead," or "forward." A cataphoric pronoun is a pronoun that replaces an NP that follows it. The uses of anaphora and cataphora are illustrated by the two sentences below:

(31)   *Linguists consider **themselves** to be scientists.*

(32)   ***He** is good. Yes, the Lord is good.*

In (31) <themselves> refers back to <linguists>. Therefore, <themselves> is an anaphoric pronoun. In (32) on the other hand, the pronoun <He> refers forward to its antecedent, that is, <the Lord>. Therefore, <He> is a cataphoric pronoun. Most linguistic research has focused on anaphora because it is the most common case of pronominalization in world languages.

14.4.1 The Binding Conditions

The use of anaphoric pronouns is governed by a set of universal principles made explicit by Government-Binding theory. These principles obey three important conditions which are stated below:

The Binding Conditions

X is bound if X has an antecedent to which it is co-indexed. (Radford 1989:367)

The Indexing Rule

Assign every NP in a sentence an index (where the index is a random integer). (Radford 1989:366)

The Matching Condition

If two NPs are assigned the same index, they must match in features (e.g. ,number, gender, person, etc.) (Radford 1989:366)

Government Condition

X is the governing category for Y if X and Y are clausemates. (Fromkin et al. (2000:249).

Within Government-Binding, pronouns are said to be either **bound** or **free.** A bound pronoun must have an antecedent with which it is co-indexed in the preceding or following NP. A free pronoun, on the other hand, is a pronoun that is not co-indexed with an antecedent in the NP preceding or following. Let us examine sentences (33) through (37) to see how the distinction applies and how it is relevant to sentence interpretation.

(33) *Jeremy hurt **himself** playing dodge ball.*

(34) *Students help **one another** study for exams.*

(35) *The person **who** finishes first can leave.*

(36) *John thought that **she** had been fired.*

(37) *Mary thought that **she** had fainted.*

In the first three examples, the pronouns <himself>, <one another>, and <who> are bound pronouns because they refer back to their antecedents, namely, <Jeremy>, <students>, and <the person>. Bound pronouns whose antecedents precede them are called anaphoric pronouns. The pronoun <she> in (36) is a case of free pronoun. This pronoun is said to be free because it does not have its antecedent in the sentence. Clearly, <John> is not the antecedent of <she> because they do not match in the feature [+gender]. Now let us consider (37). Here the pronoun <she> can be either bound or free. If it is bound, then its antecedent is <Mary>. However, another possible interpretation is that <she> and <Mary> refer to two different individuals. Free pronouns such as <she> in (37) lend themselves to ambiguity. Ultimately, only the context of the utterance can help untangle the ambiguity.

14.4.2 Pronominalization and the Deep Structure

In determining the deep structure of surface structure sentences with pronouns, one must always find out whether the pronoun is bound or free. If the surface structure sentence is bound, it means that no pronoun occurs in the deep structure. However, if the surface structure pronoun is free, it means that the pronoun occurs in the deep structure. The deep structure forms of bound and free pronouns can be illustrated by (37). If the pronoun <she> is bound to <Mary>, we have the following deep structure:

*Deep structure: Mary Past think [that **Mary** Past Have-EN faint].*

In this case (37) can be diagrammed as follows:

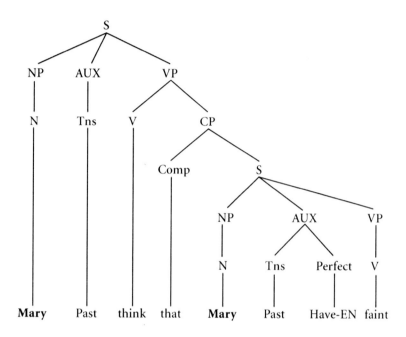

The two <Marys> are highlighted to show that they are co-referential. According to this diagram, <Mary> is the person who fainted. To derive the surface structure (37), the following derivations must take place:

Deep structure: Mary Past think that Mary Past Have-EN faint

Indexing Rule and Matching Condition: Mary^1 Past think that Mary^1 Past Have-EN faint

Pronominalization: Mary^1 Past think that she^1 Past Have-EN faint

Affix Hopping: Mary^1 think Past that she^1 Have Past faint-EN

Spell-Out Rules: Mary^1 thought that she^1 had fainted

Surface Structure: Mary thought that she had fainted

However, if the pronoun <she> is free, the deep structure of (37) is as follows:

*Deep structure : Mary Past think that **she** Past Have-EN faint.*

The tree diagram which reflects this deep structure is as follows:

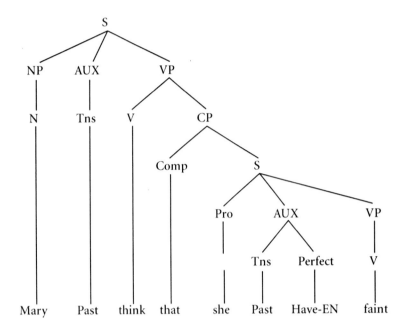

The fact that the pronoun <she> appears directly in the tree diagram shows that it is free. The derivations that lead to the surface structure of (37) are as follows:

Deep structure:	Mary Past think that she Past Have-EN faint
Affix Hopping:	Mary think Past that she Have Past faint-EN
Spell-Out Rules:	Mary thought that she had fainted
Surface Structure:	Mary thought that she had fainted

Note that because free pronouns occur directly in the deep structure, Indexing Rule/ Matching Condition, and the pronoun substitution rules do not apply. Pronouns that are usually free (occur in the deep structure) are indefinite pronouns, interrogative pronouns, possessive pronouns, and some relative pronouns (to be discussed in 14.7.1). However, the Indexing Rule/Matching Condition, and pronoun substitution rules apply for all bound pronouns. Pronouns that are usually bound are the following: reflexive pronouns, emphatic pronouns, and relative pronouns. Personal pronouns can be free or bound, depending on the context.

14.5 The Syntax of Relative Pronouns

Now let us turn our attention to relative pronouns. These pronouns have been the subject of an intense worldwide study because they have helped uncover important generalization about Universal Grammar. A relative pronoun is defined as a pronoun that occurs in a subordinate clause called a "relative clause." Relative pronouns are so named because they have "blood" relatives that occur in the main clause. In English, relative pronouns must agree with their antecedent in case and in the semantic features listed below:

No.	Semantic Features	Case	Relative Pronoun
1.	[+human]	Nominative	who
2.	[+human]	Accusative	who, whom, that
3.	[+human]	Genitive	whose
4.	[+human]	Dative	who(m)
5.	[-human]	all cases	that, which
6.	[+locative]	Unmarked	where
7.	[+reason]	Unmarked	why
8.	[+degree]	Unmarked	how, in which, by which, at which
9.	[+time]	Unmarked	when

Table 12 *Relative Pronouns*

Here are sentences to illustrate the various uses of relative pronouns in English:

> (38) *The man **who** became president was my childhood friend.*

> (39) *I met the professor **who** became a Nobel Laureate.*

> (40) *The car **that** you bought is an albatross.*

> (41) *The suburb **where** we live is quiet.*

> (42) *The reason **why** she resigned is unknown.*

> (43) *The speed **at which** she was driving is ridiculous.*

> (44) *The time **when** he will return is still a mystery.*

In all these sentences, the relative pronoun is said to be embedded in a relative clause.

14.5.1 Relative Pronouns and Embedding

Relative pronouns occur in subordinate clauses. However, unlike the other subordinate clauses discussed in Chapter 13 where the verb phrase dominates the subordinate clause, with relative pronouns, it is the NP which dominates the subordinate clause. The antecedent of the relative pronoun is found in the NP that dominates the subordinate clause, as shown in the tree diagram of (39) restated here as (45):

> (45) *I met the professor **who** became a Nobel Laureate.*

In this sentence <who> is a relative pronoun. Its antecedent is <the professor>.

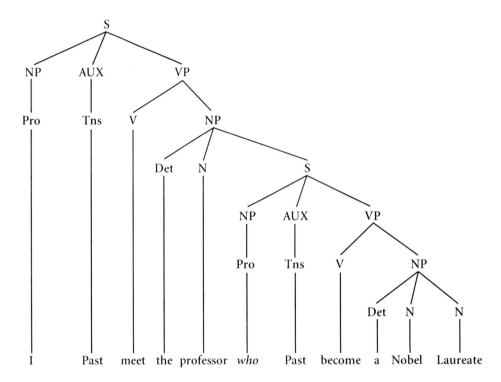

The tree diagram shows clearly that the NP <the professor> dominates the subordinate clause which contains the relative pronoun <who>. This fact has led linguists to expand the phrase structure rule of NPs as follows:

$$
\begin{aligned}
&S \; \rightarrow NP \quad AUX \quad VP \\
&VP \rightarrow V \; NP \text{ (where either the NP before} \\
&\qquad\qquad\qquad\qquad AUX \text{ or the NP under VP} \\
&\qquad\qquad\qquad\qquad \text{can be rewritten as follows)} \\
\\
&NP \rightarrow (Det) \; (Q) \; (Num) \; N \; (PP) \; (S)
\end{aligned}
$$

Sentence (45) has been diagrammed to highlight the relationship of dominance between the relative pronoun and its antecedent. Normally, tree diagrams are meant to reflect the underlying forms of sentences. In subsequent sections, only the deep structure forms will be diagrammed. Doing so helps us emphasize the derivational processes entailed in the relativization of pronouns.

14.5.2 Transformations and Relative Pronouns

Technically, relative pronouns do not occur in the deep structure. They are the object of a transformation called "**relative pronominal substitution**" which consists of replacing the antecedent with a pronoun that agrees with it in case and in the semantic features listed in Table 12 previously. Nearly all relative pronouns are anaphoric pronouns. This means that they are bound, as explained in 14.4.1. Consequently, they do not appear in the deep structure as such. The tree diagram of (45) shows the deep structure prior to the application of transformational rules:

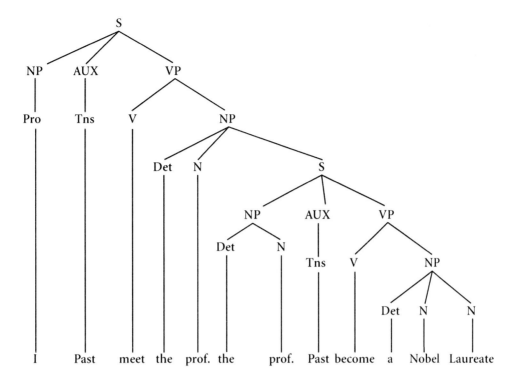

To obtain the surface structure in (45), the following derivational steps are necessary:

Deep structure: I Past meet the professor the professor Past become a Nobel Laureate

Indexing Rule and Matching Condition: I Past meet the professor[1] the professor[1] Past become a Nobel Laureate

Relative Pronoun Substitution: I Past meet the professor[1] who[1] Past become a Nobel Laureate

Affix Hopping: I meet Past the professor[1] who[1] become Past a Nobel Laureate

Spell-Out Rules: I met the professor who became a Nobel Laureate.

Surface structure: I met the professor who became a Nobel Laureate.

The personal pronoun <I> appears directly in the deep structure because it is a free pronoun.

14.5.3 Types of Relative Clauses

A distinction is made between restrictive and non-restrictive relative clauses. The two types of relative clauses differ in prosody/punctuation and in meaning/function, as illustrated by the two sentences below. Sentence (46) contains a restrictive relative clause whereas (47) contains a non-restrictive relative clause.

(46)   *The scientists **who** win the Nobel Prize are all driven by research.*
(Restrictive relative clause)

(47)   *The scientists, **who win the Nobel Prize**, are all driven by research.*
(Non-restrictive relative clause)

In oral communication, English speakers do not pause between the relative pronoun <who> and its antecedent <the scientists> in (46) (restrictive relative clauses.) However, in non-restrictive relative clauses, a slight pause has been observed between <who> and its antecedent <the scientists>, as in (47). In writing, the two types of clauses are kept distinct through the use of punctuation marks. Non-restrictive relative clauses are set off by commas (as in (47)), but restrictive relative clauses are not. Semantically, restrictive relative clauses modify their antecedent directly and specifically, but non-restrictive relative clauses "serve merely to give the hearer an added piece of information about an already identified entity, but not to identify that entity (Comrie 1981:131). In English, non-restrictive relatives have been given various labels. Some call them appositive, descriptive, or explanatory clauses. They require the use of the pronoun <who> or <which>.

Celce-Murcia and Larsen-Freeman (1999: 592) argue that non-restrictive relative clauses are derived from two compound sentences in the deep structure. However, other linguists, including Comrie and Downing, do not share this view. Downing (1978:380) notes in his cross-linguistic study of relative clauses that the distinction between restrictive and non-restrictive relative clauses is not universal. He observes that "some languages apparently have no nonrestrictive relative clauses; in others they are syntactically quite distinct; in others restrictive and non-restrictive relative clauses are syntactically indistinguishable." Whether restrictive and non-restrive relative clauses are syntactically similar or different in English is beyond the scope of this analysis. Suffice it to say that restrictive relative clauses occur more frequently in speech and in writing than non-restrictive relative clauses. Celce-Murcia and Larsen-Freeman (1999:602) cite a 1985 study done by Frodesen which shows that in a chemistry text, 77% of all relative clauses were restrictive relative clauses.

14.6 Accessibility Hierarchy in Relative Clauses

Studies done by Comrie and Keenan (1981:149) and Keenan (1987:121) show that relative clause formation is subject to a number of constraints. The constraint that we are particularly interested in in this section is called "**accessibility hierarchy.**" This notion suggests that it is easier to turn a noun phrase into a relative pronoun if that noun occurs in certain positions in the sentence than in others. After studying more than fifty genetically and typologically unrelated languages, Comrie and Keenan (1981) proposed the following hierarchy:

> **Subject > Direct Object > Indirect Object >**
> **Possessive NP> Object of Comparison[2]**

Keenan (1987:121-2) explains the accessibility hierarchy as follows:

First, the subject is the easiest position to relativize; i.e., if a language can form relative clauses at all, it can form them on the subject. Second, any particular relative-clause forming strategy which applies to the subject may, in principle apply continuously down the accessibility hierarchy, cutting off at any point. Thus, a

---

[2] Keenan (1985:147) omits "object of comparison" but makes a distinction between "indirect object" and "object of pre or postposition." The order is as follows: Subject > Direct Object > Indirect Object > Object of pre or postposition > Possessor.

human language may have (some do have) relative clause-forming strategies that apply only to the subject; others have relative clause forming strategies which apply to subject and direct object, but nothing else; still others, relative clause-forming strategies which apply to subject, direct object, and indirect object, but nothing else, and so forth.

English can relativize clauses in all these positions. Additionally, a four-way distinction has been made that combines the accessibility hierarchy and the function of relative clauses in sentences. Table 13 defines the various patterns as follows:

No.	Relative Clause Patterns	Explanation/Definition
1.	Subject-Subject (S-S)	The subject of the verb in the main clause is identical with the subject of the verb in the subordinate clause.
2.	Object-Subject (O-S)	The direct object of the verb in the main clause is identical with the subject of the verb in the subordinate clause.
3.	Subject-Object (S-O)	The subject of the verb in the main clause is identical with the object of the verb in the subordinate clause.
4.	Object-Object (O-O)	The object of the verb in the main clause is identical with the object of the verb in the subordinate clause.

Table 13 *Patterns in the Accessibility Hierarchy*

Examples will be provided to illustrate each pattern in the sections below. Subsequent discussions of relative clause formation will follow this pattern in the order presented in the table above.

14.6.1 Relativization in the Subject-Subject Pattern (S-S)

Relativization in the subject-subject pattern is a syntactic construction in which the subject of the verb in the main clause is also the subject of the verb in the subordinate clause, as illustrated by (48) and its corresponding deep structure form below:

(48)   *The professor **who** teaches this course is a Nobel Laureate.*

Deep structure: The professor [the professor Pres. teach this course] *Pres. be a Nobel Laureate.*

In this construction, the subject of the verb in the main clause is the <the professor>. The same NP is the subject of the verb <teach> in the subordinate clause. Relative clauses that fit this pattern can be represented by the following tree diagram:

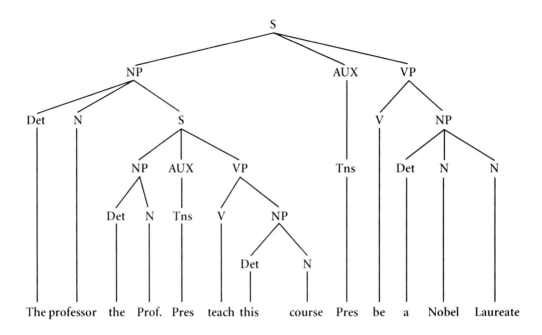

The derivational steps that help produce the surface structure shown in (48) are as follows:

Deep structure: The professor [the professor Pres. teach this course] Pres. be a Nobel Laureate

Indexing Rule and Matching Condition: The professor[1] [the professor[1] Pres. teach this course] Pres. be a Nobel Laureate

Relative Pronoun Substitution: The professor[1] [who[1] Pres. teach this course] Pres. be a Nobel Laureate

Affix Hopping: The professor[1] [who[1] teach Pres. this course] be Pres. a Nobel Laureate

Spell-Out Rules: The professor[1] [who[1] teaches this course] is a Nobel Laureate

Surface Structure: The professor who teaches this course is a Nobel Laureate.

Comrie (1981) and Keenan (1985, 1987) concur with Downing (1978) that many more languages relativize in the subject position on the accessibility hierarchy than in any other position. Consequently, ESL/EFL students are less likely to make mistakes in the acquisition of the relative pronouns in the subject position. If they do make mistakes, the non-native forms that they produce are often caused by a mismatch in features. Their mistakes have nothing to do with the subject position in the accessibility hierarchy per se.

14.6.2 Relativization in the Direct Object Position

After the subject position, the direct object position is the next easiest position for relativization on the accessibility hierarchy. However, according to Table 13, there are at least three different patterns in this position: the Object-Subject (O-S) pattern, the Subject-Object (S-O) pattern, and the Object-Object (O-O) pattern. Let us examine each one of them to highlight their structural and derivational differences.

14.6.2.1 Relativization in the Object-Subject (O-S) Pattern

In the Object-Subject pattern, the direct object of the verb in the main clause is the subject of the verb in the subordinate clause. This can be illustrated by (49) and its related deep structure:

(49) *You met the professor **who** became a Nobel Laureate.*

Deep structure: You Past. meet the professor [the professor Past become a Nobel Laureate]

The direct object of the verb <met> of the main clause is <the professor>. However, in the subordinate clause, <the professor> is the subject of the verb <become>. This exemplifies the O-S pattern. Object-Subject patterns are typically represented by the following tree diagram:

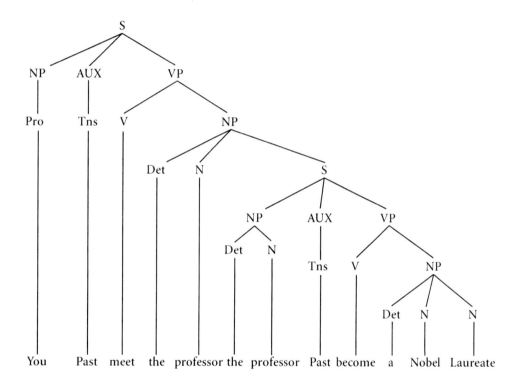

The transformational rules that apply to the deep structure of Object-Subject patterns are indicated below:

Deep structure: You Past. meet the professor [the professor Past become a Nobel Laureate]

Indexing Rule and Matching Condition: You Past. meet the professor[1] the professor[1] Past become a Nobel Laureate

Relative Pronoun Substitution: You Past. meet the professor[1] who[1] Past become a Nobel Laureate

Affix Hopping: You meet Past the professor[1] who[1] become Past a Nobel Laureate

Spell-Out Rules: You met the professor who became a Nobel Laureate

Surface Structure: You met the professor who became a Nobel Laureate.

Relativization in this position is also common and fairly easy. Celce-Murcia and Larsen-Freeman (1999:602) indicate that this pattern occurs more frequently in English than any other pattern. They quote a 1978 study by Stauble in which 234 out of 425 relative clauses conform to the Object-Subject pattern.

14.6.2.2 Relativization in the Subject-Object (S-O) Pattern

In this pattern, the subject of the verb in the main clause is identical with the direct object of the verb in the subordinate clause. Sentence (50) and its corresponding deep structure fit this pattern:

(50)   *The professor **whom** you met is a Nobel Laureate.*

Deep structure: The professor [you Past meet the professor] *Pres. Be a Nobel Laureate*

The subject of the verb in the main clause is <the professor>. We also see that the direct object of the verb <met> in the subordinate clause is <the professor>. The tree diagram below is typical of all Subject-Object patterns.

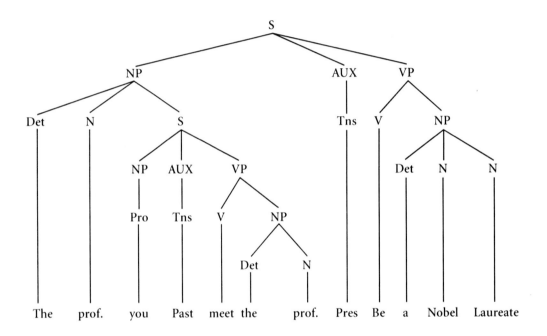

The surface structure of (50) is the result of the following derivational processes:

Deep structure: The professor [you Past meet the professor] Pres. be a Nobel Laureate

Indexing Rule and Matching Condition: The professor[1] [you Past meet the professor[1]] Pres. be a Nobel Laureate

Relative Pronoun Substitution: The professor[1] [you Past meet whom[1]] Pres. be a Nobel Laureate

Relative Pronoun Movement:	The professor[1] [whom[1] you Past meet—] Pres. be a Nobel Laureate
Affix Hopping:	The professor[1] [whom[1] you meet Past—] be Pres. a Nobel Laureate
Spell-Out Rules:	The professor[1] whom[1] you met—is a Nobel Laureate
Surface Structure:	The professor whom you met is a Nobel Laureate.

The main difference between the Subject-Object pattern and the Object-Subject pattern in the derivational process is the rule of relative pronoun movement that applies in the O-S pattern but is found to be lacking in the S-O pattern. The same study cited by Celce-Murcia and Larsen-Freeman (1999:602) shows that the Object-Subject pattern occurs less frequently in English. Only 30 out of 424 relative clauses conformed to the O-S pattern.

It is worth pointing out that English has an optional rule that frequently deletes relative pronouns in the Object-Subject pattern. Thus, if this optional deletion rule applies to (50), sentence (51) would be the result:

> (51) *The professor you met is a Nobel Laureate.*

Some feel that deleting the relative pronoun is more informal than keeping it in. Consequently, teachers should encourage their students to use the full form rather than the reduced form. If the use of the full form is encouraged, should the relative pronoun agree in the accusative case since it originated in a position where it was case-marked for the accusative? Composition rules have been somewhat relaxed these days so much so that the relative pronoun <who> is preferred to <whom> by many. Using <whom> seems more pompous than using <who> even though the former is grammatically more "accurate."

14.6.2.3 Relativization in the Object-Object (O-O) Pattern

Finally, English allows for an Object-Object pattern, that is, the object of the verb in the main clause is identical with the object of the verb in the subordinate clause. Sentence (52) and its equivalent deep structure exemplify the O-O pattern:

> (52) *I met the professor whom you admire.*

Deep structure: I Past meet the professor [you Pres admire the professor.]

The verbs <meet> and <admire> are strictly subcategorized as taking NP direct objects. However, in (52) the verb <admire> in the subordinate clause has no direct object. Technically, this should cause (52) to be ill-formed. However, it is a well-formed sentence. The reason why (52) is grammatical is because in the deep structure, the two verbs have <the professor> as their respective direct objects. The direct object of <met> is <the professor> and the direct object of <admire> is also <the professor>. This is shown in the tree diagram following:

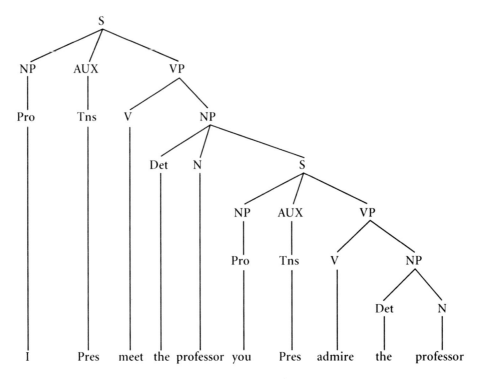

I   Pres   meet   the   professor   you   Pres   admire   the   professor

Now let us examine the derivational processes that apply to the deep structure to produce the surface structure form seen in (52):

Deep structure: I Past meet the professor [you Pres admire the professor]

Indexing Rule and Matching Condition: I Past meet the professor[1] [you Pres admire the professor[1]]

Relative Pronoun Substitution: I Past meet the professor[1] [you Pres admire whom[1]]

Relative Pronoun Movement: I Past meet the professor[1] [whom[1] you Pres admire—]

Affix Hopping: I meet Past the professor[1] [whom[1] you admire Pres—]

Spell-Out Rules: I met the professor whom[1] you admire

Surface Structure: I met the professor whom you admire.

The derivations in the Object-Object pattern are similar to the ones that we have already encountered in the Subject-Object pattern. There as here, a relative pronoun movement rule applies. The same optional relative pronoun deletion rule applies. The observations made about retaining or not retaining the relative pronoun in composition apply here as well. However, for reasons that are still not clear, English speakers prefer O-O patterns to S-O patterns. Stauble's (1978) study cited by Celce-Murcia and Larsen-Freeman (1999:602) shows that 108 relative clauses out of 429 conform to the O-O pattern.

14.6.3 Relativization in the Indirect Object Position

The third position on the accessibility hierarchy in which English can relativize pronouns is the indirect object position. The group of words <under the professor> in (53) below illustrates relativization in such a position:

(53)   *The professor **under whom** you studied is a Nobel Laureate.*

Deep structure: The professor [you Past study under the professor] Pres. be a Nobel Laureate

The word <professor> is the object of the preposition <under>. Therefore, <under the professor> is the indirect object of the verb <study> which occurs in the subordinate clause. Sentence (53) is diagrammed as follows:

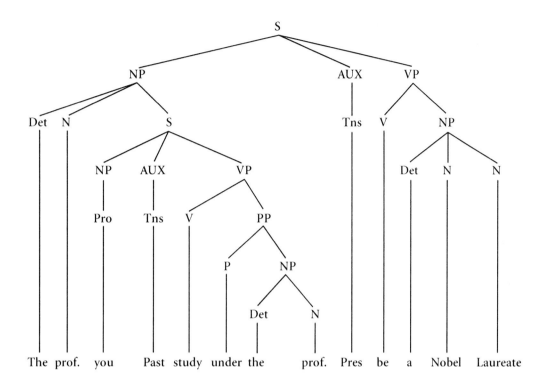

The derivational processes which help generate the surface structure of sentence (53) are detailed as follows:

Deep structure: The professor [you Past study under the professor] Pres. be a Nobel Laureate.

Indexing Rule and Matching Condition: The professor[1] [You Past study under the professor[1]] Pres. be a Nobel Laureate

Relative Pronoun Substitution: The professor[1] [You Past study under whom[1]] Pres. Be a Nobel Laureate

PP Movement: The professor[1] under whom[1] [You Past study—] Pres. Be a Nobel Laureate

Affix Hopping: the professor[1] under whom[1] You study Past — —be Pres a Nobel Laureate

Spell-Out Rules: The professor[1] under whom[1] you studied is a Nobel Laureate

Surface Structure: The professor under whom you studied is a Nobel Laureate.

This derivational process includes a movement rule similar to the one that we saw in the Subject-Object and Object-Object patterns. The only difference with relativization in the indirect object position is that in this case it is a prepositional phrase (PP) movement. Here too, there is an optional rule that can move only the relative pronoun out of the PP, as seen in (54):

(54) *The professor **whom** you studied under is a Nobel Laureate.*

This transformation results in preposition stranding. Contemporary standards in composition make (54) to be acceptable, even though some language purists cannot tolerate it.

14.6.4 Relativization in the Possessive NP Position

According to the accessibility hierarchy, possessive NPs that occur in the subordinate clause are harder to relativize than those that appear higher up in the hierarchy. This observation is true for English where the genitive relative pronoun <whose> is used considerably less in writing and in speaking than the other relative pronouns. Judging by the lack of statistical data on the relative pronoun <whose>, one would not be wrong in concluding that native speakers try to avoid it whenever they can. Relativization in possessive NP position is illustrated by (55) below:

(55)   *The professor **whose** research is controversial resigned.*

Deep structure: The Professor [the professor Poss research Pres. be controversial]
Past resign

The genitive marker Poss shows that the second <professor> is a possessive NP. Sentence (55) is diagrammed as follows:

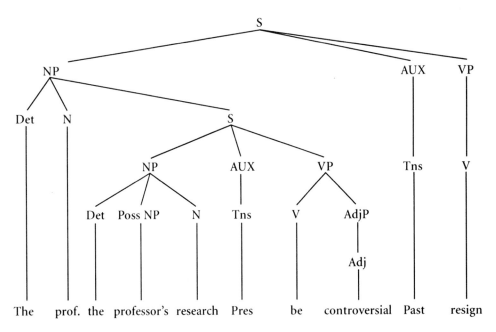

The derivational processes that help generate sentence (55) from its corresponding deep structure form are the following:

Deep structure: The Professor [the professor Poss research Pres. be controversial] Past resign

Indexing Rule and Matching Condition: The Professor[1] [the professor Poss[1] research Pres. be controversial] Past resign

Relative Pronoun substitution: The Professor[1] [whose[1] research Pres be controversial] Past resign

Affix Hopping: The Professor[1] [whose[1] research Be Pres controversial] resign Past

Spell-Out Rules: The Professor[1] [whose[1] research is controversial] resigned

Surface Structure: The professor whose research is controversial resigned.

14.7 More on Relative Clauses

The analysis of relative pronouns offered here is far from complete. Much more could be said to investigate other aspects of relative clauses. However, we will limit ourselves to two related phenomena, headless relative clauses and cleft sentences, which are partially built on relative clauses.

14.7.1 Headless Relative Pronouns

The phrase structure rules that were proposed in 14.5.1 for relative clauses indicate that NPs containing such clauses can be rewritten minimally as follows:

$$\text{NP} \rightarrow \text{(Det) N S}$$

Though this formula is generally true, there are cases where the antecedent of the relative pronoun is missing in the sentence. In such cases, there is no NP in the sentence that can be said to be the antecedent of the relative pronoun. Let us illustrate this situation with the following examples:

(56) *Mary knows **where** the Nobel Laureate lives.*

(57) *Mary knows **when** the professor received the Nobel prize.*

(58) *Mary knows **why** the professor received the Nobel prize.*

(59) *Mary knows **how** the professor received the Nobel prize.*

The use of the pronouns <where>, <when>, <why>, and <how> seems to contradict a claim made in 14.4.2 regarding the fact that relative pronouns are always bound. If they are bound pronouns, where are their antecedents in the sentences above? They have none, and yet the sentences are grammatical. For this reason, an exception has been made for these four relative pronouns which also happen to be interrogative pronouns. We know that interrogative pronouns are free pronouns. Consequently, it has been proposed that these four pronouns be considered free relative pronouns. Linguists refer to the relative clauses in which these pronouns occur as **"headless"** relative clauses.

14.7.2 Generating Headless Relative Pronouns

Two possibilities exist for the generation of headless relative pronouns. One option is to claim that in the deep structure, the relative pronouns occur with their heads. However, by the time we arrive at the surface structure, an antecedent deletion rule has deleted the head. If one follows this view, then all relative pronouns are bound. The second option consists in claiming that <where>, <when>, <why>, and <how> are exceptions and that even though relative pronouns are generally bound, in some usages they are not bound. In this way, they are similar to personal pronouns which can be either free or bound. Consequently, they need not appear in the deep structure. The arguments from both sides are cogent. The Occam Razor Principle would favor the second option because it eliminates the need for an antecedent deletion rule. However, there is something ad hoc about the second option. It raises suspicions as to why the relative pronouns <where>, <when>, <why>, and <how> are free while all other relative pronouns are bound. My own preference goes to the first option. However, analyses that follow the second option are equally valid.

14.7.3 Idiosyncratic Uses of <How>

The relative pronoun <how> has idiosyncratic uses. It has the feature [+degree] but cannot co-occur with its antecedent, as shown by the ungrammaticality of (60) below:

(60)   *The speed **how** she was driving is ridiculous.

For this sentence to be well-formed, the antecedent <the speed> must either be deleted or <how> must be replaced by a functionally equivalent relative pronoun such as <at which>, as shown in the two sentences below:

(61)   **How** she was driving is ridiculous.

(62)   The speed **at which** she was driving is ridiculous.

Thus, deletion of the relative pronoun <how> is obligatory when the antecedent that has the feature [+degree] occurs with it in the sentence. It seems that in contemporary English the relative pronoun <how> can be substituted for by <in which>, <by which>, <at which>, and <with which> if the antecedent is to occur in the sentence. Sentences (63) and (64) exemplify this possibility:

(63)   The tone **in which** she addressed the crowd was not good.

(64)   The manner **with which** his application was rejected was hurtful.

Native speakers often hesitate as to knowing the correct relative pronoun to use when the antecedent is an NP that has the feature [+degree]. Celce-Murcia and Larsen-Freemam (1999:599) note that ESL/EFL students have difficulties too: "ESL/EFL students predictably have trouble with this exception and will learn to consistently delete the head noun in order to produce a grammatical sentence when the relative adverb *how* is used."

14.7.4 Relativization and Cliticization

Cliticization is a syntactic construction which consists of moving a lexical item elsewhere in the sentence for the purpose of indicating contrastive emphasis. In speech, prosody is consistently used worldwide to indicate contrastive emphasis. Harries-Delisle's (1978:421–486) overview of cleft sentences in world languages shows that there are many ways to cliticize sentences. However, for our purpose we will focus exclusively on cleft sentences that show connection with relative pronouns, as in the sentences below taken from Harries-Delisle's article:

(65)   The man called.

(66)   It was the man **who** called.

(67)   I saw John.

(68)   It is John that I saw.

(69)   It is John I saw.

How cleft sentences of this kind are produced is a matter of intense theoretical debates. One approach suggests that cleft sentences are generated by transformation but another claims that they can be generated by phrase structure rules. According to the latter view, the following rule is responsible for generating (66), (68) and (69):

$$S \rightarrow NP \quad AUX \quad VP$$
$$NP \rightarrow It \ Be^3 \ (NP) \ WH \ AUX \ VP$$

[3] <Be> agrees in tense with the verb whose tense occurs under AUX.

In this formulation <It> is a dummy pronoun similar to the one discussed in 13.7.3. However, some linguists object to this analysis and claim that, given the striking similarities between relative clauses and cliticization, all cleft sentences of this type are derived from underlying sentences. They note that in all such cases, the relative pronoun has an antecedent, whether it appears on the surface structure or not. Accordingly, it has been suggested that the deep structure of (66) is as follows:

Deep structure: It be the man [the man] *Past call*

The tree diagram of cleft-sentences such as (66) is the following:

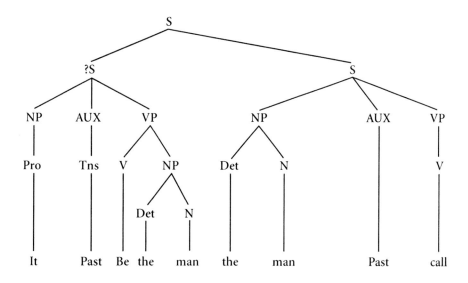

The question mark before "S" indicates that the status of <It be> is unclear. Harries-Delisle (1978:437) takes it to be an NP. However, this label is suspicious. The syntactic behavior of <It be> does not show that it is an NP. To derive (66) from (65) the following steps take place:

Deep structure: It Past Be the man [the man] Past call

Indexing Rule and Matching Condition: It Be the man^1 [the man^1] Past call

Relative Pronoun Substitution: It Be the man^1 [who^1] Past call

Affix Hopping: It Be Past the man [who] call Past

Spell-Out Rules: It was the man who called

Surface structure: It was the man who called.

The difficulties in analyzing the cleft-sentences mentioned above pale in comparison with the problems one encounters in deriving (71) from (72):

(70)   *John helped us.*

(71)   ***It was** John **who** helped us.*

(72)   ***John** was the **one who** helped us.*

It is easier to generate (72) through transformations than to generate it through phrase structure rules.

14.8 Pedagogical Issues in Relative Pronouns and Clauses

Throughout this chapter, the challenges that pronouns create for native speakers and non-native speakers of English have been mentioned and discussed briefly. The pedagogical implications for the use of pronouns, especially relative pronouns in relative clauses, are numerous. They range from number agreement to unlawful pronoun retention. Let us highlight three aspects of pronominal use in English that are particularly difficult for ESL/EFL students.

14.8.1 Pronominal Agreement and L2 Acquisition

Most ESL/EFL students have more trouble with the 3rd person singular pronoun in all grammatical cases. However, particularly troublesome are instances when this pronoun is used in genitive case <his> and <hers>. The reason for this stems from the fact that the grammatical gender of possessive pronouns and adjectives is expressed differently in English than in many other languages. In English, the biological gender of the possessor controls the use of <his> or <her>. In other words, if the possessor is male, the pronoun <his> is used. If the possessor is female, the pronoun <hers> is used. In Spanish, French, and other languages, as explained earlier, the gender of the possessor does not control agreement. Instead, it is the grammatical gender of the thing possessed that determines the kind of possessive adjective or pronoun to use. Thus, an English sentence such as <her car broke down> or <hers broke down> is almost untranslatable in French and Spanish. The French equivalent <sa voiture est tombée en panne> or <la sienne est tombée en panne> and the Spanish counterpart <su carro se accidentó> or <el suyo se accidentó> say nothing about the fact that the car belongs to a woman. Because of this, French and Spanish speakers, and possibly speakers of other languages, make many errors with gender and possession when learning English.

14.8.2 Long Distance Anaphora

The Government-Binding conditions require that in English the antecedent of the anaphoric pronoun be in the same clause or in the main clause if the pronoun occurs in the subordinate clause. This constraint is widespread in world languages. However, Cullicover (1997:289, 294) notes that in Japanese, the anaphoric pronoun can be separated from its antecedent by a large chunk of discourse. He gives the label of "**discourse anaphora**" to such pronouns. This usage of discourse anaphora in Japanese can create communication difficulties for Japanese ESL/EFL students. If they transfer the long distance anaphora feature of their language into English, it can lead to miscommunication. Their English-speaking audience may not be able to correlate the pronoun that they have used halfway through their discourse with its antecedent that occurred a paragraph or two earlier.

14.8.3 Pronoun-Retention in Relative Clause formation

We saw in 14.6.2 and 14.6.3 in the Subject-Object pattern, the Object-Subject pattern and the Object-Object pattern that when direct objects are relativized, pronominal movement follows. Typically in English, the trace that the pronoun leaves behind cannot be occupied by another pronoun. However, this constraint does not apply in all languages. Comrie (1981:134) notes that in many world languages the trace that the pronoun leaves behind when it is moved must be marked for case. This means that another pronoun must occupy the trace left behind. This is called "**pronoun retention.**" However, this constraint clashes with the syntactic requirements of English which does not allow the trace left behind to be occupied by another pronoun. Radford (1989:337) formulates this constraint as follows:

NP-Trace Condition

The trace of an NP Movement cannot be case-marked.

Celce-Murcia and Larsen-Freeman (1999:573) report that ESL/EFL students make the following errors:

(73)   *Shirley called out to the boy that she knew **him.**

(74)   *The man who you were talking to **him** is my uncle.

It can be posited that English language learners make these errors because they generalize the pronoun retention rule to English. Supposedly, such errors are common with Arabic and Chinese speakers.

14.9 Conclusion

Pronouns are important in contemporary syntactic analyses because they occur with high frequency in all languages. Pronouns are not only important for classroom teachers. They have recently been at the center of theoretical linguistic investigation because they offer insights into Universal Grammar. By bringing together issues that are pertinent to both semantics and syntax, grammatical competence in the use of pronouns can help teachers improve their students oral and written skills. ESL/EFL students will benefit from understanding how gender interacts with 3rd person pronouns. By familiarizing themselves with the accessibility hierarchy, teachers will understand why some of their students have difficulties with some relative clauses and not others. Judicious use of cliticization and anaphora can help enhance the overall quality of students' writing style.

Key Terms to Know

These are the key terms that you should be able to use and define after reading this chapter:

1. accessibility hierarchy:14.6, 14.6.2, 14.6.3, 14.6.4, 14.9

2. agreement in case: 14.2, 14.2.1

3. agreement in number: 14.2.2

4. anaphora: 14.4, 14.8.2, 14.9

5. antecedent: 14.3.4, 14.4, 14.4.1, 14.5, 14.5.1, 14.5.2, 14.5.3, 14.7.1, 14.7.2, 14.7.3, 14.7.4, 14.8.2

6. bound pronoun: 14.4.1, 14.4.2, 14.7.1

7. cataphora: 14.4

8. cleft-sentence: 14.7.4

9. cliticization: 14.7.4, 14.9

10. declension: 14.2.1

11. demonstrative pronoun: 14.1, 14.1.2, 14.3.3

12. emphatic pronoun: 14.1, 14.1.2, 14.3.5, 14.4.2

13. evidential: 14.1.3

14. exclusive pronoun: 14.1.3

15. free pronoun: 14.3.4, 14.4.1, 14.5.2, 14.7.1

16. gender 14.2, 14.2.2, 14.2.3

17. government-binding (GB): 14.4

18. headless relative pronoun: 14.7.1, 14.7.2

19. honorific pronoun: 14.1.3

20. inclusive pronoun: 14.1.3

21. indefinite pronoun: 14.1, 14.1.2, 14.3.3

22. long distance anaphora: 14.8.2

23. object pronoun: 14.3.1

24. person: 14.2, 14.2.2, 14.2.3

25. personal pronoun: 14.1, 14.1.2, 14.3.1, 14.3.5, 14.4.2, 14.5.2, 14.7.2

26. pronoun retention: 14.1.3, 14.8.3

27. reciprocal pronoun: 14.1, 14.1.2, 14.3.6

28. reflexive pronoun: 14.1, 14.1.2, 14.3.5, 14.4.2

29. relative clause: 14.5, 14.5.3, 14.6, 14.6.1, 14.6.2.1, 14.6.2.2, 14.7, 14.7.1, 14.7.4, 14.7.8, 14.8.3, 14.9

EXERCISE 1—GOVERNMENT AND BINDING

State for each pronoun in the following sentences whether it is free, bound, or either bound or free.[4] If the pronoun is bound, say what its antecedent is.

1. John talked to Susan about herself.

2. Mary talked to Susan about herself.

3. John saved Susan from herself.

4. Mary saved Susan from herself.

5. Louise said to herself in the mirror, "I am ugly."

6. The fact that he considers her pretty pleases Maria.

7. Whenever I see you, I think of her.

8. John discovered that a picture of himself was hanging in the post office, and that fact bugged him, but it pleased her.

9. It seems that she and he will never stop arguing with them.

10. Persons are prohibited from picking flowers from any but their own graves. (On a sign in a cemetery.)

11. For you, O Lord, have made me glad by your work. (Ps 92:4).

[4] The data for this exercise comes from three sources: my own sentences, and sentences taken from Culicover (1997:279–314), and Fromkin (2003:230).

EXERCISE 2—PRONOUN IDENTIFICATION

Identify all the pronouns in the text and classify them according to the categories listed below. Identify also any personal, possessive, demonstrative, and interrogative pronouns, relative, reflexive, reciprocal, and indefinite pronouns that you find in the text. [**Note:** Keep in mind that some of the categories listed may not appear in the text.]

The Gettysburg Address

by Abraham Lincoln

"Fourscore and seven years ago our fathers brought forth on this continent a new nation, conceived in liberty and dedicated to the proposition that all men are created equal. Now we are engaged in a great civil war, testing whether that nation or any nation so conceived and so dedicated can long endure. We are met on a great battlefield of that war. We have come to dedicate a portion of that field as a final resting-place for those who here gave their lives that that nation might live. It is altogether fitting and proper that we should do this.

But in a larger sense, we cannot dedicate, we cannot consecrate, we cannot hallow this ground. The brave men, living and dead who struggled here have consecrated it far above our poor power to add or detract. The world will little note nor long remember what we say here, but it can never forget what they did here. It is for us the living rather to be dedicated here to the unfinished work which they who fought here have thus far so nobly advanced. It is rather for us to be here dedicated to the great task remaining before us—that from these honored dead we take increased devotion to that cause for which they gave the last full measure of devotion—that we here highly resolve that these dead shall not have died in vain, that this nation under God shall have a new birth of freedom, and that government of the people, by the people, for the people shall not perish from the earth."

	Personal Pronoun	Demonstrative Pronoun	Relative Pronoun	Reflexive Pronoun	Interrogative Pronoun	Reciprocal Pronoun	Indefinite Pronoun
1.							
2.							
3.							
4.							
5.							
6.							

EXERCISE 3—GRAMMATICAL TERMINOLOGY

Make English sentences based on the grammatical information provided below:

1. Make a sentence with a relative pronoun that fulfills the following semantic feature [+human, +subject]. Underline the relative pronoun.

2. Make a sentence in which the relative clause on the accessibility hierarchy conforms to the S-S pattern. Underline the relative clause and the elements that are indicative of the S-S pattern.

3. Make a sentence with a subject pronoun that fulfills the following semantic feature [+inanimate, +singular]. Underline the subject pronoun.

4. Make a sentence with an object pronoun that fulfills the following semantic feature [+animate, +female, + 3rd person plural]. Underline the object pronoun.

5. Make a sentence in which the relative clause on the accessibility hierarchy conforms to the O-S pattern. Underline the relative clause and the elements that are indicative of the O-S pattern.

6. Make a sentence with a reflexive subject pronoun that fulfills the following semantic feature [+ 2nd person, + plural]. Underline the reflexive pronoun.

7. Make a sentence with a relative pronoun that fulfills the following semantic feature [+place, +object]. Underline the relative pronoun.

8. Make a sentence in which the relative clause on the accessibility hierarchy conforms to the S-O pattern. Underline the relative clause and the elements that are indicative of the S-O pattern.

9. Make a sentence with a reciprocal pronoun. Underline the reciprocal pronoun.

10. Make a sentence with a demonstrative pronoun that has the following semantic features [+plural, + proximity]. Underline the demonstrative pronoun.

11. Make a sentence with an interrogative pronoun. Underline the interrogative pronoun.

12. Make a sentence with an indefinite pronoun. Underline the indefinite pronoun.

13. Make a sentence with an emphatic pronoun. Underline the emphatic pronoun.

14. Make a sentence in which the relative clause on the accessibility hierarchy conforms to the O-O pattern. Underline the relative clause and the elements that are indicative of the O-O pattern.

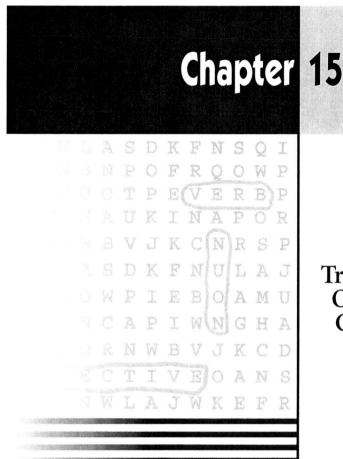

Chapter 15

Transformation Operations in Composition

15.0 INTRODUCTION

This chapter seeks to demonstrate that knowledge of the syntactic operations of addition, movement, substitution, and deletion can benefit writing pedagogy. To be sure, writing is a very complex cognitive process which includes interrelated sub-skills. Adger et al (2007:113) outline the difficulties inherent in writing as follows:

> Teaching students to write is seen as one of the most important functions in schools. But teaching writing is hard work. Students bring a range of language skills to this task. . . . One challenge concerns the need to distinguish between features that are particular to writing and those that are generally restricted to speaking. Another is the more general challenge of accommodating the special communicative demands associated with the situation. Developing written language expertise involves learning to make choices about style at different levels of language, including vocabulary, grammar, and text structure.

Given these multifaceted difficulties in teaching writing, it may seem rather odd and simplistic for this chapter to focus exclusively on sentence-level issues. The choice to do so is justified only because the sentence is the minimal unit of writing. Calderonello et al (2003:48) explain that the sentence should be attended to first because complete thoughts are expressed in sentences, not by isolated words, or phrases. Clouse (2006:125) underscores the importance of the sentence as the basic unit of writing by arguing that "Good ideas are not enough to keep your reader's interest. You must also express those ideas well. Thus, an important part of revising is assessing your sentences and words, and making changes to express your ideas as effectively as possible." The decision to focus on sentence-level phenomena in this chapter also stems from the fact that sentences are important in Generative Transformational Grammar. This entire approach is predicated upon the uncontroversial importance of the sentence. Given the centrality of the sentence both in composition and in formulating syntactic rules, it seems justified to focus on the sentence in this chapter. It should, however, be clearly understood that doing so does not suggest or imply that issues related to text structure, cohesion, the choice of the appropriate vocabulary items to match the rhetorical situation, punctuation, and a host of other issues are unimportant. They all deserve attention and they all contribute to the complexity of the writing task.

With this important caveat in place, this chapter examines the aspects of Generative Transformational Grammar that can contribute significantly to the improvement of writing skills. Most of the examples used to illustrate the claim that syntactic operations contribute to writing proficiency are taken from Abraham Lincoln's *Second Inaugural Address* and/or from *The Gettysburg Address.* These two speeches have endeared themselves to the average American's psyche so much that many people can recite some fragments from memory. Biblical examples will also be used to illustrate cases of transformations not found in Lincoln's speeches. The choice of the Bible is advantageous for two reasons. First, the Bible is readily available in print and online and can be used effortlessly to check the validity of the claims being made. Additionally, since the publication of the King James Version in 1612, the Bible has left an indelible mark on American and British rhetorical and literary traditions. Finally, when examples have not been found in any of these sources, other literary sources are used or I construct novel sentences to illustrate the point. Again, the thesis put forth in this chapter is that purposeful and explicit teaching of transformations will translate into better sentence-level writing proficiency.

15.1 *Sentence Patterns and Information Structure*

Speakers and writers rely on sentence structures to convey their thoughts to hearers and readers. It is generally assumed that the way one packages information matches perfectly the syntactic structure of one's language. Discourse analysts have coined binary terms such as **focus/presupposition, topic/comment, theme/rhyme,** and **old/new information** to account for how languages structure information. Jackendoff (2002:408) presents the architecture below to represent the levels at which prosodic, syntactic, and information structure interact. In spoken language, focus is shown through prosody. The elements of the sentence that are in focus are stressed more heavily than other elements. In the diagram below, both <Bill> and <jacket> are in focus because they receive prosodic peaks.

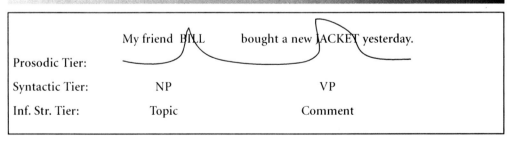

Diagram 1 *Topic/Comment Tier*

Syntax indicates prominence slightly differently. Focus is most often indicated by moving a lexical item or a phrase out of its default position. Linguists have identified six basic sentence patterns common to all the 6,000 or so languages spoken on earth today. Syntactically, then, information structure in these languages is patterned after the dominant syntactic word for each language. The six sentence patterns are as follows:

1. SVO

2. SOV

3. VSO

4. VOS

5. OVS

6. OSV

The three letters of the acronyms are to be interpreted as follows: <S> for "subject," <V> for "verb," and <O> for "object." The dominant word order pattern around the world is SVO. English is an SVO language with the following sub-patterns (Oaks and Stageberg 2000:224–242):

1. SV → Subject + Verb

2. SVC → Subject + Verb + Subject Complement

3. SVA → Subject + Verb + Adverbial

4. SVO → Subject + Verb + Direct Object

5. SVOO → Subject + Verb + Indirect Object + Direct Object

6. SVOC → Subject + Verb + Direct Object + Objective Complement

On the information structure tier, the word order that corresponds to the NP subject position is the topic and the VP position is equated with the comment. English has been labeled a topic-first language because in every pattern the topic appears first. If writing consisted only in reproducing these six patterns, written communication would be extremely monotonous. Fortunately, writers have at their disposal syntactic operations that they can use to diversify the information structure in their sentences. Clark (2003:262) notes that when the normal word order is incapable of carrying the information that speakers or writers wish to convey, they resort to **syntactic reordering,** i.e., transformations.

15.1.2 Transformations as Assets to Writers

The correlation between the knowledge of syntactic transformations and the improvement of writing skills has not yet been sufficiently established. This lacuna is due to the fact that, for the most part, theoretical linguists have not bothered to apply their findings to writing. This lack of interest has been evident since the inception of Generative Grammar. From the very beginning Chomsky (1965:127) made a clear distinction between grammatical transformations and **stylistic reordering.** He made his preference known as follows:

> *In general, the rules of stylistic reordering are very different from the grammatical transformations, which are much more deeply embedded in the grammatical system. It might, in fact, be argued that the former are not so much rules of grammar as rules of performance. In any event, though this is surely an interesting*

phenomenon, it is one that has no apparent bearing, for the moment, on the theory of grammatical structure.

Again in *The Minimalist Program,* Chomsky (1995:324–5) repeats and reinforces the same distinction by noting that "increasingly, this distinction seems to be quite real." Chomsky's unwillingness to apply his insights to writing is not unexpected. Following Bloomfield, as noted in 2.2.6, many linguists shunned written language as something unworthy of serious linguistic inquiry. For this reason, the body of knowledge that has been accumulated for the past half century of Generative Transformational Grammar research has not yet trickled down in large measures to the task of teaching writing. However, those who have taken the time to apply Chomsky's ideas to writing have been impressed by how they can revolutionize writing pedagogy. Rodby and Winterowd (2005:26) do not devote much time to transformations, but they offer an insight that underscores the importance of transformations in writing: "The verb is the pivot around which other elements in the sentence move. By substituting, adding, deleting, and moving sentence parts, we can revise our sentences and change their meaning." Taking this quote as the launching pad, we focus on four syntactic operations—addition, movement, substitution, deletion—in the remainder of this chapter. Various arguments and examples will be used to support the claim that knowledge of transformations can help to elevate an ordinary sentence into a stylistically enhanced one.

15.2 Defining and Classifying Adjuncts

The canonical word order of English sentences is SVO, as noted in 15.1. However, this order can be changed in a variety of ways for rhetorical reasons. One principal way in which the expected word order is changed is by moving sentential elements out of their normal positions. Usually, the elements of the sentence that are easily moved are adjuncts. The different positions in which adjuncts can occur are illustrated as follows:

SVO → SVO xxx
SVO → xxx SVO
SVO → S xxx VO
SVO → SV xxx O

Diagram 2 *Added Elements (Adjuncts)*

The elements represented by "xxx" are called **adjuncts.** They are defined as words or phrases that can be omitted from sentences without making the sentence ungrammatical. When all the adjuncts are removed (1), we arrive at a bare-bones sentence such as (2):

(1) *"Fourscore and seven years ago our fathers brought forth on this continent a new nation, conceived in liberty and dedicated to the proposition that all men are created equal."*

(2) *Our fathers brought forth a new nation.*

Sentence (2) has an SVO pattern. The subject of the verb is *"our fathers,"* the verb is *"brought forth,"* and the object is *"a new nation."* To this basic sentence pattern, Lincoln added at least seven adjuncts. The NP *"fourscore and seven years ago"* was provided to give adverbial information of time. The VP also contains several phrasal adjuncts, the first of which is the PP "*on this continent.*" The fragments "*conceived in liberty and dedicated to the proposition*" are also adjuncts. Adjuncts come in a variety of phrasal and clausal forms. Writers may use any one, or a combination, of the following types of adjuncts in their sentences:

1. Participial clause
2. Infinitival clause
3. Prepositional phrase
4. Adjective phrase
5. Adverb phrase
6. Appositive noun phrase
7. Relative clause

15.3 *Adjuncts in Writing and Speaking*

Adjuncts are modifiers that allow writers to provide various types of information in the sentence without resorting to new SVO sentences. The insertion of multiple adjuncts inside an SVO sentence pattern was an effective rhetorical device commonly used by classical authors and writers from previous generations. Then, the more adjuncts a sentence had, the more elegant and deep it was deemed to be. However, contemporary rhetorical practices encourage a reduction in the number of adjuncts per SVO sentence. In today's style, a sentence such as (1) would be rewritten as follows:

(3) "*Fourscore and seven years ago our fathers brought forth on this continent a new nation. It was conceived in liberty and dedicated to the proposition that all men are created equal.*"

Limiting the number of adjuncts reduces the overall density of the information. The simpler the information structure, the more grace and clarity the sentence has. Williams (2007:5, 7) complains bitterly about sentence density as follows:

Generations of students have struggled with dense writing, many thinking they weren't smart enough to grasp a writer's deep ideas. Some have been right about that, but more could have blamed the writer's inability (or refusal) to write clearly. Many students, sad to say, give up; sadder still, others learn not only to read that style but to write it, inflicting it on the next generation of readers, thereby sustaining a 450-year-old tradition of unreadable writing.

Dutton, the editor of the journal *Philosophy and Literature* chose Professor Judith Butler from the University of California at Berkeley as the recipient of the Fourth Bad Writing Contest in 1998. This unflattering award is given to authors of scholarly publications for the turgidity of their sentences. Professor Butler won the prize for the following sentence which appeared in her article "Further Reflections on the Conversations of Our Time" in the journal *Diacritics* in (1997):

The move from a structuralist account in which capital is understood to structure social relations in relatively homologous ways to a view of hegemony in which power relations are subject to repetition, convergence, and rearticulation brought the question of temporality into the thinking of structure, and marked a shift from a form of Althusserian theory that takes structural totalities as theoretical objects to one in which insights into the contingent possibility of structure inaugurate a renewed conception of hegemony as bound up with the contingent sites and strategies of the rearticulation of power.

This sentence contains ninety-three words with numerous adjuncts and embeddings! Students are now discouraged from writing sentences overflowing with adjuncts. Recently, an electronic mail entitled "*The Joy of the Hyperactive Sentence*"[1] was circulated in the English Department to highlight the kind of turgid sentences produced by students:

Shakespeare's reputation as a master of his art is again cemented in the sidewalk of history, for how many other plays written centuries ago can we claim to contain the seeds of a flower which takes three hundred years for us to bloom and really appreciate.

The professor who sent the electronic mail sarcastically wrote the following comment: "After 40 years in this business, I'm not easily surprised by student sentences, and perhaps it is the late hour, but I had to share this one."

In light of the preceding, novice and intermediate writers should be encouraged to limit the number of adjuncts to three per SVO sentence pattern. One adjunct can be used to modify the subject NP, and no more than two to modify elements in the VP. Imitating the adjunct-laden style of the previous generations of writers should be discouraged as much as possible. Just as the dress code has changed, and nobody wishes to wear the same outfits as our ancestors of previous centuries, so too should writers be encouraged to emulate the simpler style that contemporary rhetoric calls for. Today, a sentence is considered well written if it economizes on the number of adjuncts and has a simpler and straightforward information structure.

15.4 Movement Rules in Composition

Movement is the only syntactic operation that has survived the various refinements of Generative Transformational Grammar. In *The Minimalist Program*, Chomsky champions the operation called "Move α" while abandoning all other syntactic transformations. Chomsky (1993:228, 261) introduces two important principles to constrain movement rules. Culicover (1997:349) summarizes them as follows:

> **GREED:** A constituent does not move unless it has to in order to satisfy some requirement that it has.
>
> **PROCRASTINATE:** Movement occurs as late as possible in the derivation.

The last principle is not of any particular interest to the teaching of writing, but the first is certainly applicable. When applied to writing, the Greed principle can be restated as follows:

> **GREED in Writing:** A constituent is not moved unless it must, in order to satisfy the stylistic requirement of focus.

Writers frequently modify the canonical SVO sentence pattern by moving words or phrases around in their sentences. The overriding motivation behind such movement rules is focus. By moving constituents from one place to another, writers can convey subtle and not so subtle nuances of meaning. Clark (2003:263) underscores this point by noting that "Written language has no system for marking special stress; instead, a constituent must be focused by moving it to a position where it receives the stress automat-

---

[1] This e-mail was sent by Professor Phil Keith on March 15, 2007. Emeritus Professor Keith taught English at Saint Cloud State University in Saint Cloud, Minnesota.

ically." The cover term used to describe the movement rules in composition is **stylistic shifting** or **stylistic reordering**. The term encompasses a wide variety of movement rules which will be discussed in the following sections.

15.4.1 Appositive Movement in Composition

Appositives are classical illustrations of the movement operation. Writers routinely move adjuncts from the end of the sentence and place them elsewhere in the sentence as parenthetical comments. Based on Diagram 2, we assume that all adjuncts in English occur after the object of the verb. Hence, appositives are moved from the end of the sentence and are inserted elsewhere in the same sentence. The piece of information that is moved functions as an aside that helps the writer focus on a specific aspect of the sentence. An example of an appositive is found in (4):

(4)   *Then a statement, **somewhat in detail,** of a course to be pursued, seemed fitting and proper.*

Lincoln uses the appositive "somewhat in detail" which functions here as an adjective that modifies the noun phrase "a statement." Clark (2003:264) explains the stylistic use of appositives as follows: "The subject of the sentence can be given focus by placing an adverbial modifier or parenthetical phrase after it, forcing a pause at the end of the subject. Because the subject now falls at the end of the intonation phrase, it will receive a nuclear stress." According to this interpretation, the appositive *"somewhat in detail"* is used by Lincoln as a rhetorical device to reinforce the statement that he was about to make.

Lincoln's speeches are characterized by an abundance of appositives. In the sentence below, there are two appositives:

(5)   *The progress of our arms, **upon which all else chiefly depends,** is as well known to the public as to myself; and it is, **I trust,** reasonably satisfactory and encouraging to all.*

These appositives are used to add valuable side comments. Novice writers can use this same rhetorical device in academic writing to tone down strong positions or to agree or disagree with a given position. Appositives are very effective in writing book reviews or opinion-based research papers where one's personal views are important. Additionally, they help writers make side comments without having to make new sentences. Thus, addition operations in the form of adjuncts and appositives are rhetorical strategies that writers can use to enhance their style.

15.4.2 Subject-Auxiliary Inversion in Composition

Subject-Auxiliary Inversion is an obligatory transformation in Yes/No questions and in some WH-questions. But it is also used in some affirmative sentences for emphasis, as seen in the sentences below:

(6)   *"**Fondly** do we hope—**fervently** do we pray—that this mighty scourge of war may speedily pass away."*

The proposed SVO counterpart of (6) is (7):

(7)   *We hope **fondly**—we pray **fervently**—that this mighty scourge of war may speedily pass away.*

In (6) we notice that the adverbs "*fondly*" and "*fervently*" have been front-shifted. This movement (to be discussed below) has triggered a **Subject-Auxiliary** movement rule and a **DO-Insertion** rule. Extracting the adverbs "*fondly*" and "*fervently*" from their post-verbal positions without the subsequent movement of the Subject and the Auxiliary would have yielded the anticlimactic sentence (8):

> (8) ***Fondly*** *we hope—**fervently** we pray—that this mighty scourge of war may speedily pass away.*

The stylistic importance of Subject-Auxiliary Inversion cannot be underestimated. It has been said that (6) marks a climactic point in Lincoln's speech. It seems that influential orators know the locutionary force of Subject-Auxiliary Inversion and use it effectively to achieve the desired effect on the hearer or the reader. As noted in 10.9 to 10.9.2, Rev. Dr. Martin Luther King, Jr. used this transformation three consecutive times in his unforgettable "*I Have a Dream*" speech. When he reached the crescendo of his speech, he repeated "*now is the time*" three times. Stylistically, "*now is the time*" appears to be more effective than "*the time is now*."

15.4.3 The Stylistic Effects of Adverbial Fronting

Subject-Auxiliary Inversion transformation often triggers a movement rule known as **Adverbial Fronting.** In this transformation, an adverb is moved from its canonical position in the SVO sentence pattern to the beginning of the sentence. When adverbs move to other positions, they do not attract as much rhetorical attention as when they move to the beginning of the sentence. The rhetorical value of placing adverbs at the beginning of a sentence is clearly seen in (6) repeated here as (9):

> (9) ***Fondly*** *do we hope—**fervently** do we pray—that this mighty scourge of war may speedily pass away.*

Adverbial fronting is used sparingly by writers, but when they use this construction, they intend for it to have a full impact on the reader or the listener. Not all adverbs can or should be shifted to the front. Lincoln uses adverbial fronting only once in the *Second Inaugural Address* and once in the *Gettysburg Address*. In all other instances, the adverb is left either in its canonical position or moved elsewhere in the sentence where it does not necessarily receive focus, as in the two examples below:

> (10) "*The prayers of both could not be answered—that of neither has been answered **fully.**"*

> (11) "*On the occasion corresponding to this four years ago, all thoughts were **anxiously** directed to an impending civil war.*"

Adverbial fronting should be taught to novice and intermediate writers with the caveat that it should be used sparingly but powerfully to achieve a wide range of rhetorical effects. Calderonello et al (2003:259) highlights the usefulness of this transformation to writers as follows:

> . . . *Adverbials are perhaps the most flexible of the parts of speech, in that many of them are movable and can be used to provide a wide variety of information in a sentence. Adverbials can also be fun for writers because they can be used for stylistic purposes to provide sentence variety and to emphasize certain parts of the sentence. . . . Moving a sentence modifier or subordinating conjunction such as* perhaps *or* consequently *to various parts of a sentence can also change the tone of the sentence according to the information the writer wishes to convey.*

Writing teachers should not only instruct their students to move adverbs such as those listed in 10.9.2 to the beginning of sentences, they should also emphasize that such movements often call for Subject-Auxiliary Inversion and Do-Insertion. Indeed, fronting alone without the subsequent inversion transformation either results in an ungrammatical sentence or diminishes the rhetorical effect. Sentence (12) is rhetorically less powerful than its counterpart in (13).

> (12)   We hope **fondly**—we pray **fervently**—that this mighty scourge of war may speedily pass away.

> (13)   "**Fondly** do we hope—**fervently** do we pray—that this mighty scourge of war may speedily pass away."

The main stylistic difference between these two sentences is that (13) has undergone the additional Subject-Auxiliary Inversion transformation and Do-Insertion but (12) has not.

15.4.4 Adjectival Fronting and Inversion

Some of the syntactic similarities between adjectives and adverbs have been discussed in previous chapters. Suffice it to note here that, like adverbs, adjectives can undergo Fronting and Subject-Auxiliary Inversion with virtually the same rhetorical effects as adverbial fronting. When adjectives are front-shifted, they receive prominence, as seen in the Beatitudes[2]:

[3]Blessed *are* the poor in spirit, for theirs is the kingdom of heaven.

[4]Blessed *are* those who mourn, for they shall be comforted.

[5]Blessed *are* the meek, for they shall inherit the earth.

[6]Blessed *are* those who hunger and thirst for righteousness, for they shall be filled.

[7]Blessed *are* the merciful, for they shall obtain mercy.

[8]Blessed *are* the pure in heart, for they shall see God.

[9]Blessed *are* the peacemakers, for they shall be called sons of God.

[10]Blessed *are* those who are persecuted for righteousness' sake, for theirs is the kingdom of heaven.

[11]Blessed *are* you when they revile and persecute you, and say all kinds of evil against you falsely for My sake.

Adjectival Fronting is obligatorily accompanied by Subject-Auxiliary Inversion or else the sentence becomes ill-formed, as is the case of (14) below:

> (14)   *Blessed the poor **are** in spirit, for theirs is the kingdom of heaven.

Calderonello et al (2003:298) encourage the explicit teaching of adjectival fronting and its stylistic impact by arguing that "many types of adjective modifiers can also be moved to create various stylistic effects. Although single-word adjective modifiers ordinarily precede the words they modify, sometimes they can be repositioned." A word of caution is in order here. Adverbial and Adjectival Fronting tend to elevate the register from informal to formal, or even to ceremonial. Consequently, these constructions should be used sparingly in academic writing.

---

[2] The Beatitudes is the name given to this teaching by Jesus found in Matthew 5:3–11. The verses are quoted from the Revised Standard Version.

15.4.5 Preposition Preposing

Most prepositions fulfill an adverbial function, as noted in 11.8.3. For this reason, they tend to have the same mobility as "true" adverbs. Just as adverbs can be front shifted, so can prepositions. The syntactic transformation which consists in moving prepositional phrases to the beginning of the sentence has been called **PP-Preposing** or **PP-Fronting.** We keep the term PP-Preposing because it was used in Chapter 11. PP-Preposing is used commonly by speakers and writers. It is also the most frequent transformation used by Lincoln in *The Second Inaugural Address.* The following is just a sampling of the various PP-Preposing constructions found in his speech:

(15) *"**At this second appearing to take the oath of the presidential office,** there is less occasion for an extended address than there was at the first."*

(16) *"**With high hope for the future,** no prediction in regard to it is ventured."*

(17) *"**With malice toward none; with charity for all; with firmness in the right;** as God gives us to see the right, let us strive on to finish the work we are in; to bind up the nation's wounds; to care for him who shall have borne the battle, and for his widow, and his orphan—to do all which may achieve and cherish a just and lasting peace among ourselves, and with all nations."*

PP-Preposing transformation is used purposefully in these three sentences to achieve a stylistic effect that is commensurate with the importance of the message being conveyed. If the prepositional phrase had been placed after the verb phrase as dictated by the SVO pattern, the sentences would have had a diminished stylistic impact. The stylistic difference between a sentence with a preposed preposition and its canonical counterpart is clearly revealed by (18) and (19) below:

(18) *On the occasion corresponding to this four years ago,* all thoughts were anxiously directed to an impending civil war.

(19) *All thoughts were anxiously directed to an impending civil war* **on the occasion corresponding to this four years ago.**

In a survey for a class project, Deuser (2007)[3] discovered that English as a Second Language speakers and native speakers prefer sentences with PP-Preposing to sentences in which the prepositional phrase occurs in its canonical SVO position. Thus, PP-Preposing is yet another syntactic transformation that teachers can use to improve their students' written discourse.

15.4.6 Moving Noun Phrases to the Front

We have seen from the previous sections that adverbs, adjectives, and preposition phrases can be moved to the beginning of the sentence for stylistic reasons. Nouns that function as direct objects can also be moved from elsewhere to the beginning of the sentence. Linguists give the label of **topicalization** to this transformation. Fromkin et al (2007:161) define it as follows: "Many languages, including English, have a transformation that moves a direct object to the beginning of the sentence to draw particular attention to it. The transformation is called topicalization because an object to which attention is drawn is generally the topic of the sentence or conversation." Examples of topicalization abound

---

[3]Deuser sought to assess the judgment of native and nonnative speakers on 12 basic sentences. All these sentences were compared with their counterparts that had undergone various syntactic transformations. Her findings showed that native speakers and nonnative speakers preferred sentences involving movement than sentences in which movement did not take place.

both in literary language and in conversational speech. One of the most dramatic and enigmatic uses of topicalization is found in the New Testament. In Romans 9:13, we find the following sentence:

(20) "***Esau,*** *I hated;* ***Jacob,*** *I loved.*"

(21) *I hated Esau; I loved Jacob.*

The non-topicalized counterpart of (20) is (21). To derive sentence (20) from (21), the direct objects "Esau" and "Jacob" are moved to the front of their respective clauses. The consequence of this construction is that by moving the objects into sentence initial position, they receive prominence. Lincoln also used a similar literary strategy in his speech:

(22) "***The progress of our arms,*** *upon which all else chiefly depends, is as well known to the public as to myself . . .*"

It can be postulated that the non-topicalized version of (22) reads approximately as follows:

(23) *All else chiefly depends upon the progress of our arms, which is as well known to the public as to myself . . .*

The movement of the noun phrase "*the progress of our arms*" to the beginning of the sentence helps to emphasize one of the key points in Lincoln's speech. Topicalization does not only move phrases; it can also move clauses, as in the following example:

(24) "***To strengthen, perpetuate, and extend this interest*** *was the object for which the insurgents would rend the Union, . . .*"

Sentence (25) is the hypothetical base for (24):

(25) *The object for which the insurgents would rend the Union was* ***to strengthen, perpetuate, and extend this interest.***

In moving the italicized portion to the beginning of the sentence, Lincoln achieves a stylistic effect by focusing on the motivation of the insurgents. This interpretation agrees with Clark's (2003:264) observation that "topicalization focuses on a constituent by moving it to the front of the sentence." Topicalization is very similar to a construction called **left-dislocation.** If sentence (20) were: "*Esau, I hated* **him;** *Jacob, I loved* **him,**" then these constructions would have qualified as left-dislocation instead of topicalization. The main difference between the two is the retention of the pronoun in left-dislocation and its deletion in topicalized sentences.

15.4.7 Extraction of Main Verbs

A rare form of topicalization in English consists of moving the main verb to the beginning of the sentence. This is not common in everyday speech, but the writers of *Star Wars* made abundant use of it to create important stylistic effects. Yoda, one of the main characters, is often heard uttering sentences such as the following:

(26) "***Surrender,*** *you must or* ***die,*** *you will.*"

The SVO canonical word order underlying this sentence is reflected in sentence (27) below:

(27) *You must* **surrender,** *or you will* **die.**

Another uncommon transformation involving English verbs consists of extracting the main verb from its original position and placing it at the end of a sentence, as is the case of the following sentence made by Kingsbury (2007:55):

> (28) *Yet an expensive degree does not necessarily a literate citizen* **make.**

Normally, in declarative sentences the main verb remains in close vicinity to the auxiliary verb. However, in (28) the main verb "*make*" has been moved from its normal location and shifted to the end of the sentence. Stylistically, this transformation has an emphatic function. Here Kingsbury uses it to bolster his claim that money alone cannot buy a good education. Advanced composition students can be made aware of these rare but effective syntactic constructions.

15.4.8 Extraposition in Writing

Nearly all the movement rules that we have discussed so far, with the exception of the extraction of main verbs to the end of the sentence, have dealt with moving phrases to initial position in the sentence. However, movement rules can move syntactic elements elsewhere in the sentence. This can be illustrated by the following sentence:

> (29) *It may seem strange* **that any men should dare to ask a just God's assistance in wringing their bread from the sweat of other men's faces.**"

Linguists posit that the form of the sentence prior to the application of movement rules is as follows:

> (30) *That any men should dare to ask a just God's assistance in wringing their bread from the sweat of other men's faces may seem strange . . ."*

The subject of the verb "*may seem*" is "*That any men should dare to ask a just God's assistance in wringing their bread from the sweat of other men's faces.*" Syntactic constructions such as this one are said to have heavy subjects. As noted in 13.7.4, Kaplan (1995:259) argues that English prefers to place longer constituents at the end of the sentence, not at the beginning. Consequently, speakers and writers resort to extraposition to avoid heavy subjects. The avoidance of heavy subjects at the beginning of sentences necessarily leads to the use of "It" at the beginning of some sentences. This dummy "It," as it is called, is needed because in English conjugated verbs must have a surface structure subject. However, when the heavy subject is moved to the end of the sentence, the main verb finds itself "subjectless." To avoid this situation, speakers and writers resort to the dummy subject "It." Unfortunately, some Language Arts teachers tell their students to avoid "It" without taking the time to explain clearly which "It" to avoid. Dummy "It" must not be avoided because it is necessary. The "It" to be avoided is the one that denotes unclear pronominal reference (to be discussed in 15.5.4). The "It" that results from extraposition is neither improper nor stylistically inferior. Lincoln uses it in *The Second Inaugural Address* and in *The Gettysburg Address*. Williams (2007:98) encourages the use of dummy "It," saying that "when you have a subject consisting of a long noun clause, you can move it to the end of the sentence and start it with It."

15.4.9 Cliticization in Writing

Extraposition is not the only transformation that calls for the use of "It." Cliticized sentences also make use of "It." Cliticization is a syntactic transformation that is similar to extraposition. However, in contrast with the latter where an element moves towards the end of the sentence, in cliticization, syntactic elements move toward the front of the sentence. Linguists distinguish between two types of cliticization: "It-cliticization" and "Wh-cliticization." Let us focus first on "It-cliticization":

(31) *Chomsky teaches linguistics at MIT.*

(32) *It is Chomsky who teaches linguistics at MIT.*

(33) **It is Chomsky—teaches linguistics at MIT.*

(34) *It is at MIT where Chomsky teaches linguistics.*

(35) **It is MIT—Chomsky teaches linguistics at.*

(36) *It is linguistics that Chomsky teaches at MIT.*

(37) **It is linguistics—Chomsky teaches at MIT.*

The ungrammaticality of (33), (35) and (37) shows that the relative pronoun cannot be omitted. The rhetorical value of the cliticization in (32) is clear. The cliticized construction "It is ..." focuses more on the agent than its non-cliticized counterpart. The difference between the two constructions is highlighted by (31) and (32). In both sentences, Chomsky appears at the beginning of the sentence. If the element to be cliticized does not appear in the subject position, then two transformations must apply. First, a topicalization rule must move the element to the beginning of the sentence. The topicalized element undergoes a subsequent cliticization transformation by the addition of "*It is X that,*" or "*It is X where,*" as is the case in (36).

15.4.10 The Rhetorical Value of Cleft Sentences

Another syntactic construction known as Cleft sentence construction is closely related to cliticization. The stylistic effects are similar. The only difference between the two is that in cleft sentences, a Wh-word appears at the beginning of the declarative sentence. Williams (2007:98) explains the rhetorical effect of this transformation as follows: "This is another device that shifts a part of the sentence to the left, thereby emphasizing it more." Sentences (39) and (40) are illustrative of cleft sentences. These two sentences can be derived from (38) which represents the canonical SVO sentence pattern:

(38) *She needs a vacation in the mountains.*

(39) *What she needs is a vacation in the mountains.*

(40) *A vacation in the mountains is what she needs.*

(41) *It is a vacation in the mountains that she needs.*

Cleft sentences with Wh-words are stylistically effective because they highlight the part of the discourse that needs to be underscored. Cleft sentences such as (39) are different from cliticized sentences such as (41) in that in the former the Wh-word must agree in semantic features with its antecedent whereas sentences with "It-cliticization" do not have to meet such a requirement. For instance, if the antecedent of a cleft sentence is [+human], the Wh-word must be the relative pronoun "who," as shown in the examples below:

(42) *He wanted to study under Chomsky.*

(43) *Chomsky was who(m) he wanted to study under.*

(44) *Who(m) he wanted to study under was Chomsky.*

It is worth noting, without necessarily going into the details of the actual derivational processes, that cliticization and cleft sentences rely on complex transformational operations that include movement of an NP. For instance, in (43) the NP "Chomsky" has been topicalized, resulting in a preposition stranding. The derivational processes that led to (44) are equally complex. Clark (2003:263) explains the stylistic benefit of these constructions as follows: "The constituent in the focal position of a cleft is automatically given nuclear (= heaviest) stress. By choosing which constituent to place in this position, the writer can determine which constituent will be stressed." Stylistically then, sentences (39) through (41) and (43) and (44) give prominence to the elements that have moved from their position in the canonical sentence pattern.

15.4.11 Sentences with "There" as Subject

Some sentences have "there" as their grammatical subject as a result of a transformation that moves the subject NP from its original grammatical position and places it right after the verb "to be" or a modal auxiliary verb. This construction can be illustrated by the two sentences below:

(45) *Bats are in the attic.*

(46) ***There** are bats in the attic.*

"*There*" is a dummy subject. What stylistic value is there in generating sentences such as (46)? Williams (2007:98) complains that some editors have unfairly targeted "there" for exclusion because it does not contribute anything valuable to the sentence. Some teachers object to *there is/there are* in papers on the grounds that they are characteristic of colloquial or informal register. However, this objection cannot be sustained. Scholarly publications and serious academic journals allow their contributors to use the existential "*there is/there are.*" A cursory analysis of a three-page article by Joseph (2006:482-485) explaining the editorial process in *Language, Journal of the Linguistic Society of America,* the author uses "there is/there are" seven times. In one sentence "there is" appears twice! If a respectable academic journal such as *Language* uses "there is/there are," students certainly can use it in their papers. Lincoln also uses "there is/was" twice in the opening sentence of *The Second Inaugural Address:*

(47) "*Fellow countrymen: At this second appearing to take the oath of the presidential office, **there** is less occasion for an extended address than **there was** at the first.*"

Unlike the purists who do not see any redeeming value in *there is/there are,* Clark (2003:262) sees stylistic and information processing value in using *there is/there are* in some sentences. She explains it as follows: "*There* insertion moves a subject NP that introduces new information to the position following the main verb, leaving a dummy subject called "**existential there**" in its place. The existential *there* at the beginning of a sentence serves to warn the hearer or reader that new information is coming up." Some sentences simply sound better with "*there is/there are.*" It is hard to imagine how the opening sentence of *The Second Inaugural Address* could have been constructed without "*there is/there are.*"

15.4.12 Unshackling Split Infinitives

The movement of some adverbs from their canonical position in the SVO sentence pattern results in a syntactic construction that has been labeled <**split infinitive.**> This construction consists of extracting an adverb from its postverbal position and moving it to a preverbal position, between the infinitive marker <to> and the main verb. There is no split infinitive in neither Lincoln's *Second Inaugural Address* nor in his *Gettysburg Address*. Searches of electronic Bibles have not yielded any instance of split infinitives. The absence of this construction from these sources shows that the ban against the split infinitive is still in effect in some quarters. Sentence (49) illustrates the use of a split infinitive. Sentence (48), the counterpart of (49), has not undergone the split infinitive transformation:

    (48)   *He wants to destroy his enemies **utterly**.*

    (49)   *He wants to **utterly** destroy his enemies.*

Technically (48) is a more grammatical sentence than (49). However, to most people, (48) sounds stilted whereas (49) seems more natural. Stylistically, the latter seems to add more poignancy to the thought being conveyed. Cumes (1931:458) concurs with this assessment, arguing that in their canonical post-verbal position, adverbs do not usually receive stress. However, they receive emphasis when they are moved between the infinitive particle "to" and the main verb.

Generations of students have been discouraged from using split infinitives despite efforts by linguists to show that inserting an adverb between <to> and the main verb fulfills a better rhetorical purpose than leaving it in its postverbal position. Cumes (1931:458–61) defended the use of split infinitives in the last century as follows:

> *The insertion of the adverb here between* to *and the infinitive cannot even in the strictest scientific sense be considered ungrammatical . . . The split infinitive has been censured by grammarians to whom grammar is not an objective study of the living language but a fixed body of rules that has come down to us from the past. Also a number of good writers avoid the split infinitive. Since the fourteenth century, however, the split infinitive, by virtue of its decided advantages, which are unconsciously widely felt, has been gradually gaining ground, in recent times even making headway against deeply rooted prejudices, so that it frequently appears in good authors, among them many of our best, sometimes only occasionally, sometimes more freely . . . In general, it is more characteristic of our most prominent authors than the minor writers, who avoid it as they fear criticism. In the last fifty years, however, its use in literature has spread more rapidly than in any previous period of its development. It has become such a necessary form of English expression that we often cannot avoid it if we would employ the infinitive at all.*

Prejudice against the split infinitive is alive and well. Some composition and Language Arts teachers still frown upon its use. In spite of efforts by linguists to emancipate the split infinitive, there is reluctance in using it. Pinker (1994:374) complains about this outdated prohibition. He contends that "forcing modern speakers of English to not-whoops, not to split an infinitive because it isn't done in Latin makes about as much sense as forcing modern residents of England to wear laurels and togas. Julius Caesar could not have split an infinitive if he had wanted to. In Latin the infinitive is a single word like *facere* or *dicere,* a syntactic atom. English is a different kind of language."

15.4.13 Multiple Movements and Passive Constructions

Passive constructions are notorious for the amount of derivational steps associated with them. For this reason, the change from an active voice sentence to a passive voice sentence was the "poster child" of transformations in the early days of Generative Transformational Grammar. In a typical derivation of a passive voice sentence from an active voice sentence, the NP subject moves to the NP object position and the NP object moves into the position left vacant by the NP subject. The agentive preposition "by" and the discontinuous morpheme <Be-EN> are inserted by an addition rule. All this made the passive the darling of early transformational grammarians. Even though the early enthusiasm for deriving passive constructions through transformations has faded, the passive voice has not lost any of its appeal. Students still love to use it. When asked why they use passive constructions, the students in one survey responded that they wanted to appear "intelligent." It is unclear why the use of the passive voice is associated with intelligence, but it is true that "smart" people use passives. In *The Second Inaugural Address*, Lincoln uses the passive voice at least seventeen times. In the excerpt below, six passive constructions are used!

> (50)   *"Yet, if God wills that it continue until all **the wealth piled by the bondsman's** two hundred and fifty years of unrequited toil shall **be sunk,** and until **every drop of blood drawn by the lash shall be paid by another drawn with the sword,** as was **said** three thousand years ago, so still it must **be said,** The judgments of the Lord are true and righteous altogether."*

Lincoln's uses of the passives underscore two of the most important functions of passive constructions. By moving the direct object into the subject position and casting the underlying subject into the object position, the writer can emphasize or de-emphasize information at will. This is seen in the fragment "*the wealth piled by the bondsman's two hundred and fifty years of unrequited toil.*" Lincoln implicitly focuses on the wealth. In "*every drop of blood drawn by the lash,*" he emphasizes the cruel treatment that the slaves have endured at the hand of ruthless masters.

Lincoln uses another type of passive construction known as "**agentless passives.**" These are found in the fragments ". . . unrequited toil shall *be sunk*" and "*was said.*" These passives are so named because the agent is not explicitly stated. Writers resort to agentless passives if they determine that knowing the agent is not key to understanding the message. They may also omit the agent if it is believed to be known to the reader or the hearer. The agent may also remain unnamed for ideological reasons. In sentence (50) the implicit agent of the first "*as was said*" can be understood to be the prophets. The agent of the second "*it must be said*" can refer to Lincoln himself for speaking boldly against the evil of slavery. However, rather than draw attention to himself by using the pronoun "I", he turns to an agentless passive construction. Jackendoff (2002:413) notes that such a construction is pervasive in academic and legislative writing. Celce-Murcia and Larsen-Freeman (1999:354) find that agentless passive constructions correlate highly with the level of formality. The highest number of passives is found in scientific, journalistic, and administrative jargon. This information is useful to composition and Language Arts teachers. Instead of uncritically discouraging the use of passives, as some have done, teachers should correlate the use of passives with the type of writing assignment. Expository writing will in general tend to make frequent use of passive constructions, whereas creative writing will use considerably fewer passives.

15.5 Substitution Rules in Composition

Substitution is a transformation which replaces a lexical item, a phrase, or a constituent with a **proform.** Proform is the label that linguists give to a class of words that can replace other words, phrases, and even sentences. The best known words in this class are pronouns, the main focus of this section. Pronouns are a lexical category found in all languages. Their main function in languages is to provide cohesion in the discourse by avoiding the repetition of lexical noun phrases. Williams (2007:99) explains the relevance of pronouns in composition as follows:

> *This is a fine point: a sentence can end flatly if you repeat a word that you used just a few words before at the end of a sentence, because the voice we hear in our mind's ear drops off at the end of a sentence. If you read aloud the preceding sentence, this one, and the next, you can hear that drop at the end of each sentence. To avoid this kind of flatness, rewrite or use a pronoun instead of repeating the word at the end of the sentence.*

In speech, pronouns are less problematic because of the enriched discourse environment in which they occur. However, this is often not the case in writing because many of the contextual clues that make it easy to interpret reference accurately are missing. Yule (2006:126) argues that cohesion is an important part of discourse analysis. He claims that judgment on the quality of a piece of writing depends to a great extent on how things are tied together in the text: "Analysis of the cohesive ties within a text gives us some insight into how writers structure what they want to say and they may be a crucial factor in our judgment of whether something is well written or not." Since pronouns were the focus on the previous chapter, this section deals only with areas of pronominal use that have been identified in the literature as troublesome for novice and intermediate writers.

15.5.1 Free vs. Bound Pronouns

One rhetorical device that all natural languages use to implement the need for textual cohesion is **pronominalization.** Linguists distinguish between two types of pronouns: **"bound"** vs. **"free"** pronouns. The insights on how cohesion is obtained through pronominalization have been largely discussed in the linguistic literature, especially in the Government-Binding Theory, but the gains have not trickled down to teaching students how to use pronouns in their writing. Bound pronouns are defined here simply as pronouns that have an **anaphoric reference** in the text. The person, place, time, or object referred to can be identified in the text. Free pronouns, on the other hand, do not need to have a reference. Students must constantly keep the distinction between these two types of pronouns in mind when they write or else their readers are likely to be confused. *The Second Inaugural Address* offers us a wide range of pronouns. Both free and bound pronouns are used, as illustrated by the excerpt below:

(51) *The Almighty has **His** own purposes. "Woe unto the world because of offenses! For **it** must needs be that offenses come; but woe to that man by **whom** the offense cometh." If **we** shall suppose that American slavery is one of those offenses **which,** in the providence of God, must needs come, but **which,** having continued through **His** appointed time, **He** now wills to remove, and that **He** gives to both North and South this terrible war, as the woe due to those by **whom** the offenses came, shall **we** discern therein any departure from those divine attributes **which** the believers in a living God always ascribe to **Him**?*

The pronouns "*His,*" "*He,*" and "*Him*" are anaphoric pronouns because they refer back either to "*The Almighty*" or to "*a living God.*" The first relative pronoun "*whom*" refers back to "*that man*" while the second "*whom*" refers back to "*those.*" The two occurrences of the relative pronoun "*which*" are related to "*offenses.*" These are all illustrations of bound pronouns. The situation for the pronoun "*we*" is trickier. Even though there is no clear reference in the text as to whom "*we*" is connected, one can interpret it either as referring to "the American people in general" or to Lincoln himself. This usage of "we" is sometimes called "editorial we" or "royal we." The pronoun "*It*" is free because it does not refer back to anything.

Proficiency in the use of bound pronouns develops early. Guasti (2002:271) notes that the binding principles that govern the grammatical use of pronouns are acquired between the ages of 3 and 4. Reports indicate that adultlike proficiency in the use of anaphoric pronouns is definitely acquired by the age of 6 in almost all languages. Therefore, by the time an English-speaking child begins first grade, he/she does not need to be taught pronominal agreement rules. If this is so, why then does Yagoda (2006) include pronouns among the *Seven Deadly Sins* that college students make? Here again, a distinction must be made between Innate Grammar and School Grammar. School Grammar is more demanding on the use of pronouns. In written discourse, writers must navigate the referential system carefully to allow the reader to arrive at the correct interpretation of the text. Experts have identified the following three as areas where pronouns are tricky to use in academic writing.

15.5.2 The Overuse of "They"

Language influences culture and culture influences language. As societal norms change, so do linguistic norms. This is nowhere more obvious than in the use of the third person singular pronouns "he" and "she" in English. Since the mid 1970s the stated editorial policy of leading academic journals has been to ban sexism. Thus, the use of the masculine pronoun "he" as the default pronoun has been eliminated. This contrasts with the rhetorical views of previous generations for whom "he/his/him/himself" were generic pronouns for both the masculine and the feminine gender. In (52) Lincoln uses the pronouns "*him*" and "*his*" in *The Gettysburg Address* in the generic sense:

(52) *With malice toward none; with charity for all; with firmness in the right; as God gives us to see the right, let us strive on to finish the work we are in; to bind up the nation's wounds; to care for **him** who shall have borne the battle, and for **his** widow, and **his** orphan—to do all which may achieve and cherish a just and lasting peace among ourselves, and with all nations.*

The contemporary exclusion of the generic "he" has created a problem for novice writers, namely the overuse of "they." Yagoda (2006) explains it as follows:

This is one item on the list with shades of gray. A student wrote, "He asked each audience member to reconsider their stance," using the plural "their" to stand in for the singular "member."

The desire for gender neutrality in pronominal use has led to the overuse of the third person plural pronoun. This, in turn, has created an agreement mismatch between pronouns and their antecedents. Increasingly the pronoun "they" is used even if the antecedent is a genderless noun which is grammatically singular. Thus, it is not uncommon to see "they" used as a substitute for the following words: "*the jury, the government, the band, parliament, the team, the class, the family, the nation, the country, the army, the couple, the orchestra,* etc." Additionally, indefinite pronouns such as "*anybody, somebody, everybody, nobody, everyone, someone, anyone, no one*" are made to agree with the third person plural. Opinions differ as to the grammaticality of such constructions. Calderonello et al (2003:98) note that many Language Arts teachers do not comment negatively on the use of "they." However, they sound a cautionary note saying, "Despite the increasing prevalence of this practice, there are some readers who consider this usage wrong and who can be alienated by writing that contains such constructions." Yagoda predicts that the use of "they" in such instances, though not widely acceptable now, will be soon. Teachers can also let their students know that there is an alternative to using "they" in such cases. An acceptable solution consists in using the binary pronouns "his/her" to signal gender neutrality. Many academic journals, including *Language,* prefer this solution.

15.5.3 Who vs. Whom and I vs. Me

Old English and Middle English had a morphological agreement in **case.** Case is defined as a morphological system in which suffixes are added to nouns to indicate their grammatical function. However, in contemporary English, the only remnant of the old case system is found in pronouns. Of the existing relative pronouns, the distinction is found only in the third person pronouns "who" and "whom" when their antecedent has the feature [+human]. If the antecedent of an action or event is a human being, or has human attributes, the relative pronoun is supposed to agree with it in grammatical function. Thus, if the antecedent is the subject of the verb in the main clause, then the relative pronoun is <who>; if it is the object, then <whom> is selected, as shown in the two sentences below:

(53) *"The brave men, living and dead* **who** *struggled here have consecrated it far above our poor power to add or detract."*

(54) *"For it must needs be that offenses come; but woe to that man by* **whom** *the offenses cometh." . . . as the woe due to those by* **whom** *the offenses came, . . ."*

The pronoun <whom> is used less and less in academic writing, even in refereed journals. Instead, <who> has supplanted <whom> regardless of grammatical function. Calderonello et al (2003:304) give the following reason for this change: "Interestingly, however, even when speakers know how to appropriately select *who* or *whom,* they may elect not to use *whom* because they think it sounds too formal or stuffy. Many language users, hearing the sentence *The man whom we elected betrayed us,* would consider the use of *whom* pretentious even if it is technically correct."

The situation with "I" and "me" is analogous with that of "who" and "whom." In her book *Woe is I,* O'Conner (1996:10) writes the following humor-ladden paragraph about the use of "I" vs. "Me":

These days, anyone who says, "It is I" sounds like a stuffed shirt. It wasn't always so. In bygone days, you might have had your knuckles rapped for saying "It's me" instead of "It is I." Your crime? A pronoun following the verb to be, *the English teacher insisted, should act like a subject (*I, he, she, they*) and not an object (*me, him, her, them*). But language is a living thing, always evolving, and* It is I *is just about extinct. In all but the most formal writing, some of the fussiest grammarians accept* It's me. *Most of us find the old usage awkward, though I must admit that I still use "This is she" when someone asks for me on the phone. Old habits die harder than old rules.*

Though the change from "whom" to "who" is complete and widely accepted, the same is not true for "I" and "me." Teachers still expect their students to select the correct pronominal form based on its function in the sentence. Thus, a sentence such as "*Me go to the store*" is considered unsuitable in writing even though elementary school-aged children produce it freely in their speech.[4] However, teachers are understandably less strict

---

[4]Recently I overheard a teenage girl use this construction with her two friends at a restaurant while I was working on this chapter!

on the use of "*It is I*" versus "*It is me*" or the "grammatically correct" use of pronouns after comparative words, as in the sentences "*She is taller than I (am),*" versus "*She is taller than me.*"

15.5.4 Vague References

Pronominalization is a rhetorical tool to maintain cohesion in writing. When pronouns refer back to an NP mentioned previously in the discourse, the pronoun is said to be bound and the antecedent to which the pronoun refers is clear. Proper binding of pronouns is essential to sorting out the different participants who populate a text. However, Calderonello et al (2003:99) note that novice writers often fail to bind their pronouns properly. Consequently, readers may not know who or what a pronoun refers to. The seriousness of this problem in writing is explained as follows: "A far more serious problem in writing than pronoun-antecedent agreement is the problem of unclear pronoun reference. Pronoun-reference problems have the potential to render sentences and even entire passages of writing ambiguous, unclear, or confusing. Unclear reference can occur with a personal or demonstrative pronoun by itself."

Binding pronouns properly has been a major preoccupation of contemporary Bible translators. In *The King James Version* of the Bible and in many older versions, pronouns were not bound properly. It is not uncommon to see a pronoun after a section heading. Often the reference of a pronoun is found in a different chapter. Recent versions have eliminated such problems by beginning a new section with a lexical NP before using a bound pronoun that refers to it. Matthew, Chapter 13: 1–35 has four section headings. Only the first begins with "Jesus". The remaining three begin with "he" in *The King James Version*. In contrast, *The Contemporary English Version* has five section headings and each one of them begins with "Jesus" before the anaphoric pronoun "he" is used.

Teachers can help their students avoid vague references by insisting that every pronoun be bound by having its antecedent elsewhere in the same paragraph. The pronoun "it" has been found to be the main source of vague references because there are many types of "it." Some uses of "it" are anaphoric while others are dummy substitutes of the kind discussed previously. Calderonello et al (2003:99) recommend patience in teaching pronouns: "Despite the widespread occurrence of writing problems that involve pronoun reference and teachers' best efforts to teach students the importance of clear pronoun reference, problems in this area persist well into college."

15.6 Deletion Rules in Composition

The inclusion of deletion among the syntactic operations that are useful in teaching writing may seem surprising at first. An important aspect of successful writing is the ability to delete redundant or unnecessary information, especially in the editing and revising stages. Generative Transformational Grammar has proposed two constraints on deletion that can be of great help to writers and composition teachers. The first constraint concerns the deletion of function words while the second focuses on the deletion of content words. Both constraints were briefly introduced in 4.5.2.3 but they will be revisited in this section from the point of view of deletion in writing.

15.6.1 Deleted Complementizers

Complementizers are function words such as "that, when, if, whether, why, where" that help introduce a subordinate clause. None of these complementizers can be deleted except "that." Let us consider the two sentences below:

(55)   *We are sure that we are going.*

(56)   *We are sure that we are going.* → *We are sure we are going.*

Burch (2003:80) comments on the stylistic differences between the two sentences by noting that "Instead of writing, '*We are sure that we going*', for instance, the casual writer might write: *We are sure we are going,* leaving out the *that* that introduces the clause . . .'" Presumably, the more formal the register, the more likely it is for "that" to appear in the sentence (Celce-Murcia and Larsen-Freeman 1999: 653–4). In this regard, the most useful writing strategy is to teach students the syntactic environments where "that" must obligatorily occur and the environments where its presence is optional. For instance, constructions such as "*It is/seems/appears/sounds + adjective*" require the use of "*that,*" as in the sentence below:

(57)   *It may seem strange **that** any men should dare to ask a just God's assistance in wringing their bread from the sweat of other men's faces; but let us judge not, **that** we be not judged.*

With verbs of opinion such as "*to think, to suggest, to claim, to purport,*" and some emotive verbs such as "*to hope, to believe, to regret, to be sure,*" the complementizer "that" can be deleted even in academic writing. However, deleting "that" when it functions as a conjunctive adverb of purpose as in "*so that*" or "*in order that*" is not acceptable, as seen in the two sentences below:

(58)   *I have come **that** they may have life and have it abundantly.*[5]

(59)   **I have come ~~that~~ they may have life and have it abundantly.*

Novice writers need to be taught to distinguish which "that" can be deleted and which one cannot.

15.6.2 Clausal Reduction

Lincoln is fond of reduced relative clauses. He uses this construction abundantly in *The Gettysburg Address* and in *The Second Inaugural Address*. Reduced relative clauses are clauses in which the relative pronoun has been deleted. To exemplify this, let us compare (60) and (61):

(60)   *"One-eighth of the whole population were colored slaves,—not distributed generally over the Union, but—localized in the Southern part of it."*

The basic form of this sentence prior to the deletion of the relative pronouns can be inferred to be (61):

(61)   *One-eighth of the whole population were colored slaves **who were** not distributed generally over the Union, but **who were** localized in the Southern part of it.*

[5]The Gospel of John 10:10.

The syntactic transformation which deletes <who were> from the basic sentence and yields sentence (60) in the process is referred to by Lobeck (2003:316) as **Relative Clause Reduction.** The same syntactic strategy is at work in (62):

> (62) *"Now we are engaged in a great civil war, **testing** whether that nation or any nation **so conceived** and **so dedicated** can long endure."*

It has also been argued that pre-nominal participial adjectives can be generated by a similar process of clausal reduction augmented by a movement rule as (63):

> (63) *"It is for us the **living** rather to be dedicated here to the **unfinished** work which they who fought here have thus far so nobly advanced."*

Fowler (1977:20) explains the derivational steps that lead to sentences such as (63) as follows:

> *Relationships between other ranges of sentence constructions can be informatively treated in a similar way. For instance, many sentences containing adjectives have counterparts with relative clauses:*
>
> *(a) The hungry guest ate all the olives.*
>
> *(b) The guest, who was hungry, ate all the olives.*
>
> *A transformational description can handle this relationship by giving both sentences a common sequence of derivational rules up to a certain point: i.e., deriving (a) in a series of steps which would first derive (b) (both having the same deep structure on which the transformations operate, because both have the same meaning), then reducing the relative clause to the adjective "hungry," and finally repositioning the adjective before the noun "guest."*

Similarly, it can be posited that the unreduced counterpart of (63) is sentence (64):

> (64) *It is for us **who are** living rather to be dedicated here to the work **that is** unfinished which they who fought here have thus far so nobly advanced.*

All the transformations that result in clausal reduction of the types discussed here are effective rhetorical strategies because they turn long sentences into compact ones. The deletion of the superfluous elements does not affect the overall comprehension of the sentence nor its stylistic elegance. Novice writers can benefit from instruction on how to say the same thing with fewer words. Knowledge of clausal reduction transformations can help achieve this goal.

15.6.3 The Stylistic Effects of Ellipsis

Ellipsis and *gapping* were respectively defined in 12.7.1 and 12.7.2 as syntactic constructions involving deletion of the elements in the second clause of compound sentences. The distinction made between the two constructions in Chapter 12 will be overlooked here because in writing, both constructions are lumped together as **ellipsis.** This construction is particularly useful to writers because it affords them economy of expression. It is used effectively by Lincoln in *The Second Inaugural Address.* His opening and concluding sentences contain elliptical constructions:

> (65) *"Fellow countrymen: At this second appearing to take the oath of the presidential office, there is less occasion for an extended address than there was at **the first.**"*

> (66) *. . . to do all which may achieve and cherish a just and lasting peace among ourselves,—and with all nations.*

The full non-elliptical form of the opening sentence can be surmised to be as follows:

(67) *Fellow countrymen: At this second appearing to take the oath of the presidential office, there is less occasion for an extended address than there was at the first **appearing to take the oath of the presidential office**.*

Sentence (65) is obtained as result of the deletion of the italicized element in (67). The non-elliptical counterpart of (66) can be reconstructed as follows:

(68) *. . .—to do all which may achieve and cherish a just and lasting peace among ourselves, and **to do all which may achieve and cherish a just and lasting peace** with all nations.*

The italicized portions do not appear in the surface structure sentence because they have undergone deletion. In both cases, the author deleted redundant information from the sentences without affecting the overall meaning of either sentence. These two examples illustrate the use of ellipsis in formal style. Ellipsis is also used extensively in the colloquial register. Everyday conversation is replete with ellipses. Novice writers should be taught to distinguish between elliptical constructions that are not becoming for academic writing and those that are. When sentences (69) and (71) are compared with (70) and (72), we realize that the latter are not appropriate for academic writing because they belong to a colloquial register:

(69) *They are going to bed; **so am I.***

(70) *They are going to bed; **me too.***

(71) *She loves singing hymns; **so do I.***

(72) *She loves singing hymns; **me also.***

Finally, teachers will do well to draw the attention of their students to correlative conjunctions such as <either ... or>, <neither ... nor>, < both ... and>, <not ... but>, <whether ... or>, and <not only ... but also> which often involve an ellipsis. Sentence (73) illustrates the elliptical use of <not only ... but also>:

(73) Amy is *not only* a teaching assistant but *also* a graduate student.

This sentence contains an ellipsis because "*Amy is*" has been deleted from the deep structure of the second clause "*Amy is also a graduate student.*"

15.7 Conclusion

It was already noted in the introduction that writing involves much more than transformations. The fact that this chapter has dealt mainly with transformations in composition does not make all the other aspects less important. Pinker (1994:401) lists editing and revision as key ingredients in achieving writing proficiency. He makes this point very clear in *The Language Instinct* by observing that "a banal but universally acknowledged key to good writing is to revise extensively. Good writers go through anywhere from two to twenty drafts before releasing a paper." Seeburg (2007:38) focuses on accuracy in spelling as another important ingredient in successful writing. He contends that "if the text is not spelled correctly, the reader will not place his trust in any of its content." Finally, the role of punctuation in developing competence in writing cannot be emphasized enough. Three of Yagoda's *Seven Deadly Sins of Student Writers* have to do with punctuation. Yagoda is not using a hyperbole when he writes that "punctuation problems are endemic, and perhaps epidemic." At my university, the editing office called The Write Place organizes more seminars on punctuation than any other writing issue. These other issues are undeniably important. Yet, this chapter has not tried to address them because it cannot do justice to any of them in the space available. Still, it is my firm conviction that knowledge of transformations of the types discussed in this chapter along with instruction in paragraph structure, sentence mechanics, and attention to details concerning register/style, can turn a mediocre writer into a good writer, and a good writer into a better one.

Key Terms to Know

These are the key terms that you should be able to use and define after reading this chapter:

1. adjectival fronting: 15.4.4
2. adjunct : 15.2, 15.4.1
3. adverbial fronting: 15.4.3, 15.4.4
4. agentless passive: 15.4.13
5. agreement in case: 15.5.3
6. anaphoric reference: 15.5.1, 15.5.4
7. appositive: 15.2, 15.4.1
8. bound pronoun: 15.5.1
9. cleft-sentence: 15.4.10
10. cliticization: 15.4.9
11. comment: 15.1
12. do-Insertion: 15.4.3
13. ellipsis: 15.6.3
14. extraposition: 15.4.8, 15.4.9
15. focus: 15.0, 15.1, 15.4, 15.4.1, 15.4.6
16. free pronoun: 15.5.1
17. left-dislocation: 15.4.6
18. new information: 15.1, 15.4.11
19. old information: 15.1, 15.4.11
20. pp-preposing/fronting: 15.4.5
21. presupposition: 15.1
22. proform: 15.5
23. pronominalization: 15.5.1, 15.5.4
24. relative clause reduction: 15.6.2
25. split infinitive: 15.3.12
26. subject-auxiliary inversion: 15.4.2, 15.4.3, 15.4.4
27. syntactic/stylistic reordering: 15.1, 15.1.2, 15.4
28. topic: 15.1, 15.4.6
29. topicalization: 15.4.6, 15.4.7, 15.4.9

EXERCISE 1—IDENTIFYING TRANSFORMATIONS IN SENTENCES

One of the best ways to improve students' writing is to help them identify and name specific transformations used to construct sentences. A number of sentences are presented below. Use information from this chapter to identify the transformation used in each sentence. The elements under consideration are italicized. Ideally, there is only one transformation per sentence. However, in some cases, there may be more than one.

1.   *When the economy goes well,* everything goes well.

2.   "*Boys, they* are more difficult to raise than girls." (My wife's friend made this comment.)

3.   "Ask and it *will be given* to you; seek and you will find; knock and the door *will be opened* to you," Matthew 7:7.

4.   "It is written: 'Man does not live on bread alone, *but on every word that comes from the mouth of God,*" Matthew 4:4.

5.   *It is France that* invented the cinema.

6.	*Where they eventually settle down,* only time will tell.

7.	"*Surrender,* you must or *die,* you will."

8.	"*The progress of our arms,* upon which all else chiefly depends, is as well known to the public as to myself . . ."

9.	*Blessed are* the merciful, for they shall obtain mercy.

10.	"*Fondly do we hope—fervently do we pray—*that this mighty scourge of war may *speedily* pass away."

References

Adger, Carolyn T, Walt Wolfram, and Donna Christian. 2007. *Dialects in Schools and Communities,* 2nd ed. Mahwah, New Jersey: Lawrence Erlbaum Associates, Publishers.

Aitchison, Jean. 1994. *Words in the Mind: An Introduction to the Mental Lexicon,* 2nd ed. Cambridge, Massachusetts: Blackwell Publishers, Inc.

Aitchison, Jean. 1992. *Teach Yourself Linguistics.* Chicago, IL: NTC Publishing Group.

Arnaud, Kelly. 2003. Just Listen to Us. *English Journal,* January, Vol. 92, No. 3, pp. 13–14.

Baker, Mark C. 2003. Syntax. *The Handbook of Linguistics,* ed. by Mark Arnoff and Janie Rees-Miller, 265–294. Malden, MA: Blackwell Publishing.

Baker, C. L. 1989. *English Syntax.* Cambridge, Massachusetts: The MIT Press.

Baker C. L. 1978. *Introduction to Generative Transformational Grammar.* Englewood Cliffs, NJ: Prentice-Hall.

Barry, Anita K. 2002. *English Grammar: Language as Human Behavior,* 2nd ed. Upper Saddle River, NJ: Prentice Hall.

Bauer, Laurie. 1983. *English Word-Formation.* Cambridge Textbook in Linguistics. New York: Cambridge University Press.

Benjamin, Amy. 2006. What Is Your Compelling Reason for Teaching Grammar? *English Journal,* May, Vol. 95, No. 5, pp. 18–21.

Berk, Lynn M. 1999. *English Syntax: From Word to Discourse.* New York: Oxford University Press.

Bickford, Abert J. 1998. *Morphology and Syntax: Tools for Analyzing the World's Languages.* Dallas: The Summer Institute of Linguistics, Inc.

Bloomfield, Leonard. 1933. *Language.* Chicago, IL: Holt, Rinehart and Winston.

Bock, Kathryn, Anne Cutler and Kathleen M. Eberhard. 2006. Number Agreement in British and American English: Disagreement to Agree Collectively. *Language* 82. 64–113.

Bollag, Burton. 2006. President-Elect at Gallaudet U. Fails to Win Faculty Support. *The Chronicle of Higher Education,* May 19, 2006, Volume LII, Number 37, PP. 1A, 28A–29A.

Borsley, Robert D. 1991. *Syntactic Theory: A Unified Approach.* New York: Edward Arnold. A Division of Hodder & Stoughton.

Braun, Frank X. 1947. *English Grammar for Language Students: Basic Grammatical Terminology Defined and Alphabetically Arranged.* Ann Arbor, Michigan: Ulrich's Books, Inc.

Brooks, James A. and Carlton L. Winbery. 1988. *Syntax of New Testament Greek.* Lanham, MD: University Press of America, Inc.

Burch, Beth C. *A Writer's Grammar.* 2003. New York: Longman.

Calderonello, Alice, Virginia S. Martin, and Kristine L. Blair. 2003. *Grammar for Language Arts Teachers*. New York: Longman.

Celce-Murcia and Larsen-Freeman. 1999. *The Grammar Book*. New York: Heinle & Heinle Publishers.

Chomsky, Noam. 2000. *New Horizons in the Study of Language and Mind*. New York: Cambridge University Press.

Chomsky, Noam. 1995. *The Minimalist Program*. Cambridge, Massachusetts: The MIT Press.

Chomsky, Noam. 1965. Aspects of Syntactic Theory. Cambridge, Massachusetts: The M.I.T Press.

Clark, Mary M. 2003. *The Structure of English for Readers, Writers, and Teachers*. Glen Allen, Virginia: College Publishing.

Clouse, Barbara F. 2006. *The Student Writer: Editor and Critic*, 7th ed. New York: McGraw Hill.

Comrie, Bernard. 1981. *Language Universals and Linguistic Typology*. Chicago: University of Chicago Press.

Culicover, Peter C. 1997. *Principles and Parameters: An Introduction to Syntactic Theory*. New York: Oxford University Press.

Curme, George O. 1931. *Syntax*. Chicago: D.C. Heath and Company.

Davis, Stuart. 1988. On the Nature of Internal Reduplication. *Theoretical Morphology: Approaches in Modern Linguistics,* ed. by Michael Hammond and Michael Noonan, 305–323. New York: Academic Press, Inc.

Dell, François. 1980. *Generative Phonology and French Phonology*. Translated by Catherine Cullen. New York: Cambridge University Press.

Department of Linguistics. The Ohio State University. 2001. *Language Files: Materials for an Introduction to Language and Linguistics,* 8th ed. Columbus, Ohio: The Ohio State University Press.

Deuser, Cindy. 2007. ESL Writing: Adding Richness and Depth Through Transformations. Personal Communication.

Disterheft, Dorothy. 2003. *Advanced Grammar: A Manual for Students*. Upper Saddle River, NJ: Pearson-Prentice Hall.

Dobrin, Lise and Jeff Good. 2009. Practical Language Development: Whose Mission? *Language* 85.619–29.

Downing, Bruce T. 1978. Relative Clause Structure. *Universals of Human Language, Volume 4-Syntax,* ed. by Joseph H. Greenberg, 375–418. Stanford, CA: Stanford University Press.

Dulay, Hiedi, Burt Marina, and Stephen Krashen. 1982. *Language Two*. New York: Oxford University Press.

Ehret, Christopher. 2000. Language and History. *African Languages: An Introduction,* ed. by Bernd Heine and Derek Nurse, 272–297. New York: Cambridge University Press.

Foley, William A. and Robert D. Van Valin. 1985. Information Packaging in the Clause. *Language Typology and Syntactic Description 1: Clause Structure,* ed. by Timothy Shopen, 282–364. New York: Cambridge University Press.

Fowler, Roger. 1977. Linguistics and the Novel. New Fetter Lane, London: Methuen and Co Ltd.

Freeman, David F and Yvonne S. Freeman. 2004. *Essential Linguistics. What You Need to Know to Teach Reading, ESL, Spelling, Phonics, Grammar.* Portsmouth, NH.

Fromkin, Victorian, Robert Rodman, and Nina Hyams. 2007. *An Introduction to Language,* 8th ed. Boston, Massachusetts: Thomson and Heinle.

Fromkin, Victorian, Robert Rodman, and Nina Hyams. 2003. *An Introduction to Language,* 7th ed. Boston, Massachusetts: Thomson and Heinle.

Fromkin, Victorian, Robert Rodman, and Nina Hyams. 2000. *An Introduction to Language,* 6th ed. Boston, Massachusetts: Thomson and Heinle.

Gee, James P. 2003. Educational Linguistics. *The Handbook of Linguistics,* ed. by Mark Aronoff and Janie Rees-Miller, 647–663. Malden, MA: Blackwell Publishers.

Gleason, H.A. 1955. *An Introduction to Descriptive Linguistics,* Revised ed. New York: Holt, Rinehart and Winston.

Guasti, Maria T. 2002. *Language Acquisition: The Growth of Grammar.* The MIT Press: Cambridge, Massachusetts.

Haliday, M.A.K and Ruaiya Hasan. 1981. *Cohesion in English.* New York: Longman.

Harries-Delisle, Helga. Contrastive Emphasis and Cleft Sentences. *Universals of Human Language, Volume 4-Syntax,* ed. by Joseph H. Greenberg, 419–486. Stanford, CA: Stanford University Press.

Harris, Zellig S. 1947. *Structural Linguistics.* Chicago, IL: The University of Chicago Press.

Jackendoff, Ray. 2002. *Foundations of Language: Brain, Meaning, Grammar, Evolution.* New York: Oxford University Press.

Jacobs, Roderick A. 1995. *A Grammar of English for Language Professionals.* New York: Oxford University Press.

Jago, Carol. 2006. What Is Your Compelling Reason for Teaching Grammar? *English Journal,* May, Vol. 95, No. 5, pp. 18–21.

Joseph, Brian D. 2007. The Editorial Process Once Again: Behind the Scenes in the Language Office. *Language* 82. 482–85.

Jurafsky, Daniel and James H. Martin. 2000. *Speech and Language Processing: An Introduction to Natural Language Processing, Computational Linguistics, and Speech Recognition.* Upper Saddle River, NJ: Prentice Hall.

Kaplan, Jefferey P. 1995. *English Grammar: Principles and Facts,* 2nd ed. Englewood Cliffs, New Jersey: Prentice Hall.

Keenan, Edward L. 1987. Relative Clauses. *Language Typology and Syntactic Description: Complex Constructions,* ed. by Timothy Shopen, 141–170. New York: Cambridge University Press.

Keenan, Edward L. 1987. *Universal Grammar: 15 Essays.* Croom Helm: Wolfeboro, New Hampshire.

Kempton, Ruth. 1986. *Semantic Theory.* Cambridge Textbooks in Linguistics. New York: Cambridge University Press.

Kingsbury, Alex. 2007. The Measure of Learning. US News and World Report, March 12, 2007, p. 55.

Klammer, Thomas P., Muriel R. Schulz, and Angela Della Volpe. 2004. *Analyzing English Grammar*. 4th ed. New York: Pearson Longman.

Koffi, Ettien N. 1997. *Language and Society in Biblical Times*. Bethesda, MD: International Scholars Publications.

Koffi, Ettien N. 1994. Problems in Translating "Or" in some African Languages. *The Bible Translator*, 45. 434–441.

Kolln, Martha. 2006. What Is Your Compelling Reason for Teaching Grammar? *English Journal* 95.18–21.

Kolln, Martha and Robert Funk. 2006. *Understanding English Grammar*, 7th ed. New York: Pearson Education.

Kristeva, Julia. 1981. *Le Language, Cet Inconnu: Une Initiation à la Linguistique*. Paris : Editions du Seuil.

Labov, William. 1998. Recognizing Black English. *Linguistics at Work*, ed. by Dallin D. Oaks, 360–386. New York: HarcourtBrace College Publishers.

Laitin, David D. *Language Repertoires and State Construction in Africa*. Cambridge Studies in Comparative Politics. New York: Cambridge University Press.

LeTourneau, Mark S. 2001. *English Grammar*. New York: Harcourt College Publishers.

Lobeck, Anne. 2000. *Discovering Grammar: An Introduction to English Sentence Structure*. New York: Oxford University Press.

Lunsford, Andrea A. and John J. Ruszkiewicz. 2007. *Everything's an Argument*. New York: Bedford/St. Martin.

Lyons, John. 1970. *Noam Chomsky*. New York: The Viking Press.

Marion, Ed. 2000. *Chicken Soup for the Sports Fan's Soul: 101 Stories of Insight, Inspiration and Laughter from the World of Sports*. Deerfield Beach, Florida: Health Communications, Inc.

Marshall, Nancy. 2002. *Language and Literacy Development in First and Second Language Learners, 2nd* ed. Dubuque, Iowa: Kendall/Hunt Publishing Company.

McWorter, John. 2003. *The Power of Babel: A Natural History of Language*. New York: Perennial.

Mounin, Georges. 1974. *Histoire de la Linguistique: Des Origines au XXè siècle*. Paris: Presses Universitaires de Frances.

O'Connor, Patricia T. 1996. *Woe is I: The Grammarphobe's Guide to Better English in Plain English*. New York: Riverhead Books.

O'Grady et al. 2005. *Contemporary Linguistics: An Introduction*, 5th ed. New York: Bedford/St. Martin.

Oirsouw, Robert R.V. 1987. *The Syntax of Coordination*. New York: Croom Helm.

Patterson, Nancy. 2006. What Is Your Compelling Reason for Teaching Grammar? *English Journal* 95.18–21.

Penha, James. 2006. What Is Your Compelling Reason for Teaching Grammar? *English Journal* 95.8–21.

Pinker, Steven. 1999. *Words and Rules: The Ingredients of Language.* New York: Basic Books. A Member of the Perseus Books Group.

Pinker, Steven. 1997. *How the Mind Works.* New York: W.W. Norton & Company.

Radford, Andrew. 1986. *Transformational Syntax: A Student's Guide to Chomsky's Extended Standard Theory.* Cambridge Textbook in Linguistics. New York: Cambridge University Press.

Ravin, Yael and Claudia Leacock. 2002. *Polysemy: Theoretical and Computational Approaches.* New York: Oxford University Press.

Reich, Peter A. 1986. *Language Development.* Englewood Cliffs, New Jersey: Prentice-Hall.

Riemdjik, Henk and Edwin Williams. 1986. *Introduction to the Theory of Grammar.* Current Studies in Linguistics. Cambridge, MA: The MIT Press.

Roberston, A.T. 1934. *A Grammar of the Greek New Testament in the Light of Historical Research.* Nashville, Tenenessee: Broadman Press.

Robdy, Judith and Ross Winterowd. 2005. *The Uses of Grammar.* New York: Cambridge University Press.

Rymer, Russ. 1993. *Genie: An Abused Child's Flight from Silence.* New York: HarperCollins.

Scalise, Sergio. 1986. *Generative Morphology.* Studies in Generative Grammar 18. Riverton, USA: Foris Publications.

Seeburg, Dierk. 2007. Quality Assurance for In-House Translation: Tips and Tricks. *The ATA Chronicles,* Volume XXXXI, Number 2, pp. 35–39.

Stageberg, Norman C. and Dallin D. Oaks. 2000. *An Introductory Grammar,* 5th ed. New York: Harcourt College Publishers.

Walker, Williston et al. 1985. *A History of the Christian Church,* 4th ed. New York, NY: Charles Scribner's Sons.

Wardhaugh, Ronald. 2006. *An Introduction to Sociolinguists,* 5th ed. Malden, Massachusetts: Blackwell Publishers.

Wardhaugh, Ronald. 2002. *An Introduction to Sociolinguistics,* 4th ed. Malden, Massachusetts: Blackwell Publishers.

Weaver, Constance. 2006. What Is Your Compelling Reason for Teaching Grammar? *English Journal* 95. 18–21.

Wheeler, Rebecca. 2006. What Is Your Compelling Reason for Teaching Grammar? *English Journal* 95.18–21.

Williams, Joseph M. 2007. *Style: Lessons in Clarity and Grace,* 9th ed. New York: Pearson and Longman.

Yagoda, Ben. 2000. *The Seven Deadly Sins of Student Writers.* The Chronicle of Higher Education, September 8, p. B13.

Yngve, Victor. 1986. Linguistics among the Sciences. *Theoretical Linguistics,* Volume 13, pp. 257–280. New York: Walter de Gruyter.

Yule, George. 2006. *The Study of Language.* 3rd ed. New York: Cambridge University Press.

Index of Subjects

The index refers to numbered sections, not to pages.

focus: 15.0, 15.1, 15.4, 15.4.1, 15.4.6
formal analysis: 1.13, 1.14
formal descriptor: 1.14
formal register: 3.8., 3.8.1
formality continuum: 3.8.1
fossilization: 5.2.3.6
free morpheme: 5.1, 5.5
free pronoun: 14.3.4, 14.4.1, 14.5.2, 14.7.1, 15.5.1
free variation: 10.3.4
fronting transformation: 13.7, 13.7.5
functional analysis: 1.13, 1.14
functional descriptor: 1.12, 1.14
functional grammar: 3.6
future tense: 7.2.2, 7.4.3

G

gapping: 12.7, 12.7.2
gender: 1.3.2, 1.5.2, 6.2.2, 14.2, 14.2.2, 14.2.3
gerund: 8.5.8, 8.6
gradability/gradable: 9.1.3, 9.2.5
grammatical category: 1.2.2
grammatical function: 6.7
grammatical function/grammatical relation: 8.5, 8.6.1, 8.9
grammatical relation: 6.7
grammaticality convention: 4.3
grammaticality judgment: 2.3.3

H

habitual aspect: 1.4.3
head (noun): 6.5, 6.5.1, 8.4, 8.5, 8.6.2
headless relative pronoun: 14.7.1, 14.7.2
hierarchy: 4.2.6
historical linguistics: 1.1
homograph: 11.3.3
homophone: 11.3.3
honorific pronoun: 14.1.3
hypochoristic/pet name: 5.4.5

I

identity: 12.6.1
idiom: 11.3.4, 11.3.5.5
idiomatic phrase: 11.3.4
idiophone: 5.4.10
immovable particle: 11.5.1
imperative mood: 1.4.5, 7.2.4, 7.2.4.1
inceptive aspect: 7.2.3
inclusive pronoun: 14.1.3
indefinite adjective: 9.4.4

indefinite pronoun: 14.1, 14.1.2, 14.3.3
indexing rule: 4.5.2.2
indicative/declarative mood: 1.4.5, 7.2.4, 7.2.4.1
indirect object: 8.5, 8.5.2, 8.5.4
indo-European: 2.2.5
infinitive: 1.2.2, 1.12.2, 8.2, 8.2.2, 8.6
infix: 5.1.1, 5.9
inflection: 5.2, 5.2.1, 5.2.2, 5.2.3.3, 5.2.3.6, 5.9
informal register: 3.8.1, 3.8.2
innate grammar: 3.1, 3.3
Innateness Hypothesis: 2.3.7
interfix: 5.1.1, 5.9
interjections: 1.2.2
internal vowel change: 5.2.3.2
interrogative: 6.5
interrogative adjective: 9.4.3
intimate register: 3.8.2
intransitive phrasal verb: 11.3.5.6
intransitive verb: 1.4.6: 1.14, 8.5.1, 8.5.8, 8.7
irregular inflection: 5.2.2, 5.2.3.6
iterative aspect: 7.2.3

J

jargon: 3.3

L

Language Acquisition Device (LAD): 2.3.7
Latinate form: 11.7.2
left-dislocation: 15.4.6
lexical category: 1.2.2, 1.11
lexical gap: 5.3.4, 5.5
lexical insertion rules: 4.2.4
linearity: 4.2.6
lingua franca: 2.2.1
linguistic equality: 2.2.6
linguistic reconstruction: 2.2.5
linguistics: 1.0, 1.1, 1.1.2, 1.1.3, 1.7.2
linking stative/stative: 1.4.6, 1.14, 8.5, 8.5.5, 8.8, 9.6.2 9.6.5,
long distance anaphora: 14.8.2

M

main clause/independent: 1.7.2, 13.0, 13.2, 13.4.1, 13.5.2, 13.5.2.1, 13.5.3, 13.5.4.1, 13.5.4.4, 13.7, 13.7.1, 13.7.2, 13.7.3, 13.7.5, 13.7.6, 13.8